PSYCHO
ANALYSIS
IN
GROUPS

PSYCHO ANALYSIS IN GROUPS

ALEXANDER WOLF

EMANUEL K. SCHWARTZ

GRUNE AND STRATTON · New York · 1962 · London

Library of Congress Catalog Card No. 61–18677

Printed and Bound in the United States of America (B)

CONTENTS

FOREWORD

The meteoric rise of group therapy in this country within the short span of its existence is a tribute to its validity as a treatment method. Perhaps no other procedure in the solar system of psychotherapy has inspired so much interest among professionals intent upon experimenting with devices that can have an ameliorative influence on emotional problems. Almost universally, where a therapist has employed it, he has recognized its importance, not only as an adjunct to individual therapy, but as a psychotherapeutic tool in its own right. In the course of its usage, many of its practitioners have instituted their unique interpretations of theory and their singular modes of technical operation. It was to be expected that controversies would arise regarding the nature of group therapy, its values, its processes, its dynamics, the syndromes that yielded best to its influence and the preferred background and training of its practitioners. The same forces of bigotry and self interest that have blighted the field of individual psychotherapy have settled into this new domain, filling it with a spirited Babel. Amidst the din, a few eloquently rational voices have been raised. Among these are the authors of the present work, who, in this volume, contribute to the writings on the treatment of individuals in groups a welcome and hitherto lacking dimension.

Group therapy has been called the Pandora's box of psychiatry. Reaching into it, one may find more opinions about its methods and values than almost any other psychotherapeutic technique. A major need is a means by which we can consolidate the relationship between facts and theories. In this effort, it has been unproductive to take as a reference point the available knowledge about non-therapeutic group relationships, since this has neither been adequately delineated nor related in a pertinent way to treatment process. The suppositions that have been made to date are so provisional that they hardly account for a minutia of the observed phenomena. They can thus scarcely serve as starting points for further investigation and experiment to prove or disprove tentative hypotheses.

The ambiguities inherent in the concept of "group" as a distinctive entity are in themselves confusing. No clear picture exists of the psychological and sociological elements that enter into group interactions. This surely need not hamper us in an effort to explore and to attempt a definition of their nature, but we should not deceive ourselves into thinking that this is an uncomplicated task. Among the difficulties is the fact that we do not possess a simplified paradigm around which we may structure reliable and conceptually meaningful theories about group therapy. There are great problems in the sheer identification of significant variables that constitute the material under observation. We are unable to anchor our activities in previously substantiated empirical operations. Furthermore, our existing methodological weapons are crude and do not enable us to quantify the qualitative data detectable in groups. Finally, it is impossible to manipulate the group situation for the purposes of experiment to permit of replication of our results.

Formidable as these difficulties may seem, our expectations are that through painstaking observation, the careful gathering of data, the formulation of creative hypotheses which we can test with our available instruments, methodical reasoning as to the meaning of our results, and further observation and experiment to test our conclusions, we will eventually be able to arrive at a basis for separating fact from fantasy in group therapy.

A promising foundation for a scientific approach to the problems of group psychotherapy lies in the study of the theoretical concepts and technical procedures of competent professionals who have worked in the field. It is to be expected that such professionals will possess special interests and will be wedded to particular theories and methods that make for bias. Indeed, one may anticipate that while paying homage to scientific method as the best hope for our flounderings, they will not apply the criteria to themselves as remorselessly as they do to others. But this need not deter us in studying their observations and conclusions in the hope of distilling out of their formulations a more fundamental relationship between the significant variables in group psychotherapy.

This necessitates a countenancing of ideas and approaches that do not necessarily reflect accepted notions about group activities. A host of writings permeate the field, many of which on the surface are without substance. Within their fabric, one may occasionally discover a few strands of truth. However, one must resist the Lorelei that beckons the unwary toward a blanket acceptance of songs of unflagging success.

More productive is a reexamination of our more conventional approaches. Among these perhaps the most promising is that of psychoanalysis. During the past half-century, psychoanalysis has permeated into the fibres of psychiatry and psychology, and has fashioned many of its trends. So subtle has this amalgamation been that it is often difficult to define the extent and direction of analytic penetration. In the process, psychoanalysis has in turn been influenced by the more highly structured dimensions that constitute contemporary psychiatric and psychological thinking. It has lost many of its esoteric qualities and has acquired a firmer grounding in scientific experiment. Many of the classical concepts of psychoanalysis have undergone revision in the process. It was to be expected that group psychotherapy would eventually come under the psychoanalytic umbrella and, in due course, be examined by the observational methods afforded by this discipline. Among the pioneers in psychoanalytic approaches to groups are the authors of the present volume.

The volume constitutes a presentation of more than twenty years of experience in the application of psychoanalytic principles in a group setting. It details the dynamic interrelationships of the content, structure and process of psychoanalysis as modified by the contingencies of the group situation. The emphasis is on depth analysis rather than on the impact of group support and interaction. In this way, a structuring of personality is attempted as an objective, rather than a mere re-alignment of defenses to afford a more constructive adjustment with the existing personality equipment. The utilization of free association and dream interpretation and the analysis of resistance and transference are prescribed as the primary therapeutic implements. Alterations in technique are outlined to allow for special developments that inevitably evolve in the course of group treatment. Practical aspects of management are considered in detail as well as the advantages of heterogeneous versus homogeneous groups. Of great interest is the authors' exegesis on the highly controversial subjects of the "alternate group," "permissive groups" and "leaderless groups."

The book is interesting, unique, and highly provocative. It constitutes a major contribution to the field of group psychotherapy, and it introduces a number of significant hypotheses that lend themselves for future testing. The authors are to be complimented for their originality and lucidity of presentation in a field that is so much in need of clarity and direction.

LEWIS R. WOLBERG, M.D.

PREFACE

This book is a distillate of more than a score of years' experience treating patients in a group setting. It presents a consistently and objectively delineated point of view. Patients can be treated in a group, and we believe that best results can be obtained by our method of choice which is psychoanalysis.

We have synthesized our experience with patients, students and colleagues. This volume offers a systematic approach. It is technical and practical as well.

First and foremost we are psychoanalysts, and our objective is *good* therapy in any setting. What is presented here is an attempt to make explicit the concepts and procedures developed in the course of working with hundreds of patients of all types covering most of the syndromes, including neuroses, psychoses and character disorders, in private practice and in institutions.

In a sense this book reflects our own history in psychoanalysis and especially the development of psychoanalysis in groups. Ours is one kind of group therapy, but to our best knowledge it is the one reliable way of achieving enduring reconstructive results. We are encouraged by the reactions of patients, students and colleagues to our efforts. For more than fifteen years we have been teaching and writing about our work, and part of what is included here has been previously published in some form, but recast and integrated into a unified position. Yet psychoanalysis in groups remains open for further exploration; continuous review and revision are required of those who are experienced in this field. The peak interest in it since World War II makes the need for conceptualization especially timely.

We have sought to provide our colleagues who undertake to do analytic therapy in a group setting with specific guidance in regard to its methods. We hope individual therapists, teachers of psychoanalysis, social and clinical psychologists as well as other professionals outside of group therapy also will find the material here of interest.

A. W.
E. K. S.
New York City
February, 1962.

1. Basic Design

The group therapy we are about to describe is psychoanalytic. The techniques, employed in a group setting, emphasize dream interpretation, free association, the analysis of resistance, transference and countertransference. We are fully aware that, in expounding a theory and method of analysis in groups, we shall have to make out a case for it.

Active interest in group analysis began in 1938 for one of us (Wolf) who, reluctant to turn away low income patients who could not afford sustained treatment and hopeful of finding a method that would meet such a contingency, read widely in the literature on group psychotherapy. Many obvious and disturbing questions immediately presented themselves. Would not the presence of others inhibit a patient's free association? Would the traditional transference relationship between analyst and patient be sacrificed if the analyst became one of a group? Suppose the group developed a tendency to destroy the analyst's authority? Might not a neurotic group attack one of its members, thus paralyzing his resources? How could multiple transference and countertransference be handled without their becoming hopelessly enmeshed? Could a conscientious analyst do justice to eight or ten patients in joint session, and would the consequent period of treatment be unduly protracted? These and other imponderables were equally bothersome and required careful consideration.

The writings of Trigant Burrow, Paul Schilder and Louis Wender seemed particularly encouraging, however, and an experimental group of four men and four women was started in 1938. So promptly and effectively were uncertainties about group analysis dispelled, that within one year Wolf had telescoped most of his practice, and in 1940 he was working with five groups of eight to ten patients each.

Homogeneous or Heterogeneous Groups

Four years of Army experience facilitated the confirmation of numerous tentative theories and supplied answers to certain provocative questions. Al-

---

Based upon ref. 135.

though service statistics showed that there was a high incidence of neurosis, the personnel turnover was so rapid that many experiments lacked finality. Wolf was convinced, for example, that meeting patients in homogeneous groups was effective Army procedure. Consequently, alcoholics, psychopaths, morons and those suffering from common psychosomatic and psychoneurotic disturbances with similar underlying trends were regularly isolated for treatment in homogeneous groups.

The presence of so many individuals with similar psychiatric disorders, a rare opportunity in civilian life where homogeneous groups are not so easily assembled, naturally prompted such a move. The resultant identification, mutual understanding and sympathy were helpful factors. To be sure, the disadvantage of this psychic inbreeding was apparent: patients had no opportunity to cope with individuals whose character structure differed markedly from their own.

Even more significant from the standpoint of group analysis was a finding which resulted from the carefully tabulated impressions of two Army psychiatrists with whom Wolf was associated. It was disclosed that, although they agreed on certain characteristics among a few designated patients, idiosyncrasies that were different were being listed. Each therapist was evoking specific responses to his particular personality. The inescapable conclusion was that the character structure of an examiner provokes disparate responses in the same patient.

At present when an analysand leaves a therapist and comes to us for treatment, we try to determine the nature of his former transference. Not infrequently he will have seen his previous therapist as one parent, and he will see the next as another. This suggests some limitation on the depth and completeness of the therapeutic process in individual analysis where the therapist may not elicit multiple transferences. If treatment constitutes primarily the analysis of transference, is it not wiser to place the patient in a group setting in which he can project father, mother and siblings as well? Does the analyst with a single patient have the skill to analyze or evoke the many transference responses by which the patient is victimized? In group analysis the early precipitation and recognition of these multiple transferences are facilitated by the presence of numbers of provocative familial figures in the persons of the various members.

But these and other deductions from Army experimentation, even when they appear unique, are not at present our chief concern. As private practitioners who are actively engaged in assembling groups, each of us must choose members from his own limited panel of patients. Although group formation has its particular difficulties and has opened up a formidable area of research, certain conventions are being tested and established.

At present we subscribe to the formation of heterogeneous groups, as we describe in the next chapter. They reflect a microcosmic society and, of course, tend to reproduce that much abused institution, the family, which, since it probably ushered in the patient's neurosis, is the logical agency for checking it. Despite the fact that, at first, many patients do not cope successfully with dissimilar character structures, the battle is best won where it was apparently lost.

Perhaps it is misleading to state bluntly that groups should be heterogeneous, for in reality they must be balanced. This means that concessions must be made to homogeneity. At one time, it seemed wise, for example, to assemble patients of approximately the same age range. Older patients, invested with parental cloaks, become targets of neurotic attack. A very young patient elicits transferences that overprotect and immobilize him. But transferences evoked by wide disparity in age can often be effectively resolved. On the other hand, the presence of both sexes is advisable to incite and sharpen projection.

In private practice we have always combined men and women in the same group. We have no experience in the group treatment of boys and girls. In the Army, groups were composed exclusively of men, only because no women were available, and it turned out that heterosexual problems were resolved with greater difficulty. This is true also of Veterans Administration installations. The presence of both sexes enables each participant to project more readily maternal, paternal and sibling relationships out of the past onto persons in the group whose sex corresponds with that of earlier vital protective associates. Occasionally, of course, a male patient will evoke a feminine transference and vice-versa. There is some reticence at first about exposing oneself freely before members of the opposite sex, but such resistances quickly melt away. It is better to mix the sexes in a group, because the resolution of problems on the heterosexual gregarious plane is a catalytic agent in the working through of neurotic difficulty. The exclusion of either sex from a group limits the area of struggle in which the patient must learn new patterns of behavior. The inclusion of both sexes presents the patient with masculine and feminine façades which represent parental and sibling surrogates. They also offer him flesh and blood persons with whom he acquires the ability to make a sound social adjustment at the deepest levels. Since the disturbed person is in greater or lesser conflict with one—sometimes both—of the sexes, the heterogeneous group offers the patient a foil for the study of transference reactions and provides insight into the contrast between his responses to both the male and female.

It has been our experience that in forming groups certain readily identifiable types are best excluded: psychopaths, who are always dangerous and potentially group disrupting; alcoholics, who, it appears, can be more effectively treated together; morons, who retard group progress and tax their associates and the analyst to a painful extent; stutterers, who like alcoholics, are most effectively worked with in groups of their own kind; hallucinating psychotics and hypermanic patients. Any of these, however, can be organized into a group suffering from their common difficulty. Patients with neurotic character disorders, psychosomatic disturbances, psychoneuroses and ambulatory psychotics can, in general, be included. This is not to say that borderline cases of any type are inadmissible—particularly, it should not proscribe ambulatory schizophrenics, who have labile contact with symbolic thinking. Schizoids can be helpful to the analyst in interpreting fantasies, dreams and the latent meaning of behavior in the group. Having access to unconscious processes, they can often clarify material that baffles others. Every group might profitably include well chosen schizoid personalities.

The Size of the Group

The size of the group is important. It should number eight or ten. With fewer than eight members, there is often not enough interpersonal provocation and activity. This will lead to lulls or dead spots in spontaneous interreaction and lessen the effectiveness of the group procedure. However, with more than ten it is difficult for both patient and analyst to keep up with what is going on. An overly large group is especially bad for the patient's morale. He is likely to feel threatened and lost in such a setting; what little security he has had in his relationship to the analyst would disappear. Too large a group might, then, immediately produce immobility. Four or five men and an equal number of women make up a practical working group. In our experience ninety minute sessions are most effective. Our chapter on size deals with this problem in greater detail.

Closed or Continuous Groups

Groups are self-perpetuating. Although there is transplanting of patients, our groups do not disband entirely. Patients may join and leave groups, as will be discussed later. The question of closed or continuous groups has many parameters, such as the setting, the kinds of patients, and the nature and goals of the therapy.

Resistance to Joining a Group

The attitude of the prospective member is of considerably more importance than such generalizations on group formation. If he does not already know it, the analyst soon discovers that the average person views with prompt alarm the mere suggestion that he affiliate himself with eight or nine unknown patients. For the purposes of this discussion, we can assume that candidates for group membership fall into three classes: the *resistant* (the majority), the *enthusiastic*, and the *curious* or *open-minded*. The latter commonly approach group analysis with the healthiest attitude. In preliminary individual treatment the analyst studies and gradually breaks down particular resistance to joining a group. The enthusiastic may be variously motivated: from honest need for social contact to exhibitionism, voyeurism and a search for foils for neurotic destructiveness directed toward the group. Whatever the motive, it emerges and is analyzed.

Patients who resist entry into a group should not be pushed too hard. Their premature introduction may precipitate such anxiety or resistance that after one or two meetings they fail to return. It is wiser to inquire into and analyze their opposition beforehand. In time, the majority express a willingness to give the group method a trial. Usually in the first visit we propose to the patient that at a mutually agreeable time he will join a group for further analysis.

Specifically, among the most frequently encountered objections to group affiliation are the following:

> Patients shrink from what they regard as a mortifying invasion of their privacy. The idea of baring their motives and acts to strangers is so alien, that forcing them into a nudist camp might be less abhorrent. Suspicion that their revelations might be circulated by the indiscreet augment their fears.
>
> Certain patients want exclusive possession of the analyst. Alone with him they can relive and realize the repressed affect originally directed toward early familial figures; they will not willingly agree to share him with others.
>
> To some the word *group* unconsciously connotes the original family, and they refuse to subject themselves once again to its trying influence. Their difficulties started years ago in a nightmarish family, and it is the epitome of a social constellation from which they once escaped. Why return to it?
>
> Those to whom a friendly glance or an unfriendly word is devastating, who are shaken by the slightest sign of criticism, coolness or warmth, who shun the give and take of social living, resist group analysis. Why, they reason, should one sacrifice the gentle, detached, earnest and expert consideration of a private analyst for the blundering crudities and rough handling one would probably get in a group?
>
> Some patients are unconsciously afraid that they will have to relinquish a secretly cherished neurotic trend, which the analyst might allow but the group would not tolerate. They cling to the illusion that the therapist will permit them to retain this gratifying obsessive design; they may even hope that the analyst will augment the obsession.
>
> Others will protest at transferring from individual to group treatment because they "will get only one tenth the attention." Although member contributions may not be as professionally sound as those of the analyst, they are intuitively significant and increasingly valid analytically; in a sense treatment is multiplied by ten.

Some patients project such painful or terrifying masks onto other persons that they cannot easily enter group analysis. Such individuals require a relatively long period of individual preparation. And after entering a group they might even have to be desensitized in stages by permitting them to enter and leave the group at frequent intervals. They are able to remain for longer periods of time following each successive absence.

And there are some patients who experience intolerable pangs of anxiety at the freedom with which sexual material is discussed in the group. They too may have to be more thoroughly prepared in individual sessions. The analyst must gradually and persistently probe for the affect-laden unconscious conflict whose emergence they prohibit. This should be done delicately so that undue anxiety is not created. After a while, the succeeding increments of insight enable patients to attend group sessions with less alarm.

The analyst must do his best to allay these and other fears. He assures the prospective group member that, initially, he is under no obligation to reveal embarrassing facts and that his privacy will, in any event, be held inviolate. Group patients, he is told, need to know each other by their first names only. They function under a rigorous injunction of discretion. Patients are warned against gossip. While such admonition early in treatment guards against exposure outside the group, as time goes on, mutual regard and respect for the members' privacy play a major role in preserving ethical secrecy. The exclusion of psychopaths is a further safeguard that confidences will not be betrayed. The patient is always advised that, in the therapist's years of group analytic experience, no member has been dropped for disclosing intimate group afffairs.

For the patient who prefers to have the analyst to himself the therapist may have to clarify, in stages, the infantile demand for the possession of the isolated parent or sibling in the person of the analyst; the transferred rivalry with other group members for his exclusive attention, and the necessity, at last, of sharing with other members of this new family in the group a more satisfying mutual devotion and affection. For those to whom the group unconsciously represents the traumatic original family, the therapist tries to create a most permissive atmosphere. He interrupts any early possibility of cumulative interpersonal hostility and if a clash is imminent, he intervenes gently, asking for ventilating and cathartic material like dreams, fantasies, personal difficulties and even biographical data. He emphasizes the fact that all the members are present because, for some time earlier in their lives, they were not allowed to express themselves; that if the group plays a prohibitive role now, it will only underscore old traumatic influences; that we must try to permit exploration of particular irrationality and not play a prohibiting role. In this manner the therapist attempts to influence each patient toward becoming an ally of the liberating, creative, expansive and socializing forces in every other member and also an enemy of the repressive, destructive, contracting and antisocial trends.

For those who fear emotional contact the analyst may have to spend considerable time in prior individual analysis building up rapport and using this tentative affective closeness as a bridge to the group. Some patients are so afraid of the possibility of a positive or negative transference to the therapist, which painfully evokes for them repressed incestuous conflict, that they try to run eagerly into group sessions after just a few individual interviews. This is done in the hope of damming back what appear to them to be dangerous, emerging trends. Such members try to hide out in the group and attempt to use the group to resist the uncovering process.

With regard to the expertness of the analyst and the clumsiness and misguidance of the group, patients should not be underestimated for their intuitive perception. The analyst must use their resources to common advantage. The members should be made increasingly aware of their considerable usefulness to one another. They are inclined to overestimate the parental authority in the person of the therapist and to underestimate their own production. The analyst rewards each participant for spontaneous and intuitive speculation and points out how very often such prospecting leads to deep insight. Furthermore, he does not permit crude blundering which might distress others; he plays a moderating role. Gradually, as patients are rewarded with insight and respect for one another's reactions, mutual regard for what each has to offer develops.

Sometimes the benevolence of the analyst in individual treatment permits the patient to cling compulsively and for too long to a treasured neurotic pattern. The group has less of this tolerance for illness. It more vigorously demands, and usually gets a more rapid healthy response. When it puts too much pressure on a patient to abandon old forms for new, before he is able to relinquish them, the analyst must use his position to intercede in the patient's interest.

When an occasional patient requests a description of the group he is about to join, its members may be portrayed for him, as he may in turn be anonymously introduced to them. It is explained that the association may be regarded as tentative by either party. Some patients gain solace from the assurance that they may leave the group if they become overanxious or unduly disturbed while undergoing treatment. From time to time, patients do drop out temporarily after a clash of lateral transference and countertransference, but normally a few private interviews will help them return.

Preliminary Individual Analysis

Several phases of treatment are outlined in the following sections. Except for the first, all coexist. Any member may be at one stage when the rest of the group will be at others. While some may be going through different phases concomitantly, any one individual passes through them at his own

pace and in his own order. The phases are discussed here in this form for di-
dactic purposes only.

Following the initial interview the patient is usually referred to a clinical
psychologist for Rorschach, Goodenough and Thematic Apperception
Tests, occasionally the Bellevue-Wechsler. Before introducing him to a
group, it is best to interview him alone for a period of time. For some, all
that is required is a single consultation. Others need ten to thirty individual
preliminary visits. In rare cases, a recalcitrant patient may require as many
as a hundred. In this preparatory phase the analyst explores present difficulties, biographical material, dreams, present, recurrent and former night-
mares, gets an impression of the patient's day-to-day activities and strives to
prepare him for group analysis by explaining something about it. The patient is told, as early as possible, that he is being prepared for group analy-
ysis. His fears and doubts are studied. There is, of course, an occasional patient who never manages to transfer to a group because of his insurmount-
able resistance, or because his psychopathy makes him unfit for group
treatment.

This preliminary work is important in that it enables the analyst to obtain
an initial impression of the diagnosis and character structure of the patient.
He also gains insight into some of the unconscious conflicting trends and
resistances. The analyst uses this individual study period to make the transition to the group less anxious, to put the patient at ease with him, to enable
him to understand a patient's initially bizarre responses in the group, to
compare single and multiple transference reactions and to exclude psychopaths from group analysis. Every patient is informed that, if he becomes
too anxious, disturbed or panicky in the group, he has the freedom to leave it
for a while and to return to individual treatment for as long as may be necessary. In general, however, patients are discouraged from exercising this
right and encouraged to resolve their difficulties in the group milieu. In
most instances, one or two individual analytic sessions are sufficient to unravel the problem and dispel anxiety, whereupon the patient returns to the
group. It has rarely been necessary to keep a member away from his group
for more than two weeks.

Patients who have had prior analysis elsewhere and are somewhat familiar with dream analysis, resistance, free association and transference
phenomena, usually can enter a group early. The point at which a patient
will enter a group is determined by his diminishing resistance and anxiety
about joining one, and the availability of a suitable opening in a group. The
degree of reluctance to enter a group is often a direct measure of the patient's resistance. A readiness to engage in group activity is conversely
though not necessarily a frequent indicator of lesser neuroticism.

In the first or second visit the analyst should discuss fees for both group
and individual analysis. In the group more flexibility is possible and can be

determined by the patient's ability to pay. If the therapist knows he does not have to carry a patient to completion in individual analysis, even the fee in this preliminary work can be reduced. In his wish to be democratic, Wolf advised his first group, in 1938, that he required a given fee for the time extended them and suggested that they decide on the basis of their respective incomes and obligations what each should pay to make up the sum. A period of endless wrangling followed, and the members were finally unable to agree upon an amount suitable for each. At last they approached the analyst and asked him to set the rate for each participant. When he did, the haggling and disagreement became even more intense. Out of this experience he took away the lesson that it is unwise routinely to let one patient know what another pays. There are areas enough for potential neurotic rivalry without introducing this one. After that he arranged privately with each member for a fee which he could manage to pay. It was understood that payments vary, but as long as specific sums were not mentioned, no one seemed to feel himself more or less favored than another. More recently, we have tended to establish a basic rate for most patients.

As a rule, there is, in a group, a gradual absorption and harmonizing of interests. On occasion a group fails to assimilate a member. He may become so truculent and disruptive that he may be taken out of the group. Such a patient may be impossibly aggressive or dominating; he may be hypermanic or make excessive demands for recognition; or he may command focal attention by masochistic or semisuicidal gestures which unbalance consideration of the needs of each. A sadistic or psychopathic bent in one patient may tend to immobilize the larger body, hence forcing it to eliminate his pernicious influence. A person of this sort should return to private analysis for a period, to be reintroduced to his group, if it is willing. If not, he may enter another group. We have had two patients who did not improve, until they were assimilated by their third group. While it is true that rejection by a group is traumatic, it is at the same time also therapeutic. For the patient discovers the provocative trends in his personality which make him socially objectionable. He is then able to struggle at a new level of adjustment, in succeeding groups, to modify his personality in order to be accepted in the new milieu. If he should be discouraged and embittered at being put aside, the therapist should return him to individual treatment for a period long enough to reassure him. The analyst should work with him all the while to analyze those elements in his character which led to his being cast out. In this way a second rejection by the next group can be forestalled.

First Meeting of the Group

When eight or ten patients have been prepared by individual analysis for entry into a group, the therapist schedules an opening meeting. They have all been asked to reveal only their first names, partly to preserve anonymity and partly to create an easy atmosphere of informality. Before the session begins they assemble in a waiting room, introduce themselves and invariably converse. Spared inhibiting formalities, they almost always enter their first meeting chatting, more or less relaxed and wondering what happens next. An occasional patient will deliberately come too late in order to avoid what he may envisage as an awkward or stuffy preliminary, but normally the group can be relied upon to break the ice adequately in its own way.

The analyst does what he can to prolong the informality. When the meeting opens, he seats his patients in a circle which he has joined himself. No activity is urged upon anyone during the first meeting. It gives the patients a chance to relax in the knowledge that they will not immediately be called upon to participate. They also take this time to appraise one another secretly in sidelong glances. A part of the session may be spent in answering patients' questions with regard to details of procedure that are still unclear to them. The therapist assures them that, without permission, he will not expose a specific historical event disclosed to him in confidence during prior individual sessions. He insists, however, on his right to introduce, as often as necessary, the underlying psychodynamics which led to this particular historical event, so long as the psychic process is identifiable as resistance or transference.

In the exposition of the theory and practice of group analysis, the therapist would do well to sound a note of warning with regard to sudden infatuations and their potential involvements. Not that patients will all act out their incestuous wishes, but the record suggests that some of them will. The fact that the analyst knows that neither advice nor edict will rule out seductions should not prevent him from trying to keep group relations as uncomplicated as possible. The analyst neither forbids nor encourages sexual intimacy within the group. Were he categorically to deny sexual freedom to the group he would duplicate the parents' castrating role. If he gave his assent to it he would obscure transference phenomena, which must be worked through before such a relationship is freed of destructive neurotic elements. Here, as elsewhere, he cautions against neurotic ties, sexual or otherwise, which obscure the full significance and realization of what should become a healthy relationship.

Each patient is warned that if he exposes mutual confidences heard within the group to outsiders, he may be dropped from treatment if the problem cannot be worked through. Anonymity must be preserved in the unavoidable discussion that takes place between patients and friends and relatives.

In recent years we have recommended that newly formed groups begin analytic work with the very first session. A good topic for starting is the anxiety each felt in anticipation of the first group meeting.

Rapport Through Dreams and Fantasies

Even at the first session, patients are requested to recount a recent dream, a recurrent dream or an old nightmare. They are asked to free-associate around the dream content and finally to speculate about and interpret the dream. If a dream is not recalled, some peripheral aspect of their problems may be presented if they feel so inclined. In lieu of dreams the therapist encourages the group to present fantasies, reveries and day-dreams. He asks members to avoid censorship of fanciful speculation about one another's productions. In this fashion, personalities begin to emerge, and in succeeding visits the analyst concentrates on developing mutual rapport. He can accomplish this best by his own spirit of warmth and optimism; by not advocating too deep interpersonal or spontaneous inter-reaction of an aggressive or hostile nature prematurely; by a sympathetic, permissive attitude toward each patient's ventilating his frustrating problems, dreams and aspirations.

The therapist will find that certain patients are catalytic agents whose behavior stimulates the group in early meetings when natural reticence might keep it in check. It is practical to include one or more such individuals in every group. The healthiest of these are patients who simply wish to do constructive work and get on with the process of mutual discovery and wholesome inter-relatedness. Many others, however, are neurotically motivated in the way they spark the group. Nevertheless, the analyst can employ this activity to constructive ends. Concomitantly, he can expose gradually for group study the neurotic character of the forces that impel them to participate. Among these helpful provocateurs are exhibitionistic persons who do not hesitate, subtly or otherwise, to boast of their exceptional attributes and accomplishments, exposing themselves and arousing group responses in the process. Some elicit reactions by conscious or unconscious seductive objectives; by making covert allusions to their sexual prowess or libertinism. Others are so insecure, in such need of general approval, so fearful of the slightest criticism, that they repeatedly paint rosy self portraits which elicit ever more penetrating group inquiry. Then there are chronically anxious patients who cannot endure a painful silent hiatus and feel, therefore, impelled to speak up in a quiet period. Even habitually detached individuals are conflictful with regard to being outsiders and in order to gain a feeling of belonging or to get their share of attention, sometimes project themselves desperately into the group with an articulate now-or-never attitude.

Still other types of catalytic agents are compulsive organizers, who are unable to tolerate any wasteful or chaotic waiting and make meticulous reports on themselves. Or, obedient to the therapist's request and under his protection, they follow his prescription and give detailed, relatively uncensored reactions. There is also a kind of compulsive sociability, superficial and dissembling as it is, which impels them nevertheless, to grope formally for contact with the group. Even patients with somewhat psychopathic trends may provoke constructively participant group reactions. While such members may try anarchistically to exploit the group in order to express their irresponsibility, lack of discipline and moral laxity, such behavior tends to evoke vivid responses and mobilize feeling in defense against it. Patients who chronically feel misused often carry their triggered fear into meetings at which they must get their money's worth out of every session. They are driven to participate and project themselves into the work, anxious that not a moment be wasted. Hypomanics are obviously stimulant, and the schizoid facility with unconscious material has already been mentioned. The group analyst must be mindful of the latent catalytic potential resident in each patient, and endeavor to draw it out if it will serve some constructive purpose.

The astute analyst will look for or make opportunities to take advantage of such provocative trends in patients. Despite these maneuvers there are always several removed persons who are ill at ease, who look askance at group membership from the beginning, who sit tight-lipped until they are provoked into participation by some extraordinary act. One of the most successful ways of reaching these isolated individuals is to urge them to tell a recent dream. This is an indirect approach which engages the unwary. A patient is often less resistive to reporting dream material, of whose content he is unaware since it is safely obscured in symbolic forms. It is easier for him to tell what he believes may be less directly revealing than to admit publicly to his psychic impotence, his perverse sexual pleasures or overt homosexuality. When reports of dreams are followed by reactive and interpretive comment, inter-reactive responses are generally forthcoming. By extension of this same process, the analyst invites accounts of fantasies and daydreams which are subjected to similar study.

All else failing to engage a patient, the therapist may ask for brief outlines of personal problems. This should come as a last resort since it duplicates what has taken place in previous individual sessions and is commonly a resistive device employed to evade unconscious material. With notable exceptions most patients are prone to recite their current difficulties and case histories, and it is just this penchant that successful group treatment discourages. However, as an early meeting primer it may be justified.

Any of the above devices will contribute to the unending process of identifying emerging personalities. The therapist's permissive attitude toward the emergence of unconscious material infects the group. It becomes for each patient the new permissive family, whose tolerance and understanding fosters the essential development of generalized positive transference, group cohesion, and morale. With the recessive role of the old, original family diminished, the enfranchised patient makes the exhilarating discovery, that, in joining a communal group he has, at the same time, added to his own freedom and stature.

Members are advised in prior individual sessions the number of group meetings that will take place each week. They are told they will supplement their regular meetings with alternate sessions at which the analyst is not present. These meetings are held at the homes of patients who are centrally located and have no objection to their last names being known. After a few meetings there is sufficient rapport to find such willing members. On occasion, sessions are organized outdoors or under similar acceptable auspices, provided serious attention is given to analytic work. Sponsored by various patients, they add materially to a friendly, sympathetic atmosphere in which uninhibited participation is vastly stimulated. Attitudes toward the analyst are ventilated at alternate sessions and subsequently brought into meetings at which he is present. These sessions precipitate the early emergence of transference attitudes toward the therapist, and thus may shorten the duration of treatment. The unprohibitive atmosphere of meetings in the absence of the analyst stirs the deepest sort of reactions to him. These responses are introduced inadvertently or quite consciously at sessions the therapist attends.

Alternate meetings activate those who are reserved when the therapist is present. The shy become bolder, and the deviously aggressive exploit the opportunity to criticize. It is illuminating to note the group's reactions when a member stays away. In his absence he gets an eloquent appraisal. When the absentee is the therapist, the otherwise guarded patient is often unreservedly outspoken. With this in mind, the therapist encourages fanciful speculation and ventilation about himself or any member absent from an alternate meeting. This too accelerates treatment by forcing more basic affect and transference attitudes into the open at an early date. During these meetings the patient expresses both rational and irrational attitudes toward the analyst. The majority of these estimates could certainly be blocked by the projected domination of the therapist in regular sessions.

There is rarely unanimous agreement on the analyst and his abilities at alternate meetings. Some think he is dull; others, domineering. He may represent the reincarnation of an old, repressive parental image, and the members may join forces to unseat him. The process of taking him to pieces is cathartic and liberating. The insight that follows from such an experience, which is brought into later regular sessions, proves to be invaluable. For self-destructive restraint in the presence of the therapist is a neurotic admission of the latter's overwhelming power. It is simultaneously a confession by the patient that the illusion of transference is a reality for him. On the other hand there are patients who stoutly defend the analyst, endowing him with exceptional capacities. As one would expect, however, he is invested with multiple qualities by all patients, reflecting the images of both parents and other significant figures.

How does the analyst know what has been said of him? Inevitably in later meetings, the group members divulge such matters, whether consciously or not. The patients' reactions to these violations of implied confidence is one of anxiety followed by obvious relief when the therapist not only is not annoyed on hearing them, but rather welcomes critical and aggressive reactions to him. Later on, he may point out their transference character—in the main—and invite further development while he is present.

Let us examine one instance in which a young woman's hostility at an alternate session was encouraged and brought into a regular one. In the therapist's absence the group had discussed him. She felt he was too smug and self-complacent. Her forwardness in criticizing him led to the development of two camps. One was very critical; the other, overly defensive. Her leading the pack in depreciation of the analyst was accidentally exposed, but with unconscious intention, by another patient at a regular meeting in the therapist's presence. His persistent friendliness and warmth enabled her gradually to express enormous stores of resentment without fear of counterattack. The permissive atmosphere of an alternate meeting allowed for the eruption of wells of aggression which was then shunted into a regular session. There the analyst welcomed affect which she might otherwise have feared to express. By sponsoring her repressed animosity, many facets of it emerged, so that it could be subjected to analytic study. The analyst knew from her dream material and previous individual treatment, of her early erotic interest in a brother. He knew also of her having been sharply checked in this and other affective impulses by maternal authority for many years. He knew, he said, how hazed and rejected she must have felt under such discipline. Although he was more tolerant than her "hateful" mother, he suggested that he might similarly epitomize a kind of pressure which was infuriating to her. He proposed that she was transferring the bitterness which she felt earlier for her mother to him. While for some time she continued to make irrelevantly hostile comments about him, she eventually saw their repetitive and compulsive character and, finally, managed to erase the mother image from the face of the analyst. Countless similar attitudes toward the analyst which, if restricted to regular group sessions, might be submerged for protracted periods of time, are often first uncovered in the less inhibited atmosphere of alternate meetings. There is a more comprehensive discussion of the alternate session in Chapter 5.

These matters of procedure, although important, are ancillary to a fundamental in the group analytic process: the interpretation of dreams which continues through all stages of treatment (see Chapter 7). Dreams are discussed because they reveal essential unconscious data so reliably and with such demonstrative and liberating effect. The analyst asks for them in detail. He is interested especially in dreams which involve other members of the group. Patients are asked to associate freely to one another's dreams in order to develop intuitive interplay at the deepest levels. Dreams including other patients occur with surprising frequency and arouse the keenest sort of attention. The group becomes engrossed in dream analysis with its attendant associations, catharsis, sense of liberation and mutuality, all of which contribute toward the group interaction which is so important in the first stages of treatment. Patients who have difficulty in remembering dreams are urged to give their fancies free play and to bring in uncensored reveries and daydreams about one another. These often prove to be as useful as dreams themselves. From the outset the analyst attempts to engage the patients in intuitive and imaginative comment on this unconscious material. It is always impressive how a group of untrained people, in an unprohibited setting, by spontaneous, but somehow involuntary perceptive study of dreams, tend to explore their significant possibilities. Only occasionally does the analyst have to introduce a guiding hand.

Where the patients fall short of the mark, they study the analyst's interpretation of dreams. And by increments of cross association among group members about successive dream material, they become more skilled in translating it. Knotty symbolism or excessively vague latent content is sometimes left to the therapist. Even here he will sometimes be at a loss, and find himself obliged to a schizoid, intuitive or otherwise discerning patient for the unraveling of certain aspects of a dream. The fact that the analyst fails at times where a patient succeeds has its therapeutic value. It is a corrective to a patient's predisposition to regard the therapist as an omniscient parent. It puts the patient on the level of a co-worker whose inner resourcefulness and creative powers are so highly regarded as to give him increasing self assurance. The therapist tries not to leave dream analysis in the hands of a few "experts." He encourages the less venturesome to take experimental steps in seeking for inner meanings. He urges them to engage their unexercised natural resources and attempts to stimulate initiative where there seems to be very little. To this end, he contends that it does not matter that a reactive interpretation is far wide of the mark. It is important only that it be a spontaneous and affective response. With these qualities it will throw light on the speaker's problems, though it may be of little direct use in clarifying the immediate issue. Through this reciprocal examination of their dreams they develop insight into their mutual aberrations. This is a first step toward their disposal.

A patient's dreams are of paramount importance as a guide to the progress he is making. Conflict is continually reflected in them, and a patient should not be allowed to leave the group until his dreams certify to his progress. For the restless or resistive member who would flee the group under the guise of an apparent recovery, it is rewarding to ask for last night's dream. It can be used, if need be, to illustrate for the patient, where his unconscious says he stands, and thus frequently forestall his premature escape from treatment. Conversely, for a dejected, despairing patient, the therapist can often find suggestions of healthy, unconscious struggle in a dream that will raise his hopes considerably and give him justification for continuing with renewed effort.

Inter-Reaction Through Interpersonal Free Association

If good group rapport has developed out of the permissive atmosphere fostered by the expression of dreams, fantasies and critical problems, the second stage of group analysis has been accomplished. The therapist can then lead the group into another phase of treatment: a period in which each patient free-associates about the next. Now the spontaneously inter-reactive process still makes good use of dreams and reveries. But more attention is given to this new procedure. It is controlled by limiting it to the expression of spontaneous, uncensored speculation about other members of the group. Moreover, to admit of wide group participation, a flexible time limit can be imposed on each person associating.

Patients and analyst alike commonly refer to the procedure in which each member takes a turn at free-associating about the next as "going around." Out of this technic, which elicits the most electric kind of unpremeditated inter-reaction, a number of psychodynamic processes emerge. Patients are asked to be alert to these trends and to assist one another and the therapist in identifying them. This suggestion arouses their curiosity and alerts them for mutual examination. By making them active participants it provides them with reassuring status. It is suggested that, if a patient will say whatever comes into his head about another, he will intuitively penetrate a resistive façade and identify underlying attitudes. In the group we call this "ringing a bell," "hitting a target," "touché." Patients under examination are urged to admit freely to the striking of an inner target. This is partly to establish their basic identity and partly to reward the associator. Every neurotic so sadly underestimates his real potential, that he needs to be told when he puts his finger on something valid. Furthermore, he is usually so guarded about his spontaneity, so reservedly unspeculative and compulsively perfectionistic that rewards for unpremeditated accuracy having social value are of the utmost therapeutic benefit.

A patient is requested by the analyst to acknowledge the penetration of a façade if he feels something especially perceptive has been said to him. For the most part, he will admit to it, and his affirmation is used as a basis for further exploration. He may, however, resist insight or showing evidence of touché. In spite of his resistance, his unconscious will not usually be denied. And evidence of a bell's having been rung will present itself in a dream, a nightmare, a slip of the tongue, halting speech, a psychosomatic symptom, some other irrational or affective constellation. With continuous piercing of the shell of resistance under the group's concerted free-associations, the inner character structure and identity of each patient gradually emerges. In fact both the patient under examination and the associator benefit. The member under scrutiny profits from the insight offered him. The speaker is applauded for his intuitive perception. Up to this point, his resources have been minimized and his capacity to make a socially valuable contribution belittled by others and himself. Accordingly, with praise for his spontaneously productive accuracy, earlier feelings of inadequacy give way to a consciousness of his growing strength. The average patient is extremely wary of his unpremeditated reactions. He likes to review and polish his comments to make them unassailable. He strives for faultless performance in a compulsive fashion, because he feels so inadequate or because he dreads the expression of unrestrained affect which may invite counterattack or castration. An extremist in self depreciation, he underrates whatever comes naturally. If called upon to speak impromptu, he may stammer and break down ignominiously. When he does talk, he is inclined to applaud other speakers, especially the therapist, whose pronouncements he accepts as *ex cathedra*. The pragmatic give-and-take of group intercourse is a healthy, demanding reality he resistively withstands. But the assaults made on his defenses by group associations and the rewards that follow his initial impulsive expression pave the way for his liberation from neurotic restraint.

The following is an illustration of how at an early meeting of a group, the naive, free association of one patient about another penetrated resistance and provoked a dream which elaborated deep, vital material. Bea, a young woman, had been treated in individual analysis for three years by a therapist who had ignored her sexual problems. After she joined a group, Jack, a fellow member, commented about her: "You're awfully tense and tight and ill at ease. You remind me of an overwound watch spring. I'm afraid you'll suddenly uncoil and snap at me. You seem so bound up, you remind me of an armed fortress with loaded cannon pouring over the parapets, ready to fire. I get the feeling you're unconsciously afraid of being raped." Bea hotly resented this characterization, but at the following session she told of a dream which had been prompted by Jack's reactions. The setting of the dream was years earlier, and she was a little girl at home. Suddenly the sinister figure of her father was before her, and as she ran from him he tore off her dress. In stark terror, she leaned from a window, and there below her she recognized her previous therapist. She cried out to him for help, but nothing she did could attract his attention. On that frantic note the dream ended. The dream, instigated by Jack's intuition, had brought to the surface a significant, unconsciously obsessional fear of, and concomitant wish for sexual contact with the father. Her earlier analysis had left this underlying trend untouched and submerged. At succeeding sessions the deeper intricacies of her early erotic interest in and fear of her father were elaborated. It is interesting to note, however, that an untutored patient can uncover highly valuable repressed data which more expert hands sometimes fail to bring to the surface.

An inevitable byproduct of the going around technic is the penetration of façades to reveal each member's inner, conflictful trends thereby establishing his unconscious identity and character structure. Out of this procedure each patient's position becomes delineated. He comes to know where he stands in the eyes of his fellows and why. This does not proceed in a superficial way, but elicits reactions at the deepest levels. He learns which characteristics please the group and which disturb them. His discovery of what his real status is in relation to others is reassuring, for down deep he is apprehensive that he will be less welcome than he turns out, in fact, to be. He is given added security, because he discovers what he is and develops a sense of self, an identity which affects others. He learns to modify this newly recognized self so that it functions with increasing appropriateness in the group.

An illustration of this group-imposed status and its consequences occurred in a group where a schizophrenic had been enrolled. Since we had discussed her before her appearance as a member, the group was not unprepared for her idiosyncrasies. But the members felt obliged to handle her delicately for fear of further traumatizing her. They withheld reactions that would have been expressed with any neurotic patient. At her first meeting she lay on the floor instead of sitting in the circle with the rest of us, and as the session progressed, she ran a whole gamut of abnormal actions—all of which the group seemed indulgently to ignore. In later meetings she bickered persistently and irrationally with everyone, again with apparent tolerance from the group. One evening a man against whom she had railed with unusual bitterness voiced the pent up anger of the group in a sharp retort which ended in a vigorous criticism of her. The effect was extraordinary. While she gave evidence of resentment of his censure, she admitted at the same time that his observations had a certain logic and validity. With surprising clarity and self control she surveyed the group and replied to the irate member who had attacked her. "At last," she told him, "you are being honest with me. Now, thank God, I know where I stand in the group." By expressing his deeply felt response the man had finally come alive for her; he was no longer (as was the entire group) evasively protective. Her realistic response was so gratifying to the group that she was thereafter quickly absorbed as a full member toward whom each participant could react. This one man's explosion acted as a release for the other members. They no longer resented her, because she did not force them into overprotective, inhibited roles which denied them mutual freedom.

Expressions of feeling are one concomitant of the new permissive family that the group comes to represent. As members learn that it is safe both to give and accept spontaneous responses, they realize that something formerly denied them in the old family has been added—tolerance. In this kind of atmosphere it becomes stimulating to plumb the causes of frustration and, communicating in a language that is dynamic, to liberate and develop resources temporarily stunted by earlier familial influence.

The naturally cautious analyst may legitimately ask: Is the average precariously balanced patient safe in the clumsy hands of aggressive patients who may expose unconscious drives too swiftly or attack too cruelly the weak and defenseless? In the group's concerted attack on the defensive character structure, will it not be too rapidly shattered, leaving the patient dangerously insecure and with such weak ego reserves that he may be forced into psychosis? It is certainly true that the atmosphere is sometimes charged and subject to an explosive kind of inter-reaction. Will these intense situations become traumatic? The answer to this question is, indeed, reassuring. Nothing really inimical to the patient's interest ensues. If a member seems to be growing unduly anxious or overwhelmed, the analyst can return him to individual treatment for a short period. Patients are fortified against destructive attack by support from the therapist. They are cautioned to make the distinction between the real and the transferential in what is directed at them. When a member invests others with qualities they do not possess—when he projects—the therapist exposes his irrelevant and irrational distortions of reality as unreal. The patients themselves become adept at elaborating these enlightening differences between fact and fiction.

Pained though a dissected member may feel, if the appraisal of him is unjust, he is usually so well fortified by well disposed group opinion that his ego survives it substantially intact. As he progresses in treatment and learns to appreciate the neurotic character of aspects of ill-considered judgments of him, he develops an increasing immunity to them. If he had been wary of his own aggression, he learns to flail out where provocation invites it. But he educates himself best by extracting from neurotically tinged reaction to him, that kernel of information which is useful to him as insight. The patient who is the target of free association learns why and in what ways he gladdens or irritates the group. He discovers his provocative role. He may have, up to now, always regarded himself as the victim of other people's aggression and cruelty or wondered why people fled him in distress. When they tell him face to face just how he provokes them, he develops acute insight into the way he evokes the environmental responses that in turn startle him. With an awareness of his provocative traits, both he and the group are impelled to search for the unconscious motives which arouse critical reaction in the others. Unflattering as some judgment of him may be, it is associated with an essential sympathy and friendliness from the majority of the group.

In the demonstration of a patient's provocative role the group is a natural and effective agent. In individual analysis the therapist is hardly so responsive as to clarify the patient's stimulating conduct with the same completeness as the group. The various members are so sensitized by their particular neurotic constellations that they can discern and point up each participant's exciting peculiarities. Under individual treatment patients are impelled to review historical and present abuse at the hands of others. And the probing, sympathetic analyst is occasionally misled by the patient's complaints, unless he sees him in the animating current of the group. This has been proven to us many times after introducing a member to a group following a preliminary period of private treatment. In the social setting he often seems a quite different person. The presence of others elicits many diverse facets of his personality. In this regard, it is instructive to introduce a new patient following the recovery and discharge of an old one. Almost everyone shows a new aspect of himself, hitherto unseen, in response to the character structure of the newcomer.

The Analysis of Resistance

The fourth phase of psychoanalysis in groups arises when, as patients continue to free-associate about one another, their resistances emerge with increasing clarity. In this stage these defenses are discovered, studied, delineated and the forces that support them are examined. Finally, each member is offered increasing evidence of mutual regard and security, in an attempt to break down these defenses. Resistance manifests itself in the myriad forms encountered in individual analysis. But the group setting provides a special environment that lends itself to the elaboration of resistive forms peculiar to it.

For the patient "in love with" the analyst, being in the group is enlightening. She is soon as emotionally attached to another group member as she was to the analyst. Her "unfaithfulness," the rapidity and completeness with which she moves from one man to another, confronts her with the irrational and compulsive character of her behavior. The nature of her activity becomes obvious to her as transference. For the patient rigidly blocked in neurotic interest in the analyst, who insists she is truly in love with him and that she would be neurosis-free if only the therapist would return her genuine feeling, the group experience dispels the illusion. There, if she does not transfer her affective claim to another patient, she is led to examine her feelings more deeply in the fact of similar resistance and transference on the part of other members. Their falsification of reality makes its impression upon her. In most cases, she is brought face to face with the "infidelity" that impels her to exchange the analyst for a patient and is obliged to plumb earlier emotional attachments. She then discovers the neurotic resistance implicit in every such episode.

Another manifestation of resistance is the compulsive missionary spirit. Here the provider persists in looking after group members in a supportive, parental way, using this device subtly to dominate and attack the other members and to repress more basic psychodynamics. The group resents this false charity and demands and evokes more spontaneous participation by rewarding the messianic for unguarded slips of feeling and by rejecting dogmatic helpfulness. This does not imply, of course, that warm and spontaneous offers of assistance are rejected. The contrary is true: as long as supportiveness is not compulsive, but thoughtfully sympathetic, it is welcomed as a sign of good health. An interesting example of this kind of resistance is provided in the following case. In one group a professional teacher habitually preached to his fellow analysands until their hostility bordered on the explosive. Later he reported that during coitus, sometimes an hour passed before his sexual partner had an orgasm. To him, the sexual act, like his compulsive stewardship in the group, was a gesture of generosity. The other patients encouraged him to be less providing and to strive to enjoy his wife's allure with more spontaneity and pleasure for himself. At the next session he reported an ejaculation within three minutes with a corresponding simultaneous orgasm from his partner. The group conjectured that his earlier largesse concealed unconscious hostility to which his wife had been responding with equal frigidity. They also suggested that his benevolent preachments and ostensible advice contained the same kind of irritating and unprovoked aggression. He was urged in this situation as well to abandon his compulsive role for one that was more spontaneous and acceptable. After some time he became aware that his specious charity was a form of resistance preventing the development of real feeling. Variants of this theme appear in the self-appointed do-gooder, in the overprotective, typical "mom" in the group. It is also eminently displayed in the "mother is always right" dogma.

Some patients go blank when asked to free-associate about others in the group. If they are blocked in this way, they are urged to compose fantasies about everyone in the group just before going to sleep at night. They are asked to go around the group in the safety of this isolation, and then to bring these speculations into regular meetings. Away from the inhibiting presence of other members, associative paralysis gives way to lively flights of fancy. The analyst asks such persons to visualize each member of the group, including him, and to project them into imaginative and extravagant conduct. These inventive productions are then reproduced for the group, where they stimulate provocative discussion in the same way as dreams. By cultivating this technic patients manage to break down this particular kind of resistance and react freely in the moment without the preparatory homework. However, all patients are requested to review for the group such dreamy thought which comes to them before going to sleep. For at this time much repressed and preconscious delayed reactions well into consciousness.

Voyeurism is resistance that is more general in group analysis. Some patients try to escape personal examination and engagement by taking grandstand seats which give them a gratifying view of what may be the equivalent of the primal scene or its lesser familial counterparts. They seem willing and even eager to allow others full inter-reaction, while they assign to themselves a tremulous watchfulness. Instead of engaging in interpersonal exchange, they peer at it from a distance. But looking can be a sort of prelude to participation. The group has little tolerance for nonparticipants. It engages the voyeur by its welcoming self exposure. It moves him by inviting and provoking him to become involved in the warm emotional life of the new family. His resistance begins to melt when the sideshow to which he was drawn by dubious surreptitious motives, becomes a wholesome drama in which he is impelled to take a legitimate part. Projected aggression gives way to a recognition of reality, and he is prepared to act more appropriately in this unforbidding environment. In this fashion, voyeuristic resistance develops from an end in itself to a first step toward a normal relationship.

Hiding oneself behind the analysis of others is a common form of resistance in psychoanalysis in groups. The group may provide a convenient setting for the exercise of this specific kind of resistance. It is characterized by a concentration on the neurotic behavior of other patients and accompanied by an evasion of analysis directed toward oneself. Such a patient cleverly shifts attention from himself to the associator in order to defend himself against disturbing examination. If he is adept, he will, when threatened by an observation that might become alarmingly penetrating, neatly parry the proffered insight. He manages to redirect the group's attention to any individual who dares to analyze him. He handles what is said of him, for example, by remarking that his critic had an interesting overtone in speech that he ought to examine. By endless devices he deflects what could add up to deeper insight and tackles his examiner. Sometimes he produces brilliant, if compulsive, analyses in his own defense. Usually his technics are so able as not to be easily broken down under critical attack. However, the group gradually dissolves his resistance by expressing its gratitude for his incisiveness and by simultaneously demonstrating to him that behind his emphatic lecturing he makes himself inaccessible, in terror of humiliation, to the helping hands of the group. It is pointed out that fear of castration or its equivalent by the parental substitutes in the group is forcing him into this compulsive role. To the extent that the members understand the frantic insecurity that underlies his bravado, they extend a reassuring friendliness that enables him to relinquish his insistent critical study of others for self examination. The maintenance of a compulsive complacency which regards the other patients as neurotic inferiors cannot withstand such an approach from the associated members. Their understanding enables them to become friendly enough to help him give up his program of evasion.

The use of history as resistance deserves special comment. There is probably nothing in individual treatment more uselessly time-consuming and basically harmful to both patient and analyst than the practice of rehearsing the patient's past. Long irrelevant biographies, usually distorted by the narrator, can be a form of continual evasion. Even a recital of yesterday's events can assume this character. In its most unsatisfactory form the relationship between patient and therapist may be reduced to a day-by-day report of frustration which demands nonanalytic advice on ways of circumventing it. This insistence on guidance instead of therapeutically valuable transactions is also used as resistance. The refusal to face the present with one's own reactive emotional and mental processes withstands only in extreme cases the impact of group stimulation. Talk of what happened in childhood, and even accounts of last night's dream become vicarious and pallid when compared to the dynamic interpersonal reactions pronounced by a suddenly articulate contact. Such dramatic provocation cannot be resisted by escape into the day before yesterday.

Of course, we do not mean that we regard history as unimportant. On the contrary, it is of the utmost importance. History has the greatest significance when evoked and recalled by the discovery and analysis of resistance and transference in the moment of their occurrence—that is, when history has a bearing on the present which is meaningful to both the patient and the analyst. The present neurotic behavior is envisioned as a multi-dimensional photograph of the *significant* past. Careful scrutiny of the immediate moment will recall pertinent traumatic events. Personal flashbacks may be vividly illuminating, and the exploration and understanding of the past in terms of its influence on the present are essential to the creation of a wholesome present and future. But allowing a patient to indulge these proclivities is encouraging him in resistive subterfuge, his attempt to escape the resolution of similar conflict in the present.

Some patients, perhaps a majority of them during the early stages of treatment, discuss sexual material with patent reluctance. This is a kind of diffidence we try to dispel. Slighting or repressing sexual data reproduces the prohibitive role of the original family. Unless the patient frees his own sexuality he cannot make an adequate recovery. Access to sexual material is obtained partly by intuitive free-association in going around. Once the initial resistances are broken down in this process, there is usually little difficulty in getting patients to discuss this fundamental matter.

There exists an intimate relation between abnormal social behavior and abnormal sexual behavior. Access to sexual material is obtained by illustrating how a variety of interpersonal conduct that appears in the group has its sexual counterpart, perhaps as yet unseen. Since the average patient is wary, at first, of revealing his sexual predicament, and since he is hardly aware either of its extent or complexity, group members are urged, early in analysis, to examine the interplay of their personalities on the social level. Then the analyst may begin to suggest that for each of the character traits revealed by cross association there is a sexual analog. The analyst's ease in taking the parallel for granted, without criticism, tends to infect the group with a like tolerance for otherwise socially prohibited intimacy. The analyst might indicate that a manifestation of social impotence implies the existence of a corresponding sexual impotence; that they are both signs of a similar psychodynamic problem in the analysand. Similarly, for example, excessive attitudes of male supremacy suggest a corresponding compulsive sexual excess, organized to conceal deep-rooted castration anxiety. A statuesque poise on the social level is probably accompanied by some form of sexual frigidity. Thus, by schooling the group in the effort to uncover the usually concealed existence of these sexual correspondents of social forms, the members make numerous accurate guesses about hidden sexual data. Exposed in this fashion and by intuition, one after another uncovers sexual material. In the light of this relationship, nuances in curious social conduct are clarified in turn. One exposure excites release in others, until in a surprisingly short time, the cautious lose their caution and proceed to unburden themselves of the most intimate details.

A group afforded an illustration of an instance in which psychic impotence was accompanied by social ineffectiveness. One of its preeminently male members, physically powerful and imposing, exhibited evidence of extreme shyness. His emotional reactions were, to say the least, deficient. References to plays, art and literature both annoyed and embarrassed him, and when pressed for an explanation, he characterized them seemingly as effeminate manifestations of weakness. He secretly regarded any display of feeling as soft and feared he might be seduced into affective response by any emotional stimulant. At an early age he had lost his domineering father and had been forced to go out on the streets to sell newspapers in order to support his mother, sisters and himself. Attacked repeatedly by antisemitic hoodlums, he spent years toughening himself, until tenderness, sympathy and by extension, any emotional symbol that did not connote hard struggle, were ruled out of his life. In group activity it was noted that he evaded those social responses which might betray any underlying emotional attitude. He was formally considerate, proper and unreactive, except for a compulsive need to display his masculine excess. This latter consisted in exhibiting his masterful virility whenever possible, in missing no opportunity to engage in intellectual debate in which he excelled, and in a general supportiveness simulating strength which invited the dependence of other members on him, but which was unconsciously intended to dominate and exploit them.

During various sessions, the group speculated about the sexual counterpart of his deficiency in feeling and gradually led him to a not-too-painful admission of his impotence. He was moved so deeply by the friendly reception accorded his confession of weakness that he burst into tears, the first crack in his resistive armor. With this disruption of neurotic defense against emotional expression he began dreaming, free-associating and going around at deeper affective levels. This enabled the group, in time, to analyze his masculine conceit and striving for power as defenses against castration and passive homosexual submission. He was able to acquire insight into his compelling preoccupation with erotically tinged struggle between himself and other men that removed him from sexual engagements with women. He was able to trace his aggression toward men to his domineering father, and his later and repeated compulsive strivings with them as the ambivalent expression of submissive and aggressive conflict. He learned, too, how the loss of his father removed a masculine image with whom he needed to identify, leaving him with three feminine figures who played their part in further emasculating him, partly out of their playing a penile role and partly by providing him only with feminine example. This was added to by their own ambivalent eroticism with regard to him. To all this conflict he reacted with repression, attempting ever to surmount unconscious affective claims that would not be denied until he was both impotent and apparently unfeeling. But with the group's action, which inserted a wedge into his formerly impenetrable façade, he relaxed restraints successively and steadily built up lively and cordial contact. With the return of feeling it became possible for him to relate to others with intensity, to fall in love and to consummate an erotic relationship with full potency.

One such confession has a catalytic effect in producing similar uninhibited discussion by others. With varying degrees of stubborn opposition, the members finally yield to the potentiating influence of self revelation induced by the permissive aura pervading the group. Emboldened by avowals from all sides, each sees around him his counterpart in sexual embarrassment and exposes his particular variant of the sexual theme.

In the study of sexual and social counterparts the therapist must be careful not to generalize too broadly from one member to the next. A collective interpretation tends to obscure specific differences that vary with each patient. It helps him resist deeper and more refined interpretation. If the analyst probes every aspect of a member's reactions on the social level, he will be rewarded with rich and diversified allied sexual duplicates. The generalization that one can expect to find these correspondents should be utilized by the group to explore their ramification. By playing insights back and forth, from the social and sexual planes in the procedure of going around in dream, fantasy and unreserved speculation, the details appear. Social insight leads to sexual insight and vice versa. The emphasis on their interplay breaks resistance and leads to deep understanding. The patient's liberation in these two areas has a startling effect on his formerly inhibited resources. His spontaneity and creativeness expand freely, so that he finds himself effectively mastering reality in fields where he was once constrained.

The varieties of resistance that appear in the group cannot be discussed here, for they are as manifold and distinct as are human beings. Some resist by trying to hide in the group, whether by attempting to escape into group analysis from individual treatment, or by coming late and missing meetings. Some leave the room on various pretexts. Others cannot recall their dreams or fantasies. A few exploit their tears and other devious emotional or psychosomatic releases to evade more direct response. Some maintain a compulsive complacency among patients whom they regard as neurotically inferior, hence, not to be entrusted with important private matters. Their resistance takes the form of supercilious silence or contempt. Some try to overwhelm the group with endless outpourings of irrelevant talk that is neither self-revealing nor permissive of emergence of others.

Occasionally alternate meetings are conducted in a picnic atmosphere at a beach, park or summer or winter home of one of the participants. Eating and drinking may reduce resistance by creating a casual and intimate atmosphere. But sometimes it is intended to stuff the mouths of prospective participants and thus block inter-reaction. The analyst persistently tries to alert the group to be on guard against any activity of a nonpsychoanalytic character which may interrupt the specific function of the group and act as resistance. Almost inevitably various members are drawn to one another and become friends. They tend to enjoy and share the same social functions. The therapist takes a neutral attitude towards these developments but always warns against the repression of transference attitudes in such relationships. The attempt on the part of some members to preserve a relationship at the expense of analyzing it must always be challenged as resistance. While the analyst may at times be perplexed by the variety of individual or concerted obstacles to the invasion of multiple unconscious reservoirs, he uses his own ingenuity and the group's involuntary, accidental and intuitional reserves to penetrate them.

The Analysis of Transference

Closely allied to resistance is one of the most important aspects of group analysis, the identification and resolution of transference. The projections of parental and sibling images onto other group members are phenomena requiring exhaustive study. The analysis of transference is the largest single area of concentration. Under the analyst's leadership, patients discover the extent to which they invest one another with early familial qualities. In the group setting, where a member may not only project a significant historical figure onto the analyst, but may also single out members of the group for the same purpose, the field for transference is appreciably extended.

Certain truisms about transference are stressed. The analyst explains that all human beings carry out of childhood a heritage of responses which impel them to endow the present with old forms; that we see others in terms of our own circumscribed experience; that investing others with attributes they do not possess is revelatory of distorted character structure in the investor; and that therapeutic progress is measured by the success with which a patient can revise these erroneous imputations and by the tolerance with which he can accept similar unwarranted and invalid appraisals directed against himself. Patients are alerted in their analytic role to recognize and point to transference reactions whenever they appear. The qualities of transference are described to them so that they can more readily become conscious of its nature. It is demonstrated how every transference reaction has the qualities of irrelevance, compulsion, repetition, irrationality, and that these are accompanied by emotional disturbance and a sense of helplessness.

The discovery and analysis of transference is the most important work of group analysis, since it repeatedly interferes with the patient's true estimate of reality. Transference prevents each member from being able to accept another by conferring traits on him which originally stood in the way of a full relationship to a member of his original family. Accordingly patients must be schooled as to its derivation, qualities and purpose. It is indicated that the transference response is unconscious and that as a result the patient making the investment will usually resist recognition of his projection; that transference is inappropriate to the situation at hand, since the patient is responding to a mask which exists in *his* mind, rather than to the objective actuality. It is noted that transference has the elements about it of the illogical, unreasonable and absurd, that these qualities aside, the patient inevitably persists in his untenable position with compulsive insistence and that he reproduces his irrelevant projection over and over. It is specified that the transferring patient experiences and usually exhibits some affective disturbance, such as mild anxiety, irritability, depression, fearfulness which may mount to the most unrestrained panic and terror. It may be erotism, infatuation or romantic sentiment. It is associated with enormous feelings of helplessness which overwhelm rational considerations. Even though all its disarming and disadvantageous features are repeatedly demonstrated, the patient seems unable to control its imperative recurrence. It is revealed that the transference response is always excessive, well beyond that called for by the provoking circumstance and hence, overcomes and renders the member ineffectual. It tends simultaneously to startle, upset and inhibit persons in the immediate environment by the enormity and suddenness of its appearance. Its unyielding quality makes it difficult to modify and it takes a fixed course of its own, which the patient and analyst seem for a long time unable to disturb or deflect. All of these characteristics have an immobilizing effect on the patient. Bound by these limiting restraints he cannot react with the freedom and plasticity demanded by diverse environmental stimuli. It is suggested that any transference reaction, in the moment, should be traced, if possible, by historical flashback to the earlier experiences which determined the nature of the present response.

By example and illustrative demonstration from material at hand, the analyst repeatedly verifies the singular features of transference outlined. To this end, he avoids no opportunity to clarify any one patient's investment of another or the analyst. In the beginning whenever a reaction appears which has the characteristics of projection, he points out to the reactor the transference character of his response. With increasing experience, patients become more adept in identifying one another's transference reactions. The extreme disparity of various investments confronts each member with the patently illusory nature of these responses and he learns to see his own particular masking of others with parental or sibling surrogate cloaks as equally inappropriate. It is emphasized that transference must be dealt with in the moment of its occurrence. Anything short of this is resistance.

In some respects the transference is so rigidly fixed in the character structure that the patient projects the same distortions regardless of the personalities around him. But there are penumbral variations in his reactions to every patient and to the analyst that are a part of the transference. That aspect of investment which is so fixed as to be the same regardless of the personality on which it is projected is fairly readily discernible. Those nuances in the transference which vary, depending on the nature of the provocative personality, are less obvious; they require vigilant attention. But the close pursuit of these shadowy variants in transference relationships is most rewarding. It is the analysis of these trends, peripheral to the central transference, that makes group analysis an intensive process. While in individual analysis a patient may project onto the therapist at different times father, mother or sibling images, the analyst is less likely spontaneously to arouse these multiple investments than a group of people with variously stimulating personality peculiarities. The central or thematic transference reaction, most generally elicited, appears as a reproduction of a relationship to a more significant parent with whom the patient was more ambivalently and affectively bound. Lesser peripheral or penumbral transferences, appearing with more subtlety and often altogether neglected in individual analysis, reproduce conflictful but less painfully traumatic relationships to the less significant parent and siblings. The multiplicity of ways in which a patient dresses up the other members accurately reanimates the old family, disclosing in the action both his history and the richly divergent facets of his personality.

In individual analysis it is often difficult for patient and therapist to follow the projection onto the therapist of the roles played by a number of significant members of the family. The group provides all the familial actors and lateral transference possibilities. Not only the number of patients but also the presence of men and women expose and more rapidly precipitate aspects of transference relationships to both male and female parental and sibling surrogates. The presence of patients of both sexes facilitates the appearance and resolution of early conflicting unconscious trends formerly elicited by father, mother, sister and brother. The group recreates the family unit in which the patient can more freely reanimate the impelling and denying emotional demands whose contradictions he was once unable to solve. As he gradually becomes able to dispose of compulsive investments and discerns group members in fact, they become the social bridge to the establishment of normal interpersonal relations.

A patient will not infrequently select several other participants who represent for him diverse aspects of the same parent on whom he projects the psychological heritage of the past. The choice of a particular patient or of the analyst as a target for a specific aspect of the transference depends on the extent to which certain trends in the provocative personality most nearly resemble special characteristics of an earlier familial associate. The likeness may be near or remote. The approximation is in terms of sex, age and primarily phases of character structure. The evocation of particular facets of transference by specific patients itself becomes a matter for study from the point of view of the provocateur's unique neurotic and healthy qualities that inspire revivals of outmoded forms in other members. For some patients it does not matter in the slightest what the age or sex of a given member is, with regard to eliciting a transference—they will project the mother image onto a man and the father image onto a woman. For them, as for most, the important element evoking a particular familial mantle is the behavior in the moment, or fragment of character structure in the provocateur rather than his gender.

One of us (Wolf) had the opportunity, some time ago, to alternate sessions with a female analyst, both conducting a meeting together once a week. The purpose in organizing a group with multiple therapists was partly to teach and learn and partly to see the effect of introducing what might turn out to be maternal and paternal images in the persons of the two analysts. There was no uniform response to them. For some both evoked parental projection. Occasionally negative transference was directed by a patient toward the male therapist if there was historically greater hostility toward the father, and toward the female therapist, if there was early resentment of the mother. But just as often, it appeared that parental roles were reversed by members. And perhaps just as frequently patients did not use the analyst as father and mother surrogates at all, but utilized one another instead. This experience seemed to show that there is no special advantage in introducing two analysts of opposite sexes. When a single therapist conducts group meetings for the duration of treatment, patients may choose some member of the group of a sex opposite to that of the analyst as a representative of the missing parent. Sometimes if the analyst is seen as a mother image, the patient may choose another male or female member as a father image. Occasionally a patient discovers two or three father and mother surrogates in the group and variously any number of sibling substitutes. Sometimes the analyst is not regarded as a parental equivalent but as a sibling or child, and parental proxies are chosen entirely from the patient membership. However, there are some few members who never seem to unsex others in projection. For them the presence of both sexes among the membership provides a target for the investment of heterosexual transference reactions which are elicited with more difficulty when patients are obliged to project them onto a parent or sibling deputy of the same sex. Thus a mixed group enables each patient to excite, evolve, study and analyze projected relationships to meaningful figures of both sexes in his past.

An aspect of transference that receives repeated emphasis in the group is the analysis of such an action in the moment of its occurrence. It will not do to let a patient evade a consideration of his present irrational behavior by looking backward into history to seek the origin of peculiar conduct. It is a valuable exercise to search out critical causes. But the persistent probing into historical beginnings can become obsessional. It can enable a patient to neglect grappling with the forces that compel him even now to reconstruct the past against his better judgment. In individual analysis where the tendency may exist to explore biography in excess, transference attitudes are not always revived with the startling vividness encountered in group analysis. This is true, in a measure, because in individual analysis the therapist probes, while in group analysis the patients react and interact. Inquiry leads to insight, but inter-reaction has a boomeranging, repercussive effect that stirs echoes of former times with resurgent clarity. In individual analysis a patient can unconsciously falsify his record by reanimating perjured likenesses of parental figures. No such distortion is possible in the group, if the therapist holds the patient to his projection in the moment of its occurrence. And while it is true, in individual analysis, that the analyst can likewise insist on interpreting transference responses to him as they appear, he is frequently so unprovocative and so commonly bent on searching, that the reactions to him are often minimal or else such subtle transferences that they are too obscure to be interpreted.

Once again, this does not mean that the therapist and the patients neglect history altogether; they look upon biographical records as of central importance, but only insofar as they clarify transference, and only to the extent that they appear in significant bursts of recollection in association with the analysis of transference. By utilizing history in this way, long, irrelevant excursions into biography which are largely resistive, are eliminated. There is a curious correlation between biography and transference. To the extent that history is studied outside the context of immediate transference it is relatively unrevealing and useless as therapy. To the extent that history is studied within the context of immediate transference it provides understanding and is useful as therapy. Furthermore, the recollection of valuable fragments of the past is enormously facilitated by free association around and examination of an acutely neurotic reaction in the moment of transference. And there is a rewarding interplay between history and transference, one elaborating the other until their close relation is established in detail. In spite of the therapist's emphasis on this procedure patients manage in early alternate meetings to ventilate many aspects of previous experience. As they come to see the misleading character of extensive biographical rambling, they abandon this form of resistance. To the degree that the analyst is able early in treatment to effect such concentration on the analysis of transference, he shortens the duration of therapy. The handling of immediate projection stirs and highlights the salient repressed past—and it is this history suddenly welling into the present under the stimulus of transference that has illuminating value.

There is an element in the group setting that facilitates the analysis of transference, namely, the confrontation of each member with his disparate projection on the same person. It is often baffling in individual treatment to try to convince a patient that his estimate of the analyst is far from realistic, but is rather a reproduction of an unresolved conflictful attitude toward a parent. The neurotic person stubbornly insists that his feeling for and impression of the therapist are accurate. And while the analyst may grant their tenability, he has great difficulty in persuading the patient that they are also an attempt to maintain archaic familial constellations. His obstinacy melts more easily in a milieu where he is faced with divergent impressions of the same person projected by many present. He is forced to reexamine his perceptive faculties. He cannot maintain so readily his critical obstinacy that the analyst is brilliant, strong and all-providing when another patient insists just as mulishly that the doctor is stupid, weak and unreliable. He is obliged to reconsider his original investment of the therapist for possible misrepresentation. And in his reactions to other patients he is also forced to reinvestigate his projective devices.

There is another element in the group setting which is conducive to the fuller evocation of transference possibilities. And that is the variously provocative characteristics of the multiple personalities in the group. No matter how versatile a therapist is, he is still bound by the limitations of his character structure. This has an unstimulating effect on the patient as far as calling forth the multiple projective potentials in him are concerned. The disparate personalities in the group furnish a larger number of exciting agents whose particular differences elicit wider and more subtle facets of transference than is attainable by the analyst alone. If he is skillful, he may, by uncovering successively deeper levels of the patient's personality or by playing different roles, evoke less obvious and more many-sided penumbral transferences, but in general these shadings are lost. With little effort on his part, but with mere attention he can discern how naturally one patient animates another into revealing peripheral sides of neurotic investment that would otherwise be missed or extracted with great difficulty. This fact is underscored by the discharge of a recovered patient or the introduction of a new one. Under these circumstances the absence of an old or the insertion of a new infectious element stirs each member unconsciously to present a fresh side of his nature, projected or normal. This has the effect not only of enlarging the view of transference but of giving the patient an opportunity to test his developing healthy resources in ever-widening circles of society. Further striking evidence of the provocative effect of the group, as compared with the therapist alone, becomes manifest following the movement of a patient from individual to group analysis. From a comparatively static, single-sided individual he turns into an active, complex person with multiple facets that challenge investigation.

Each patient's provocative role must be explored in terms of the healthy and neurotic responses he elicits. Members are asked to assist in discovering one another's inflammatory tactics. This becomes apparent gradually as eight or ten patients continually tell each other what he does to them in emotional terms. But how then can he distinguish what is truly provocative, originating in the provocateur, and what is neurotically derived from the reactor? In the interplay back and forth of mutual inter-reaction there are healthy and unhealthy forces at work between any two people. The therapist may take the lead, in the beginning, in demonstrating this. He shows that in every interpersonal encounter there is the possibility of developing vigorous and bilaterally rewarding interchange; but he also points out how, by pursuing neurotic investments in transference and countertransference, any two individuals may end up in attempts to dominate, control, exploit or separate from one another. To intercept mutually destructive or detaching interplay, he is continually alert to transference and countertransference possibilities. It is sometimes very difficult to discover the actual initiator of a neurotic circus movement. It is, however, most important to intercept and analyze the movement once it is under way, and to establish the healthy and neurotic deportment of the players in mid-scene.

We have already seen how dreams may lead to insight, provoke elaborate free association and cleave through resistance. But in the clarification of transference, dreams are also valuable therapeutic adjuncts. A member may, for example, project an associated woman patient in a dream, in a dual role: both as a menacing figure and a loveable one as well. He may do this before free association or biographic acknowledgment has given us any indication of his mother's ambivalent attitude toward him. Interpretation of the dream enables him and the group to discover the castrating mother image with which he compulsively invests the woman. As he recognizes the transference features of his vision of her, and sees her, in fact, as a friendly associate, he is able to divest her of her threatening aspect and she becomes more loveable. As he progressively analyzes the compulsive character of his attachment to her, he dispels even this maternal hold and she becomes simply an engaging friend, stripped of maternal qualities, but with an attractiveness of her own. In these instances, reality proves much richer and rewarding to the patient than his illusion.

Perhaps the citation of a few examples of the transference process as it occurs in the group will be illuminating. In prior individual treatment Helen evidenced erotic interest in her analyst that was associated with some fear and anxiety, mixed unconscious feelings directed toward her father in childhood. These were never conscious or expressed. During an early group meeting, the analyst complimented George on his brilliant intuitive appraisal of her. She felt, at once, that he was being favored, and reacted with jealousy, feeling that he was more highly regarded for his intellectual talent. Immediately anxious, she challenged his statement and reacted with marked hostility toward both throughout the duration of the meeting. Despite her competition with him for the analyst's esteem, she felt that he would inevitably do better than she and that the therapist would just as certainly always promote him because he was a man. The compulsive nature of her conduct together with its interesting sequel came out at the next session. Helen told that upon leaving the previous meeting she had gone automatically to a florist to order an elaborate bouquet for her mother. Suddenly confounded in the flower store, she stopped and tried to realize what she was doing. There was really no occasion for sending her mother a bouquet, for the latter was not ill, nor was it a holiday or an anniversary. Understanding followed directly. She knew then that in the group the analyst had changed from a father to a mother image; George, the man the therapist had complimented, had become a brother substitute with whom she had been in perpetual rivalry for her mother's attention. Praise of him elicited the projection of the mother image onto the analyst. It also aroused a keen hostility toward the patient and especially toward the analyst. The gift of flowers was to propitiate a mother who was annoyed by her conduct, to conceal her welling resentment and to appease her conscience for coming so close to fully expressing her anger against her mother. Of striking interest was her abandonment of the father image in the therapist, as soon as the group provided a situation in which the analyst could reward a man who was at once invested with brother quality. Apparently she was able to re-create the father image as long as the analyst was alone with her. As soon as the original family was reanimated by the group setting and more particularly by the authority figure's approval of a man, a particular familial constellation was revived that necessitated a revision in her earlier investment on the analyst. A high estimate of a man, unconsciously recalled greater admiration of her brother and disapprobation for herself. Her mother was the prime agent in the construction of this historical configuration.

Later meetings brought out her mother's actual preference for Helen's brother because he was a boy. Helen's compulsive penis envy, her disregard for her feelings and excessive regard for excelling intellectuality, in the company of which she always felt doomed to come off second best, reproduced her relationship to mother and brother. By attention to the aspects of her shifting transferences to the analyst and to George, we were at last able to help Helen relinquish familial claims on her and to react in her own and other's right.

In thirty preliminary sessions, Joe and the analyst got on famously. He was brilliant, serene and exceptionally friendly. There was good rapport on both sides; they liked one another. He made rapid progress. There seemed to be no resistance. He interpreted a dream, and the analyst would add an additional point. He accepted it, usually with a modification that seemed appropriate. There were no stumbling blocks—it all seemed too unneurotic. The analyst proposed that he join a group, where certain areas of his personality might reveal themselves more adequately. It took the first group meeting to provoke the only indication of negative transference that could be discovered. He was a changed man. The harmonious relationship, his appreciation of what the analyst had done for him and his willingness to act upon suggestions had vanished. He challenged substantially everything the analyst said, and his keen intuition, although extremely helpful in analyzing group personnel, was unconsciously intended to forestall and belittle the analyst's contribution.

Whereas in prior private sessions there had been easy exchange, in the group he would hardly allow the analyst to speak. He interrupted, he anticipated and predicted (often accurately enough) what the analyst was about to say. The analyst held his tongue for the time being. But very soon the group noticed his compulsive behavior and began discussing it. When the analyst called to his attention the contrast between his former complacent demeanor during individual analysis and his subsequent truculent attitude toward him in the group, he expressed surprise and embarrassment at having been guilty of such behavior. But even as he spoke, he was struck with a flash of historical insight:—he recalled with what pontifical dignity and Victorian strictness his father held court at the dining table when Joe was a child; how one had to tiptoe about the house, when his father was napping on Sunday afternoons; how he was not allowed to speak unless spoken to in his father's presence. And he remembered other indignities extending to his not being allowed to enter the bathroom as a very little child when his mother was bathing—a privilege, however, that his father permitted himself. At subsequent meetings he explained how all his life he could talk freely and easily with one person, just as he used to do with his mother. But in the presence of a group he felt driven to excel, to be the genius in the drawing-room. In every social gathering, he habitually recreated the family milieu and automatically strove to become its guiding intellect. The group suggested, and Joe acknowledged, that he might now be playing an assumed paternal role in the new family. Then he remembered how as a child he had been almost irresistibly impelled to challenge his father in everything the latter did or said, but he had never quite dared to carry it off.

The reproduction of his relationship to his mother when alone with the analyst and to his father and family when in the group became apparent and led to deeper insight into his Oedipal conflict, his attachment to his mother, his repressed rivalry with his father and his compulsive replacement of the father in every regenerated family. Certainly, Joe's transfer to a group revived old family ghosts that could not have been so easily discovered or dispelled without reproducing the household unit.

There are at least three salient points involved in Helen's and Joe's stories. The first illustrates the sudden appearance of occasionally unforeseen bursts of transference toward the therapist or another member after a patient has been introduced to a group. The second throws light on the inevitable appearance of previously latent facets of personality, new and multiple transferences in the recreation of the old family, so that movement into a group changes behavior. The third illustrates how significant incidents in early life are recalled by the flashback method in relation to the analysis of immediate transference.

In difficult marital issues, the group setting has proved effective. Through an unorthodox experiment which led to the treatment of husband and wife in individual analysis, with good results, one of us (Wolf) went even further beyond the realm of standard practice by organizing in 1940, a group of five married couples.

The analysis of husband and wife in on-the-spot observation was most illuminating. He had treated a man for some months and listened most sympathetically during this time to his embittered accounts of domestic strife. When a dream fragment appeared suggesting that he was not altogether the innocent in their relationship, the analyst suggested a Rorschach for his wife and arranged for an interview with her. Later they joined a group together. It soon became apparent that he would, artfully and unconsciously, needle and humiliate her. He accomplished this with such subtlety that neither he nor she were, at the time, aware of it. This would go on for a week or so until she flared up and attacked him in return. For him this attack clinched his point. He appealed triumphantly to his fellow group members to support him in the contention that she was an impossibly aggressive woman. The group managed in time to demonstrate his provocative role to his satisfaction.

Marital differences are not always resolved so satisfactorily. Occasionally, when a couple seems to be hopelessly at odds in bilateral transference, we start by treating them in separate groups. They are brought together in the same group when they are more aware of their projective mechanisms. It is usually not too difficult to persuade couples to join the same group. When they do, each invests the other with historical familial qualities, and the happy resolution of their difficulties is determined by the effectiveness with which their mutual transferences can be dispelled.

In the married couple group each participant was sensitive to the difficulties peculiar to marital conflict. Members were able to crystallize quickly for one another the unconscious core of what was struggling to reach awareness. One couple that had managed successfully to cope with a problem would guide another to an equally gratifying solution of a similar impasse. Perhaps it should be added that, in the group composed of five married couples, two finally divorced each other, in their cases a wholesome dénouement. It is relevant to indicate that the therapeutic goal is not the preservation of a marital relationship at any cost. In this regard it is equally pertinent to remember that the current national divorce rate numbers one out of every three couples.

In 1949 one of us (Wolf) had the opportunity to treat an entire family jointly in a group. The experiment was short-lived, only six months. One of the sons who was a compulsive server asked that other members of the family share the cost of treatment. At this point the group broke up before the problem could be analyzed. More recently the other of us (Schwartz) has been working with a family group for more than a year.

Conscious Personal Action and Social Integration

In a later phase of group analysis, the technic of spontaneous interreaction must be supplemented by conscious, methodical sifting and planning of verbalized responses in the best personal and mutual interests of the members. This is a period of intense struggle with one's own transference reactions, when they cannot be justified and conciliated; when insight without acting on it cannot be tolerated; when character change must replace explaining and when self and group discipline demands personal reformation. It is the period of working through.

One test of readiness for discharge is a patient's ability to analyze and dispose of his own transference investments and his skill in not making lateral countertransferences to other patients who are disturbed by their projections onto him. A growing aptitude in detecting the component of irrelevant investment in another person's behavior enables him to avoid being drawn into countertransference. This is enhanced by rational resistance to impulsive reaction and the choice, instead, of responding to the real person behind the façade.

With time, patients become more and more adept in spotting their own transferences, and they contribute just as skillfully in the interpretation of the transferences of others. Their inter-reactivity brings vital projection to the surface, material which is analyzed by them as illogical investment. Once having discovered and studied the nature of each patient's multiple transferences, all members struggle to reach beyond this illusory veneer and to identify the genuine person behind the counterfeit front. For it is this more substantial self, embryonic though it often is, that is the emerging, healthy and likable side of a personality. As patients grope for this solid side of themselves, transferences atrophy from disuse, and the irrational emotion of earlier meetings is gradually replaced by mutual friendliness and realistic regard.

At this point it is easy to see that the six stages outlined blend one into the other, but in the strictest sense, there are really no stages at all. There are no sharp demarcations of time at which one begins and another ends. They may indeed proceed concurrently, each augmenting the other. One may think of them, rather, as levels of development in the course of reaching the point, called the sixth stage of group analysis, where constructive personality change is advocated and carried through. As noted above, dream analysis and free-association run like threads through all of the levels of progress and constantly serve as reference points in each patient's course. Yet the sequence enumerated is valuable, because it allows for variations in movement, dependent on the quality of the analysand's state. If resistance and transference can, in the judgment of the therapist, be analyzed in the second stage without jeopardizing the patient's progress, the analyst may choose to do so. It is wrong to think of these stages as closed or boxed-in technics employed in segments of time. Still, if the analyst ventures into going around prematurely in some groups, he may find intense resistances and hostile transferences and countertransferences developing that are hard to break. He may then be forced to return—as he should—to the second stage in which the emphasis is purely on personal dream and fantasy ventilation in a permissive atmosphere. He does this to recover that harmony which is necessary for adequate interaction. In a closed group, the stages described are more easily identifiable. And the initial rapport so necessary for the newly admitted patient speaks for the wisdom of working with closed groups. However, we have almost always kept groups going continuously, discharging the recovered and introducing the sick. So that membership kept changing as the group went on. Apparently it is possible to do this, if the therapist is patient enough to wait for initial, generalized positive transference or rapport. Then, what resistances and negative transferences do appear later have less strength and intensity, so that a newly introduced person is not traumatized by them. And he is rather impressed with the high level of group activity which soon includes and sweeps him along.

The Role of the Group Analyst

What, it is pertinent to ask, are the particular qualifications and functions of a successful group analyst? At present, since he is working with a technic that is relatively new, any answer will, of course, be tentative.

As Foulkes has pointed out, psychoanalysts are not ipso facto good group analysts, and, he goes on to say, it in no way impugns the former to emphasize that special attributes are required of the group analyst. He must first of all be a psychoanalyst. He must have adequate training, intuitive insight, a capacity for empathy and an ability to dispose of countertransference attitudes. He must expect concerted efforts to deflate him. He must have the capacity to withstand neurotic attacks on him with composure. He must not be discouraged or thrown off balance by the intensity of interpersonal enmity which occasionally develops in early meetings. Such outbursts are largely projective in character, and his function is jeopardized if he fails to react to them with appropriate analysis. Even the most timid will assail him from their vantage point among the group, and destructive patients will test his tolerance of neurotic frustration and aggression to the utmost. In spite of the therapist's attempt to create a new, more benevolent and permissive family, the old one with all its rivalry, aggression and dictatorship may assert itself and tax the new parent in the extreme.

He ought to be able patiently to welcome the manifold variety of transferences with which he is invested and not be misled to accept them as real by inappropriate reaction. To be sure, the analyst is afforded the same group protection as his patients. If he is unreasonably attacked, some of them will come to his rescue and support him when the occasion seems to demand it. For, acting upon his injunction, they are continually engaged in reacting spontaneously to everyone present including the analyst. He, too, must expect both blame and praise according to their changing concepts of his desserts.

He must be strong enough to acknowledge his errors and secure enough to relinquish the initiative to the group or to a patient as the situation at the moment demands. It is distinctly no position for a practitioner who would evade the interpersonal give and take that is the very basis of group analysis. He must not approach the group with the missionary's urge to convert, with the supercilious spirit of the benevolent patron or the oppressive dictatorship of the pedagogue. He cannot be pretentious, and any suggestion of pomposity will get short shrift from the group members, for he is a leader who at the same time must sit among his patients as an equal. The dual role is not an easy one. In short, his neurotic tendencies should have been dealt with in his personal or group analysis.

The function of the group analyst is to guide his patients to fuller awareness and social integration. He can best accomplish this by avoiding conceited and compulsive leadership. He can more surely achieve such a goal by attentive regard to what group members can teach him. The therapist alone need not know all to provide adequate leadership. His nuclear, professional and leading position is not by itself enough to provide his patients with the full insight they need.

Experience with him is not comprehensive enough to insure healthy social restoration. Therefore, it is necessary that he supplement his clinical knowledge with an understanding of the interaction of the various group members. This means that he must constantly maintain an alert and intimate connection with the rich reservoirs of understanding which are potential in the group, catalytically interplaying their intuitive insight with his own. He must attend the least small voice as well as the loudest. It will not do for him to detach himself at his desk and hand down well prepared instructions. While he seeks solutions to neurotic problems, the proper answers cannot be found without vigilant regard to group experience which is continually testing his leadership. While he plans operations for the resolution of conflict, he cannot achieve his objectives without the help of the patients. The patient members are an essential and final check on the extent to which therapeutic aims are being fulfilled. The patients' interactivity with each other and with the therapist guarantees status to each individual and finally enables him to utilize his own resources and those of the other members.

The group analyst's view of things tends to be one-sided. He sees patients and their behavior from above. Accordingly, his impression of what is happening is limited by his paternalistic, relatively nonparticipant position. While he engages in group activity, the quality of his participation is different and modifies his perception of events. The group, on the other hand, appreciates interpersonal forces at work from another side. Its awareness is likewise limited by its position and function in the group. To accomplish that harmony which will lead to integrated group activity, the analyst and patients must interweave their complementary roles. Leadership which achieves this is therapeutic.

The successful analyst learns never to underestimate the significance of the contribution that can be made by the members to mutual insight and social integration. Patients sometimes show themselves to be close to the unconscious truth. If the therapist is wise, he consults them and often supplements his experience with theirs. It may be said that neurotic conflict in part develops in the child out of contradictory influences imposed on him by his parents, who are exploitative, dictatorial, selfish and at the same time cooperative, democratic and supportive of the child's developing resources. In the new, permissive family of the group, to the extent that the therapist is authoritarian and detached from the group, he duplicates the destructive role played by the original parents. In this way he may reinforce the patients' difficulties and undermine their actual effectiveness. To the degree that he is continually attentive to the emerging intuitive potentials in the various members, he helps to create a new family unit of the group, in which each participant can realize increasingly gratifying levels of adjustment.

The therapist must be aware of unfeeling attitudes on his part in the group. Such an approach is evidence of his lack of specific attention to each member. There is danger in the group of thinking of it en masse rather than of each individual patient—his needs, his problems, his growth. Without special attention to each person, the therapist may act at random, either commending them as a whole or disapproving of them in toto. Such insensitivity to particular individuals breeds dissatisfaction and bitterness. It leads to the formation of neurotic cliques of malcontents who may wreck the group. The therapist must be alert to individual differences, the falling behind of a given patient and his possible personal confusion. If not, a member here and there becomes increasingly disaffected and disgruntled, and becomes a focal point of defection leading the group into disintegration.

The analyst who regards himself as the most active, critical thinker in the group and the patients as a relatively inert mass is likely to be led far astray. With such a misconception, he tends to overestimate himself and look down on the group; he has the illusion that success or failure depends pretty much on him and that the group is lacking in creative, contributory power. He believes that his acuteness alone determines the successful outcome of treatment. Such a view condemns the group to passivity and excludes the membership from the active participation essential to its recovery. It also reduces the group activity to a series of dictated or accidental psychodynamics whose ebb and flow are determined by the prescriptions, needs and fantasies of the authoritarian therapist. The fact is that the therapeutic process in the group proceeds in accordance with definite laws. While the development of the group moves on according to certain principles, the therapist and each patient are constantly modifying its progress (See Chapter 10). The therapist can play a most significant catalytic part in facilitating patient movement by seeing further ahead than his patients. He can do this also by desiring and struggling to accomplish healthy integration more vigorously than they. His effectiveness lies in his deep contact with each member, in his ability to understand them, in his skill in foreseeing the historical course the individual takes and in his confidence in the potential resources of the various members.

The course a group takes is primarily determined by the various character structures of the participant members, itself a product of their previous history. The personal qualities of the analyst modify this course. This does not mean that the contributions the analyst can make should be ignored. Nor does it mean that group progress is exactly predetermined by the constitution of the patients in it. If this were so, it would make no difference whatsoever on the movement of the group, if one therapist were substituted for another. And the role of the group analyst would be a passive one in the face of the group's fatalistic course. But the influence of the therapist cannot be reduced to this kind of insignificance. He must possess skills which make him most capable of resolving intra-group conflict; of interpreting the problems presented by the patients' previous history; of pointing up the new needs created by the preceding development of the group's interactivity, of taking the initiative in satisfying these needs.

In this relatively new field of group analysis the therapist must be a person who is venturesome, for there are many new, experimental areas to explore. He should, therefore, avoid assuming dogmatic attitudes in the group's interest as well as his own. If he is authoritarian, he prevents the group's full emergence and contribution, which may enlighten him also. He seeks to be capable of admitting his own mistakes openly, of examining the reasons for them and of analyzing the conditions which gave rise to them in order to correct them. He needs to be able to show his own shortcomings, if necessary, and so be an example to the others.

The psychoanalyst cannot encourage an inspirational atmosphere which represses unconscious factors and creates unstable illusions of success which are bound to be shortlived. He promotes a spirit of deep, mutual examination and review of personal strengths and weaknesses. Such a procedure does not destroy the patient but explores his neurotic character structure.

At times when the group falters, the analyst must remain firmly and consistently optimistic. He takes a stand against any one patient's exploitation of another. He must avoid in himself and discourage in the members the intellectual cliché that obscures the simple, richer and more elemental meaning for which the patient is groping. A calculated, scholastic approach leads to an evasion of affective contact indispensable for rehabilitation. Here, as elsewhere, he can turn to the group for the naive phrase which is poetic, refreshing and apropos in order to escape the compulsive use of the more restricted language of professional associates. He should set an example in simplicity, honesty and straightforwardness to encourage those patients who underestimate their large ability to make meaningful contributions. He does not always emphasize what is said, but rather how it is said. He tries to treat complicated questions without complexity. He should not strive for the eloquent phrase. His thoughts need to be clear and distinct—their intent plain. While he plays a leading role, he strives to help the members feel he is one of them—not apart. He ought not teach too much, for if he does, he will find himself governing rather than liberating. In this regard it would pay him to lend an attentive ear to what is said of him in the group. There he will find his severest critics as well as his staunchest defenders. Regard for what they say will help him to enlarge his understanding of himself. Again, he should not hesitate to show his appropriate feelings in the group. In doing this, he sets an example of freedom and emotional contact that is infectious. If he hides affect, the group will respond in kind. His sadness or gaiety will strike healthy reactive chords in the others. But, if he is well, he will be realistically optimistic.

The analyst is on guard against alliances in the group which conceal deeper, unrealized and unspoken attitudes, which should be ventilated. Two patients, both fearful of criticism, may evolve a superficial and precarious neurotic amity, which undermines the therapeutic process. Their fraudulent harmony is resistance and works to prevent the exposure of facets of character structure. Patient progress cannot take place in an atmosphere of insincere and evasive peace and good will. It can move on if the analyst presses for mutual exertion and cross exposure, which develops contradictory positions. Then, when intra- and interpersonal conflict is exposed, the group can proceed to overcome these seemingly irreconcilable attitudes. The neurotic character structure must sooner or later be exposed, not coddled. Otherwise it fights for its existence and defends an outlived cause. At the same time the new and healthier personality is also struggling to emerge. The analyst must ally himself with the healthy and make himself the implacable opponent of the outmoded pathology. He can do this by openly and honestly exploring unconscious conflict and screened attitudes and encouraging the group to do likewise. In examining the neurotic framework of the personality, he must concentrate his analysis on oppressive or prohibitive trends, on overprotective and exploitative tendencies and on ever-present penility, whether it shows itself in men or women.

Conscious and unconscious overestimation of what is generally regarded as masculine plays a part in the evolution and resolution of every neurosis. The analyst resists the obvious and insidious ways in which the masculine is overvalued. To this end, he takes every opportunity to establish the complementary equality of the sexes in difference. He exposes the devious and subtle ways in which the equivalents of masculinity are taken for granted as superior. He shows each member how, unconsciously, he has hardly progressed from the phallus-worship of his ancestors. Among male patients, the analyst indicates how this may manifest itself in compulsive pursuit of women to prove sexual prowess and to relieve castration anxiety. Among female patients, he points out how male supremacy notions are reflected in what amounts to the same thing: the manifold varieties of penis envy. The analyst exposes the social counterparts of this overevaluation of the male sex organ as an incessant power drive that shows itself in diverse, antisocial efforts to establish individual dominance. He traces these sexual and social correspondents to their common cultural and personal origin. He challenges psychopathic values. In this way the therapist persists in analyzing aggressive interactions. Members must be schooled not to value each other only as men or women to be exploited as competitive sexual objects.

The analyst can foster harmonious accord if he takes pains to oppose every psychopathic alliance against healthy mutuality. He strengthens individual growth by trying to expose the destructive quality of such unwholesome compacts. He is alert to the fact that not all affinity in the group is necessarily salutary. The devils too may be in league. Under the pretext that "it is necessary to express hostility"—at times a true enough observation—patients deviously, compulsively and sadistically attack and provoke discord and regression among others who are progressing. The analyst supports forces in the group whose interests are not partisan, but generally and reciprocally emancipating. He stands firm against and thwarts clannishness and narrow self interest. He analyzes attempts on the part of one patient to misuse another by exposing the act and its motivation. He resists appeasement of pathologic tendencies which would dominate or manipulate members. Such concessions will inevitably bridle and delay patients' progress.

The analyst constantly seeks a theoretic base to keep pace with his practical work. A flexible theoretic background, continually modified by concrete experience in the group, gives patients and therapist alike the power of orientation, clarity of perspective, faith in the work, and confidence in ultimate recovery. But he must be equally strong in practical work. Study of theory and practice will enable him to see a long way ahead and thus anticipate successes and impasses in the patients' best interest. Attention to the interplay of hypothesis and fact leads to the continuous elaboration and modification of each, establishing ever clearer insights into reality and corresponding changes in technique.

Every form of therapy is limited in what it can accomplish. While the analyst hopes to help the patient develop and realize his full possibilities, both he and the patient are partially blocked by a frustrating reality. Yet even within the present social context, certain things can be achieved. The movement of a patient from individual to group analysis is a considerable step toward his socialization. It is a vital step away from any misleading glorification of individualistic acts which merely subject each of us to a compulsive competition and isolation. To this unsound emphasis on detachment and individuality, the therapist offers genuine regard and relatedness to each patient in the group, with a chance to liberate and coordinate unrealized reserves. The therapist opposes purely narcissistic interests at the expense of others. He sees that no individual really gains anything at the cost of others.

An important function of the group analyst is to make clear in the terminal phase of treatment the relation between the individual patient's freedom to act as he pleases and the needs of others in any group of which he is a part. He needs to become aware that his compulsivity demands a lack of freedom to behave in any other way. He learns that his real needs and those of others are not necessarily always in opposition. He does not feel restrained or controlled by interpersonal demands. He finds this lack of freedom to be only apparent and unreal. His seeming restraint is really an increased consciousness that roles and fulfillments are complementary. He becomes able to relinquish his detached, masturbatory egocentricity. The neurotic's compulsive insistence on personal liberty frequently masks a wish to exploit and dominate, which needs to be analyzed. When he can recognize the congruence of self realization and interpersonal fulfillment and can act accordingly, he is on the way to getting well.

An example may clarify this notion. A patient insists on his right to masturbate. It is only when he is alone that he feels free enough to enjoy an ecstatic orgasm. He is inhibited during coitus, when his penile skin feels anaesthetized. As he is liberated from unconscious prohibitions, he learns how to reach new heights of personal pleasure in mutually gratifying sexual intercourse, more pleasurable to him because it also delights his partner. Rid of the illusion that contact involves demands, he realizes himself interpersonally.

Destructive Patterns in Group Analysis

An unfavorable situation which may arise in a group is the development of intense generalized neurotic resistance, accompanied by hostile bilateral transferences, and the formation of allies in groups of two or three, leaving some individuals isolated except for a relatively warm relationship to the analyst. Sometimes even this association becomes strained, because the patient blames the therapist for having been exposed to such a trying antagonistic environment. Such forms of resistance must be analyzed, otherwise the group may fall apart. Attendance may become low and demoralize those present. The therapist, while taking an analytic view of absenteeism, confronts those who stay away with the possibility of being dropped. He explores transferences that force aggressors into belligerent roles and points out their illusory character. He is equally vigilant with regard to projective devices that impel the compulsively withdrawn to retreat further or to submit to the domination of other members. He seeks to uncover the causes for resistance to participation on deeper levels, pointing out explicitly the destructive character of particular defenses and encouraging free emotional ventilation. If the situation is unwholesome enough, he may for a while, suggest no going around in order to interrupt unanalyzed, aggressive attacks and propose a retreat to an earlier phase of treatment: the exclusive presentation of dreams and fantasies. A return to the airing of the personal unconscious material which is interpreted with the help of the group is preparation for a new mutual understanding. All else failing, the analyst may be obliged to remove a patient here and there, one at a time, at varying intervals, introducing each retired member into a more constructive group. Such a crisis can usually be avoided by not organizing a group with a majority of strongly sado-masochistic patients. Too many such members in the same milieu provide an unfavorable climate for the evocation of the positive resources that should be expressed if the group is to proceed efficiently.

In our early experiences with group analysis, we felt a good deal of uncertainty as to the practicality of using free-association and of trying to handle lateral transference reactions among numbers of patients. Might not a patient's resources be paralyzed by the attacks of others? Might his feelings of anxiety, exaggerated by mounting neurotic aggression in the group, force him into further withdrawal or irrelevant countersorties of his own? With a weak ego structure to start with, would he not beat a further psychic retreat in a setting that encourages free, interpersonal, affective responses, some of which are bound to be charged with hostility? How easily might he tolerate an atmosphere in which sexual matters are freely discussed, without running for cover? However, repeated clinical experience has reassured us. For a patient under inappropriate fire finds support in the analyst and some other member or members of the group. Their support fortifies him against hurt and isolation. If a penetrating remark made in free-association hits a target and makes him falter, the other members sustain him, until he can usefully tolerate insight. If an acute observation is lost on him, because it is aggressively colored and he hears only the hostility, the therapist encourages discrimination of what is valid and what is neurotic attack. Then others analyze both the patient's peculiar attention to ill-will that compels him to lose sight of what may be useful to him in terms of further self understanding, and the character trend of the aggressor in terms of his projection that impels him to design his comments in such a destructive way, that it becomes difficult for others to extract what is very valuable from them, and to accept them. This calls for analysis of the constructive and destructive content of the latter's comments. And it also involves study of his provocative role and transference devices. Attention to these details tends to dispel anxiety. The patient finds that careful exploration of psychic recesses is ultimately less terrifying than shutting one's eyes to them, so that the therapist's insistence on frankness is bound to be rewarding. Spectres of the past vanish when the unconscious closet is thoroughly inspected.

Another occasionally troubling problem is the temptation of some patients to consummate intimate sexual relations. It has happened that a couple will have intercourse within the first half dozen meetings. If the analyst forbids such intimacy, he duplicates the original parental proscription against incest. Men and women who become so engaged do so compulsively and may drift into physical familiarity whether the analyst prohibits it or not. Then the therapist is faced with their sense of guilt, a tendency to hide aspects of the relationship and a secret defiance that complicates and obscures the significance of the act. Furthermore, patients who leap into bed with one another do so rather extensively with people outside the group. In the therapeutic setting, the repetition of the sexual act has the advantage of subjecting compulsive promiscuity to examination. Whenever members reach out for one another in sexual release, the relationship is inevitably brought up for group discussion and analysis within a few sessions.

But the analyst does not encourage sexual intercourse. He takes a neutral position. In the beginning of group treatment, he presents the position outlined above, and thus guards as best he can against playing the repressive role of original familial figures. If nevertheless patients still indulge in intercourse, the analyst and the group try to understand the meaning of the act. Later on in the course of treatment when patients' embryonic, libidinous urgings emerge in healthier give and take, a more wholesome union may take place. As long as yearnings are the expression of genuine affection or love, the therapist must not match the original, castrating parent. However, for the majority of patients tabus against incest are so strong and the family unit so sharply reanimated in the group, that excursions into sexual contact are forbidden to them by old and stringent incorporated disciplines.

The immediate investment of the group with frightening, familial transference in the first or second group meeting is difficult to handle. When it happens, a patient may run out of a session in terror, as if fleeing demons. Trying to induce such a person to return to the group to face and analyze his projections can turn out to be a formidable task. Such a member has probably been prematurely ushered into the company of other patients. The analyst must try to discern in advance his sensibility and prepare him better to cope with his distortions of reality. This may be accomplished by waiting for the development of more positive transference in prior individual treatment, followed in this case by more intensive preliminary study of his particular projective devices. Apparently such an individual straightway recreates his own ugly family in any small cluster of strangers, where original conflict is forced speedily and dreadfully near the surface, so that he takes flight hurriedly. A patient who behaves this way is commonly shy, withdrawn and schizoid. He is fearful of a collection of people who may renounce etiquette and the superficial social forms that offer him some safety. He runs from the brutality he himself is repeatedly reincarnating. He is more comfortable in an outside world that assures him a precarious security as long as it remains conventional or distant. He rarely shows up in a group, or if he does, his resistances finally give way to analysis, so that he constitutes no serious indictment of the group analytic technic.

Is there not an ever present danger that the group, functioning as a re-created family, may become pathogenic as a family per se? Without adroit management, or even with it, some groups undoubtedly might wind up this way. The therapist watches for the elaboration of self-sufficient, inbred and incestuous trends that bind members together as neurotically as in the original family. A recovering patient, for example, may be attacked as unready for discharge by a compulsively overprotective member who is parentally castrating. If a man and woman gravitate toward one another with erotic interest, they may be invested with father and mother roles, and other patients may react to them with detached respect, voyeuristic aggressive interest or moralistic disapproval that corresponds to earlier ambivalent curiosity with regard to intimacy between the parents. These investments can be dispelled only by persistent analysis. Occasionally a member or two will exhibit some reluctance to permit a patient who has recovered to leave the group. They demonstrate the same kind of envy or jealousy earlier directed toward a sibling and feel the family group or parental therapist is favoring the cured member with special regard which his performance does not deserve. The majority, however, generally welcome the improvement of any one and take pleasure in his progress. Transference which denies discharge to a patient who has recovered is also analyzable.

Then there is the patient whose love for the emotional climate of the group borders on the ecstatic. He revels in the luxury of what he considers an absolutely honest relationship. He is, *mirabile dictu,* in a family whose projections, having become at last analyzable and understandable, no longer alarm or hurt him. The danger in his case is that he runs from real life to the fabricated safety of an unreal laboratory. He finds the group warmer and saner than most associations on the outside. He must be instructed how to carry the affective closeness he has consummated in the group to larger segments of society, beyond the confines of his fellow members. This, by the way, is a common objection to working in concert with other patients. How, it is asked, can one transpose the good fellowship of the group to areas outside it? Group analysis lays no Pollyannaish or grandiose claim to making the world a big happy family. But group analytic technic offers the patient a means of making conscious, trends that stand in the way of his vigorous affective contact with others, whether loving or hating. We say hating as well as loving, because there are some psychopathic influences in the world which can appropriately be hated.

Constructive Patterns in Group Analysis

A constructive use to which group analysis is put, is the demonstration to each patient that he shares his problems with others. He loses the illusion of isolation and of the uniqueness of his neurosis. How many times has the analyst working alone with a patient, heard him inquire whether the therapist ever encountered such an unusual and complex case before. It is the discovery of common human difficulties that often leads to freer self exposure. The group is also a buffer against despair of recovery. If the patient falters or is set back, the improvement and recovery of others encourages him to go on. His fear that he will receive only a fraction of the attention available in individual treatment is dissipated by the actual experience, when he is transferred from private to group analysis. Here he finds himself scrutinized by the searching inquiry of people, whose perceptive skills multiply with successive visits. The group comes quickly and accurately to the heart of a problem by progressive increments of cross association and intuition.

There are social rewards obtainable in a group that are not as accessible to a patient in private analysis. The members of the group appreciate proffered insight and acknowledge such favors with regard and affection. The patient who intuitively produces a bit of valuable information, hitherto unseen, learns to respect his inner reserves out of the esteem of others. This approval does not encourage compulsively brilliant performance which excludes affect. In this way a patient learns to appreciate his natural and uninhibited resources at the same time as he cultivates them along appropriate lines. This group experience also rewards the participant by making him feel increasingly helpful, a function he cannot so easily play in individual treatment.

The group has a constructive effect in recreating the family—but with a new look. By cultivating a permissive atmosphere in which mutual tolerance and regard can flourish, the earlier prohibitive character of the original family is projected with less intensity and is more easily dispersed. Furthermore, the general acceptance and sense of belonging that follow make it possible to achieve similarly easy transition to correspondingly untroubled social relations beyond the confines of the group. The other patients, out of their numbers, provide more familial surrogates for transference evocation. Each member comes to a realization of the extent to which he recreates his own childhood family in every social setting and invests others with inappropriate familial substitute qualities. The number of participants also clarifies the variety and multiplicity of central and penumbral transferences. While in individual analysis the therapist tries to see clearly what perceptual distortions the patient makes of outer reality and what internal factors contribute to this social disfigurement, the analyst is often misled, because he does not see the patient in action. In group analysis, the therapist also is interested in what is happening at the moment so that the patient's unconscious warping of fact can be observed in motion. He can then be confronted with his projective trends and the inciting role he plays in precipitating the environmental disturbances he resents so much.

The group setting facilitates the emergence and acceptance of insight by confronting each member with his disparate investments of other patients and the therapist. In individual analysis it is most trying to persuade the patient to regard his endowing the analyst with parental or sibling characteristics as illusion rather than a true estimate of fact. When, however, he joins a group, he finds that each patient unconsciously warps his perception of the therapist and of the other patients as well. He begins to question the reality of his view of people in the group. As he studies his transferences, he becomes aware of his provocative role, too. In individual analysis the therapist does not often react spontaneously to the patient, but the members of the group do. Each member tells him frankly what effect he produces, so that the character of his provocation and the part he plays in creating environmental responses become clear to him. Individual analysis offers no such microcosm in which the patient can discover in action the interplay of unconscious forces. If occasional individual sessions are indicated, because insight has been imposed too quickly and the patient cannot easily handle his newly exposed conflicts for example, the therapist offers support in a temporary return to individual treatment. If deep insight is tolerated, the analyst underlines that trend in the conflict which has a healthy interpersonal as well as a personally gratifying objective.

The group has a curious effect in the way it stirs the unconscious into activity. The analyst alone with a single patient appears to gain access to the repressed by probing analysis that is slower and more painstaking. The group, by its inter-reactive and spontaneous free-association, bursts the seams of resistance in a sort of chain reaction. It is as if the presentation of a nightmare to an assemblage had a socially agitating effect on unconscious energy, until now in check, that forces it into release. This animation in turn vitalizes others, and so on. It is startling to see one patient after another getting flashes of insight from the fantasies and dreams of successive free-associators. The stimulating power of each member's provocative inner self rakes up repressed trends around him. Evidently, there is so much closely shared unconscious material that the uninhibited imagery of one person stirs the deepest levels of another.

The comments of the analyst are sometimes too loaded with interpretation and too intellectual. This may remove him, if he is not careful, from an essential affective connection with the patient. Emotional detachment can not prevail in the group. Here the freely inter-reacting unconscious excitation of patient by patient is a source of provocation and interconnection, that furnishes material for analysis. The stimulative effect of exposure to the naked, unconscious trends of other people is difficult to resist. Going around establishes a freely flowing generalized absence of restraint, so that resistances break down and deeply conflictful material is exposed. The awareness of another's buried impulses and contradictory strivings agitates the observer profoundly and forces him to participate on his own deeper levels of emotional conflict. If, as rarely happens, the patient insists on not exposing some of these personal matters to the group, he may discuss them initially with the therapist in private.

Resistances seem to melt easily in the potentiating, catalytic atmosphere of mutual revelation in the group. The searching approach of the analyst who hardly reveals himself makes the individual analytic relationship one-sided and may have an inhibiting influence on the patient. And many of them complain of just this inequality. The necessity to expose oneself to another person without a corresponding disclosure by the therapist makes some patients self-conscious. They may feel the difference in status to be unfair. Their standing naked before a clothed examiner reinforces their sense of helplessness and inadequacy. Such a patient may become resentful or withdrawn and aggressively or deviously resist laying bare successively deeper levels of his personality. In the group each member is stimulated by the partial but always increasing self revelation of another to expose more and more of himself. The discovery that the next person not only comes to no harm in showing himself but wins social approval besides, encourages one to uncover as well. The general feeling of shared divestment in a benevolent atmosphere may enable a patient to show himself more freely. This experience is confirmed by the psychic climate of a group after three or four months of operation. An observer would be amazed at the high level of interactivity and unmasking that takes place.

Every patient resists uncovering certain unconscious trends in himself. When similar tendencies are exposed in another person, he may be better prepared to accept them in himself. Then, he has the further example from direct observation of how to cope with these same unconscious conflicts and benefits vicariously from their analysis. He may not sit passively by, but often works together with other members to disentangle and understand their common problems. Resistance that takes the form of irrelevant and evasive autobiography cannot be so easily used in the group. Freud alluded to his distrust of the self-told histories of neurotics. He felt that their reminiscences inserted inaccuracies intended to intercept disturbing, demonstrable relationships between significant early history and present symptoms. Even without the therapist's pushing for immediate responses and against elaborate background, the group climate is so electric that it produces more and more varied on-the-spot reactions that contain the past.

Another form of resistance that is bypassed in the group is the evasion of sexual material. This is managed by initial attention to the social counterparts of sexual trends, to which the members thereby gain indirect access. For attention to the characterological, interpersonal forms of behavior leads to speculation concerning corresponding sexual equivalents that are thus drawn into discussion for analysis.

Still another constructive advantage offered by group formation is that it removes the patient from the danger of prolonged dependence on the therapist. In the isolation of private treatment the analyst can encourage the patient to pursue his deepest personal longings. It may turn out that these aspirations are egocentric and indulging them leads to detached, antisocial self assertion. The gratification of his particular yearnings can amount to being allowed to exploit familial substitutes for neurotically satisfying ends. Humoring these impulses is bound to bring the patient into provocative, neurotic conflict with his associates who will not tolerate such infantile actions. Accordingly, he is impelled to turn more and more to the permissive therapist as the only agent who allows him this immature privilege. In some instances, such a positive transference develops out of the patient's discovery of an all-tolerant and loving parent in the analyst that the therapist can use the rapport to turn the patient toward more self-reliant and social contact. However, the patient may misuse his dependency to prolong and entrench his childish pleasure in the analytic relationship. The group process encourages reliance of one person on the next, and more quickly demands and gets an abandonment of prolonged, possessive and parasitic attachment that excludes the possibility of mature kinship.

Perhaps one of the most valuable aspects of group analysis is that it facilitates giving up the ideal of having a relationship to the single-parent analyst. Instead of offering the questionable shelter of a private relationship to one omniscient ego-ideal it presents the patient with a group of persons in whose common effort he can join; whereas the basis of a private relationship may well be evasive of social reality and tend to create an aura of isolation, the group serves in just the opposite way. Instead of enhancing the average patient's tendencies to neurotic isolation and his anarchic wish to act out his pathology, psychoanalysis may help him realize his full potential as a social being. This is an added bridge to the establishment of healthy social relationships outside of analysis. Rather than strengthening the egocentric ideal—typified in the neurotic's mind by the notion of the omnipotent therapist—group analysis helps to resolve the false antithesis of the individual versus the group by giving the patient a conscious experience that his fulfillment can be realized better in a social or interpersonal setting.

Certainly in noting the characteristics of psychoanalysis in groups, it must be pointed out that this method allows for a greater flexibility in fees and the reaching of more patients. It also allows the therapist to treat those who might otherwise be unable to afford the high cost of sustained individual psychoanalysis.

It seems rather obvious that psychoanalysis in groups even at its present state of development, is a natural outcome from the previous theory and practice of psychoanalysis. It enables the analyst who possesses an adequate understanding of the social character of man to unite this awareness with his methods of treatment of individuals who have been immobilized by conflicts. It provides a means for the elimination of interpersonal dominance and exploitation among patients. It teaches them that appropriation of one another is immobilizing to all concerned. They learn, at least on this level, to throw off the binding sense that self aggrandizement is the means to security and happiness. The patient socializes himself as best he can on the level of interpersonal relationships. Rid of the vapid illusions which he had embodied, he is able better to attune himself with reality. By training each participant to be sensitive to the unconscious strivings in oneself as well as in others, group analysis provides a practice ground for deep rapport with others. This ability to establish an inner attunement provides group analysands with psychic antennae which are a social asset in the extent to which they help to establish a profound emotional closeness among themselves and subsequently with strangers outside the analytic circle. Group analysis is a balance between self study and social study, between the personal and the interpersonal. Their dynamic inter-relation reveals and promotes the whole man.

2. Structure

We have presented in the preceding chapter an overview of the dynamic inter-relationship of the structure, process and content of the psychoanalytic treatment of patients in a group. Before the analyst in groups can address himself to problems of management and technique he needs to assemble a group of patients. An immediate consideration is: How shall the group be constituted? We have already suggested the syndromes which, in our clinical experience, are appropriately treated in a group. But the problem of selection is also complicated by the analyst's attitude concerning the structure of the group, and especially the varieties of patients to be assigned to any one group. Is the therapy facilitated for the analyst as well as for the patients if the group is organized with persons who are more nearly alike? A random group will have homogeneous and heterogeneous aspects, because human beings, like nature of which they are a part, are both homogeneous and heterogeneous. The analyst is aware of this reality, and one of his goals is to help each person understand his appropriate and inappropriate identification with and separateness from others. The intentions and convictions of the therapist with regard to this problem are central to the ways in which he will express his preferences for homogeneity and heterogeneity in the group.

Patients are so complex that any homogeneous quality we emphasize can only be along certain lines. On the other hand, no matter how heterogeneously we organize our groups, we always find several patients who share a thought, a feeling, an experience, a fear, a conflict, a hope.

Is there an absolute homogeneity or an absolute heterogeneity? Is there any homogeneity in the physical universe? Research at the molecular level suggests that even molecules of supposedly identical tissues are, in fact, heterogeneous.[57] If there is no absolute homogeneity, what positive function does an artificially imposed homogeneity achieve? If homogeneity does exist, where is it, and where is it not? No two snowflakes are exactly alike, but they are all snowflakes. No two hysterics are exactly alike, but they are both hysterics. Among animals we distinguish the category human from the category ape. And among human beings we distinguish men from women. Categorizing has a usefulness which is integrating. It helps one level of communication to be able to refer to snow without describing each snow-flake, but it obscures another and denies reality never to explore just one snowflake. Without organizing nature into unifying abstractions, we become fragmented, but it can be equally inappropriate to invest objective reality with a subjective homogeneity. If difference is viewed as dangerous, the threatened may hasten into a narcissistic, paranoid or homosexual maneuver that would make the other like himself. What is me or mine becomes safe and good. And what is unlike me—you and yours—becomes unsafe and frightening. While it is practical to classify patients, we need to be aware of the hazard of dehumanizing them in pseudohomogeneity.

Homogeneity and heterogeneity are relative conceptions. Every therapeutic group has members who have some things in common and others which are disparate. Groups are never completely homogeneous or heterogeneous, but the possibility exists of movement toward more likeness or more unlikeness in some dimensions. The distortion is that any group is capable of achieving an unqualified identity or diversity in any or all directions.

The therapist who subscribes to a comprehensive heterogeneity may reject any selectivity with regard to patients. He may introduce every applicant to his groups with no discrimination. If he chooses one patient and rejects another, he may develop anxiety about not being permissive enough to the point where he becomes bewilderingly nonselective. If a group therapist endorses heterogeneity, he has to be reasonably selective. He may prefer divergence but he cannot negotiate an all-inclusiveness. Heterogeneity does not mean that everybody should be put together with everybody. An infinite homogeneity is just as inept. For as a group becomes more homogeneous, it becomes more limited and limiting.

If complete heterogeneity is not possible, the therapist will ask: What kinds of homogeneity should I encourage? Heterogeneity does not mean that there are no similarities among people, no communalities, no necessity for having a family whose members belong together and have a common name. We identify them as having something homogeneous about them.

Patients in a group are often helpful to one another, mutually interested, sustaining and insightful. They frequently see themselves in place of the other, whether or not their histories are parallel. And the therapist appreciates the reparative role of productive homogeneity. He welcomes the constructive use of empathic patient interaction. But he does not demand only the homogeneous expression of considerate and tender feelings or the equally one-sided ventilation of hostile affect. Such pressure would be contrary to an understanding of unconscious motivation. It would impose a one-dimensional standard not in keeping with analytic practice.

Human beings project stereotypes, namely transferences. Although the content of transference may be different from patient to patient, transference reactions are to be found in all patients, and they benefit from grasping the essence of transference as it occurs in all persons. The additive impressions deriving from the examination of multiple transferences in the group provide a matrix for quantitative and ultimately qualitative change. We are homogeneous in that we all make distortions, we have a past, a history that determines in degree the character of our responses at the moment. But the experiential detail and the particular biography of the transference is one patient's alone.

The same may be said of working through. While all patients are repeatedly called upon to struggle to resolve distortions, the resolution has a different content for each. The group setting in which every member is witness to the other's striving to overcome his pathology provides strong unifying support. Group members are homogeneous in this necessity to work through, but heterogeneous as to means and ends.

In order to facilitate communication of course we need to be able to speak a common language. But one might speculate about the utility of a multilingual group where each understood the other's native tongue. We have all acquired traditions which, if followed, assure us freedom in social intercourse, such as the alternating right to speak without rude interruption and the right to be listened to attentively. Homogeneous privileges to talk and be heeded should be extended to each patient.

While adults, adolescents and children are generally treated in their respective age groups, there is a movement toward the treatment of families together, as exemplified by the work of Ackerman, Bell and Grotjahn. Psychopaths as a rule are excluded from out-patient psychoanalytic groups, but many patients exhibit traits indicative of some psychopathy. Severe alcoholics who cannot come to meetings sober may have to be treated individually until they can attend sessions in sobriety. Seriously disabled stutterers, who in their too halting speech try the patience of the group, may have to wait to join a heterogeneous group until they can articulate more easily. The paranoids as well, who include group members in their systematized delusions, may have to be barred at first. The intensely masochistic patients who manage session after session to seduce others into aggression may have to be extracted from the group. Cardiac patients who suffer anginal pain under emotional stress ought not to be subjected to the heated exchanges that go on in a group. The senile are too much out of contact to participate in such therapeutic groups; the very depressed and suicidal are often too disturbed to take part; the gravely autistic generally cannot become involved; and the rigidly obsessive-compulsive may be so preoccupied with their rituals as not to engage responsively.

The mental defective is better not placed among patients of average or better intelligence. He becomes a burden to the group and tends to be patronized. If we put mental defectives together with geniuses both of whom have separately a certain homogeneity, simply because we set store by heterogeneity, is only to destroy the best potential of mental defectives and geniuses on their respective levels.

Those patients then, who cannot immediately be admitted to a heterogeneous group may, for a time, have to be treated individually or in a homogeneous group, until their difficulty is sufficiently relieved for them to enter a heterogeneous group. However, if the therapist works analytically, any homogeneously constituted group becomes more and more heterogeneous as treatment proceeds.[39, 40]

In the therapeutic group each member at first tends to look for shared attitudes, and in this sense he searches for homogeneity. But as he becomes stronger, he gets the courage to struggle for wholesome individuality. It is part of the natural history of a therapeutic group to proceed from greater homogeneity to greater heterogeneity, although the analytic experience itself contributes some parameters of homogeneity. As we unearth the latent particularity of each patient, we also cultivate personal growth, therapy replacing a manifest homogeneity by a latent heterogeneity. This does not mean that we should try to organize homogeneous groups in the first place —we are rather describing a security operation among patients who may believe that they cannot be accepted unless they submit to the other.

Therapists inclined to treat patients in the same way forfeit this subtlety required in the therapy of each. Every patient in a group needs to be dealt with through a special plan depending on his specific needs, his character pathology, and his constructive potentialities. Then the analyst can make those appropriate interventions to effect therapeutic change.

The therapist who pursues homogeneity is seeking counterparts in some one aspect. He emphasizes similarity in diagnosis, symptom, character structure, personality or psychodynamics, in sex or age, in economic class or color. We are concerned, however, about the attitude of the analyst who, when he promotes homogeneity, obscures differences and generalizes from the particularity of homogeneity to the totality of homogeneity. Such a therapist assumes that patients are altogether alike because they have affinities, and indeed they may, for this therapist, no longer be people. He may misperceive them as one, as depersonalized; in this illusion he may disregard anyone who is distinctive and minister to the group as a whole, to a congregation.

The Literature

A sampling of the literature reveals conflicting opinions about homogeneity and heterogeneity. Slavson[120] in discussing the selection of patients remarks that

"a true psychotherapeutic group presupposes the planful choice of patients and grouping of them on the basis of clinical diagnosis . . . " He notes that "there is still little awareness of the need for selection of patients in points of age, sex and clinical diagnoses, and, one finds that schizophrenics and manic-depressives are grouped with anxiety hysterias and other neuroses, with psychopaths, convulsives and other neurological conditions as well as with other types of mentally and emotionally disturbed patients. One should expect very little in common among this variety of syndromes and pathology and therefore little that the patients can do for one another. It is also inevitable that anxiety neurotics would become even more anxious in the presence of psychotics and convulsive patients and that their basic trauma could not be worked through in the presence of others who cannot identify themselves with their special problems and experiences."

Slavson observes elsewhere that in some heterosexual groups,

"discussions of sex are over-emphasized while in others the subject is shunned because of self-consciousness of the men and women. This is not the case to the same degree in one-sex groups. Inhibitions are not likely to occur in such groups." He deplores the possibility of acting out in a mixed group that "prevents the treatment from taking root, especially when it is not disclosed and discussed by the group." He maintains that "most group therapists adhere to a narrow age range among their patients. . . ."

Slavson[122] notes further that

"identification is particularly important in therapy groups for it makes possible vicarious catharsis and spectator therapy. It is for this reason that patients assigned to the same age group should have, as far as possible, common central or nuclear problems even though their symptoms and clinical diagnoses may be at variance or dissimilar . . . 'Mutual identification is at once the most potent and the most nearly universal socializing influence in society.' "

Rosow and Kaplan[91] report on a group of patients who

"were selected because of the similarity of symptoms, personality structures and relatively similar degree of insight; consequently, they were not overwhelmed by the productions of the group . . . Not only did the patients empathize with one another, they also gave each other meaningful insights and interpretations . . . In a more diversified group a premature discussion of such topics (as masturbation, homosexuality, or fellatio) might have been too anxiety-provoking for some individuals. This homogeneity might be an important factor in preventing turnover such as has been described by other writers."

Shames,[116] in a nonanalytic group psychotherapy setting, providing specific speech habit retraining, socialization, group mental hygiene, individual counseling and carry-over of new speech habits into social situations found that

> "when individuals in a speech therapy group resemble one another in age, education, sex, socio-economic level, type of speech problem, and types of social and psychological difficulties, they will attain, on the average, greater success than individuals in a group in which there are wide ranges among the members in age, education, types of problems, etc."

This study suggests that a homogeneous group may be better for non-analytic group psychotherapy than a heterogeneous group.

Glatzer[42] reports that more rapid therapeutic progress is made by grouping diverse personalities. She notes elsewhere[43] that

> "in homogeneous groups where individuals with some predominant personality characteristics are grouped together, the patients have less chance to see their own patterns as different from or the same as the others. In the C-group (composed of patients with primarily compulsive characteristics), the women experienced a repetition of their own aggressions and vindictive behavior in the group which seemed to increase their tension and reinforce further 'defensive blindness.' "

Glatzer remarks further that

> "there is more dynamic interaction in a group with varied personalities . . . The personality characteristics in the mixed group were more clearly articulated and highlighted than in either homogeneous group. It was noted that the C-(compulsive) patient could better grasp the nature of the therapeutic task by using the H-(hysterical) patient as contrast and the H-patient could do likewise. The more energetic interplay in the mixed group implied that although the H-group was less 'blinded' than the C-group, they were not as able as the mixed group to recognize and critically to evaluate each other's problems probably because of their 'overfondness' for each other . . . Mrs. A's C-personality had interacted in the C-group with similar negative and rigid personalities, a combination that produced an almost impermeable structure . . . The dramatic changes in Mrs. A. immediately after she was transferred from the experimental C-group (where she had made relatively no progress) to the mixed group point strongly to the fact that judicious grouping of varied personalities is important for optimum therapeutic movement."

Furst[40] notes that in homogeneous groups, "because of the absence of interaction factors the level of therapy is relatively superficial"; that "despite the removal of symptoms, character structure is relatively untouched"; that "the opportunity for reality testing is lessened by the absence of interaction with heterogeneous personalities"; that "the opportunity to develop multiple and shifting transferences in accordance to needs is lacking." He notes further that "heterogeneous groups by their very nature tend to take the therapist, whether or not he so desires, into deeper levels of therapy"; that in such groups "character structure as well as symptom formation are influenced by the process of therapy"; that "reality testing is more adequate and thorough"; that "intra-group transferences of a diverse and shifting nature can be formed readily in the heterogeneous group in accordance with individual needs." Furst concludes that "heterogeneous groups are necessary . . . for group psychoanalysis," that "it is difficult to do deep therapy with a homogeneous group" and "difficult not to do deep therapy with a heterogeneous group."

Joel and Shapiro[53] claim that groups constituted of equal numbers of psychotics and neurotics make the best progress. In an experimental study, Bendig[9] concludes that heterogeneity leads to discrimination and that homogeneity introduces bias which impairs judgment.

The search for homogeneity implies that if patients do not have a sizeable commonality, they cannot become intelligible to one another. But this view runs counter to our clinical findings in heterogeneous groups. When one patient turns his back on another because of his dissimilarity, we regard this as a piece of unhealth to be treated rather than supported.

Slavson[122] and Kubie[61] do not think that group therapy offers the patient as deep an experience as individual treatment. Their view may in part be due to the kind of therapy done in a homogeneous group, where the resistance of patients is supported by the therapist's indifference to the individual patient. Shallowness of therapy results from the lack of exploring each member in uniqueness.

Values

The therapist's preference for the homogeneous or heterogeneous medium is some indication of his values. Treating people as if they were identical is sectarian. Differentiating them is humanitarian. Homogeneity sees disagreement as irreconcilable. Heterogeneity sees disagreement as a basis for fruitful exchange. Homogeneity breeds egocentricity, the inability to tolerate complementarity. The heterogeneous group is a practice-ground that helps the patient become secure with the stranger. It is partial to the love between opposites: man for woman, parent for child, one for the other. It is more enlightening, for while there is some initial misapprehension, a disharmony of ideas can lead to fruitful discussion and insight. These cross purposes impel members to explain themselves more clearly in challenging exchange.

A homogeneous group evolves a set of customs, in the fact of which patients may become apathetic. The introduction of two or three atypical members stirs the group out of its torpor and analysis proceeds apace. Occasionally, the earlier patients at first resent the remedial newcomers as too foreign to the homogeneous ideal. They prefer to remain encysted in defense of group-as-it-was, a rigidity that thrives wherever individual vitality is at a low ebb. If the analyst values and supports the new invigorating elements, they stimulate the group.

Treatment is directed toward the interpenetration of opposites, toward heterosexuality. Its aim is not facsimile, unisexuality. The therapist or the patient may reject innovation or exception as divisive. But there is usefulness in discord as well as in concord.

In a homogeneous group there is little provocation to compare or contrast. But in a heterogeneous group the therapist probes conflict and helps the antagonists to arrive at a collaboration in which bilateral regard is possible. They learn to cooperate out of comparison and contrast. They distill some of their aspirations, yield ground on both sides and give up archaic compulsion. The value here is not just contention, but meeting one another halfway, giving and taking, coming flexibly to terms, partial satisfaction instead of totalism.[147]

There is less opportunity to choose in a homogeneous group than in a heterogeneous group. Therefore there is greater freedom in heterogeneity. To have freedom, first, choice is necessary, and second, choices must be available to the chooser.

Many alternatives are disclosed to the patient in a heterogeneous group, additional ways of choosing illusion or reality. If he has the freedom to select among many inclinations, he is more likely to adopt the better way. Possibilities are not so evident to the patient in a homogeneous group. As a result, he can less easily become aware of the avenues for choice and change that might otherwise be open to him. The patient needs to distinguish between reasonable counsel where he still has the freedom to decide and absolutism where he has none. Choice is not to be confused with compulsive nonconformity. It is more closely related to autonomy and independence.

One aim of psychotherapy is to confront the patient with alternatives to the compulsion which leaves him no choice. When the therapist limits the patient to others similarly compelled blindly to pursue a course, the reinforced, unhealthy custom tends to prevail. Where the patient is witness to many optional ways of being, even though for each member some aspect is compulsive, the wholesome exercise of some discrimination is enhanced.[146]

The analysand emerging from a heterogeneous group, while aware of his residual psychopathology and in ongoing exertion against it, is less self-involved than the graduate of a homogeneous group. The latter's egotism is likely to be entrenched by his own kind, whereas the former moves toward reciprocity. The veteran of a heterogeneous group can avoid persons who simply duplicate and feed his vanity. Instead he looks for new horizons —he may not be so provincial as one subjected to homogeneous treatment. He attends to what the other has to say, knowing that no one person has all the answers. He evaluates what the other has to contribute, extracts what is plausible and comes to more clarity than before. The patient is led by his experience in a homogeneous group to be ruled by precept and become obsessively protestant against suggestion that is not his or of his kind. It is more difficult for him to learn, addicted as he is to partners in similarity, who can teach him little.

Homogeneity in therapy is an extension of the cultural concern over being contaminated by difference. Group sameness may make the patient feel that his difference is abnormal deviation merely suffered or disparaged by the assumed norm.

E. J. Anthony notes that " 'scapegoatism' is a regular phenomenon in all therapeutic groups. . . The scapegoat may be selected in the first place on the elemental basis of being different. He may be isolated because of differences in age, sex, religion, class, race, etc. . . . . The 'passing stranger' in anthropological literature was often seized and sacrificed. . . The stranger in the human group feels the rub of strangeness until he finds acceptance and can blend with his surroundings. The next newcomer reactivates the past uneasiness and challenges the present familiarity with his obtrusive strangeness. It is disturbing to the self-satisfaction of the group, and they must deal with it either by assimilation or extrusion. The persistence of strangeness is intolerable to the group."[31, pp. 205-207]

The scapegoat and the stranger are more likely to appear in a homogeneous group. Their exclusion is less probable among patients who respect differences in a heterogeneous group. We need not only to permit unlikeness, but also to encourage it. In the name of coordination, distinctions may be discouraged. Segregation into homogeneous communities is not the aim of the therapeutic group. While a like-minded group may find temporary comfort in sameness, their uniformity makes for insecurity with the unfamiliar.

Though patients have equal privileges, each is different from the other, in sex, in age, in degree of sickness or health, and this disparity ought not to be rendered ambiguous. We are not unmindful of the obsessive pursuit of difference which becomes an irrational devotion to deviation and disintegration. An absolute glorification of uniformity or diversity can be equally unreasonable and fallacious.

Some therapists, however, seem to abhor differences. They will not distinguish one patient from another, or themselves from their patients.[79, 129] They try to render the group leaderless by levelling the therapist with the patient. This is a struggle for homogeneity. It would eliminate the heterogeneous differences between therapists and patients. While more reasonable treatment also seeks equality, it does not strive for parity in illness. Its aim is to allow each patient and the therapist similar opportunities to develop their uniquely separate resources. The analysands learn to cope more reasonably with actuality. The analyst enlarges his expertness as a therapist. They are peers, but with different functions and objectives. We would say with Kallen[56] that "Union . . . is the team play of the different (while) . . . unity . . . is liquidation of difference. . ."

The patient's original family demanded conformity of him. It impressed him with the dangers of offending by being different. Difference was equated with being disturbingly eccentric or pathologic or self-interested. The original family contended that only we and our group are good, safe, normal. It is, therefore, unwise to pursue the ways of an alien.

The homogeneous therapeutic group reproduces this restraint of personal expression, of individual differentiation and discriminating treatment depending upon particular patient needs. In this sense, the homogeneous group is re-traumatizing.

The group, if it is to be called therapeutic, must give patients a first ongoing experience of hope and fulfillment that out of their exertions together each can realize the evolution of his own unique resources in a many-sided climate. For patients have come from prior experience that has impressed them with the fact that group life has been the breeding ground of their neuroses. The therapeutic group experience then must give them a fresh conception and a more sanguine view of group life.

The Heterogeneous Group is Structurally Reparative

The heterogeneous group provides a structure which by its nature has greater reparative potential than the homogeneous group. We are not referring to some mystical force deriving from group dynamics. We are describing structural attributes rather than qualities derived from process.

The open group, which discharges a recovered patient and admits a new one, by virtue of its ever-changing variety is more heterogeneous than homogeneous. The closed group, which lets not one patient go nor admits a newcomer, by virtue of its unchanging membership and disregard of individual needs for length of treatment is more homogeneous than heterogeneous.

The patient is stirred to change by stimulation and provocation. The homogeneous group can be too agreeable for him. It may not challenge his pathology but endorse it. The excitement of a heterogeneous group will incite and animate him. The gropings of other patients urge him to clarify their confusion. Their indistinct and conflicting needs move him to try to answer their anxiety. In such a challenging atmosphere he feels called upon to exercise a more active role. He feels his opinions on their problems will be welcome. But of what use are his views in a becalmed group where everyone has the same apparent problem and solution, where everyone is tranquilized in the demand for ongoing concurrence.

The members of a heterogeneous group seem not to be content until they understand one another better. The motivation for this complementary exploration is compounded in large measure, of a natural human curiosity about the foreign and the unknown and an attraction toward the opposite and incongruous. A heterogeneous membership also tends to elicit and promote multiple transferences more readily than a homogeneous group which generally sponsors identification rather than diversified interaction. A member of a mixed group cultivates and states his personal preferences but he will encourage his associates to take similar liberties with their own choices. In a heterogeneous group there is a common consent to accept divergent views. A persistent homogeneous group sets itself against the aberrant nonconformist. A heterogeneous group, in its regard and respect for the deviant, becomes joined in diversity.

While a heterogeneous group is more readily able to elicit the multiple transferences, the varied psychopathology of each patient, as well as his concealed resourcefulness, the diversity of the membership also makes it difficult for the patient to assign to it the fixity so characteristic of transferential reactions. The discrepancy between the rigidity of his transferences and the variety of personalities to whom he assigns projected roles strikes him before long as being too disparate and urges him to re-examine his appraisals for their distorted content. There is more likelihood in a heterogeneous group that the patient will find there readier facsimiles of familial surrogates as well as figures unlike his original family.

The heterogeneous group can provide more opportunities for reality testing and working through. Interaction, movement and change are fostered by the varieties of stimulation. The patient is encouraged to test the positions he takes in the light of many points of view. The acceptance of variety is reassuring to the fainthearted who are thereby enabled to take an initiative they would otherwise have withheld.

The patient will find more reparative allies among those members who are not copies of himself rather than among his own kind. In their incongruity he will find his ingrained irrational dogma challenged again and again. Those who express considered differences have little regard for the resignation that characterizes the compulsively submissive patient who has to subscribe to group canons. The novelty of these people so foreign to himself elicits a fresh sense of release from the customary and redundant remarks of his inbred group. With these new manifold horizons he is able to develop interest in all sorts of people.

The Homogeneous Group is Structurally Nonreparative

At least one way in which homogeneity is an asset in group psychotherapy, is when a patient sees reflected in another those neurotic qualities which he finds in himself and then proceeds to struggle to work them through instead of disparaging the other or himself. But this advantage is available also in the heterogeneous group.

But it is not easy for like patients to grasp one another in depth. For each is more or less troubled and confused in just those areas to which they have least access. Just as their pathology is reinforced in approximation, so is their resistance. It may require more separation, detachment and unlikeness on the part of outsiders to see where the trouble is. The homogeneous group is too flattering of each patient's conceit. Persons are not easily critical of qualities they share. Moreover, the likeness of members tends to become an inducement to acting out.

In these and other ways, the homogeneous group tends to defeat the individual patient. For he begins to look upon his variance as an expression of his contrariety and resistance, as a personal limitation that obstructs his own and "the group's progress." So he may accommodate himself to a collusion that betrays him. He becomes the acquiescent, silent, inexpressively hostile member, insensible to his own strivings. Even if he is articulate, his voice is not active in his own or another's behalf so much as it moralistically supports certain repressive "group practices." In the fear of being called *outré* he becomes a passive group member. Joined with other patients sharing his anxiety, his uncertainty, his helplessness, his sense of inadequacy, or his loneliness, he turns dependently to the group or the therapist for direction. The group becomes an ideal community for disposing of what little ego he may have left until he is its lifeless instrument.

It is important that the therapeutic group not manipulate the individual to comply with a consensual position. To permit such usage routinely, encourages the group often to disregard the patient's obligations to other groups, his family, his professional colleagues, his employers, his co-workers. For the therapeutic group, so endorsed, may be homogeneously emboldened to give itself and its decisions a primacy not only over the patient but over all other groups in the patient's life. If the homogeneous group offers the patient little or no freedom in *its* setting, it offers him less on the outside. Tenancy in the group ought not to remove the patient from a variety of all-important extra-group relations. Yet the homogeneous group often acts as if any independence of its authority is a kind of disloyalty. The homogeneous group often directs the patient to leave the parental home because of its conventional demands, but then imposes customs just as forbidding, just as intolerant, and even less reasonable.

The conforming patient jealously impoverishes the potential of the newly admitted patient. Assimilated himself, what right has another to the privileges of heresy. In this connection we are reminded of a homogeneous group which developed a cult of smart, sophisticated banter that resisted every individual attempt to communicate more genuinely. It was only after the membership was dispersed among several heterogeneous groups that they were able to settle down to analytic therapy. Another homogeneous group made up of depressed, isolated, detached, withdrawn, obsessive-compulsive and schizoid patients, was unable to establish interactive contact until they were separated and placed in groups which were readier and more eager for interpersonal relations.

Every patient, no matter how much he would shed his neurotic maneuvers, wishes in some part to justify and rationalize them. If he is injected into an environment that largely mirrors his disorder, his resistance is compounded in multiple vindication from every quarter. A group which allows for no swerving from the prevailing position soon deteriorates as a productive force. The deviationist in such a group, who might invigorate it with his departure from convention, is often intimidated into silence. As a result, the enlivening transfusion of new thoughts is intercepted. Resistance is thereby encouraged and therapy obstructed.

To what extent are homogeneity and heterogeneity apparencies and realities? Surely the members of every group have some things in common and others apart. We ought not in our valuing heterogeneity to reject what we share. And in endorsing homogeneity we ought not to disregard individual uniqueness.

But there is a tendency among group therapists to invest the group with an apparency of uniformity which it does not, in fact, possess. A group may appear to behave in the same way, but if the analyst uses his expertness to explore underlying attitudes, he discovers varying motivations, thoughts and feelings behind the seeming unity. Some clinicians[130] imply that patients improve who go along with the group, and conversely, patients who do not improve, seek individual solutions. Such therapists are preoccupied with the group activity, the manifest distortion, rather than the relevant, personal, latent content. Individual motivations and the diversely concealed unconscious material are frequently neglected and the pertinent intrinsic reaction is overlooked. The apparency of likeness, the external foreground is attended. Despite any appearance of homogeneity of reaction, patients are too inherently diverse for their similar behavior not to have disparate underlying motivation and significance. The patient who gains insight into the dynamics of his unconscious processes learns more about himself than he ever can from an awareness of group dynamics. There is little therapeutic point in striving for cohesion if each member does not explore his own associations.

Scientific investigation is a constructive search for patterns in nature that will force it to yield its secrets to our understanding. The history of science shows that it seeks to find regularities in ever larger and more diverse aspects of nature at the same time as research uncovers unprecedented subsciences that underscore the heterogeneity of the universe. Man fears that he may not be able to control nature in its vast variety. While there is value in discovering the designs in the world around us, we want to be reasonably sure that in our anxiety for answers we do not compulsively project inappropriate pseudosolutions. We need to be careful that we do not impose on an actual heterogeneity a false homogeneous illusion. We may find ourselves rejecting diversity simply because it does not fit our limited and subjective perception.

Homogeneity as a Pathologic Subculture

There is a tendency for people who are neurotic, to look for help among equally disturbed persons rather than from more reasonable sources.[129,146] The disordered often seek one another out hoping to establish a consistently pathologic subculture of partisan benevolence that will tolerate their dislocation, irrationality and acting out. Such a group makes a virtue of its psychopathology, castle-building it into freedom, artistic sensibility, a *cause celebre* against tyranny and whatnot. And such a denouement is one fruit of a homogeneous community. To the extent that heterogeneous elements are added, these grandiose presumptions are opposed.

A homogeneous group of persons tends to develop a hauteur, a complacency that defeats the nonadherent. The derision with which it regards the opposition is hard for dissenters to take. But any therapeutic group which develops such generalized pretension is bound to fail in its function by assuming its infallibility. It fails because disparagement of individual points of view leads to the dissenter's submission, revolt or flight and the group members' increasing pathology.

There is a kind of illusion of invulnerability in feeling one with the crowd, a part of its unitary scheme, a cog in its machine, free of the anxiety and responsibility of having to choose for one's self. To the patient, exhausted by neurotic maneuvers that have failed to gratify him, the vision of belonging to an undeviating group suggests a knowledge of the way to tranquility that is hard to resist. But the tranquility of homogeneity is the peace of insensibility.

Homogeneity as Narcissism

A patient's genuine capacity to accept others does not demand that they be cast in his own image. If he insists that others be like himself, else he cannot endure them, he is narcissistic. By surrounding him with patients with similar pathology, we cater to his disorder rather than challenging it. The healthy person is not so rejective of difference from himself.

In sponsoring the individual in the group, we do not seek to reinforce his egotism or his arrogance, but to increase his self respect and to strengthen his ego. As we see it, psychoanalysis in groups is impossible without preserving individual freedom. When the search for personal dignity degenerates into the compulsive pursuit of contentious impudence, when the search for legitimate standing becomes the insistence for the center of attention, analysis of the pathology is indicated. We cannot, however, in the fear of cultivating a group of insulated egotists, go to the opposite extreme and demand absolute dependence on a "group will." For no healthy consciousness can emerge between puppets and puppeteers.

Homogeneity demands exclusivity. The insistence on sameness is a kind of narcissism that repudiates love. Its segregation suggests an illusion of the superiority of an in-group and the inferiority of the out-group, a breeding ground for grandiosity. Its reflection of self in the other would seem to support egocentricity, homosexuality and xenophobia. Heterogeneity seems to sponsor opposition to narcissism, self love—it is the breeding ground for true love.

Homogeneity as False Belonging

Homogeneity implies that a patient cannot belong unless he is part of a like-minded group, that where the members do not have a good deal in common, cohesion, the feeling of being part of a group is lacking. And restorative powers are ascribed to the feeling of belonging. The lonely patient now feels received at last.

But the analyst, as usual, is interested in the subtleties of belonging. He asks to what, to whom, under what conditions, to what end and over what period does this or that patient want to belong? Will belonging here or there serve him at this time in sickness or in health? The analyst makes distinctions. He cannot simply accept belonging as uniformly health-giving and solitude as invariably sickening. We refer to the belonging, which is valued by some group therapists as *false belonging,* whenever a patient's feeling that he is an integral part of the group is won at the cost of his integrity, whenever he has to sacrifice a restorative psychodynamic for a crippling group dynamic.

A nondiscriminative drive to belong might lead a patient to become overly involved with a homogeneous group that sanctions but does not seek to resolve a common disorder. This morbid connection might embed the patient in subordination to the shared pathology. Indiscriminate concession to the need to belong might prevent the patient from engaging in social activity which is not centered in the therapeutic group. This pseudo-integration requires of the individual a surrender to the collective will. He can possess the group so long as it possesses him.

To center attention on belonging is liable to distract the individual from his particular objective. The whole group has no aim, which is the same for each member. When, in fact, a patient consciously devotes himself to the reconstruction of the group, he is generally acting out an earlier role in the original family. The target for each patient is his personal rehabilitation and recovery.

Under the guise of belonging there is an injunction to assimilate and dance attendance. The thesis seems to be that if the patient can be induced to submit to the consensus, his neurosis is dissolved in the therapeutic magic of belonging, that, if he does not belong, he cannot get well. We rather see nondiscriminative belonging as a sign of sickness and discriminating belonging as a sign of health.

Homogeneity as an Isolating Experience

The coterie of a homogeneous group is isolated and isolating. It is unsympathetic to all but its own kind. It frequently offers only a shallow and petty hearing to disagreement. And the acceptance it tenders the conformist is worth little to him in the end. In the homogeneous group the patient is more removed from awareness of differences present in the rest of the culture. The demand for homogeneity promotes insulation, detachment and segregation.

It may seem to some that by emphasizing the individual we are proposing narrow, egoistic solutions which are no solution at all, or that we are even basically opposed to psychoanalysis in groups. This is far from the case; but the patient is already limited and shut up in a fearful, neurotic world. Simply to surround him with his kind offers him no way out—a sort of iatrogenic claustrophobia. If we present him with people who are different, he can move out of the narrow world of self into the larger world of self and of others. If he is one of a series of mirror images, he is still alone.

It is claimed that homogeneity dispels isolation. But a person may become part of an authoritarian group and still be essentially alone. A ruffian may join a gang of rowdies and still feel alien. So, too, the patient may discover himself more alone than ever in a homogeneous group. The grouping of equivalents can result in a deceptive propinquity, beneath which isolation goes on. On the other hand, dissimilarity need not necessarily mitigate against the group's interest and favor, as long as the group values a selective right to appropriate dissent as one of its aims. The member of the homogeneous group must accommodate. In such a reality, the price of belonging is isolation from one's true self.

To be sure, an enforced heterogeneity may be equally isolating and destructive to patients. Therapists who indiscriminatively insist upon difference deprive persons of benefiting from healthy human commonalities. It is forcing an absolute choice as if between two mutually exclusive alternatives that destroys the therapeutic possibilities of group analysis.

Homogeneity as Authoritarianism

The homogeneous requirement subordinates the patient to group dictation. The group thereby exercises a hierarchic dominance or control over the individual member. It is invested with an irrational authority to stultify elements of diversity. The greater the demand for homogeneity the more the need for thought control and brainwashing of the dissenting minority.

While it is not actually possible for a therapist to coalesce the members of a group, to render them identical, he can nevertheless be a powerful force for homogeneity, in the selection of patients, in his emphasis on group dynamics, in tolerating only impulsive reactions, or in approving only emotional or intellectual responses. He may restrict the group only to historical material or limit them largely to an exploration of motivations. He may be narrowly interested in ego functions or reject dream material and insist that only conscious reactions are relevant. To the extent he imposes a one-dimensional operation, he abandons analytic therapy which requires the individual's emergence in all his complexity.

In the homogeneous group, the proposal of reconstructive alternatives to the pathology, whether offered verbally or by example, is limited by the consistency in the group. So suggestions for alternative ways and means have to come largely from the leader. Since the alternatives come from the authority figure, they often tend to be submitted to—or resisted.

Homogeneity as Diegophrenogenic

The homogeneous group provides a climate ready-made for the borderline state. The patient makes a diegophrenic adjustment, accommodating to the majority, seeking their approval, refusing to swerve from the conforming role the mass assigns him. The uniform group often insists upon a torpid, noncommittal compliance instead of working through pathology. While conformance to the demands of a stereotyped group may be reassuringly agreeable and beguiling, it is at the same time oppressive in prescribing agreement. It is an atmosphere that breeds resignation. Where submission to convention is dictated by the therapist himself, there is little hope for the patient to escape his own subordination.

The trend toward homogeneity is an attempt to support faltering egos by attaching them to a large movement, greater than they individually are. But the patient cannot get well unless he rejects such authority over his own ego. If he glorifies the group, his own status has no solid base. It rises or falls in a reflection of group status. Patients whose resistance to suggestion is lowered, can too easily succumb to the coalescent view. They can be too readily seduced by the repressive inspirational appeal of "group values" which so derogates the individual as to make him feel that self interest leads only to impotence, uncertainty and guilt.

Every patient seems to try to evade personal accountability, and the homogeneous group is an ideal medium in which to continue to exercise this pathologic maneuver. The patient needs to be encouraged to strengthen his ego by saying what he thinks and feels and to assume responsibility for what he says and does. He ought not to be sponsored in the illusion that it is all right for him to act out as long as he hides behind group skirts, where he makes the group responsible rather than himself. But why should anyone assert his individuality in a uniform group that depreciates the independent mind and rewards the conformist?

Homogeneity as Identification, Mimicry, and Inbreeding

There is a good deal of encouragement of identification in homogeneous groups and considerably less in heterogeneous groups. In one current view of identification which is receiving increasing support among some analysts, it is always regarded as an unhealthy manifestation. This seems to us an indiscriminate attitude. If a patient compulsively identifies with the other and thereby loses his independence of mind, initiative and autonomy, such fidelity is surely unhealthy. If he represses his own resources and is repetitively inspired by the omnipotence of another, his identification is a sign of disturbance. If he renounces his own for the ego of the other, he is diegophrenic. But, if on occasion, he discriminatingly and consciously aspires to achieve the qualities of an admired pattern, such activity need not be considered abnormal.

It depends on how we define identification. In the former example, identification is unconscious; in the latter, conscious, selective and freely chosen. Where does this understanding lead us in defining the relative efficacy of homogeneous and heterogeneous groups? It brings us to the conviction that consciousness, and particularly consciousness of difference, is a most important goal of treatment. Even when an awareness of sameness in pathology occurs, it is the patient's realization that he has the potential to be different that impels him to struggle to change. Therefore, the exploration of the problem of homogeneity and identification teaches us that health lies in the individual's movement from compulsive likeness to free difference and from compulsive difference to free likeness.

The patient does not come to group therapy to be mimicked, to have his own illusions reflected back to him by the identically sick—he does not seek an imitation to mock him. He is looking for human beings who have had other kinds of experience, whose different development may open doors until now closed to him, whose different ways in perception may help him to reinterpret his dilemma. While Rogers' mimicry is said to be therapeutic, it is a consciously and selectively applied device, a technical intervention, not a happenstance or a way of life, as it tends to become in a homogeneous group.

Homogeneity would make the group a dreary community. For what adventure is left to us in a society of men without women? What animation stirred by members who are images of ourselves? What excitement stimulated by a monotonous sameness? We are levelled in sameness only in death, and a therapy that extinguishes differences extinguishes life. It is true, of course, that a therapy which denies the essential commonalities of human experience, also denies life.

Homogeneity as Antianalytic

The detailed exploration of each patient's unconscious processes, his psychodynamics, his conflicts, his motivations brings insight, the ability to distinguish the rational from the irrational and to choose to act upon the appropriate. The stress in group therapy upon homogeneity diverts us far from these interests, for while attending group processes psychoanalytic investigation tends to be bypassed.

The homogeneous assumption suggests that by modifying the surrounding climate, the neurosis thereby dies of attrition. While this is conceivable, it is not psychoanalytic treatment. It is a daydream of group therapy. In this millenium, every patient is cooperative, helpful, uncritical and identical; in this golden dream group members never differ, never distort, never ambivalate and never resist. This is a fool's paradise of consistently dreary automatons. A homogeneous group may be useful in circumstances other than psychoanalytic treatment. Rigidity, rules and regulations are conceivably helpful in various settings: education, scientific research, business, professional and social groups.

The heterogeneous group tends to encourage interpersonal transactions rather than intrapsychic preoccupation. Intrapsychic exploration is, however, stimulated by the difference among patients, their curiosity about one another, and the therapist's promptings. The homogeneous group tends to focus the patient on intrapsychic material. Interaction is dulled by the sameness of the other. There is a turning inward as mutual identification limits stimulation and communication. But examination of intrapsychic processes is not deep as the patients tend not to penetrate to their latent differentiation but remain fixed on their more manifest uniformity.

The psychoanalyst attends the individual's intrapsychic operations. He studies how these latent psychodynamics improve or disturb his interpersonal relations. The therapist who indiscriminately prefers homogeneity would explore the prevailing group consensus that he is at the same time imposing. But such absorption distracts him from scrutinizing individual aspirations beyond awareness. Both the intrapsychic and the interpersonal tend to be neglected when the therapist stresses homogeneity as a therapeutic instrument.

Individuality and Commonality

Homogenizing influences misunderstand the patient's reactions as collective responses. Personal behavior is discounted except as a manifestation of group influences. The activity of a single patient tends to be regarded as pathologic. Consensual reactions tend to be looked upon as healthy. An unselective approval evolves which sees every shared view as wholesome and every minority view as sick. The joint position becomes the helpful one, and the distinctive position becomes the hurtful one. Such a point of view is nondiscriminative. Private and group life have both constructive and destructive possibilities. The movement toward homogeneity exalts the value of the group. It is necessary also to affirm what is fruitful in the person and noxious in the group, as well as the reverse.

One of the problems of psychoanalysis is the tendency to apply generalizations to the patient, to try to make him understandable in terms of a preconceived theory. This may have some validity. But we are likely to be misled unless we realize that, although two patients have similar backgrounds, each really behaves differently. We may inappropriately fuse them missing the specificity required in good analysis. The homogeneous group encourages the loss of specificity. The loss of particularity is one of the serious criticisms of group psychotherapy.

It is looming as an important task in group psychotherapy to re-emphasize the necessity to attend the patient if we wish to treat him. We need, despite our enthusiasm for therapy in a group, to return to the psychoanalytic emphasis upon the individual, the individual in interaction. It is not possible to treat a group. We need to keep the patient the center of attention, not an abstraction lost in a sociologic ideal. We need to help him avoid that kind of groupism in which he loses autonomy and belief in his own competence to renew and reconstruct himself. We need to aid him resist that form of involuntary conformity that negates his conviction that he is not the blind victim of the inevitable forces of circumstances.

Group therapists, in an attempt to justify the group as a reparative instrument, have become so group-centered that they look upon individual attention as sacrilege against the "group ideal" or as a rejection of therapy in a group. They seem to regard concern for the members as distinct patients as a seedy return to individualism.

Role of the Therapist

The need to generalize represents an attempt to find an over-all explanation in fact or in fancy. In the face of an absolute heterogeneity, man would have no means of understanding nature, no way to cope with or control it. The therapeutic problem is how to deal with the complexity, how to cope with the group without damaging the person. A parent may regard his offspring homogeneously as children, but they need to be seen as different children. The therapist, like the parent, may become anxious or guilty that he does not feel the same way about each patient or treat all his patients in the same way. He may confuse equality with sameness. The therapist or the patient may impose a homogeneity in order to relieve his tension. The therapist may make a facile but irrelevant generalization to alleviate his anxiety.

Homogeneous structure or heterogeneous structure is a consequence of the position taken by the therapist. He may believe that mental health comes from individual submission to the group.[24] Under these circumstances it is not the group that strives for such homogeneity, it is the therapist. For the group, given its head, even if it is originally relatively homogeneous, achieves a more wholesome heterogeneity.[39, 40] It is the therapist's drive for homogeneity that is the significant force. This imposition of a make-believe unity is a projection of the therapist.

The therapist may be a progressive idealist with visions that psychoanalysis, and particularly group psychotherapy, are the answer in social reform.[136] He may believe that the democratic group will change man. But in doing so, he misinterprets parity as identity and democracy as psychotherapy. Here the unconscious aim in homogeneity, is the democratic goal misconceived as subordination to group will.

The treatment of diverse patients as if they were identical helps the therapist to evade the necessity for the differentiated therapy of each one. It is quite possible that he is looking for an abbreviated form of group therapy. He may expect that the group, its climate or its dynamics will somehow heal the patient with less need on the therapist's part to intervene. He may, like the patient, hope to evade the large number of conflicts, the struggle to resolve distortions of patients so often at cross purposes. By ignoring their disparity or levelling them in similarity he can be relieved of the differentiated necessity to work through their divergent problems. Some therapists fear subjecting the patient to alien experience, as if they would protect him from the new and unknown.

The group therapist inclined to homogeneity is essentially cynical about the constructive and realistic possibilities in patients. He seems to believe that, given the opportunity, they are more than likely to run amuck, to hurt one another, to act in pathology, to become irrational rather than more reasonable. Accordingly, he tries to establish "group precedents," a "group authority," to control an inherent tendency to misbehave. He may see the homogeneous group as a way of restricting acting out to the therapy situation. Or, he may have the clinical experience that interaction of any kind, whether appropriate or acting out, is reduced in an undiversified group. In either case, the therapist is likely to prefer homogeneity.

He may misjudge singularity as compulsive nonconformity, and uniqueness as pathological deviation. He may try to render his group homogeneously irrational with a view to establishing "therapeutic" psychoses.[129, 146] Here the aim is to obscure the difference between patient and therapist.

An unconscious objective in homogenizing a group may be the therapist's need to manipulate it. A group can be more readily dealt with, if it is made coalescent, if it is one mind, if the individual members have been conditioned to follow. The homogeneous group may be used by the therapist to bludgeon the patient to conform to the consensual view. The group can be more adroitly handled in the mass than in the man. But if the patient is to be lost in the group, his irrationality must be stimulated, encouraged and intensified. For he will resist his drowning in homogeneity with whatever sound reserves are still available to him.

It is quite possible that the group therapist's insistence on establishing a priority of homogeneity is an acting out of his own need authoritatively to prevail. Or, it may be that the imposition of group uniformity represents the group therapist's acting out his own submission to a suprahuman father force, invested now in a defied conventionality from which no one is exempt.

A therapist who ignores the heterogeneity of patients is likely to be authoritarian. He may think that restorative influence rests entirely with him and in extension of him, his homogeneous group. He is rejective of group therapy, of interaction among patients, of the alternate session.[148, 149] He may feel it necessary to dominate the patients or they will anarchically disintegrate. He feels obliged to maneuver and manipulate the group. His attitude is patronizing. He regards patients as altogether pathological with no remedial resources of their own. He acknowledges that unless he is in absolute surveillance of the group, it will fall apart. Its members are viewed as defective or entirely given over to id impulses in his absence. To be sure, both healthy and unhealthy attitudes and behavior assert themselves whether the patients are in treatment or not. It is the therapist's fancy that they become unbridled unless they are under his watchful supervision.

The pursuit of homogeneity may be in part derived from the therapist's quest for certainty.[111] The compulsive banding together of patients who have similarities may be reassuring to the leader out of some matching necessity of his own. Or, he may feel more inappropriately secure in the presence of patients who are less anxious among their own kind. He is likely then to rationalize his preference for homogeneity in an illogical conviction that consonance is essential to the group. The projection of a homogeneous cloak over the heterogeneous qualities of patients may make the therapist feel more sure of himself but does not correspond to the realistic needs of patients.

One homogeneous aim is infallibility. In this view the therapist can be positive if the group's even tenor is unquestioned. Homogeneity then has the quality of massive conformism. It creates new problems by encouraging infectious parapraxes. The nature of psychoanalytic practice requires that we question the motivations of patients and our own as well. Otherwise we are homogeneous with their resistance. When the right to question our patients, for them to question and disagree with one another and the therapist, to be different from one another and the therapist, is disavowed, we are forced to accept homogeneity and an illusory assurance.

Often the expectation of the patient is that the members of his group share his feelings, thoughts and behavior, that they have convictions identical with his own. He experiences their differences from him as something of a shock. It is as if their not being like him represents a rejection of all he stands for. This is such a common point of view that even the therapist may be misled into attempts to cater to it by organizing as nearly homogeneous groups as possible. One function of the therapist is not to submit to the expectation that each member reflect the other's mood, values, reasoning or conduct but to analyze such a presumption as irrational and work through to the acceptance of constructive differences.

A pitfall the group therapist needs to guard against is the formation in the therapeutic group of a clique of elite patients who underline the analyst's values or manage to establish a homogeneous bias to which they demand the remaining members conform. There is a danger here of the group's becoming noxiously homogeneous, for example in its insistence that the only acceptable material for expression must be affect-loaded; or in the rule that no experience of a patient outside the group is relevant; or in the dictum that historical data is immaterial and that only the here-and-now counts; or in the attitude that dreams are of little consequence—and a bore besides; or in the position that this or that new member is not bright enough, not up to the group level. With such a development the therapist must analyze as thoroughly as possible the psychodynamics of each patient party to this autocratically harmonizing influence, until the multiple individual and divergent aspirations in the group recover. Otherwise he caters exclusively to the majority and neglects the necessity of the individual patient.

Sometimes a therapist fosters a hierarchical setup in the group in which a ruling clique can maintain its control. In such a climate there can be little shift in participant privileges from the upper echelons to the lower and still less genuine communication between the leading and the led. Their seeming intercourse and reciprocity is counterfeit in which the dominant members govern the more passive who tend to yield to dictation, increasingly reluctant to take a first step in opposition. Not only must the therapist analyze the motivation of each member who joins the ascendant clique but he should just as carefully attend and support those patients who with some help can resist the commanding circle and develop their own initiative.

It seems to us that what often passes for concurrence in the group is itself the expression not so much of constructive cohesion as it is of diegophrenic pathology. The split ego is so characteristic of our time that many patients passively follow the more assertive leaders, lending the group the appearance of homogeneity. This manifest accordance, so liable to be sponsored by the therapist as a salutary "group climate," needs to be analyzed as it shows itself in each dominant-submissive dyad. Each group may have one or two members whose personalities strongly sway the others. They are frequently the most verbal and active, but not necessarily reparative in their insensitivity to others. In order to support weakened egos it is a function of the therapist not to be misled by an apparency of uniformity and to analyze any compulsive passivity and leadership.

Patients seem to have preferences for particular ways of being for each member. And the group tries to get the patient not to deviate from the verbalization and behavior congenial to this role. If he tries to depart from his familiar pattern, the group tends to become rejective. This is particularly true of a homogeneous group. To the extent that this tendency exists at all, the therapist should analyze it in the members.

If a therapist is inclined to foster homogeneity on the grounds that the patient's weak ego cannot tolerate the vigorous approach of a heterogeneous group which might undermine his confidence, we would say that it is the function of the therapist to analyze these judgments when they become pathologic assaults. While we too want the patient to believe in himself, we do not think this self regard ought to be based on any common pathology. We would like to see each member's ego resources encouraged to grow. We do not wish to affirm and reinforce what is sick.

Each patient has different needs at different stages of his treatment. Therefore, the nature of the therapist's intervention at the beginning is not homogeneous with his intercession at a middle or terminal phase of therapy. It would be equally erroneous for the leader to apply a uniform approach to a whole group in the misconception that their needs are the same at any one moment.[139]

An insightful observation about one patient is sometimes useful to another as well. A new awareness may be shared not only out of similar history and experience, but out of comparison, contrast and an appreciation of differences. The analyst ought to be cautious about assuming that what he says of one patient is necessarily valid for another, for his assumption that a sweeping explanation is generally applicable may play into individual resistance that would conceal personal variations. If the analyst finds one person stirred by another's probing or remembering, he is likely to find that, while one patient stimulated another out of a seemingly similar manifest content, the underlying psychodynamics has latent uniqueness for each.[135]

There is a common misconception that individual analysis occupies itself more with genetic etiology while analysis in a group is engaged largely in the current, momentary interaction. This is a limited, one-dimensional and homogeneous notion of treatment, whether individual or group. What happens in therapy is influenced by the analyst. He can facilitate the group experience as historically oriented and the individual one as essentially current. Either aproach, exclusively applied, defeats the treatment in homogeneity. More appropriate multidimensional therapy explores historic, present and future paths in the patient's development, regardless of the treatment structure.

There is a tendency on the part of combined therapists to be intrigued with homogeneity. They are inclined to treat the group as a single unit in group meetings and just as homogeneously to differentiate them in individual interviews. Such an approach acts as a damper on interaction at group sessions, where little or no analytic therapy is done. Deep therapy is reserved for individual sessions where the patient is distinguished from the group.[114] In chapter 9 we shall discuss combined or concurrent therapy at length.

The leader discriminates between patients in order to discover their different illnesses and to be able to work through for each the specific way to enlist their cooperation and help them resolve their disorder. By this discriminating means the therapist gives each member particular insight, so that patients do not expect the analyst to approach them in a homogeneous way. Sometimes a therapist is disconcerted by patients' objections that he does not treat one member like another. When the leader is sure that patients are heterogeneous and need to be treated differently, he ceases to feel disturbed by such complaints. And he soon discovers that patients stop insisting on identical treatment from him and instead appreciate his distinguishing their respective needs.[139]

What is the role of the therapist in the face of a developing homogeneity, a common dynamic, a shared motif in his group? It is the analyst's function to accept and understand the manifest, but also to penetrate the resistive, generalized façade to each patient's concealed, unconscious and differentiated interest.

It is important for the therapist to value multiformity, to appreciate diverse thoughts and feelings and to demonstrate to his patients the productive import to each of the heterogeneous organization. For, as group members discover the worth of parity in difference, they permit and encourage appropriate dissimilarity in others. Then the patients themselves cultivate a climate of mutual examination that is cordial to unlikeness. This receptivity toward divergence encourages each to unfold his particularity, which in turn enriches the group experience of all. The group's interest in the discordant view fosters a medium of friendly candor in which the patient can expose himself and have more choice in determining his destiny.

Summary

Mark Twain once remarked that "It is not best that we should all think alike; it is difference of opinion that makes horse races." Apart from clinical considerations our philosophical bias is with heterogeneity, because it is in keeping with nature. The only solution for a democratic society lies in the recognition and acceptance of the pluralistic character of the population. Only in a monolithic society can the heterogeneity of man be levelled in homogeneity. Child-rearing, education and psychotherapy ought not to be the same for all, unless we are robots on an assembly line (*see* chapter 12).

The insistence upon homogeneous grouping may in part be the consequence of American adulation of magnitude with too little respect for personal craftsmanship and qualitative distinction. The indissoluble wholeness of American culture has made the American countryside so lacking in diversity that one town is hardly distinguishable from another, succeeding each other in appalling monotony. We need not demand the same self effacement of one another. If we look and think and feel alike, we negate the fertile complementation that makes life worth living.

A danger of the homogeneous group lies in the appeal it makes to the potentially dissident minority. And this appeal is very potent in a society trained to concede to the majority opinion, sensitive to being outside the in-group. In order to "belong," the American tends to sacrifice his private views—for there is no greater sin in America than to stand apart.

We live in a time when it is regarded as dangerous not to share a common view. Liberty of mind is more frequently a fancy than a fact, for the person who takes exception jeopardizes his right to belong to the group. We seem rather to welcome aberration, peculiarly irrational departures that are not to be confused with rational originality. Group therapy ought not to become another sanctuary for like-minded, disturbed patients.

The neurotic patient characteristically has a low tolerance for honest evaluations of himself, for disagreement with what he thinks and feels and does. And he often enough moves in circles where he can avoid such unpleasantness. Why, in what should be a therapeutic environment, ought we to surround him again with the same therapeutic embalmment? He has seldom been frankly confronted before with what he is, so why subject him to an approving audience of like minds who demand no changes from him? Such a group merely reinforces the illusion that he is fine as he is by compounding an unconscious majority. For the homogeneous group regards itself with benevolent blindness; it goes its sacrosanct way, the members hardly touched with any insight into their insufficiencies or resources. The heterogeneous group, on the other hand, does not let the individual rest in unrealistic contentment with the way he is.

The patient subjected to a group with approximately uniform ideas and feelings is likely to renounce his own wishes for those of the group. Analytic therapy would provide the patient with a setting in which he can uncover his repressed wishes. How can he even begin to approach these guarded aspirations in a climate which is massively opposed to his deviation from the ordered theme?

The formation of a homogeneous group is the attempt to fuse human beings into a unit, an instrument, an abstraction, a thing. And in the process patients are likely to become A, A', A'', and so on rather than to retain and develop their characteristic personalities. Impersonal, circuitous speculations displace the therapist's interest in psychodynamics. What holds his attention is less his patients than an aura peripheral to therapy. He gives primacy to the *idea* of a group. The effectiveness of any therapy is dependent on the prominence given to the persons in the group. In a homogeneous group they are merely shadows. Therapists whose patients grow as their individual psychopathology is worked through will never be content with such an outcome. Homogeneity would make the patient incidental to a group essence. The realistic therapist begins and ends with his patients and their ways of interrelating. He does not project them into a cloudy mass, a formula without personal thoughts, feelings, curiosities, histories, qualities, motivations, values, aims, opinions and activities. Patients reduced to contemplating one another merely as part of an ensemble become phantoms for each other and the therapist as well. They hover in an undetermined expanse without boundaries. They become group ghosts rather than distinctive people.

The homogeneous disposition is not psychoanalytic in its inattention to personal distinctions. It disregards each patient's particular needs and means of development. The critical question of proper timing of analytic interventions becomes more confused by treating "the group as a whole." The approach to patients as group with little regard for a particular member's receptivity at the time may reinforce resistances, prematurely deal with defenses or institute inappropriate behavior. Homogenizing the patients improvises a demeanor of consistency but suppresses the actual ventilation of multiple transferences and the development of rational uniqueness. In a search for common ground, we are likely to overestimate the commonplace. In quest of the golden mean, we are liable to end with the mediocre. The homogeneous vision is contrary to the variety of nature. It is unreasonable in one-dimensionality. It stresses the framework but overlooks the essential ingredients, their origin and interaction. It is not clinical or therapeutic in its discarding of individual history and differentiated psychodynamics. Effective therapy is not possible in a group which disregards heterogeneous development, motivation and kinship, but prizes conformism and isolation.

3. Size

An early question arising in the mind of the psychoanalyst contemplating treating patients in a group is—*how many*? The assumption is often made that a certain fixed number is to be preferred to all others. There is marked difference of opinion as to what that number is and for what reasons. The clinical experience and inner necessities of the analyst frequently determine at least in part his choices in theory and technique. Size becomes not only a management problem but also a rallying point for personal investment and commitment.

Slavson,[123] like Bion,[15] values the number eight. Therapeutic groups are defined by him as "not exceeding eight persons." Interaction is a prime mover, but if the size of the group is more than eight, Slavson believes that true therapeutic interaction cannot occur. If the group is less than five, he states, benefits will be minimal, since "countertherapeutic processes" will not occur. On the other hand, the actual number of persons in a treatment group is not vital for Slavson, since he treats the group as if it were one patient. Under such circumstances, the size is unimportant since he homogenizes the patients, and is thus really giving individual therapy.

Slavson claims there is evidence from the group dynamics investigators that eight is the optimal number for interaction, but "five to six patients will yield better results." "The present writer's own introduction of therapy through the group was based on the concept of a small group of eight. The number eight has since been universally accepted by therapists everywhere."

Goldfarb,[44] too, holds the belief that eight patients constitute the ideal number, based upon the therapist's feelings concerning the interaction and level of intimacy among the membership. Loeser[66] believes groups of four to eight are best for handling acting out. Smaller groups cannot tolerate acting out and groups larger than eight will not accommodate it. Lorge and Solomon[68] suggest that ten seems to be a realistic upper limit beyond which groups will not attempt to work out problems. They offer an interesting theoretic model for evaluating the possibility of correlating changes in group size with the possibility of individual solutions in problem solving situations. Westman[128] extends the upper limits and states, "In the practice of group therapy, from eight to twelve members have been found most workable."

Size, however, cannot be seen mechanically as a separate, unrelated determinant. Considerations of magnitude need to include many other factors such as the kind of therapy, the nature of expected outcomes, the motivations of the persons involved, and the dynamic interaction between size and other group properties. But Loeser[66] holds that size is central. "As the size of the group increases or decreases, certain fundamental changes in patterns of function take place of a predictable, observable nature." And he offers the following classificatory system: (1) dyad; (2) triad; (3) four to eight —the ideal therapy group; (4) eight to thirty, the ideal educational group; (5) thirty to several thousands, the audience group; (6) crowds, masses, unlimited numbers.

We would like to draw the obvious cautionary against a rigid view of some ideal number for some ideal group. Would ten neurotics make a less well functioning, interpenetrating, interactive group than five depressed or delusional, psychotic patients? Number and function are related to the realities of who these patients are. In the cocktail party group, all may be witty and sophisticated but massively resistive to any kind of meaningful interaction. A class of forty students who are bright might be a much better educational group than a class of five morons or four idiots. A homogeneous group of eight to ten patients may not be as effective as a heterogeneous group of three to four.

Rickman[89, 90] draws sharp distinction between the number of persons and the kind of psychology present. For him, the dyad and triad are most important no matter how large the group. One-person psychology is largely neurophysiology and inner processes. Two-person psychology is the interaction between two human beings, classically perceived as the reciprocal relationship in child rearing and individual psychoanalytic work. Three-person psychology is that of the Oedipal situation with both parents and the child. Four-person psychology introduces into the triad the other child or sibling. All other combinations beyond the tetrad are for Rickman multi-person groups. In the dyad, he believes, either one-person or three-person psychology applies.

On the other hand, the chances are that a one-person psychology does not exist. At least one person and probably two others are included. Theoretically, one-person psychology might apply to the infant before he really relates or is aware of the other in the first year of life, more or less. The narcissistic relationship of the infant to the mother before awareness that persons other than mothers exist might be conjectured as two-person psychology. Three-person psychology, the Oedipal, is a contribution of psycho-analysis. Rickman, as well as others, are convinced that the three-person interpretation is essential for cure, no matter what the size of the group. He suggests that in the two-body, dyadic situation of individual analysis, three-person or four-person psychology is probably always at work by virtue of transference.

Perhaps from this point of view there is no optimal size of group. For each group analyst the number of persons that can be adequately observed may vary. Rickman stresses that the range of group sizes in which the therapist can effectively work relates to the number of persons he is able to observe and not to the category of psychology or work. Within the limits of certain basic capacities, however, with experience and training the range of simultaneous interaction the therapist can observe may be increased. Rickman feels that a range from seven to ten patients provides sufficiently for individual variations in analysts.

In our opinion, Rickman has raised some of the crucial issues pertaining to size of group. But individual variations exist not only in therapists but also in patients. The appearance of real or fantasy figures in any constellation may intensify or attenuate the nature of the interaction. With some persons, isolation, the one-body situation, the monad, is more secure even if a second person, or a third or more persons are present in fantasy. For others, the presence in reality of a second, third or even fourth person is much more secure than the fantasy of such people. In the dyad, for example, the fantasied presence may be more secure or more threatening than the real presence, and the reverse is also true for some.

In this connection we are stimulated by the possibility that in the technical handling of the patients in a group, the analytic work may not be specifically related, within certain limits, to the number of patients present. It may be that how the analysis proceeds in the group is only slightly colored by whether five or ten patients are present. In general, the analytic work deals with the interaction between two or three or at most four, and is largely the attempt to resolve recurrent efforts to triangulate human relations by incorporating them into the original family and thus resurrecting the incestuous situation. The emphasis is on working through the introduction of the third member in fact or in fantasy, thus to be able to see the true nature of the provocative, interactive, dyadic relationship.

If repetitive triangulation is a primary mode of interaction requiring the continuing attention of the analyst, he may become anxious to reach the individual member and do individual analytic work. On the other hand, he may want to include all the members or amalgamate them, no longer seeing them as individuals, but as a mass. He may then resort to group dynamic approaches. In the first instance, if the analyst wants to do individual work, why do it in the group? It is wasteful in that setting. And the group dynamic approach is, as we shall discuss later, antianalytic. In this connection, Rickman keenly recognizes group dynamics as invaluable for anthropology or some other science of the future but of questionable value in psychoanalytic therapy.

The nature of dyad and triad psychology is basic to an understanding of group analytic processes and the problem of size. The choice of the dyadic relationship, apart from certain considerations which in themselves should be explored, seems to be an attempt on the part of either partner to resolve the competition, the anxiety, the threat of aggression inherent in the triangular or Oedipal situation. It may represent the hope or the fact of a sexual solution, and the chances are that the dyadic operation is more likely a homosexual than a heterosexual one.

It is our clinical impression that the dyadic experience is in general more serene than the triadic. It is confirmed, it seems to us, by the reluctance of most therapists to do analysis with couples and groups. And when analysts work with couples or in groups there is greater show of aggression and sexual activity. Group therapists report experiencing more anxiety when dealing with a couple or with a group, except those who do individual analysis in the group. In this case, the group becomes either an extension of himself or of the patient.

Analysis of the hostile nature of the triad has been explored carefully by Ernest Jones in his essay, "A Psycho-Analytic Study of the Holy Ghost Concept." He proposes that the resolution of the hostility problem is accomplished in the Trinity of the Christian religion through denial of the three-way system. The mother is removed from the father-son situation by the introduction of the non-sexualized Holy Ghost in place of the Mother-Goddess figure. In this way the hostility that is to be expected in the Oedipal situation is diminished by Christianity.

It must not be assumed, just because therapy is done in the group, patients are allowed to interact with one another. The individually oriented group analyst working in the group setting may, for example, prevent interaction by controlling patient to patient transactions for fear that there will be aggressive or sexual acting out. He might seek to maintain exclusive, dyadic relationships only with him. On the other hand, an individual analyst working in a dyadic setting may encourage many more kinds of interaction than only the exclusively dyadic relationship by permitting or encouraging the patient to have relations with persons other than himself. Triadic and tetradic transactions become available for analysis just as soon as the analyst no longer rigidly insists upon focussing on the one-to-one relationship with him. In the group, this means the willingness to encourage peer interaction rather than a non-discriminative demand for an exclusive vertical relationship only with the analyst. One criterion we use to discover whether or not a group therapist is committed to the value of peer interaction is the answer to the question, does he use the alternate meeting? If a combined therapist, for example, permits the alternate session, we view this as his recognition of the therapeutic significance of peer vectors. Refusal to adopt the alternate session is one indication of the possibility that the therapist is too authority-centered, is overemphasizing hierarchical vectors.

A therapist, despite a manifest preference for the group as a setting in which to work, may, at times, be latently more committed to dyadic relationships than some individual therapists who support the patient in multilateral experience. It is possible that there are some therapists, whether they function in the dyadic or group setting, who are so insecure and distrustful of difference or so omnipotent with underlying fear and helplessness, that they cannot tolerate even a dyadic relationship but insist only on monads.[129] They feel more secure if there is only "unconscious to unconscious" contact, that is, isolation, or only if a patient is a replica of the therapist or an extension of him. In this sense the therapist who insists on a homogeneous group may be insisting on a monadic indentification with himself rather than any relationship of patients to himself or to one another in difference.

Loeser[66] believes that the dyad is capable of achieving the highest degree of "spiritual values." He also states that hostile reactions are more intense, more prone to be acted out in a dyadic relationship than any other kind of setting. This position seems to be contradicted by human experience. Wars are rarely fought between the two leaders of warring nations. Wars are generally fought by large armies of persons who go out and kill each other. The experience in psychoanalysis in groups indicates that the increase in stimulation, provocation and reactivity of all kinds including hostile reactions approaches geometric proportions in groups of eight to ten, as compared with the dyadic relationship either between the therapist and the patient or husband and wife.

The general opinion, expressed by Loeser and others, is that in the one-to-one relationship, the individual analytic setting, for example, quantitatively and qualitatively more hostility and some say also more love are expressed than in the analytic therapy group. This needs to be questioned. For most patients, the freedom to express the full extent of their feelings toward authority figures as well as others when the vertical vector is stressed, as in individual analysis, is much less likely than the same person expressing the same degree of feeling toward authorities, peers or subordinates. Since the dyad is so intense an emotional experience, say Loeser and others, additional patients are added to the treatment setting to dilute the intensity. Loeser prefers the larger group because here emotional interactions can be dealt with more safely. Still others agree that the smaller group is more intense, but find it preferable for that very reason.

When we go beyond the dyad to the triad, we increase the possibilities for rivalry, for the manifold development of new transferences. In the original family beginning in a dyad, when there is the birth of a child, one or the other parent or both may go into rivalry with the new born infant for the possession of the other parent. When a second child is born additional rivalries enter into the situation, and so on. At the same time, there appear on the scene new objects for support, for love, for choice, new freedoms as well as rivalries. So it seems that as we add new members to the therapy group patients are given new opportunities for making transferences and for making healthy alternative choices.

For Geller[41] a direct relationship exists between the size of the group and the depth of therapy achieved. Yet our experience has been that regardless of the size of the group depth will vary with the kinds of patients, the individual necessities of the members of the group, and the aims, attitudes, theoretic commitment and techniques of the therapist. The size of the group does not ipso facto determine depth. This is too mechanical a view. A small group, even a dyad, can provide superficial therapy, as in brief or non-analytic therapy or counseling, whereas in a psychoanalytic group depth may be accomplished, even though there are eight or ten patients. Can it be said automatically that depth is less in a group of eight than a group of five or a group of three; or that depth is greater in a dyad in which counseling techniques and objectives are employed than in an analytic group of three, five or eight? The idea that "depth of therapy decreases as the size of the group increases" is probably true only if the size differential jumps from 2 to 20, 50 or 100; but if the steps are 2, 3, 4, 5, 6, 7, 8, it is doubtful that the principle still holds. Should some correlation actually be found between the size of group and the depth of therapy, we would feel, from clinical experience, that this may be an artifact rather than a dynamic relationship.

Depth or intensity of therapy are related mostly to such items as the syndromes or categories of patients included in the group; individual differences among patients, their conscious and unconscious motivations and interests; and their availability for and commitment to therapy. To this order of consideration need be added those dimensions determined by the techniques employed by the therapist, whether he is doing counseling, directive, inspirational or analytic therapy, for example. For us, the qualities of therapy are not determined by size but rather by the qualifications, competences, predilections and personality of the therapist as well as the patient. In fact, other things being equal, optimal size may be determined by the depth of therapy sought by the therapist rather than the reverse. Of course, we are committed specifically to psychoanalytic therapy in a group setting, which provides the frame of reference for our discussions. It is the psychoanalytic commitment that influences the intensity of the work. We are not referring to other kinds of groups which may be therapeutic in outcome, such as social or orientation groups, or even inspirational groups where the size factor will have different consequences.

Psychoanalysis in groups encourages the participants to attend the feelings, actions and considered opinions not only of the self but also the others. As in the case of the analyst, so too for each patient in the group the range of number of persons whose reactions are perceived may be increased through experience. There are those who state that seven plus or minus two patients make the ideal therapy group; others recommend seven or eleven; or ten, the basic unit of the decimal system. Still others think twelve the most versatile number. Experimental evidence in group dynamics suggests that the size of successful small groups is curvilinear, that is, of the progression five to ten, groups of five, seven and nine are to be preferred to those of six, eight or ten. For us there is no magic in numbers.

Our experience has been largely limited to groups ranging in size from eight to ten patients. In one group of ten, an eleventh patient was introduced with no objection and with no apparent diminishment of therapeutic effectiveness. It may be possible to go beyond ten patients, in some instances, without the group deteriorating into a crowd in which the individual is lost. If in a group of three patients there were a monopolist who made it very difficult for the two others to participate, there could be opposition on their part to the introduction of a fourth member. They might feel they were having enough difficulty as it was. Experience with a group of seven members originally numbering ten, illustrates the opposite. Three of the seven patients were extremely difficult. John and Sam were schizoid, withdrawn persons; and Paul was a very verbal but autistic schizophrenic who would not relate in a constructive way. The other four members lost patience with the withdrawal of John and Sam and the inappropriate participation of Paul. They demanded that three new patients be added with whom they could better interact. John and Sam were not stimulating enough, and Paul was too distracting.

There may be value in considering to what extent the size of the group is dependent upon the dimensions and shape of the room, and how the seats are arranged. If the group treatment room is too long and too narrow, so that patients cannot see one another, it might cause problems. If three patients sit side by side on a couch or bench with their backs to the wall, they cannot very well see each other. We, on the other hand, have a preference for a circular arrangement where everybody has the possibility of seeing, being stimulated by and interacting with everybody else. If the room is too small, patients may complain that they feel jammed in. If it is too large they may feel lost. While the therapist needs to be aware of such factors, they are perhaps not as important as analyzing specific reactions to the size of the room. In a small room, some patients feel very cozy; in a large room, some do not feel as intimately related, but more expansive and free. If more persons are in a small room or fewer in a large one, different kinds of reactions may be invoked. But up to a point, group composition and the therapist's attitude are really the most important factors in determining size. There probably is a point at which size becomes a central problem.

Although the more general problem of size of groups is instructive, we need to keep in mind that we are not discussing groups in general but therapy groups, and specifically psychoanalytic treatment groups. We have been concerned specifically with the question: What size, under ordinary circumstances, for most situations and for most patients will provide the optimal outcome therapeutically speaking? For a therapist with a loud voice, a roomful of 50 persons might be a possible therapeutic setting. But it is certainly not optimal, because the therapist cannot practically know and work with the individual psychodynamics of so large a group. Moreover, the membership would probably voice disappointment about the real and neurotic gratification they seek from the analyst.

If the objective is therapy—that is, the health of the individual patient who comes for treatment—and if patient and therapist accept the group as the setting, under what circumstances can this experience be facilitated? What size of group will maximize benefits? Clinical experience suggests that if one keeps the size of the group within a certain range rather than rigidly set on a certain number, benefits will be derived for most people, under most circumstances, with most group therapists. This does not mean that if a patient drops out or an additional one is added, therapy will be facilitated or impeded. Of course, we are excluding from this consideration special cases of countertransference as, for example, when a patient is dropped by the analyst out of his own prejudice or subjective necessity; or to avoid the resentment of the group; or as a mechanism to disrupt an interaction rather than to analyze it.

Although we recommend a group size of from eight to ten patients, any rigid view can be misleading. Research findings are necessary before a fixed number of patients might be decided upon for all kinds of patients, for all therapists, under all kinds of conditions. In the meantime and for a long time to come, we suspect, we shall have to be experimental under a variety of clinical conditions and keep in mind that size probably involves a range of numbers of patients. Group size is not an absolute number or an absolute concept, but a dynamic, interconnected variable in psychoanalysis in groups.

We should like to share a fantasy with our readers. Perhaps the problem of size can be approached symbolically. What is a family, how large is it? Three is the minimum number of members in a family. Until there are three, there is no family. Anything less than three is not a group by definition. The average number of children in the family, in most families, is three or four children. Most persons would say a family consists of father and mother, and three or four children. If one is brought up in a particular culture, one might say half-a-dozen children; and in still another, one might say one or two children. But in our culture, when a person talks about a family, he generally thinks of three or four offspring. That would be the projected family size, namely, five or six. When someone says, I have a dozen children, one is at a point where he begins to hold his head and feel, "That is no family, that is a mob." With 14 or 16 members, it is no longer a family group that can easily maintain itself economically, emotionally and socially.

The fantasy continues. A family consists of parents and children totaling five, but a healthy family group experience is possible only if there is contact with some extrafamiliar figures. If the family group does not relate to a few strangers of different age and sex, the incestuous problem tends not to be resolved—the experience of loving a stranger is missing. As a symbolic basis for group size, then, we once again arrive at the family group with a few friends. This fantasy may even have anthropologic or sociologic validity. The ideal treatment group size may be visualized as a family group plus a few strangers. What does this mean to most analysts—6, 8, 10, 20, 30? For us, psychoanalysis in groups provides an experience in which a person has the opportunity to reconstruct the nuclear family with the possibility also of accepting the stranger. This is another way of approaching the problem of group size.

4. Other Variables

We have already discussed such important parameters of psychoanalysis in groups as size and structure. Many other variables come into existence when treating patients psychoanalytically in a group. Some of these will be discovered later in the chapters on the alternate meeting, group dynamics, contrasts and values. We wish here to elaborate three fundamental dynamic elements which need to be kept in mind if we are to understand the nature of psychoanalysis done in a group and to improve the level of therapeutic work. We shall attempt to demonstrate the usefulness of these three in approaching various theoretic and technical problems.

First are the *hierarchic factors* which can be seen in the interplay of horizontal and vertical reactions in status relationships. They are revealed in the quality of one's transactions with authorities and peers. Second are *multiple reactivities* indicating how one utilizes other members of the group and the leader in healthy and neurotic ways. Third are *intra-communication* and *inter-communication*. The one stresses self knowledge leading to personal integration, the other knowledge of the self and of others leading to personal and social integration. The balance and contrast between intrapsychic focus and interpersonal transactions are included here.

Everyone in our culture has problems in peer relatednesses and in authority transactions. No one escapes the hierarchic experience of a class society, whether in family life, in the community, at work, or other areas of living. None of us has completely worked out his difficulties with parents and siblings, with authorities and subordinates, as well as with peers. The group experience creates opportunities for direct experiential observation of these differences, and by this scrutiny their nature is clarified. It is easier in the group to learn to understand peer and authority attitudes than in any other kind of experience, not only because peer and authority figures are actually present but also because multiple reactivities are encouraged in psychoanalysis in groups. Any therapy that limits the emergence of the activities of

---

Revision of ref. 109.

the human being is not very effective. Many forms of therapy actually prevent the appearance of certain kinds of material and their utilization. Finally, communication in its broadest sense is the matrix of all human existence. Alienation and aloneness, which are so common as to become a national malady, can be worked through successfully in the group where the interpersonal interaction is at least as important as intrapsychic attention. Awareness of self and awareness of others are in ongoing focus and the one is not stressed to the neglect of the other.

Individual Psychoanalysis and Psychoanalysis in Groups

The absence of the group makes it possible for the individual analyst to maintain some real or neurotic position of superiority with regard to the patient. Because he comes for help and the therapist is the helper, it is hard for the patient to acquire a sense of equality of his own with the analyst. When supervising psychoanalysts, we have been impressed how often they tend to interpret any attempt of the patient to equalize the relationship as hostility and resistance to accepting the authority position of the therapist.

"Therapeutic-like behavior of members suggests that reparative resources do not reside in the therapist alone. The leader may capitalize upon this possibility and seek to release the therapeutic potential in other group members . . . (who) may make major contributions to the therapeutic activity in a group."[25]

The nature of the individual therapeutic situation calls for testing of reality and of experiences largely in terms of the values and experiences of the analyst. Multiplicity, it seems to us, allows for creativity. Individual analysis, in a sense, exposes the patient to a homogeneous experience. He can relate only to one person or one kind of person. In analysis in groups, however, eight to ten other unique individuals allow for differences to appear and for other kinds of people to be accepted. The other members as well as the analyst become the social ideal and measure of oneself, with whom one identifies and from whom one learns.

In the individual analytic situation, then, little opportunity is given to the patient or to the analyst to examine, develop and work through peer relationships. Moreover, neither the therapist nor the patient gets an opportunity to see in action the multiple transference and countertransference reactions or the movement of transference from one person to another.

Psychoanalysis tends to emphasize intracommunication. Traditional training and the personality of the more orthodox analyst favor intrapsychic patterning and intrapsychic activity. Turning within the self makes for intracommunication, that is, the attempt to understand and to communicate with the self, to examine the self and inner activities rather than interactions with others. The group demands, at least equally, intercommunication as well as intracommunication.

Some individual analysts criticize psychoanalysis in groups on this very basis. They claim that in the group setting less free-association is possible; therefore, less unconscious material is available. It is true that less free-association may occur in the group, but we think this can be good. Overemphasis upon inner processes may be unhealthy. The consequence, however, is not less unconscious material which can be derived also from dreams and the analysis of resistance and transference, and other behavioral manifestations.

Individual analysis takes place under conditions of isolation, more or less. This is due partly to the neurosis of the patient and partly to the method. The isolation stemming from the neurosis of the patient is not altered merely by changing from individual analysis to psychoanalysis in groups. Some patients remain isolated, for a time, even in the group. On the other hand, the methodologic isolation implicit in individual analysis is modified in psychoanalysis in groups. In individual analysis, a person tends to behave as he or she would in isolation, whereas group members resist this trend. The patient cannot long remain in the group totally isolated—no matter how he tries. The interactive, interpersonal, intercommunicative demands in the group are difficult to deny.

It seems clear that optimal therapy provides a harmonious balance between the opportunity to work out the horizontal and vertical transactions, the individual and multiple reactivities, and the inter- and intracommunicative needs. The nondiscriminate and exclusive emphasis upon one direction on each of these three continua results in a one-sided or a lopsided kind of psychoanalysis. These limitations will be apparent as we proceed in our examination of variations in group therapy.

Combined Individual and Group Therapy

Combined therapy seems like a natural and happy resolution for those who would like to preserve the benefits of individual and group therapy without sacrificing what may seem like the special advantages of each. Unhappily as we shall see in detail later, in practice combined therapy turns out generally to be individual therapy with "some group experience" like the social group or fun session. The group is not used therapeutically in our sense but rather as a place to have experiences to be analyzed later in the individual session. The group may be misused, also, quite out of keeping with its nature, as support for the authority of the therapist. For example, when a patient in the individual session resists an interpretation of the analyst, he may bring it to the group for confirmation. This can only make the patient more hierarchically oriented in all human relations, for even the peers are seen as on the side of authority. This curtails also the possibility for differences to emerge and for the multiplicity of reactions usually to be found in group therapy settings. The indiscriminate use of individual sessions by the patient sets up an irrational opposition of analyst against group, whereas their real objectives are identical.

This state of affairs is a consequence of the therapist's attitude that "real" therapy goes on in the individual session; the group experience is merely a catalytic agent for the work to be done alone. Such an arrangement limits the interaction and the intercommunication which can and ordinarily do occur in psychoanalysis in groups. Sometimes, even in the group, individual therapy is done where the group is ignored or the activity and interactivity of the peers are limited. If the analyst is committed to group therapy, individual sessions, where necessary, need not interfere with the group experience. But in general practice as we have seen it, having individual sessions routinely along with group sessions is a deterrent to the proper utilization of group resources. The individual session can be used destructively by impeding interaction, by setting the tone, or by limiting expression in the group situation. But it may be used constructively if one is aware of the ever-present relationship between the individual session and the group session and its implications. The individual session must never be employed by either patient or analyst as resistance to the group experience.

Heterogeneous and Homogeneous Groups

For a variety of reasons which we have already discussed, homogeneous groups can give rise only to a limited and limiting form of therapy. In heterogeneous groups there is opportunity to work through the problem of difference. The person gains a new value and a new security. He can accept and be accepted by different people, persons who are different from each other and different from himself. His isolation is reduced and the possibility exists for working out relationships with peers as well as with authorities. Often the individual who feels different relates this difference to status, assuming that the hierarchic relationship is somehow intrinsic to human transaction. Those who are different from oneself are seen as either higher or lower than those who are the same as oneself.

In the heterogeneous group the individual has the opportunity to experience multiple reactivity possibilities and so move out of his isolation. As he emerges and interacts, he moves among peers who are different, as well as among authority figures who are different, because some of the other patients are projected as authority figures like the therapist.

We raise the question whether one needs only authorities in order to work out one's authority problems, and whether in the group one works out only one's peer differences. In some of the studies with children there is indication that the socialization process occurs through the peers.[85] The probability exists that one works through both kinds of problems both with authorities and with peers. In the group we might expect to work out inter-locking authority attitudes by greater scrutiny of relationships to peers; in individual therapy we hope that by stressing authority problems in the transference, we will work out interlocking peer relatedness problems as well.

So far as multiple reactivities are concerned, in heterogeneous groups we can expect to find less mirror imaging and less identification. In the homogeneous group there is likely to be more hostility in seeing oneself in others. In heterogeneous groups more transference and countertransference reactions may arise, but also more reality testing and working through. Because of the varieties of stimulation in heterogeneous groups, interaction, change and movement are facilitated. There is clinical and experimental evidence of the advantages of heterogeneous groups over homogeneous groups in encouraging multiple reactivity and more interaction among the members.[39, 40, 43]

At least superficially, the heterogeneous group encourages interpersonal communication more than intrapsychic preoccupation. This is quite different from what occurs in the homogeneous group which limits intercommunication because you start with the assumption, I am like everybody else here. There is less stimulation or provocation to compare and to change. In the heterogeneous group intrapsychic communication is stimulated by virtue of the comparison of individual with individual, because of differences. In the homogeneous group the interpretive interventions of the therapist focus the patient on intrapsychic examination because of the so-called sameness of the members.

The homogeneous group, like the very permissive group or leaderless group, seems to set up a pathologic subculture which excludes the rest of the culture. Patients who are alike are admitted; those who are different are not. In the homogeneous group there is a greater tendency to act out whereas in the heterogeneous group, patients may act out more in the beginning, but ultimately solve their problems. This is not as true for the homogeneous group which tends to be more isolating from reality, from differences, and from the rest of the culture. One of the advantages of the heterogeneous group is that differences or alternatives do not have to come only from the authority figure—it is possible that alternatives may come from the peers. Sometimes when alternatives are offered by the authority in the individual or homogeneous group situation, they are resisted or submitted to but never accepted on a basis of equality relationship as from the peers. It may be that a teaching group or some form of social group may be more efficient if homogeneous, but it does not seem so for the therapeutic group.

The Alternate Session

The three primary parameters under discussion are brought into sharp focus in the meeting of the group without the analyst. "Alternate meetings represent, in general, a phase of testing, exploring and consolidating, wherein the patient learns to separate himself from parental dependency in its various forms.[55] The alternate session sometimes is seen as leaderless, but this view is erroneous. Even though the analyst is not present, there are expressions with regard to him and attempts to work out the hierarchic relationship with him. In the alternate session, patients talk about their feelings with regard to the analyst. This comes out later in the regular session. Moreover, the experience with alternate meetings demonstrates that individual members take over leadership. By virtue of transference, there is available leadership or authority. The alternate session is an antidote to the traditional detachment of the analyst.

Although in the alternate session emphasis is greater upon peer transactions, there is also examination of feelings and reactions with regard to authority figures. Support of the peers helps the individual work out some of his authority feelings and gives him courage to face the authority in the session when the analyst is present. It is true that in the alternate session leaders may be more easily made and unmade. Nevertheless, leadership does occur and some of the vertical problems are worked out and worked through. In the alternate session as in the session with the analyst, multiplicity of healthy and unhealthy reactions is typical. The alternate session affords opportunity for both intrapsychic and interpersonal activity. New fantasy material can emerge, and interpersonal or intercommunicative activity is quantitatively greater when the therapist is absent.

On the communication continuum, individual therapy is really groupless therapy in that one communicates largely with one person or, even more orthodoxly, with oneself. At the other end of this continuum is the alternate session which is leaderless therapy only in the sense that the analyst is not physically present, although there is awareness of the relationship to the therapist, and parental surrogates may give leadership. The absence of the expert, however, seems to permit freer intercommunication and to lessen the necessity for intracommunication. There is, therefore, greater possibility for interaction and integration on the peer level.

Consider the case of the group therapist who does not permit alternate meetings. This kind of therapist is somewhat unrealistic because in our experience patients seek out individual sessions with one another unless these are absolutely forbidden. Even then there may be some who may take the chance. The therapist who will never allow them to meet together forbids their exploring real and fancied attitudes toward one another.

The group therapist must be flexible. He needs to be free enough to let the group meet without him and to be able to meet with a patient alone when there is real need for an individual session. The group therapist who never allows an individual session is like the one who allows no intercommunication except under his surveillance. If he never meets his patients individually, he actually forbids them to explore their vertical relations to him. Some patients are afraid to express feeling in front of others, whether about the therapist or members of the group. Others cannot express their feelings when in a face-to-face relationship. Still others are able to express themselves more freely only in the alternate session. The group therapist who fosters only intercommunication and interaction in the group can immobilize in that he isolates his patients and limits the possibility of a one-to-one relationship with the analyst. This is what happens with the Israeli sabra brought up in a crêche on a kibutz. As a child he has no opportunity for an intimate one-to-one relationship with a parent; as an adult, therefore, he shows more anxiety and difficulty in one-to-one relationships than in group situations.

The therapist who forbids the patients getting together increases hierarchic relatedness and limits peer interaction. He blocks patients experiencing and experimenting with the quality of peer transactions. He cuts down on the multiplicity of reactivity and the working through of both horizontal and vertical distortions. The therapist's rationale is that it reduces acting out, that if he permits patients to get together they will act out. The fact of the matter is many patients act out even in individual therapy, and it limits his effectiveness as a therapist if he has to forbid acting out. Forbidding patients to meet limits interaction in that it sometimes reflects the therapist's wish that patients relate only to him. Transference phenomena that can occur when the patients are free to interact with regard to the peers are curtailed. Communication is also blocked in that it forbids patients to be either intracommunicative or intercommunicative without the presence and the approval of the parental figure. There is no real resolution, therefore, of either intrapsychic or interpersonal problems.

Authoritarian group therapists of both the id-dominated and superego-dominated varieties reject alternate sessions. In the id-dominated group every expression is intense; in the superego-dominated group all intensive affect is forbidden or looked upon as acting out. Very permissive as well as very repressive therapy deny the meaningfulness of the group experience.

The Permissive Group

Let us examine the nature of very permissive therapy done in a group. The permissive group is one in which anything goes, which encourages acting out. It is essentially pseudopermissive in that it masks an authoritarianism. So far as the hierarchic situation is concerned, the so-called permissive group emphasizes the vertical relationship; it is characterized by domination by the id. The therapist assumes he should maintain the distinction of being more of everything than the patient. He believes it is necessary to be more of a patient than the patient. He claims that he is able more easily to enter into a kind of "therapeutic" psychosis; that he is able more directly to communicate his unconscious feeling to the unconscious feeling of his patients. Such a view promotes the superiority of the therapist, even in pathology.[146]

So far as multiple reactivities are concerned, there is in this kind of therapy a tendency toward greater and greater isolation. Patients are encouraged to isolate themselves one from another as well as from the therapist. In the core phase of therapy the patient as well as the therapist are in individual isolation, each in his own pathologic privy. This contamination with pathology without a working through is directed to creating a pathologic subculture based upon intrapsychic pathology and individual isolation.

As a consequence of this isolation the patients' communications are blocked. There is no intercommunication. There is probably also no intracommunication in the sense of the word as it is used here. There is reliance on a kind of communication that exists, so far as we know, only in the minds of men, that is telepathic, unconscious-to-unconscious, noncommunicative communication. It is best described by one of these therapists when he suggests that the highest form of communication exists when the therapist sleeps and has a dream about his patient.

The Leaderless Group

We are led to a consideration of the leaderless group from the point of view of these parameters. In the leaderless group there is the apparent wish to have horizontal relationships with no vertical relationship. The leaderless group is an attempt to achieve therapeutic goals and work out problems without the presence of an expert. There is, therefore, no harmonious working through of any vertical vector since there is, theoretically at least, no leader in the group. It is our experience, however, that a leaderless group either breaks up, as, for example, if the therapist is sick or on a holiday too long, or it will seek a leader because the members of the group are not solving their problems. They are indeed communicating with one another, but they are communicating pathology without arriving at an understanding and working through of their problems. There is, therefore, a pseudomultiplicity of reactivity in that there are many members of the group, but the kind of activity is always the same, namely, the communication of pathology without the attempt to improve the nature of the interaction. There is also, of course, little reactivity in the vertical direction. As for communication, there is interpersonal contact without necessity for intrapsychic awareness. In a leaderless group communication actually breaks down because of the continuous communication of pathology. This happens because there is no guidance, no leadership, no direction, no expert, no analysis and no integration.

In light of our discussion, training, treatment and research in group therapy must emphasize the general and specific implications of these three parameters. They are in fact dimensions of the group psychotherapeutic process and reflect its nature. Attention should be paid, then, to these and other variables. They need to be kept in mind and consciously utilized as guides for the kinds of material to be stimulated and scrutinized and the kinds of intervention to be made. The group therapist will want to know more about the ways in which patients relate not only to authority figures but also to peers. He will want to know the typical ways in which patients act and interact, the provocative roles the patients play as well as the kinds of reactions to which they are provoked by different kinds of persons both on the hierarchic as well as on the peer level. He will want to know, therefore, also the kinds of healthy as well as transferential reactions that patients may have to other kinds of persons within the group, when the therapist is present as well as when he is absent. Finally, we think he will want to encourage patients continuously to exercise not only self knowledge, that is, intracommunication, but self knowledge derived from the real experience of intercommunicating one's own feelings and having these feelings reflected, accepted, or rejected when in interpersonal contact in the group as well as in the individual situation.

5. The Alternate Session

We propose to describe the nature, dynamics and therapeutic implications of the alternate session,[149] that is, the session of a therapeutic group unattended by the analyst. More than 500 patients participating in analytic experience in a group setting over the past two decades provide the clinical material for this presentation.

Opposition to therapy in groups has diminished considerably since the Second World War. Papers in increasing numbers have appeared in the literature endorsing treatment in a group setting. Opposition to psychoanalysis in groups is still strong, but it is gradually losing ground. Opposition to incorporating the alternate session into group therapy is, however, still vigorous. The alternate session remains one of the most misunderstood and controversial innovations in group psychotherapy. Even those who appreciate the value of the alternate session are not clear as to its nature and use.

It was first introduced by Wolf[135] in 1938 as a vital part of the group therapeutic process. It was subsequently evaluated in an article by Kadis.[55] It is a scheduled meeting of the members of a therapeutic group without the therapist, such sessions alternating with regular meetings when the therapist is present. The therapist asks the group to meet without him once or twice a week, usually in the homes of the various patients. In this way, an atmosphere is provided in which free interaction and participation are stimulated. Patients are told by the analyst that part of getting well requires that they meet at regular intervals without him. They are not instructed to carry on the analytic process in the alternate session as at the regular meetings. Nevertheless, the alternate session frequently becomes an extension of the regular session and tends to preserve its atmosphere and interaction,

---

See ref. 148.

with patients speculating about each other and the absent therapist. At the alternate meeting, patients speak about what they think and feel, and scrutinize their communications.

Purpose of the Alternate Meeting

It is important in group therapy that patients' reactions be directed not only toward the therapist but also toward each other in the presence and absence of the therapist.[145] One purpose of the alternate session is to facilitate interaction in the absence of the therapist. Members learn that they can disagree and still be friends without the continuous guide of authority.[147] Many patients seem freer to interact at alternate meetings when transferences to the therapist are less threatening. Projections developing at the alternate sessions are attenuated by peer realities. Patients experience, and sometimes see and define different transferences in the absence of the analyst. Often when the therapist is away, it is easier for a withdrawn patient to attach himself or a dependent person to relate to a peer-authority in the figure of a co-patient.

The alternate sessions provide an opportunity for the patient to be helped by his peers and to exercise, as well, a constructive role as a helper. In this respect and in others, the alternate meeting comes closer to an experience in life where the patient plays a great variety of roles, as husband or wife, parent and child, employer and employee, ally and antagonist, giver and taker, helper and helped.

A function of the alternate session is the opportunity to compare the behavior of the individual in different settings. Comparison is the basis of all analysis as, for example, when we compare fantasy and reality enabling the patient to choose reality. There is no possibility for drawing conclusions except by contrast. The regular and alternate meetings become a special field for the discrimination of behavioral differences. The two settings confront the patient with disparities in thinking, feeling and acting in the authority's presence and absence, for members relate differently to the analyst and co-patients at regular and alternate sessions.[135]

Together the two climates represent a field which cannot be experienced in the one or the other group atmosphere alone. By comparing differences in conduct and analyzing the transferences involved, the patient is able to work through more completely in both settings. A clear picture emerges of the patient's transferences on the therapist and his fellow patients, and of the means to resolve them. The patient develops the freedom to express himself with less distortion in the two climates. Essentially, the alternate meeting is felt to be a session without the parent, the teacher, the authority.

The struggle for a more realistic perception of one's self and of others requires the scrutiny of differences.[147]

With the alternate session, increased amounts and new forms of healthy and unhealthy material emerge. Not only the negative but the positive as well is stimulated. This is a constructive movement, for there is no fruitful interaction unless egocentricity and hostility give way to empathy. If a patient is able to express only destructive feelings in the therapist's presence and constructive feelings in his absence, it is the therapist's function to analyze this compartmentalizing and to encourage positive as well as negative feelings to be expressed in his presence. The reverse also may be true, that a member displays only friendly attitudes at regular meetings and unfriendly reactions at alternate ones. Here again the therapist's role is similar.

Among other things, feelings about the therapist are often brought to the surface at alternate sessions and then revealed with group support at regular sessions.[135] By precipitating the early emergence of irrational attitudes toward the analyst, alternate sessions may shorten the length of treatment. The relatively less inhibited climate of the alternate session may provoke intense responses to the analyst. These reactions are communicated either consciously or unconsciously in regular meetings. A patient may reveal what he or another member has said apart from the analyst, and it is the therapist's responsibility to determine whether and when to interpret this. For patients blocked in the analyst's presence, the meeting unattended by him can hasten the uncovering of repressed material.

Patients do not have the knowledge of timing in interpretation, which is certainly a problem in all group psychotherapy. Occasionally, anxiety is provoked by patients trying too assiduously to penetrate resistance. The fact, however, that understanding or misunderstanding comes from co-patients, from projected siblings in the main, makes it less threatening. In general, the anxiety is less, and the patient is able to cope with it more easily, when a peer offers reactions or interpretations, than when the expert does. The patient under scrutiny often defends himself against premature insight by protesting that his fellow patients cannot really distinguish significant psychopathology or illusion from reality. The patient so guards himself constructively and realistically against the anxiety of penetration. He gains security in the alternate session by demanding that the group wait to hear what the therapist has to say about the matter at hand.

In the analyst's absence members develop a relationship to each other on their own without being bound by or to him. The opportunity to air contradictory feelings about the leader frees patients and tends to hold the group together. If patients are induced to act and interact together, they are thereby motivated to remain together. So alternate sessions mitigate against premature desertion of the group.

The alternate session reveals to patients that human beings basically want to and can help each other. It adds a new dimension to the therapeutic experience. It gives patients an opportunity to function on their own, to test new found personal strength[145] with support from peers rather than authority. It enables them to try their ego resources without the backing of the analyst. It builds the ego, for the analyst says in effect: "I trust and believe in you, and you can interact without my watching you."

The alternate meeting is ego-building also in that it is ego-demanding. The analyst demands of patients that they alternately stand alone together. The identification and incorporation that occur at these meetings are superego strengthening as well. The patient is impelled to assess his own worthiness without the therapist. He is forced to examine his neurotic and healthy ties to the leader. He is moved to initiate his own activity. He is given a chance to positive role playing on his own. His growth and independence are facilitated.

The alternate session is a trial period without the parent, a preparation for living in the world. The patient is encouraged to esteem his own adequacy, to see that he can brave the world without his father and mother. Yet, the alternate meeting is not simply a session of a peer group outside the home or away from the parents and authority figures, for leadership exists in the group itself. Co-patients are still projected parental figures. Moreover, members are still aware of their relationship to the absent therapist and their transferences are still operative. In the alternative setting, however, their authority-directed projections on the analyst are quantitatively and qualitatively weaker.

The alternate meeting enables members to study one another in their respective homes and to bring in new relevant material. This semistructured atmosphere approximates life experience more closely. The alternate session is a transition and a preparation for successful termination. By meeting now in the home of this member, then in the house of another, patients see how each behaves differently as host and guest.

It can even happen that a neurotic spouse is drawn into therapy by his attendance at socials following alternate sessions. His initial resistance to psychotherapy may give way before the friendliness and humanity of the group members. But he cannot join the same group as his marital partner without consultation with the analyst, who can then weigh with the parties involved the wisdom of their functioning in the same therapeutic group.

At the alternate session, the patient can be less selective about what he says, and he functions in a healthier or more pathologic fashion. In the absence of the analyst, the patient feels he has more opportunity for initiating the exploration of new dimensions and the freedom to associate. When the therapist is present, on the other hand, he counsels the patient to make appropriate associations, as when he asks for associations to parts of a dream. Generally, greater focussing and more structuring exist at the regular meeting. At the alternate meeting, with less focussing and less structuring, there is more interaction and spontaneity as well as more inappropriate responses and impulsivity. The regular session has the advantage of getting down to business sooner, of helping the patient to be self-disciplined, to store impulses, to have an outgoing relationship and to delay immediate gratification for future gain.

The regular session may have the disadvantage of letting the therapist determine what he considers appropriate. He limits spontaneity and cuts out what he thinks is unimportant. The alternate session has the advantage of providing an atmosphere that is more catholic, a freedom to roam, permitting more to come through. It encourages the patient to accept human experience as useful even if sometimes inept. It makes the patient more tolerant of a good feeling and a good thought. It enhances social interaction relieving tension from extended work. It stimulates play which has a place in life but must not become a substitute for life. Play has a place in the life of the adult, but his life must be more goal-directed, more historically fulfilled.

While it is our conviction, based upon theoretic and clinical considerations, that the addition of the alternate session contributes significantly to therapeutic outcomes, we should like to point out the need for its experimental use and evaluation. We are aware of the necessity also for a good research follow-up comparing the results of psychoanalysis in groups with and without the alternate session. Moreover, the alternate session has already undergone variations and modifications, some of which can be mentioned here briefly.

We have described how patients gather for the meeting without the therapist in the homes of individual patients. This is the routine arrangement. The occasion, however, has arisen in which the alternate session was held in the analyst's office either directly before or after the regular meeting. Other group analysts, too, have had experience with this kind of arrangement. We are not sure that the best use of the alternate session occurs under these circumstances, because it remains—like the regular meeting and the individual hour with the therapist—too artificially removed from life and too therapist-centered. We have the impression also that such limitation may encourage specifically rebellious forms of acting out. It seems to prompt resistance to fuller peer interaction in that it is temporally too closely connected with the regular session, and patients may withhold full intercommunication until the analyst appears, as, for example, in the telling of a dream, in order to get the therapist's interpretation. We do, nevertheless, recognize that necessity may make such an arrangement seem desirable; it may, moreover, have advantages for certain kinds of patients under certain kinds of conditions. Research study of such variations, however, needs to be undertaken. Other variations in the clinical use of the alternate session we have already suggested elsewhere.[114]

Some group therapists have held their alternate sessions just before the regular ones, using the meetings without the analyst as "warm-up" periods, so that by the time the therapist has joined the group, interaction is at a high pitch. Our experience with such an arrangement has been that some patients may be eager to have the analyst witness their reactions, support them in distress or interpret their material. Accordingly, they suppress their responses until his arrival. And others, just as eager not to be seen by the therapist, hurry to present themselves before his entry.

Some group analysts hold the alternate sessions immediately after regular ones. We do not believe that pre- and post-meetings are alternate sessions in our sense. We have had no difficulty with unanimated regular group sessions, unless the membership lacked heterogeneity.[109] "Warm-up" periods have proved unnecessary in our experience, for most groups move easily into interaction. The problem of scheduling the alternate meeting is best solved by separating it in time from the regular one, because this puts defined limits on both of them.[146]

Another variation of the routine we have already described[135] is to assign leadership roles to patients meeting without the therapist. Chairmanship for the alternate session may be assigned to one patient for a period of time or rotated successively among patients. Our experience with rotating leadership assigned by the analyst is that it tends to formalize and to structure too much the nature of this experience and deprive it of one of its basic benefits, namely, the greater freedom in self determination by the peers. Nevertheless, in this connection too, we think experimentation and the careful reporting of comparative findings will encourage group analysts to become increasingly aware of the potentials for enriching the therapeutic experience through the alternate session.

Three Primary Parameters

As we have described earlier, group therapeutic interaction involves at least three primary parameters, namely, authority and peer vectors, multiple reactivities and inter- and intracommunication.

Psychotherapy deals with authority and peer vectors and requires a working through of problems with regard to them. In group therapy the patient has reactions to his peers, to his fellow patients, and to the authority figure in the person of the analyst.[109, 145] The group is an especially happy medium for resolving the individual's difficulties with peers and authorities. The therapist encourages patients to interact and thereby helps them to work through their problems in these two directions. If the analyst holds to his vertical position unyieldingly and forbids contact with himself or among co-patients in the horizontal vector, he denies them an opportunity to explore and resolve their distortions and to experience the development of their healthy potentials. If he denies the members the opportunity to meet without him, he displays a lack of respect for their resources and their ability to grow and to make decisions on their own. Intercommunication among peers and with authorities is facilitated in the therapeutic arrangement that includes the alternate session.

Not to permit the alternate meeting circumscribes the examination of actual and illusory attitudes among patients in both peer and authority directions. In so doing, the analyst reinforces hierarchic difficulties and restricts peer interaction. He prevents members from becoming acquainted with the true character of their peer transactions. He limits the resolution of both the horizontal and vertical distortions. He forces patients to relate primarily to him and curtails the interaction, intercommunication and transference reactions they have to one another. He tends to confine patients to communication in the vertical vector instead of giving them the freedom to interact in both directions.

Even though the alternate session emphasizes peer relatedness, nevertheless, at such meetings considerable attention is paid to ways of responding to hierarchic figures. It is not a leaderless session—support from co-patients enables the member to face part of his vertical problems and gives him the strength to express his feelings toward the therapist in regular sessions. Some confrontation of the patient with his difficulties with power figures takes place at alternate sessions, since some of the peers are invested with parental quality as well. Confrontation by a peer projected as authority is weakened in its impact by some awareness of equality.

Peer interaction is greater at alternate sessions where the immediate source of help is from the patients themselves. The sense of being able to give and take without a governing control, the impulsion to support and be supported by compeers, gives the members greater self esteem. Forced to be more helpful to one another and to assume more responsible roles, they develop a healthier interdependency. The alternate session increases interaction and intercommunication, and reduces the authority of the therapist.[5] In this way, neither the regular nor the alternate meeting becomes leader-centered.

Some group therapists who do combined therapy with all their patients,[114] say that members communicate more in individual hours than they do in the group, where they are too fearful of eliciting negative responses and consequently seek protective sanctuary with the analyst. Such therapists and their patients see the analyst as the exclusive chaperone of security. But patients, too, exercise supportive and protective functions with one another. Real and positive transferential ties impel them to offer each other safeguards against attack. Commonly, therapists who assign overprotective roles exclusively to themselves reject the alternate meeting and offer regular individual hours, thus infantilizing the patient in the process. In such instances, it is necessary for the therapist to work through his overprotective anxiety, and for the patient, his excessively exclusive dependency on the analyst, so that both can tolerate the alternate session.

Any group treatment which directs reactions too exclusively in the hierarchic vector is not good therapy. The therapist who forbids alternate meetings curbs multiple reactivities among patients, the emergence of shifting transferences and countertransferences and the development of ego-building healthy potentials. By facilitating the communication of new material reflecting additional aspects of unconscious process, the alternate meeting stimulates both interpersonal and intrapsychic activity and its scrutiny. The addition of the alternate session, then, facilitates the evocation and resolution of peer and authority problems, promotes multiple reactivities and emphasizes intercommunication rather than intracommunication.

Integration of the Alternate Session into the Therapeutic Process

We do not believe that the patient's therapeutic experience should be limited to individual sessions or to regular sessions or to alternate sessions. He should be allowed to participate in all three climates. They are three aspects of a total therapeutic process. All three are directed toward the same goal, the cure of the patient. Multiple media are valuable in treatment, because more facets of the personality appear in a heterogeneous atmosphere. Some patients have a greater need for the exclusive support of the analyst at individual sessions. Others flourish better in regular group meetings. Still others have a greater need for alternate sessions.

The diversity of patients demands different kinds of experience. Any one kind of transaction should not exclude the possibility of other modes. Uncovering requires that we provide diverse environments to find that medium which will allow the whole person best to emerge. Ultimately everything is funneled back to the regular session, the heart of group therapy. For some therapists, the core of treatment lies in the individual session, the group meeting playing an adjunctive role,[114] but for others, the most significant therapy goes on in the alternate session.[146] For us, however, though the individual and alternate sessions are invaluable complements, the regular session is still the center of psychoanalysis in groups.

The three settings have different qualities. These qualitative differences make for different influences on the patient. The alternate session may stimulate one patient and inhibit another. The therapist has to understand the particular patient's dynamics to know why for this patient something happens at the alternate meeting and not at the regular one, or the reverse. Patients may function differently in different situations. Some act out only when the therapist is around; others only when he is absent. It cannot be assumed for all patients that at alternate meetings there is more acting out, more motor activity, more freedom and more affect. One must relate behavior to the special setting at the particular moment in the patient's life. The analyst provides a variety of special settings: individual, regular and alternate. Being alone with the therapist is for some dangerous, for others secure; being in the group with the therapist is for some threatening, for others safe; being in the group without the therapist is for some frightening and for others reassuring.

The alternate meeting has been variously referred to by other group therapists as the social gathering,[5] the autonomous meeting, the fun session, the coffee klatsch or the post-session. These are misnomers. By an alternate meeting we mean a regularly scheduled, planned session as an integral part of the therapeutic experience, alternating with regular meetings at which the therapist is present. Calling the alternate session a pre- or post-meeting regards it as extratherapeutic, whereas it is for us, in fact, a part of the continuum of therapy.

A sharp distinction must be drawn between social gatherings and alternate meetings. The objective of the alternate session is therapy. The social gathering has no such objective. To call the alternate session a social gathering reflects the therapist's ambivalence with regard to the therapeutic usefulness of the alternate session.

It is true that in social gatherings people talk in twos, threes or fours.[5] But this is not what we mean by an alternate session, where the group functions as a whole group. Our groups protest, in fact, against pairings apart. The therapist who regards the alternate meetings as social gatherings may think of them as opportunities to act out, as separating in subgroupings, as meetings in a restaurant. Our groups may have a coffee klatsch after a regular or alternate meeting, but such a get-together must not be confused with the alternate session. Social gatherings may be resistive subdivisions of the group or subpairing individual meetings. Unlike some group therapists,[5, 80] for us in alternate sessions the whole group gets together and attendance is mandatory. There should be no misunderstanding of what the alternate meeting is. It is not a getting together to act out, but a formally structured part of the therapeutic process.

To encourage two members to split off from the group at a social gathering, as Bach does, we believe to be anti-therapeutic. He says, in effect, that bilateral problems cannot be shared and worked through with the group.[5] In such subdivisions, we think where each patient develops his private co-patient therapist, group therapy no longer exists. Besides, if a patient is healthy enough to be a therapist, he no longer needs treatment, and keeping him in the group becomes exploitive. Co-patient therapists in pairs at a social gathering is not what we mean by the alternate session.

While not every joining together of two people is resistive and may have positive aspects as well, all bilateral alliances and subgroup, coalitional cliques are potentially resistive. The moment two members get together for seemingly therapeutic purposes and exclude the analyst or the group, it extracts them from the therapeutic process and becomes resistive. The exclusion can be made useful to the pair and the group only if it is analyzed. Pairing may be acting out, or a positive experience, or both. Individual sessions in combined therapy may be similarly used as resistance, acting out, a positive experience or all of these together.[114]

Bach,[5] we believe, encourages resistance and acting out when he recommends coalition pairing. He expects the coalition pair to bring their resolved problems to the group after it "has had a chance to work through threatening material (p. 108)." We do not find this is therapeutically necessary or desirable. If the pair has worked it through, there is little value in bringing it back to the group. Moreover, it is our clinical experience that such interaction between pairs of patients is generally reported back to the group. They tend to bring it in when their acting out reaches an impasse in frustration. Bach's use of the social gathering is conceived in resistance.

For us, the group's getting together at a social or in pairs is a happenstance. At the alternate meetings, the whole group assembles by plan at regularly stated intervals. And patients complain if the whole membership does not attend, or if they do not get down to work. As an example of a post-session, Bach cites a birthday party.[5] But this is not an alternate session. Not that our groups have not had an occasional party, but this is not therapy. What goes on there can be reported later and analyzed. But the party is not an integral part of therapy, nor is it an alternate meeting, in our sense.

One of the aims of therapy is to become free of the therapist. Termination is facilitated by the alternate session, an experience without his direct support and guidance. His being away enables the patient to test moving and directing himself on his own. He gets an opportunity to use his own resources mobilized in the regular sessions, and the reverse. The alternate meeting is an apprenticeship without the immediate help of the expert. It gives the patient the freedom to use what he has learned in regular meeting, but now in the absence of the authoritative guide. But this alternating experience is always part of a planned therapeutic continuity. The alternate session is an alternate therapeutic meeting that is part of the treatment process. It is not just socializing. It has a relationship to and a continuity with the regular session. The alternate meeting is part of a regulated, strategic experience, consciously and purposefully determined, an experience-giving part of the therapeutic scheme. One can be just as resistive to the therapeutic implications of the alternate session as to the regular one. Our concept rejects the anarchic, chaotic impression of the alternate meeting. It is an organized experience, part of a well thought out design of the analyst. It is an integral part of the group therapeutic experience.

Inception of the Alternate Meeting

There was a time when we used to postpone the inception of the alternate meeting, until we felt there was adequate rapport in the group.[135] Subsequent clinical experience has taught us that generally the first alternate session can be safely introduced immediately after the first regular one, that the group does not need extensive preparation in meetings with the therapist in order to meet without him. To view the group as needing to be readied for the alternate experience is to deny that the members of the group have any positive resources of their own.[142]

Readiness for the alternate session is not group cohesion. Patients are almost always ready for a new experience in interaction. Cohesiveness is based on the good, positive feelings apparent in groups and not only on their tolerance for frustration and hostility. A heterogeneous group is ready to carry on alternately without the therapist except for the fragmented, the isolated, the detached and the withdrawn, and even these may often welcome the opportunity to participate in an atmosphere of peers. Occasionally there is a problem for the new patient required to join a group that has been meeting for some time. He may find it difficult at first to engage in the uninhibited give and take of the alternate session. But this may happen in the regular session as well, where the patient joins a continuous group.[135] Or it may even occur in a newly organized group where some members cannot participate as quickly as others.

Whether the therapist is at ease or not in introducing the alternate meeting is not a criterion for timing its inception. The primary question is whether or not it is therapeutic for the patients. Anxiety is contagious, and the therapist's overprotective concern may provoke anxiety in patients with regard to their beginning or attending the alternate session. The therapist may duplicate the overly shielding parent who cultivates the child's helplessness and dependency. The therapist may transmit his apprehension, so that patients mistrust one another to the point of sabotaging or refusing to attend the alternate meeting. If they feel the leader is not solidly behind them in his security that they can function together without him, they feel threatened. If, at the alternate session, they sense the analyst's conviction, they proceed with less timidity. The analyst's anxiety over whether they may act out in his absence is allayed by the clinical experience that therapeutic groups set limits on their pathologic behavior.[145] Once the therapist is convinced a patient can participate in a group with the therapist, it should follow that the patient can utilize the group without the therapist.

Resistance to the Alternate Meeting

We shall now attempt to formulate and to respond to the major objections to the alternate session, for a number of group therapists take exception to it.[13, 121] Some of their resistance is ascribable to an overprotective concern, a need to control, direct and supervise, and a lack of confidence in patients. The therapist may be catering to the patient's neurotic need for, or the therapist's equally inappropriate need for an omnipotent, restrictive parenthood. The therapist may be afraid of losing his authority; he may be impelled to make the patient dependent on him alone; and he may even fear that patients will act out their own or his distortions.

Furthermore, the analyst may be concerned that little or no work will be done at the alternate session. But reparative application does go on there. For patients shortly protest and resist any deterioration of the alternate meeting into a nonworking session. They come to see that one of the good things about the alternate session is that, at times, it offers the various members a relationship, not apart from therapy but as part of it. Some group analysts similarly forbid social relations between meetings. We do not regard all social relationships as necessarily resistive. We would attempt rather to analyze only those alliances which are neurotic pacts. For us, a social relationship often reveals resistances and often, as well, positive facets of character not otherwise seen as part of the therapeutic experience.

One set of criticisms of the alternate session is that it encourages wild analysis and inappropriate interpretations, which are related to such problems as timing, who shall interpret, responsibility and acting out. But interpretation is not the only therapeutic activity, whether offered by the analyst or the less expert patient. And a badly timed, or a misconceived, inappropriately formulated interpretation by a peer can be more easily discarded than one suggested by the therapist. It must not be assumed that the analyst's timing is always good, that his interpretations are always correct.

Moreover, an insight proferred by a co-patient may be more easily accepted or rejected, because it is less threatening in the horizontal than in the vertical vector. The fact that an interpretation comes from a peer is a safety valve, because the explanation is coming from another patient. So the construction can always be delayed for confirmation, acceptance or rejection at the regular meeting. Whether an interpretation is appropriate or inappropriate and accepted depends on the particular psychodynamics of a given patient, the special material being examined, his resistances and transferences at the moment, as well as on the way the understanding is offered, in friendliness or hostility.

The alternate meeting may provide opportunity for new insight and the re-experiencing and reinforcement of old insight.[5] If the group concentrates its help on one person with an emergency problem, for example, and forgoes its immediate needs in a selfless way, there may be reinforcement of insight.

Some opponents of the alternate session misconceive what patients do with one another as psychoanalysis. If the conscious role of the therapist and the nature of therapeutic intervention are clearly defined and communicated, then patient-to-patient interaction is never seen as analysis, for it stems from patient needs. The therapist who fears what patients will say to one another and who must restrict them to a sterile environment reflects an overprotective and controlling attitude. It is an historical atavism, long since discarded, to keep patients isolated, for such a technique can only fail.

The alternate session provides patients with an opportunity to experience one another more concretely in action as against the more verbal exchanges in the regular meeting. There is more tangible giving and taking at the alternate session as, for example, when the host provides some food. Ice-boxes are opened, some of the members bring snacks to the meeting, and significant attitudes toward feeding and being fed emerge. Occasionally, acting out which might otherwise not have become manifest is revealed in this way. A voyeuristic patient, for example, had this aspect of his problem exposed by a member who protested against his opening her ice-box and closet doors. It developed that several other patients resented this behavior in their homes, but had suppressed it as too petty to speak about. Valuable material for both the voyeur and those who were offended by his behavior was thus revealed. Similar intrusion into drawers, chests, playing with the dials of radios and hi-fi sets are objected to, discussed and analyzed.

For the therapist concerned with the possibility that there is no reparative pressure at the alternate session, it should be said that the urge toward health persists in the therapist's absence, partly out of inherently constructive strivings resident in all patients, partly because the leader is projectively present at the alternate meeting. The patient knows in the alternate session that he is in a therapeutic group, that his behavior there will be questioned, studied and scrutinized both in alternate and regular meetings. It must be said, however, that there is less therapeutic pressure at the alternate session and that working through is possible primarily in sessions with the expert. The session without the analyst permits certain material to come out and to be worked with but in different quantitative and qualitative degrees.

Certainly there is more analysis, more positive change when the therapist is present. But this does not exclude constructive activity when he is absent. The group therapist who forbids the alternate session may fear that only the sickest elements in the group will take over leadership or get hurt when he is not there, but these patients may use their defenses by failing to attend one or more alternate meetings as their pathologic behavior is resisted by the group. Patients are not all so helpless and do not have to be protected so constantly and nondiscriminately from being hurt in their assumed vulnerability. It is theoretically sound that no one should undergo suffering unnecessarily. But a large body of clinical experience indicates that the alternate session is not so painful. Patients who give leadership in the alternate session are not the most pathologic. They are among the healthiest. The group rebels against leadership by the most disturbed and brings such a problem into the regular meeting. The healthy influences ultimately take over, provided the analyst is unequivocally on the side of health.[146, 147]

Some group therapists express concern about the fact that they will miss out on a relevant mass of material ventilated at the alternate session. But to tell a patient that he must tell the analyst everything is to flood the therapeutic situation with irrelevant matters. The selection of material is therapeutic, if we scrutinize it. There is no time in analysis to tell everything. We must discriminate with the patient in being selective about what is to be worked through, about what is important and useful to tell. To ask the patient to tell all makes therapy nonselective, inefficient and chaotic. It does not teach the patient to be discriminative; it does not tell him what is appropriate in therapy and what is inappropriate, what is useful and what is not useful.

Catharsis in and of itself which is nondiscriminative verbalization is not therapeutic. Abreaction is valuable only if significant repressions are broken through and analyzed. It is unnecessary and impossible to know everything about a patient and grandiose to think one can. To demand that the patient tell all simply befuddles him. What the analyst needs to know is enough to set up hypotheses to explore the present and the past, to predict the future and to discover methods for changing patterns of behavior in the present and the future.[81]

The therapist who believes the patient must tell him everything cannot tolerate the alternate session. We do not urge on the patient the necessity to tell all or not to tell all. The parent who demands of the child total self revelation controls and castrates him, but the parent who allows the child some independent existence is more likely to secure his confidence. By providing the group with alternate sessions the therapist says to the patient in effect: Be as honest as you can be with me, the analyst. Maybe there are things you'd like to tell me, but don't feel strong enough to tell me till you have discussed them with your group, your peers, friends, siblings, the gang. If then the patient does not bring into regular meetings what happens at the alternate ones, he may be resisting. Even if relevant material should not immediately be reported at the regular session, unresolved problems present themselves again and again in dreams, in fantasies, in acting out, in interaction. Whatever is of significance ultimately comes through at regular meetings. The therapist cannot or should not expect that everything that happens at the alternate session should be reported back. The therapist who wants to know all that occurred in his absence encourages resistance.

Furthermore, communication does not have to be immediate. Even in individual treatment we cannot expect everything to be reported immediately nor is it necessary. If good therapy is being done, what is important will be directly or indirectly revealed. Only an analyst in countertransference will be continuously afraid that he is going to miss something. Where there is freedom to communicate in different atmospheres, it is likely that what is important to impart will be brought in sooner or later as the patient grows stronger and his trust in the therapist is confirmed.

It is a denial of individual differences[147] to assume that, if patients get together, they will homogeneously agree to withhold information. In our experience such activity is rare and always resistive. People are generally too heterogeneous to agree to behave in only one way. A group is made up of different kinds of persons. They will, therefore, react differently to the same experience.

Clinically, it is common to find that disturbed behavior at alternate sessions is brought up in succeeding regular meetings. Some members inevitably want to tell the parental figure in the person of the analyst what the siblings did while he was away. Whatever is of hurtful, or of constructive consequence to the patient at the alternate session comes up at the regular one. If a member never reports what happens at alternate meetings, it is the function of the analyst to inquire into this. It may be a transference problem of the patient, for example, his fear of a punitive parent projected onto the analyst.

Analytic study will reveal whether review of alternate sessions at regular ones is either compulsive or constructive. In the therapist's presence patients will provide the evidence in review, leading to further interaction and insight into their reactions. What actually happened at the alternate session is not routinely and microscopically scrutinized; on the other hand, the analyst should not always discourage a review of what happened at the alternate session. For sometimes what actually happened may be as important to know as the affective reaction. It is nondiscriminative for the therapist always to urge patients not to tell him what happened in reality, but only their feelings about what occurred. What really happened is also important in order to clarify emotional distortions.[146]

Some therapists imply that it is healthy always to behave in different ways in the regular and in the alternate session, and that it is unhealthy not to behave differently in the two settings. This view holds that new values, new psychologic phenomena, a new kind of experience is introduced at the alternate session. This is only in part true, because there are differences and similarities in functioning. The important question is the emphasis, what is the same and what is different in the two contexts. The quantity and quality of healthy and unhealthy experiences are different. Nevertheless, the person is essentially the same. It is not only stereotyped forms of behavior which lend a constancy to a person's functioning under varying conditions, but also his freedom to select positive and constructive alternatives in whatever situation he finds himself. The patient will ultimately want to show similar kinds of healthy behavior and be able to function in similar ways, given similar provocations, even in varying contexts, for example, when the therapist is present or not.

The way in which the analyst perceives the group and the individual encourages particular patient activity and determines to an extent the way in which patients tend to act at regular and alternate sessions. To assume that groups go wild, act out and become delinquent at alternate meetings and are decent human beings in sessions under the therapist's surveillance is a misconception of human nature. There may be some variations in behavior, but there is also constancy in both constructive and pathologic directions. When the therapist suggests that the patient is one person with the therapist and another without him, this cannot be entirely true. It denies, among other things, that there are parental transferences on other members of the group during the alternate session. It also denies the existence of strengths and positive resources that transcend the specific context. One factor which makes for some difference in behavior in the two settings in that transferences may be more or less intense and more or less binding than those on the analyst. But as treatment goes on, patients function more and more in a healthy way in both sessions, as projections on the therapist and fellow patients diminish.

Individual treatment, too, has always proceeded on the assumption that the patient will behave with the therapist as he does with others, and that one outcome of treatment is that the patient be as healthy with others as he has become with the therapist. So in group therapy, it may be assumed that patients in general function in regular meetings very much as they do in alternate ones, with variations in emphasis. It is just as logical to deny the patient a life experience apart from the analyst as it is to forbid the alternate meeting.

A group therapist may foster the patient's resistance to the alternate session. Groups that refuse to meet without the analyst are generally responsive to his conscious or unconscious wish. The parent who says to the child, "You can go out and play, but watch out for ever-present dangers," infantilizes and controls him. So too, the therapist, who encourages the group to have the alternate session but warns the members to be very careful, imposes his problem on them. An occasional patient may want to remain in transference with the analyst who, like the patient, worries about what will befall the patient.

On the other hand, pathologic motives in the therapist may lead him to encourage the alternate session, to sponsor acting out, irresponsibility, irrationality and psychosis.[146] Here the therapist abdicates accountability and fragments the patient. And the therapist is relieved of his anxiety with regard to his unconscious wish. Patients then may express the leader's problem, who misuses the alternate session to induce patients to act out the therapist's id which impels them to borderliness and diegophrenia[137] and denies them the right to develop their own egos. Or, the analyst, fearful of or overwhelmed by patients' pathology, may try to get them to express their destructiveness at alternate sessions in his absence and their constructive attitudes at regular meetings.

Some critics assume that the alternate session is contemptuous of authority. Such an assumption really masks a contempt for the value of peers; their activity and interaction also have value. If the therapist himself is scornful of expertness he may abuse the concept of the alternate meeting by converting the regular session into an alternate one. Patients and therapist alike may function this way, with contempt for authority and respect for peers, or vice versa.

Let us consider briefly the patient's resistance to the alternate session. We find that, for most members, once they have accepted the idea of group therapy, they welcome the alternative absence of the therapist. Some very few wish to preserve their anonymity by hesitating to show themselves away from the therapist's office and in their own homes. But they discover shortly the disadvantages and resistances implicit in their self concealment and reveal their real identity in due course without confusing their roles and relationships. A small minority are anxious at first without the projected, protective parent and may hesitate to participate in the alternate session. Frightened to be out on their own, they may become irresolute in anxiety over being able to explore, express and test more. The patient's resistance must be studied for what the alternate meeting means to him. He may see it as separating him from the source of security and gratification, knowledge and insight, the therapist. He may feel abandoned or rejected by the analyst. He may fear exposure to the hostility and warmth of siblings or projected parental figures. He may resist the alternate session if he has joined a group as a way of avoiding self exposure and individual analysis. Whatever his resistance means, it has to be analyzed.

Alternate Meeting and Acting Out

A charge against the alternate meeting and group psychotherapy as a whole is that acting out is encouraged. It is feared that patients may aggress against or sexually exploit each other, and that such activity will damage the patient and reflect upon the group analyst's authority and reputation. Such a therapist seems to be concerned especially with his responsibility to patients and with the need to protect them from one another. He believes they are dangerous to themselves, to the group and to society and, therefore, need to be limited. The alternate meeting with its more permissive climate is assumed to encourage exclusively pathologic activity.[13, 121, 144]

Even the well meaning and conscientious therapist who forbids the alternate session, does so in the conviction, he says, that he will thereby reduce acting out. The fact is there is a good deal of acting out in individual treatment, and the therapist's effectiveness is limited, if his only available intervention is to forbid acting out.[109] He need not forbid it, except in extreme emergency; neither should he encourage it. It is self-limited anyway at alternate sessions. Limits are established there by the healthy aspects of individual egos, by knowledge that what happens there will be reported in regular meetings, by personal frustration in acting out, by curbs the group sets upon itself and by leadership in the group. It is frequently overlooked that in all patients self-corrective needs exist which, in the first instance, propelled them into treatment. To view patients as having no constructive potentials is to deny reality.

The alternate session provides a proving ground for putting into execution new designs for living, new ways of relating. Whatever occurs there becomes more immediately available for further working through. Acting out, should it occur, is no longer done in secrecy but among peers and projected parents. It is generally easier to conceal acting out in individual therapy. In the group, because at least two patients are involved, it is more likely that one of the two, or both, or other members will refer to the acting out at the regular session. Therefore, psychoanalysis in groups offers greater opportunity for more immediate scrutiny of this psychopathology.

And since most patients tend to act out anyway, a therapeutic environment is provided in which it can be examined. Since it occurs in the group, there is greater likelihood that it will be brought in sooner for analysis. When it occurs bilaterally in individual treatment between patient and therapist, treatment is at a standstill. The presence of the group acts as an inhibiting or controlling force on the therapist limiting him from acting on his countertransference. In the group, the realities can be distorted with greater difficulty, because the participants submit their behavior for study by a larger number of observers.

For the group therapist to fear most a physical acting out is to misconceive the nature of acting out. To emphasize that there are special motoric aspects in acting out at the alternate session is to countertransfer. There is no greater stimulation for motoric functioning in the absence of the analyst than in life. Some people have more and some have less motor responses. There is nothing inherent in the alternate meeting to facilitate this special kind of activity.[55] If the therapist knows a patient to be homicidal, he does not put him in a group or in society at large. If the patient is given to sexual promiscuity, he is not kept out of a therapeutic group or out of society, unless he is a rapist. Behind the rejection of the alternate session may be a countertransference, a view that the therapist's function, like the parent's, is to prevent the siblings from making contact with one another, from murdering each other or destroying the house and family. Or the therapist in his anxiety about his own dangerous acting out may project his apprehension onto the patient, again a countertransference problem.

It seems to us that some analysts are too fearful of any activity on the patient's part, confusing all action with acting out. Apparently such therapists, passive and inactive themselves behind the couch, make a nondiscriminative virtue of their detachment and would limit their patients to a like reclining passivity, so long as they confine their activity to talk. But psychoanalysis has graduated, in the main, from its original restrictions which, in some instances, demanded no sex, no marriage, no divorce and no children in the course of therapy.

We believe that good therapy should provide opportunities for activity, thereby enabling the therapist to struggle with the patient to make this a movement toward health. Even if acting out should increase in the alternate session, why the fear of it? All activity increases at the alternate meeting. This is not to say that we are in favor of acting out, only that the alternate session provides us with the opportunity to scrutinize pathologic activity. Acting out increases and decreases in all therapy. And some patients behave more pathologically in regular than in alternate meetings. With others, the reverse is true.

The authoritarian group analyst may believe that reparative powers lie exclusively in his hands. Such a therapist is likely also to deny the heterogeneity of patients.[109] He does not really believe in group therapy, in the value of peer interaction, so he does not sponsor an alternate session. He believes that to prevent patients from running riot he must impose his control. Such a therapist is a puppeteer with a condescending, unsympathetic view of people, seeing them only with negative potentials and no self-corrective ones. He says there can be no constructive activity unless he is present. But patients are not decorticated when he is not there. Normal and abnormal activity occurs in or out of therapy. It is a projection of the analyst that patients run amok. There is no evidence that more acting out occurs in group therapy with alternate sessions than in group therapy without alternate sessions, or in group therapy as compared to individual therapy. It may even be that more acting out goes on in individual than in group treatment, because the therapist is free from social scrutiny and can thereby maintain the illusion of omnipotence no matter how he acts.

Some group therapists believe that the alternate meeting is an exclusively acting out session. It is a mistake to regard this interaction as an encouragement to act out only in pathology. For not all contact among patients leads to acting out. There is also much appropriate behavior, positive constructive relating and interacting. Many individual analysts think that the therapist treating patients in groups at all is acting out even without alternate sessions. Many group therapists believe that the group analyst who provides alternate meetings is acting out. This is grandiosity, for it suggests that only he can control the acting out of his patients. This is a resistance of the therapist. It implies that unless he maintains absolute surveillance, his patients will act out. It says that when he is present, there will be no acting out and when he is not around, acting out will take place. This is in itself an acting out.

An occasional therapist may be afraid to let the members get together without him, because they may then jointly come upon repressed awareness of his actual controlling, overbearing character. Such a therapist fears the group will in private concert confirm his domination, which may have a basis in reality. The therapist here denies the group an alternate session where they are liable to come upon, challenge and resolve their problem with his real, overexercised authority. This is a caesarian view of division and subdual, which encourages isolation and noncommunication, in which no questioning of the analyst's omnipotence is tolerated.

Some group therapists are especially concerned that the alternate meeting is particularly dangerous for psychotics and adolescents. But the hazard is not so great as is generally believed. Such patients may need some supervision, but this depends on the kind of psychotic or adolescent patient. The alternate session may do very controlled psychotics and adolescents much good. It has even been reported that combined psychoanalytic therapy in groups with the alternate session "is the treatment of choice for borderline schizophrenia," because "interaction on the peer level (especially facilitated by the alternate session) can be considered a specific or optimal technique of treatment for schizophrenics . . ."[46, pp. 57 ff.]

Some of the confusion about acting out arises from the fact that a number of group therapists regard the alternate session as a setting whose exclusive function is to provide an increased intensity of emotional experience. But such an approach makes for what is really resistance to therapy. The alternate session is organized to enrich the group therapeutic experience, not make up for a deficiency of the regular meeting. In general, the level of affect is higher at the alternate session than at the regular one, but there is also more intercommunication and interaction of both constructive and destructive kinds. The important thing is not more or less affect, but more or less of what kind of affect, inter-reactivity, communication, in what kind of patient, and what is done with it.

There are, for example, more peer feelings of a positive and negative kind in the alternate session and less peer feelings in the regular one. There may be greater intensity of hostile feelings directed toward the therapist in the alternate meeting. There is, to be sure, less examination of such behavior in the alternate session than in the regular one. But group members learn from the analysis of their conduct at regular meetings to scrutinize their transactions also at alternate meetings. Some fewer patients express more affect toward peers or the analyst in his presence, because they expect to get protection from him, or because of their emotional involvement with him at certain stages of treatment. Fear of the siblings or peers will enable some members to show more affect at regular sessions. Some show more hostility to the analyst with peer support, such hostility having been mobilized at alternate meetings and then brought into regular ones. This may be true also of warm feelings toward the analyst.

It is of some interest to speculate about the possibility that patients may unconsciously predetermine the setting in which they tend to act out based on their childhood experiences. It may well be that if a child acted out at home, he will be more likely to do so at regular meetings. Whereas, if he acted out outside the home, he will tend to do so more at alternate sessions. If, as a child, he behaved constructively in the family setting and pathologically outside the home, he will be likely to act more positively at regular meetings and more destructively at alternate sessions. If, in earlier life, he was more disturbed in the familial setting and more constructive in the larger society, he may tend to be more pathologic at regular meetings and more wholesome at alternate ones. Similar parallels may also hold for contrasting behavior in individual and group sessions.

One objective of treatment is to enable the person to function with equal freedom in all atmospheres. By providing relative intra- and extra-familial climates in the regular and alternate sessions respectively, the patient is given greater opportunity to reveal healthy and unhealthy characteristics. Then the analyst becomes aware of and attempts to resolve this disharmony. The patient who exposes his pathology in regular meetings has the advantage of the analyst's presence in order to work through. The patient who reveals disorder in alternate sessions shows himself or is uncovered by other patients or by their reactions at regular meetings.

In psychoanalysis in groups, at regular, alternate or individual sessions, acting out is the same as we see in individual treatment and has to be dealt with by the same techniques as in individual analysis. The alternate session no more encourages acting out than the regular session or the individual hour. Patients know that the objective of the alternate meeting is therapy, not an indiscriminate giving in to psychopathology. If the analyst sees the alternate session only as an opportunity to act only when the forbidding therapist is absent, he really regards the alternate meeting as a chance to act out and may convey this impression, fear or wish to his patients. It is not just a setting in which the patient can inappropriately rebel against the analyst, but a place where he can also act positively and constructively on his own. In the next chapter, acting out is explored in detail.

Exclusively Leadered Groups

It is the patient's relationship to the therapist which establishes the therapeutic experience. The way in which the patient relates to co-patients always has some relation also to the analyst. It is primarily the experience with the therapist that permits the patient to have a host of other experiences with fellow patients and non-patients. Even though children may have good relations with other children, with neighbors and teachers, they have only one mother and one father. Similarly the patient has only one therapist. So what goes on even at the alternate meetings has some relation to the analyst. Though this connection is fundamental we do not believe it must be artificially maintained by denying the patient experience apart from the physical presence of the therapist.

As one patient put it, "Individual and regular sessions give me the key, the insight, because the therapist knows more. But patients help too at alternate meetings, because I feel they're trying. Alone with the analyst, I miss the complexity of real life that the group provides. We're forced to help one another and become stronger when the therapist is not here. We get less protection from him and have to stand on our own feet. Our observations are less profoundly analytic, but we say lots of common sense, reasonable things to one another. The alternate session is a tentative step between treatment and life itself."

Those who conduct exclusively led groups contend that the alternate session may become resistive. And they cite the danger of socializing as one alarming form of resistance. Such resistive maneuvers may appear in the alternate meeting, but clinical experience has demonstrated that they can be dealt with effectively. Some patients come to us referred by their individual analysts specifically for "socializing." Some of these patients who are timid in social intercourse may even refuse to join a therapeutic group, or having joined one, leave it shortly afterwards. Socializing may be resistive, but it also has constructive value.

The group therapist needs to be flexible enough to allow the group to meet without him.[109] The group analyst who never permits any alternate sessions says, in effect, there must be no communication among patients, except under his supervision. In forbidding the alternate meeting he denies those who are able to express themselves more freely primarily in his absence. His authoritarianism may be in the superego-dominated vector, so that all intense feeling is forbidden or regarded as acting out.[13] Or his control may be in the id-dominated vector, so that only extravagant affect is cultivated.[129] In either case the group therapist rejects the constructive use of the alternate session. Very repressive and very permissive treatment equally subvert the essence of what a group therapeutic experience has to offer.

Some authoritarian therapists not only reject the alternate meeting but also take the position that the patient must suffer to get well.[10] This is a medieval, prepsychotherapeutic, preanalytic point of view. It would beat the psychopathology out of patients and beat sense into them. Such an approach makes a grand inquisitor of the therapist who sadistically submits patients to purification by ordeal.

The therapist's tolerance or intolerance for group therapy in general or alternate sessions in particular has to do with his view of his and others' roles. Reparative roles should be allowed to others besides the therapist. He is not the only one who has restorative gifts. Patients, too, have reparative power with one another, but of a different quality. They are less self-conscious, less planful, less goal-directed, less conscious, less expert, less aware of reality, but sometimes no less helpful. In the therapist's skill there is greater self consciousness, more planning, more goal-direction, more reality awareness, more expertness, more consciousness and rationality. Patients, it might be said, give each other nourishing food—the therapist gives them specifically curative medicine.

Patients do not consciously apply therapy. The analyst consciously applies therapy. Working through is a rational pursuit by the therapist of greater consciousness on the part of the patient. Working through is the repetitive confrontation of rationality and consciousness as alternatives. It is pointing out to the patient his potentials for acting on his positive resources and his ability to relate reasonably and appropriately. If a patient always tries to do this with other patients, he is in resistance, because he is denying his own affective reactions and his own realistic patient needs. He is playing the role of therapist. An occasional assumption of such a role, however, is constructive and helps group members to give and take; but always to do this makes the patient an exploitive, isolated person who does not really interact. He consigns himself exclusively to interpretation of the behavior of other group members. Moreover, interpretation as an exclusive activity, whether on the part of patient or therapist, becomes acting out and may facilitate acting out.

The overdirective group therapist who views patients as dominated or as running wild without his supervision, who commands them not to function without his direction, fosters their infantilization.[145] His domination discourages them from making contact with one another, from establishing a coexistence and community which build a positive climate in which growth can take place. It is our belief that the restrictive analyst who will not permit the alternate session is, in general, acting out his own need to dictate. In this respect, he subjects the patient again to what may have been traumatic in his earlier family experience, the denial of the right to some activity independent of absolute parental control. An indiscriminate emphasis by the therapist upon those activities he approves results in a pathologic adaptation which resists the resolution of basic authority problems.

Is therapy enhanced by an experience without the therapist? Would it be better if all sessions were with him? For some few, treatment might be improved if all meetings took place with the analyst, should such an arrangement be economically possible. But for most, therapy is moved forward by the alternate session. Patients who have a rich, interactive life outside of therapy and who can bring their reactions into sessions, who can play, who are impulsive but need more discipline, who are disorganized and cannot get down to work, who behave inappropriately, for these perhaps, only regular sessions are necessary. But such patients are less common. Even for them, to see that they can play and yet learn discipline without giving up the play is an important experience. For the isolated, lonely, hard-working, compulsive, over-disciplined person the alternate meeting is useful if not vital.

Leaderless Groups

A common objection to the alternate session is based on the assumption that the therapist foregoes responsibility and leadership because he is not physically present. This is another misconception of the nature of the alternate meeting and the role of the therapist. He cannot renounce responsibility for what goes on in therapy, an integral part of which is the alternate session. While the alternate session may be the antidote to the traditional detachment and position of omnipotence of the therapist,[109] he cannot be dispensed with altogether. We would doubt very seriously the implications of the statement that "in the group-centered atmosphere of alternate meetings, where the stimulation is much more personal and powerful, there is even greater likelihood that individuals' perceptions will be altered."[55] If this were true, why then should there be a need for a therapist at any time?

Clinical experience with autonomous groups which have attempted group therapy without a therapist have failed so far. They have deteriorated with more and more acting out. Or, having recognized their imminent disintegration without a leader, they have sought one. The alternate session is leaderless only in the sense that the analyst is not physically present; even then, group members realize their relationship to the therapist. Although he is absent, they continue to react to him and try to resolve the hierarchic vector in relation to him by virtue of the support and interaction with peers. The recommendation that psychoanalysis in groups include alternate sessions as part of the therapeutic continuum is not a plea for leaderless treatment. It does not deny responsibility for and analysis of what transpires in the total therapeutic process.

The alternate session is not a therapeutic medium which increasingly confers responsibility on patients, as the analyst gradually surrenders responsibility.[55] The therapist never renounces responsibility, so long as patients are in treatment with him. He may surrender control over them, but he never relinquishes expertness as the therapist, nor does he resign his liability for what occurs. He forgoes ascendancy over what happens at the alternate meeting, but he does not abdicate his accountability and leadership.

The patient is no more or less responsible for his behavior at the alternate session than at the regular one. At the same time, however, the patient must be made increasingly aware of his responsibility for his own behavior rather than assigning the consequences of his pathology to other patients or to the therapist. It is an encouragement to irresponsibility and irrationality to believe the patient or the therapist is not answerable for his behavior.

It is self-deceptive to think that the patient is responsible for his conduct only when the analyst is absent, and that the analyst is responsible for what happens only when he is present. No therapy can be achieved with such an approach. The therapist may for a time support a deteriorating ego with such an arrangement, but it must shortly be analyzed and worked through. The therapist does not assign or distribute leadership functions to patients. They have auxiliary roles in which one member is helpful to the next. But the fundamental responsibility for therapy is always the analyst's. And he cannot deny his expert role even if he strives irrationally to achieve the status of patient.[146] Even though there is an alternate session in which patients have adjunctive, reparative functions, it is the leader who is the responsible expert, the therapist. By leadership, we do not mean, however, that all authority, activity, initiative and creativity originate and end with the therapist.

Discussion and Conclusions

The way the therapist perceives or misperceives the group determines how he uses or abuses it. If he sees the group as an extension of himself, he may use the alternate as well as the regular meetings to confirm his judgment. If he views the group as a forum for his own acting out, he may encourage the alternate session for still more provocation of unconscious pathology. He may even convert the regular meeting into an alternate one. If he sees the group as subordinate to him and unable constructively to work together as peers, he will very likely forbid them the alternate session and limit patients to resolving vertical and horizontal problems only in his presence.

If the therapist sees the group as made up of patients who are permitted to relate only to him, and if he denies peer interaction, he is doing individual therapy in a group setting, not group therapy. He does not perceive the membership as a number of individuals with the right, freedom and ability to act on their own. If he sees the group as a medium in which he can detach himself, hide out or voyeuristically observe, without being seen, he may sponsor the alternate session and evade in this way the evocation and resolution of patients' problems with authority.

The alternate session does not loosen the relationship of the members to each other or to the therapist. It intensifies patients' interaction with one another, because it lets them be free of the governing source of control. It also intensifies their interaction with the therapist. The alternate meeting enables them to be more trustful and hopeful with regard to authority. Like good parental care, the alternate presence and absence of the analyst provides them with wholesome attention and wholesome inattention.[113] In sponsoring the alternate session the therapist tells patients he trusts them. This creates in them a sense of appropriate responsibility, respect, affection and reciprocity, a therapeutic pressure for health. In yielding to patients a temporary opportunity to govern themselves, the therapist may surrender control but not his responsibility, authority or expertness to give the best therapy possible.

If patients can get along in a group in the analyst's presence, they can in turn function together in his absence from the alternate meeting. If they can live twenty-three hours a day without him, they can work together a few hours a week without him. Only if a patient needs twenty-four hour supervision should he be excluded from alternate meetings and very likely from any form of out-patient therapy as well.

There are many ways in which the alternate session brings the patient closer to reality. It gives him more experience in therapy, in part overcoming the limitations of time, funds and available therapeutic personnel. It offers the general advantage of reaching more patients in less time.

There are qualities in human functioning which arise out of the experience in the alternate meeting which open the door to reality. Treatment becomes a human transaction not in isolation, but an experience that goes into each member's home, where he plays other than merely patient roles. There he loses some of his pathologic anonymity in the more wholesome roles of host and guest. There he can determine the time limits of the session without the analyst's supervision. There he can be subjected to a heterogeneous set of experiences in different climates. There he has more opportunity to get acquainted and catch up with other group members, with their historic, biographic material and problems, enriching mutual knowledge and experience. In this way, the alternate session is not a movement toward unreality and irrationality but a step in the direction of reasonableness and reality.

If the behavior in the alternate session is not healthier activity, if the old ways predominate, if even unhealthier ways begin to arise, this then becomes subject matter for further exploration and analysis. One value of the alternate meeting is that whatever occurs there becomes available for further scrutiny and working through. Acting out, if it should occur in any form in the alternate session, is no longer something done in secrecy but is done in the group, among the peers, in projected parental situations, and available then to many rather than only to those directly involved. It is, therefore, available for working through in terms of a larger number of reactions and interactions.

We do not doubt that psychotherapists, individual and group therapists of all variations, believe in good fellowship and in basic human values; that they are dedicated to encouraging human equality of the differences among men, and that they believe human beings can learn to live together in a more equitable fashion as they resolve the distortions and problems of their lives. That this is their conscious wish and aim can be accepted in the very fact that they are therapists. It is our prejudice that the group therapist in accepting the possibility of doing therapy in a group is even more consciously aware of the value of a democratic procedure and democratic relatedness among human beings.[147]

But apparently there exists unconsciously and in the character structure of some group therapists of the authoritarian, dominating variety, a scepticism about the potentials for constructive, human interaction, a doubt about ordinary people's capacity to relate to one another in positive ways. Such therapists are compelled to hover like overprotective mothers about their brood of patients, denying them wholesome access to one another in the absence of the therapist. This is not unlike the cultivation of borderline pathology by parents who want their child to grow up, provided it is actually carrying out their unconscious wishes.[133] The belief that everything the therapist does is necessarily constructive and everything the patient does is necessarily destructive is a distortion on the part of the therapist. If such distortions exist, then the formulation and organization of therapy may be a reflection of the unconscious pathology of the therapist rather than a consequence of any theoretic or clinical justification.

On the other hand, we are not unaware of the fact that there are therapists who accept the alternate session for pathologic reasons. It seems to us that the nondiscriminate attitude toward the alternate meeting must be examined in terms of how it is conceived and used in the framework of the total treatment process rather than to react to it as if it were an isolated phenomenon removed from the totality of therapeutic actions. We are aware that therapists of the id-dominated as well as the superego-dominated variety may reject or accept the alternate session for equally pathologic motivations.

The assumption is made by such therapists that only they are really in contact with reality, only they know what reality really is, and that patients have no knowledge of the nature of reality. This is part of the superego-dominated idea that contact with reality can be made only through the intermediation of the therapist. This, too, is a further encouragement of the trend toward borderliness. If only the therapist knows what reality is, if only the parent knows what reality is, then the ego of the patient or the child must be given up, and the ego of the therapist or the parent becomes the ego of the patient or the child. Such an attitude on the part of parent and therapist denies the right of the child or the patient to develop an ego of his own. This in itself is disruptive of the healthy development of the human being. The fact of the matter is that the group very often provides for the id-dominated as well as the superego-dominated variety of therapist, a foothold in reality. The group resists the distortions of therapists and the repetition of countertransferential reactions.

There is a view among some analysts that any kind of communication among patients, among peers, whether it is verbal communication, social intercourse, the exchange of feelings and ideas, is always and exclusively pathologic. Such therapists are not too different from the ever-present, all-knowing, all-dominant and all-powerful parent who must supervise and control all the activities of the children, forcing them into conspiratorial activity or into submission. An indiscriminate emphasis upon only those kinds of activities that meet with the approval of the therapist results in a pathologic adaptation on the part of patients, leading to resistance to the resolution of basic problems with authority figures. To make the point of view exclusively the therapist's, to expect patients to behave just as the therapist wishes, to demand of them that they function in the way the therapist sees it and wills it, must of necessity result in further damaging of human beings and ultimately in rebellion and resistance.

We conclude that psychoanalysis in groups is a harmonious balance between individual and group experiences. The regular session is the core of treatment; but individual sessions are available when really needed; and patients are permitted regularly to get together also when the therapist is not present. The alternate meeting permits, among other things, exploration of feeling with regard to authority and peer figures, the emergence of new material, and more interaction and intercommunication. The alternate session is not a leaderless session. Awareness exists that patients have therapeutic objectives and are related to the therapist. Healthy as well as transferential authority reactions appear in the alternate meeting, so that leadership is provided. Should acting out occur, it becomes available sooner for scrutiny and working through in regular sessions.

Finally, we have attempted to describe the nature, purpose, dynamics and therapeutic implications of the alternate meeting. We have examined the parameters of authority and peer vectors, multiple reactivities, and inter- and intra-communication in relation to the alternate session. We have suggested how the alternate meeting is integrated into the therapeutic process. We have discussed the inception of and the resistance to the session without the analyst. We have considered the dangers of acting out when the analyst is not present. We have described exclusively leadered as well as leaderless groups. We have discussed the nature of leadership in the alternate session.

We are convinced that the alternate session is a happy historic addition to psychoanalysis in groups, as a better way of relating the therapeutic process to the realities of living. The alternate session must not be considered only in terms of unconscious resistances or the utilization of it for pathologic purposes on the part of therapists or patients. It provides opportunity for freer interaction among the peers. A more rapid and effective working through of hierarchic problems can be accomplished where security and interchange among members on their own are encouraged. The alternate meeting is a clinical therapeutic measure contributing significantly to an enlarged view of the nature of healthy human relations. Therapy is facilitated in intensity, direction and time by the proper utilization of the alternate session as part of the therapeutic procedure of psychoanalysis in groups.

6. Acting Out

The age of anxiety has become the age of violence. Mickey Spillane, whose novel "The Big Kill," for example, sold two and one half million copies, is so successful, partly because his hero, Mike Hammer, combines sex and violence.

The kinds of patient activity provoking greatest anxiety in the therapist are gross manifestations of violence and sexuality. Tolerances vary among therapists as to how much of these forms of behavior will be permitted in the treatment setting as well as outside. What is not tolerated is often automatically labeled *acting out*. Such loose use of a psychoanalytic construct obscures the understanding and handling of acting out behavior.

There is confusion between acting and acting out, and between acting out and other forms of pathology. Activity arising in the course of treatment is often viewed as acting out only if the impulses or compulsions are grossly sexual or aggressive. Attitudes toward acting out vary considerably and range from forbidding to encouraging.

Acting out evades sharp definition because the term is used in both a technical and popular sense. Popularly, eccentric or deviant behavior is described as acting out. Nations as well as individuals have been said to be acting out if they do things that are contrary to the values of the local group or world community. This misconception of acting out has spilled over into treatment. Frequently the term is employed as a value judgment to condemn any patient activity not in keeping with the values of the therapist.

What the patient will do in therapy depends, to some extent, on what the therapist will tolerate and sponsor. For example, some group therapists believe that sexual relations between patients can have healthy components. They are, therefore, tolerant of sexual activity among patients. Some of these therapists, however, regard physical violence as necessarily always acting out and prohibit it. On the other hand, there are therapists who encourage physical violence.[146] One of these described a first session in which he assaulted the patient and grappled with him on the floor. So far as we know, these therapists who sponsor violence in themselves or in their patients do not encourage sexual activity. Another therapist encouraged a girl of sixteen to set up an apartment away from her parents, which she then used as headquarters for a narcotics ring.

Other therapists take a rather neutral position about activity outside the therapeutic situation, but forbid the same activity in the treatment setting. Some therapists take no stand or are relatively antidisciplinary with regard to a patient's getting drunk at any other time but insist that he come to therapeutic sessions sober. Still others hold that a person can engage in all the sexual activity he likes outside but not inside the therapeutic setting. Conversely, a therapist may have sexual relations with his patients or encourage them to become sexually involved with one another and be upset if a patient has a sexual relationship outside treatment.

There are many standards, many differences as to what patient activity falls within permitted limits, and what is not within the tolerances of the therapist. This differs from patient to patient and from therapist to therapist. Sexual activity generally provokes the greatest amount of anxiety in the therapist. Physical aggression and motility also tend to disturb the therapist, but they seem to mask a more fundamental concern about sexuality.

The phrase *to act out* is a technical term and needs to be restricted to specific forms of behavior of patients in psychoanalytic treatment. All transference reactions, regressive phenomena, defensive maneuvers, resistance manifestations, and symptom formations are not necessarily acting out. It becomes a nonspecific meaningless mark of approbrium to designate all activity, even if only all the pathologic activity of a patient, as acting out.

Historically, psychoanalysis was perceived as a relationship steeped in passivity. The patient was relatively immobilized on the couch and the analyst was nonparticipant. Any activity was antitherapeutic and, therefore, acting out. It is the nontherapeutic aspect that distinguishes acting out; it has two qualities, namely, it is *on transference* and *in resistance*. Acting out is resistance–transference activity.[106] We, on the other hand, view the therapeutic transaction as one in which patient and therapist are not immobile and passive but active and interactive in reality and in therapy. The problem then arises at what point is what kind of activity detrimental to the analytic work. An activity determined by transference and motivated by resistance is acting out.

Patient activity, then, must be scrutinized for its manifest and latent motivation and conscious and unconscious content, so as to understand its meaning in the light of the patient's psychodynamics and psychopathology. Acting becomes acting out when it serves the function of acting out; namely, that it is behavior on transference and in resistance to ongoing treatment, to change. In this sense, societies do not act out, nor do children with their parents or teachers.

In psychoanalysis in groups patients have room for more mobility. There is more mobility in the sitting position; patients in a group may stand up and aggressively shout at or threaten one another; patients may smoke, give one another cigarettes, candy, or a handclasp; they may move about in the group and even embrace one another; they may hold hands. These degrees of freedom do not exist in individual analysis.

The two most feared forms of acting out are sexuality and violence, but are they not always associated? We live in a culture where everyone is more or less castrated and castrating. Is not the promise of sexual fulfillment, the act of such fulfillment and the attempt to gain gratification by means of such fulfillment always followed by fear of the father, no matter how benign the father (or phallic mother) is, and no matter how much analysis is done? Is not sexual activity always, at least unconsciously, connected in some degree with physical violence? Do we not, therefore, as analysts attempt, in part, to limit our patients to thinking and feeling, and are we not much more wary of their acting? Once patients get into motion and act, and engage in a sexual act, for example, do we not in our identification with them wish to overprotect them out of fear that they may be punished? Have any of us, as analysts, completely worked out our own anxiety about this fear of being maimed, punished violently, or castrated?

Sex and violence seem to be in a reciprocal, dynamic relationship. Every sexual act in this puritanical culture has some component of violence. "'Lay," "fuck" and "screw" are good examples of how these attitudes have infiltrated our very language. These concepts carry with them the underlying idea that sex is an attack. The expression "to violate" is in effect a further example of the latent connection between sex and violence. When we fear patients' motor activity that combines sex and violence, are we not more anxious because the differences between the two have become obscured? If indeed we live in a culture that is largely sado-masochistic, it is possible that every act of violence carries with it some component fantasy of sexuality and that every sexual act carries with it the hidden component of violence. Behind the fear of motor activity is the assumption that any forward-moving growth or development is a rebelliousness which brings with it violence and retaliation from the gods, the fates, or the authorities in society. These implications concerning motor activity merit further exploration in education and family life as well as in the treatment of Oedipal and pre-Oedipal problems.

The analyst's demand that the patient take no independent action and make no major changes or decisions in his life before consulting the analyst reflects the fear and anxiety under discussion. An unconscious attitude exists, at least in the therapist, that any independent action by the patient must ipso facto be bad or pathologic. Then a jump in logic is made to the conclusion that such activity is acting out.

For some patients, of course, being cautious about activity may be quite antitherapeutic, since many come to therapy with a large introspective, obsessive, ruminating tendency, but blocked in activity. On the other hand, there are patients who are impulsive or compulsive in their activity, who do not spend sufficient time in thinking through their problems, or exploring their feelings. We must keep in mind the necessity to be discriminative about what the patient needs. Moreover, some patients may use activity in the service of resistance, such as, the compulsive pursuit of repetitive patterns; the avoidance of feeling and fantasy; anxiety about planning and an impatience about careful examination of alternatives in making a rational choice. If in addition these behavioral manifestations are on transference, we are then dealing with a form of acting out.

We must ask whether the group setting provokes more acting out, and what values we are applying to patients in a group. Some analysts believe that any sexual behavior during analysis is acting out. There are probably some who feel that having sex seven, seventeen or twenty-seven times a week is acting out. Others may think that not having sex is acting out. At what point is the particular sexual activity acting out, that is, contrary to the best interests of the patient's growing development, to the resolution of neurotic conflicts, and to the discovery of new, more fulfilling and healthier ways of behaving and living?[144]

When is masturbation a forward movement and when is it acting out? Let us consider cases. A young man has never masturbated, never has had a conscious experience of sexual feeling or fantasy, or a sexual relationship with another person. The exploration of his sexuality leads to the beginnings of masturbatory activity. The expression of himself in masturbation, though on transference and perhaps ultimately in resistance, may, at the moment, be considered forward moving. It becomes resistance if, for example, he refuses to continue to struggle to develop a heterosexual relationship, or after having established one, returns to masturbation.

A young man had a large number of girl friends. His sexual activity was pathologic. He was a Don Juan who would have a one-time-contact with each girl and end up in bed with her. After he came into treatment he separated himself from women and concentrated on masturbation as the only source of sexual gratification. This was, in part, a healthy development. There came a time when to continue to do this was resistive to forward movement, to constructive change. It was an attempt to maintain the status quo, his struggle to resist. He used masturbation to overcome the repetitive seduction of one girl after another and to avoid early confrontation of his fear of the father. It became clear that he was now using masturbation to resist having a sexual relationship with a woman and resolving his problems. His isolation from women was in resistance. He feared facing the anticipated violence for being sexual; he was in transference. The analyst was the forbidding father. Rather than come to grips with his own felt and projected violence regarding the castrating father and resolve the conflict, he sought to avoid it. The persistent masturbation had to be approached by the careful analysis of these two factors, the resistive element and the transference element, and the relationship between the two.

The psychoanalytic attitude is that violence or sex between the therapist and patient is always bilateral acting out, because it is always on transference and in resistance. Some group therapists similarly regard any sexual relationship between two patients as bilaterally pathologic. Are there any instances in which this is not entirely so? Obviously there must always be some unhealthy element in it, and it may indeed be pathologic, but is it necessarily acting out? The crucial criterion is whether such activity is therapy facilitating or impeding.

A patient used to lie on the couch and masturbate during his session. Was this acting out? He was restricting his activity to therapy and it was, therefore, available for analysis. This is the generally accepted position. "If you are going to act out, act out in the therapeutic setting, don't act out outside." If a patient acts out in the treatment room, the analyst feels it is not as serious as when he acts out outside, because the material is thought to be available for scrutiny. Psychoanalysis in groups offers the advantage that acting out, even in the alternate session, is generally reported, because it is shared or seen by eight and the probability is greater that it will become available for analysis.

Let us return to the patient who masturbated during the course of his sessions. Was he reporting this activity and his fantasies to the therapist? Was he doing this to distract himself from the therapist? Was he in contact with the therapist? He kept his hand in his pocket, and the therapist was not aware of the patient's masturbatory activity for a long time after he had begun the practice. Was this acting out? The patient did not report it for eight months. The therapist did not know about it. The patient finally revealed that every time the analyst began to talk about a certain problem, the patient felt violently resentful and was unable to express it. What he did was to have a fantasy and masturbate. The therapist admits that the patient might have left treatment if he had not found some way of expressing his hostility and removing himself from the particular communication of the therapist. The behavior that isolated him from therapeutic contact and analytic work was acting out in that it was in resistance and on transference.

But as a defense, it made it possible for him also to remain in therapy. This part of his behavior was not acting out. It was pathologic in that it was based upon distortion, but the part that kept him in treatment was thereby therapy facilitating and not acting out.

It is generally felt that the group sponsors more activity, both healthy and pathologic, including acting out. It should not be overlooked, however, that in the individual setting the patient has much more opportunity to act out outside therapy without the analyst becoming aware of the activity, unless it is reported in associations or dreams. We have discussed elsewhere self-imposed limits to acting in therapeutic groups.

A careful exploration of the conscious and unconscious manifestations of the two activities most feared by therapists, sex and violence, reveals a hidden connection between the two, and that every expression of either one presupposes the presence, in reality or in illusion, of the other. A proper analysis of grossly sexual or aggressive behavior requires that we investigate the latent presence of the other. Not all pathologic sexuality or pathologic aggression arising in the course of treatment is acting out. Only that activity which is on transference and in resistance should be viewed as acting out. Both components need to be scrutinized, worked out and worked through in order to resolve the conflict in motivations.

Some therapists new to the group setting report after they have introduced patients to groups, that such patients make sudden and more consistent progress. We believe that one of the variables that furthers this movement is what we call forced interaction imposed by the presence of other persons in the group setting, a process that leads to more healthy and unhealthy activity, including acting out. In part, such activity leads to patient improvement, because more constructive as well as destructive activity confronts the therapist and the patient earlier and with less possibility of suppression. Perhaps the main point we are making is that on the couch the patient is limited largely to thinking and feeling. In the group he is put in a position where he must act and interact, whether he likes it or not. He is forced into activity which naturally includes thinking and feeling. This patient activity arising in the group setting adds a new dimension to therapy, new problems, new anxieties in both patient and therapist, and new forms of expression, but always resulting in more material more immediately available for analytic work.

7. Dreams

This discussion is included because we call our method of treatment psychoanalysis in groups. We are convinced that being a psychoanalyst has very little to do with the trappings, the rituals or mechanics of treatment. It has even less to do with the settings in which it is done. For us, a psychoanalyst is one who is committed to psychoanalytic theory, values and practices, to an analytic view of human nature, to psychoanalytic psychology. We shall not here review the philosophy and techniques.[73] Nor do we propose to restate what Freud has already so brilliantly discovered about the dream.[35]

From a psychoanalytic standpoint, we approach dreams as any other production in that we seek the latent meaning, to discover and make conscious what is unconscious, to recover the repressed. Many psychoanalysts and group therapists deny that this is possible in the group. They offer such arguments as the attenuation of the transference neurosis, limitations upon regression and the interruption of the free flow of associations, if free association can at all occur in a group. It is our experience, however, that the analysis of transference, resistance and dreams can and does take place even in the presence of peer participants provided the analyst is committed to doing analytic work in the group setting. This does not mean, as we have so often stated, doing individual analysis in the group. We refer to working analytically with the individual patient as part of an interactive system in which his rational and irrational productions are seen, elaborated and worked through with co-patients as well as analyst.

The help of the co-patients takes largely the form of free-associations, provoked and responsive to the thinking, feeling and activity of the other. If a patient functions as if he were the analyst, he is in resistance as a patient. When a member tells a dream, for example, he is encouraged to associate to it. In fact, his associations take precedence over all others, and at this point the analyst may have to inhibit the instantaneous reactions of other members. After the dreamer has given his associations, other members

---

Based upon material in refs. 104 and 107.

are invited to associate. These contributions are more often facilitating and stimulating of further associations by the dreamer than they are distracting. The task of focusing is the responsibility of the analyst. The contributions of the co-patients not only provide additional material to understand the dream and the dreamer but also to work on and work out the dynamics of the other contributors from their associations. We refer here to lateral transferences and countertransferences too. The geometric increase in benefits, quite apart from the interventions of the analyst, constitutes an additional dimension in psychoanalytic therapy.

A motivation for including this chapter is related to a personal experience of one of the authors (Wolf) which is added here as a historical note. In the course of his psychoanalytic training he was supervised by Karen Horney. He was struck by the fact that in her writings she appeared to be disinterested in dreams. But in a two year control analysis she always inquired about the patient's dreams, was very much concerned and perceptive about them. We, therefore, wish our commitment to psychoanalysis to be more open.

What follows then are some of our ideas concerning the use of dreams in treatment. We have only very briefly dealt with some aspects which reflect our attitude toward specific problems. We have retained a modified dialogue form reflecting an edited version of our associative interactions regarding the dream. No attempt is made here to provide a handbook on the interpretation of dreams in individual or group analysis, but to encourage group therapists to recognize the essentiality of dream analysis and its appropriateness in the group setting.

In our culture dreams are generally rejected; they are ordinarily of no great consequence. Since the eighteenth century, dreams have been seen as having little or no usefulness in reality. Little attention is paid to dreams except in very rare instances where, for example, dreams have been regarded as omens of the future or reflections of psychic experience, such as precognition or telepathy.

It is true, perhaps somewhat less today than twenty-five years ago, that the person coming to an analyst for treatment does not look upon dreams as significant. When the analyst asks the patient for dreams, it is within the context of his relationship to the analyst that dreams begin to become important. In one sense, all of the patient's activities after he starts treatment have some effect on or are in some way affected by the relation with the analyst. Whatever the patient does from the moment he enters analysis and even in anticipation of the first interview, is related in fact or fancy to the analyst. For example, the sudden changes and flights into health, called transference cures, are often done for and or against the analyst. Dreaming in analysis we view as the beginning of a hoped for, partly appropriate and realistic, partly transference relation to the analyst. The patient's movement toward health, the rejection and sloughing off of pathologic modes of behavior and the attempts at new alternatives which frequently give rise to greater anxiety are at least initially steps taken for the analyst. Getting well or remaining sick, and engaging in healthy or pathologic activity are to some degree for the analyst or to affect the analyst in some way. Figuratively, the analytic experience can be thought of as a large fantasy on the part of the patient who includes the analyst and the analysis in his fantasy. What the patient does is motivated at least in part by the wish to get the analyst to play roles prescribed in the fantasy, whether the role is to punish or gratify the analyst, or to be frustrated or fulfilled by him. A complex of motivations is involved in the fantasy. Dreams, then, can be viewed in a sense as connected to the therapist in terms of what it is that the patient wants to convey, how he wants to control what roles the analyst plays or is expected to play within the fantasy, the images of which are the dream itself.

The question of the dream as images in contrast to fantasy, thought and feeling as words, needs to be explored. The relationship between image and word is similar to the difference between art and science, emotion and cognition. The word is in itself an advanced form of image. Images in this context are visual, and it is likely that visual images are more primitive, more basic ontologically and phylogenetically than language but not sound. An interesting problem is whether a person can express in images, problems, forms, feelings and conflicts ordinarily not expressible in words.

But this is getting us too far away from our daily work with patients and their dreams. Does one dream all the time? And what has this to do with the incidence of dreams in the course of treatment?

When you ask, all the time, do you mean every night and day, waking and sleeping? There may well be streams of consciousness, preconscious activities of which we are only dimly aware and which break through in moments of reverie, relaxation, and in the semihypnotic state during repetitive, mechanical or automatic acts. This is when dreams apparently dreamed earlier but recalled later seem also to come into consciousness.

Whether a patient in analysis brings in dreams depends on many things: the patient, the dream, the therapist and the relation among them. The kind of patient, the attitude of the patient about dreams, his feelings toward the analyst, the attitude of the analyst about dreams, and more, also play roles.

Forgetting, remembering and reporting dreams are related to the real and illusory problems with the analyst. But technically, he can encourage or discourage dreaming, and even selective dreaming, by the conscious and unconscious application of gratification (reward) and frustration (punishment).

Sometimes how the analyst deals with the dream, with hammer and tongs, with scalpel poised to disclose only pathology, the negative in the patient's productions, will discourage the patient. I have often asked beginning analysts in supervision with me, "Can't you find something positive in this dream?"

In psychoanalysis in groups, if a co-patient is aggressive toward the dreamer, his dream or his associations, it is good practice to explore the provocation for the attack in the dreamer and in the aggressor. In this way we attempt to arrive at some understanding of the encounter, so that the dreamer may be encouraged rather than discouraged about reporting further dream material. Generally, some members of the group see the positive in the dream. If, as on occasion happens, there are only negative reactions, the analyst ought to explore with each member this homogeneous manifest response and search for differentiated latency. At the same time the analyst may wish to emphasize what is constructive in the dream.

Patients may use a dream to break through or support resistance. Dreams may also be used as resistance by a patient. A patient, Irene, comes to each session with a dream. While these dreams are revealing of her psychodynamics and we work with them, resistance takes the form of not expressing personal reactions to the analyst. This dynamic is acted out in her life in two ways. Irene maintains great distance from her father, really wanting him all the time but isolating herself in a remote part of the house and hoping he will come to her. Secondly, she never really relates to a man. While in treatment, she finally began to build a relationship with a man. She has not yet reached orgasm in intercourse. That some part of her problem still exists is expressed by her putting the dream in the way of her relationship to the analyst. The fact that she tells her dreams, however, is in itself positive.

The therapist, too, may use interest or disinterest in dreams as a countertransference problem. Analysts who are consciousness-bound in the antiunconscious, repressive inspirational school, tend to be less interested in dreams and often present cases in which patients have been in therapy for many years and have not reported a dream. Where the therapist shows no interest in dreams, it is felt generally as a communication to which the patient may respond by being indifferent to dreams, that is, to unconscious material.

On the other hand, the analyst's interest in dreams may be a resistive demand. Let us imagine in the case of Irene, for example, the analyst may be willing to go along with her dreams each session and never raises questions about other dimensions of her life: her relationship to the analyst, his relationship to her, her relationship to others. Perhaps he permits her to focus too exclusively on this dimension of activity.

You point out that Irene used the dream as a way of resisting a real relationship with the analyst and working one out with anyone else. This reflects a more general problem that many patients have not only with regard to dreams. Many use a single dimensional way of relating to a person, to things or to the world around them. The dream that Irene uses is a kind of intermediary, a filter, a compact but depersonalized way of reaching toward the analyst. Another patient, John, is a professional photographer. His contacts with reality are limited. He experiences people through his camera. He has no close relationship with anyone except the persons who sit for portraits. With these subjects, through the camera's eye, he has intense relationships. But remove the camera and he cannot relate. He can relate to others only through the intermediation of the camera. What you seem to be saying is that Irene can relate to others, the analyst, to a man, to her father only through the intermediation of a fantasy. The dream *is* a relationship to the analyst, not a non-relationship. But it is a kind of a funnelled or focussed relationship. She does not permit any other kind of relatedness to come in, but there is relationship. This is one reason she improves.

Are there other patients who keep most or certain kinds of relations only on a fantasy level? Crudely formulated, analytic relationships, theoretically, are really fantasy relations—illusory, since complete fulfillment in reality is not possible between analyst and patient. One might ask, is there really a difference between Irene, who relates to the analyst by means of a dream, and a patient who relates to the analyst on the basis of transference.

I think there is a difference. A patient who relates in terms of transference is also relating more personally, because every transference is also contaminated (if you can use that inappropriate word) by reality.

Isn't every dream also contaminated by reality?

That's true, every dream is. But it seems to me that there is more readiness to interact more directly when a patient in transference gets angry with the analyst or loves the analyst, or loves and hates him. There is more readiness to relate. For example, when I come out into the waiting room and greet Irene and at the end when she goes, there is just a flirtatious look at me that has quite a different quality than the way she behaves in the session when she gets down to work and concentrates on the dreams. That is, in the moment of meeting and parting there is some kind of nonverbal reaction to me which is quite direct or at least more direct.

I wonder why you as an analyst who works deeply with unconscious material, I wonder why you reject the dream as a meaningful way of relating. Transference you take as a meaningful way of relating. You say it is more meaningful, you feel it is more direct. But, I have the feeling that when a patient tells me his dream and his associations, he is communicating his transference feelings and reactions to me, whether he loves me or hates me. Yet you seem to reject this as direct contact.

I think you are right, that it is contact, but for me it is more indirect. I can think of one illustration, but it is really simplified and made more mechanical than it is. Let us say a man right at the beginning of therapy has a dream in which he cannot find his key to put into a keyhole. This is not so disguised and it may be much more disguised than this. He can't find it. As he goes on with treatment, he finds it. Or as therapy goes on, he may find somebody else's key and then as therapy continues still further, he finds his own key, and then he can't find the keyhole. Or if he finds it, he can't get it into the keyhole, or somebody else has his key in there. Toward the final phases of therapy he has greater and greater ease in finding his key and getting it into the keyhole, and there is less blocking and anxiety about it. At the conclusion of his analysis, he has a dream of being in bed with his wife and embracing her and making love to her and he becomes aroused. He wakes up sexually excited, embraces his wife and makes love to her. The dream is telling us something. It contains the resistance and the blocking and the anxiety and the distortion. But as the patient gets better, there is more direct communication in terms of person-to-person instead of symbol-to-symbol. And this is the sense in which I mean that the patient's reaction to the therapist is more contactful. It may be argued, of course, it may be equally distorted and equally irrational to the extent that it is contaminated by transference.

By the end of an analysis you want to work through the transference as well as the symbolic relationship in the dream. But the fact is that he does not relate to the analyst by waking up from the dream and having intercourse with him. He makes love to his wife when he wakes up from this dream. Why should activity, this is the question we started from, why should activity that is on transference be more contactful than a dream?

Let me put it this way. It is not that I think the transference is more contactful; the transference is not. Well, the transference is also an attempt to make contact, but in an archaic way.

So is the dream.

And perhaps the dream is too. But I feel that when a patient is transferring, there are always also healthy aspects apart from transference in the reaction to the analyst. You say that is true in the dream too. Isn't this man's struggling to achieve heterosexuality a healthy struggle?

Can we go back a bit? Did I understand you to suggest that a transferential interaction is person-to-person, whereas the telling of a dream to the analyst is fantasy-to-fantasy? My feeling is that when a patient in analysis remembers dreams, the patient is doing this not for himself or herself but for the therapist. Persons in our culture throw away their dreams. They have to be educated in treatment to think that the dream is valuable. One way that we make the person a patient is by having him bring dreams to us. They facilitate the development of a transference neurosis. They are the patient's gifts, his way of making contact with us. I think the proof of the pudding is that you would also consider it resistance if the patient did not bring you dreams. If a patient brought you no dreams, you would say he was trying to avoid or limit his contact with you.

It may be a fact. I do not know about this. Maybe the dream—well this sounds a little mystical—is more an attempt to communicate about the unconscious reality than the interpersonal reaction. Maybe they are the same, but maybe a dream has another function. For example, Marge, a young girl of 17 told me the other day that she loves her mother and her mother loves her. The Rorschach report says there is tremendous hostility toward the mother and fear of the mother, and competition with the mother, on both sides, both from the mother and from the girl. She denies all this, however, in her interpersonal reactions with her mother, and she denies this aggression in her reports to me. But in her dreams, she fights gun duels with women, she is in invasions of islands, and these are all fights among women, so that, in a sense, the underlying communication in the dream is more appropriate to her real feelings than to her conscious reactions. Maybe this contradicts the point I first made. The dream is telling the analyst more of what is really going on than any conscious verbalization, unless it is free association. Maybe even there it is not as genuinely revealing as the dream despite the dream's distortion.

But we were talking in the context of how the dream is used as resistance. Patients will flood with dreams, for example. Now flooding with dreams is obviously a resistance, maybe a resistance to allowing you to come in and interpret, or refusing to communicate intercurrent material which may be of equal or greater importance. The patient can take up the entire time with dreams. A patient can flood you also with free associations. A patient can flood by reporting day-by-day activities. A patient can use almost anything resistively. Therefore, the reaction that your patient was resisting by means of dreams is really nonspecific. A patient can use anything resistively, including dreams. But it is not that the dream is in itself resistance by virtue of the fact that it is a dream. Irene, you feel, uses the dream to resist communicating or resists relating or resists doing other things that you, the analyst, feel are important. But, does this make the dream resistance per se? Does this make telling the dream as a psychologic process of interacting in and of itself characteristically a resistive maneuver or a resistance phenomenon?

Could we discuss for a moment, what is the nature of dreaming? What is the usefulness of the dream for the patient, for the analyst, for the relationship? Because I, too, feel that we can encourage or discourage reporting dreams in treatment, as you pointed out. If the analyst starts with the assumption that the dream has no usefulness because he does not know what it means, or because he does not know what to do with it technically, then he will reward non-dreaming, he will punish dreaming. If he sees the dream exclusively always as being resistance, he will not use dreams well. If he sees the dream always non-discriminatively as a transference expression, again he may not use dreams well. If he sees the dream rigidly always as being a communication directly to the analyst, then again he may not use dreams well. So it seems we ought to ask: Why do patients dream? Why do patients bring in dreams?

Well, I would say that they (I am talking about patients in analysis) are dreaming partly because they really want to communicate something deep to the therapist. They are conflictful and ambivalent about this because they also censor and distort, condense, evade and resist in the dream.

But they are trying to communicate something that is unconscious and important and significant to them. It is interesting that with regard to Irene, I let it become known to her that while I was interested in her dreams, if she continued to work only with them she was leaving out a certain dimension of her interaction with men, historically with her father, with other men, with her boy friend. As I said, she has improved. She is now enjoying sexual relations with her boy friend as she never enjoyed with a man before. Nevertheless, she still is not having orgasm. A development, as I began to press her for more reactions to me, was that she consulted a medium, and I am not sure that this is unrelated to my pressing her. She began telling me that she believed in mental telepathy and tried very hard to convince me that there is something to mental telepathy, that I should not be so rigid and dogmatic about it, that I should have an open mind about it. This mental telepathist told her that she was in treatment with somebody who had my first name, named all the members of her family, and described her relationship to her boy friend, remarkable things about her, her past, the present, the future. Irene was tremendously impressed with this. She did not confirm or deny anything that the medium said, but she came to me to report it. I am not sure I know exactly what this means, but she is saying that there is some kind of communication, maybe unconscious-to-unconscious, and that she is going to preserve the dreams this way rather than to relate to me as a person.

I have an association. She went to the medium and then came to you and asked you not to be rigid, to accept mental telepathy, because there are things that she does not want to communicate to you consciously in the form of words. Perhaps there are things she feels she cannot communicate at this point in terms of an open direct statement to you. "Look. I want to have intercourse with my father! I want to kill my mother!" How can she say this to you, assuming that this is her problem? So what she has done is, she has brought in dreams, telling you things in a disguised fashion; hoping that you will be able to read through the symbolism and begin to understand what it is she would like to communicate. Otherwise, she would not communicate her dreams either, if she did not want you to know; or she would not come for analysis and continue to come if she were completely resistive to communicating. She is in contact with you in her self-selected way because this is the only way, at this point, she feels free enough to be able to communicate. You put pressure on her. "Now look, I want you to talk to me, not about dreams, but about how you feel and what you think, about me and others." She comes in and says to you, "Look, can't you read my mind without my having to say it to you? Must I let the dirty words cross my lips? Will you compel me to say these things that I cannot say, that I cannot say openly and directly to you?"

This leads us to another question. What does a patient do when he says to an analyst, "I had a dream last night." What is the patient doing? Is the patient sharing a dream with us? I doubt it. From our own individual, subjective experience with dreams, we know dreams are visual images like hallucinations. When a patient tells his dream, we do not see his dream. We only hear his verbal description of his visual images. Two people looking at the same play, film or painting do not see the same thing. When two people tell about what they saw in the theatre, the movies or in a painting, you cannot know what the play, the film or the painting really looks like, how it is really experienced.

For example, my wife will go to the museum and see a nonobjective painting and come home and say that she sees it full of activity, full of the expression of feeling, full of tensions being resolved, in conflict and in struggle, and an attempt to come to a harmonious resolution of such conflict. Then I go and look at it and see it as an exaggerated Rorschach plate. You go and look at it, and say, "I saw a bunch of lines and color that didn't mean anything." The next person looks at it and says, "I see a mass of blotched areas; in fact, I don't see anything in this painting but a mass of slopped-on paint."

When the patient tells a dream, he is not sharing with us a moving picture of the same visual experience. He is sharing with us an already censored, selected communication, a transposition into verbal symbols what were visual images. So we are getting the dream transposed into what the analysand thinks makes sense to him and will make sense to us in terms of the analytic relationship, which, for me, is verbal. This is secondary elaboration. Despite the talk about nonverbal and unconscious-to-unconscious communication, the fact of the matter is that even if the patient is speaking about a non-verbal communication to himself, namely an imaginary experience for himself, the only way we shall ever "see" his dreams, unless the brave new world people will invent a machine so that we can look directly at the dreams of other persons, is through extrasensory perception. In fact, one theory about telepathy is that the way in which I communicate to you telepathically is that I can directly stimulate your central nervous system without the intermediation of the senses. In other words, I don't have to go through your peripheral nervous system to reach your central nervous system. My central nervous system can immediately influence your central nervous system. Until we get such a machine or develop our extrasensory perception, we are not going to see anybody else's dreams, and I do not think we ever shall. We are only going to be able to hear verbal descriptions of dreams.

Of course in art therapy we can ask the patient to paint or sculpt the dream. And in Lowenfeld's world technique the patient can "act it out" by objects.

Now, if I set the problem in this way, it complicates our picture considerably because we have to ask ourselves, Why does the patient dream? Why does the patient tell us this dream? What is the patient doing when the patient tells us this dream? What is the nature of the communication? And, perhaps even before that, What is the difference between verbal communication, or verbal psychologic process, and visual imagery? It is a very unique, individual and individualistic experience that man is able to dream, that he can have visual images seemingly devoid of verbal content. Comparatively few dreams have speaking going on in them, in which you have, "And he said to me and I said to him." This is not what the dream usually deals with. The dream generally depicts activities, not language.

My experience is, that is not so rare, and maybe this is a reflection of the number of people that we have in groups where there is a good deal of speaking to one another.

Can you recall a dream some patient brought in which there was verbal communication between the participants?

Well, I heard one yesterday where the devil speaks to a man; he speaks to the patient and says: "You like expensive clothes, don't you?" And while the patient says, "I'm dubious about that," he finally admits it. Often patients will say they have been speaking in the dream but they may not remember the exact words. They may paraphrase what is said. Sometimes they remember the words.

Can you give me another one? You see, I have a feeling that the chances of a dream with conversation being reported is relatively small, because such a dream really represents a shifting of modalities. A dream is a visual experience. It is difficult, in your mind's eye, so to speak, in the visual to hear the voice. An auditory hallucination is generally not confused with a visual hallucination. This is a kind of mixing of modalities that is not common. It does happen, but it is rare that a person has an inner experience of hearing sounds, hearing voices, who has daydreams and reveries in which sounds go through his head, like a Beethoven, for example, who could hear in his mind's ear, orchestra playing. Such persons would tend to have diminished visual fantasy. They hear the rustling of the trees. They hear the pastoral scene. They don't see the pastoral scene. When you talk about seeing a dream, it is not easy to see somebody talking to somebody else and hear what they say simultaneously. It is, I think, because of the nature of the modality; not because I think it is impossible for people to speak in a dream, but in the nature of the modality, the dream being visual, it emphasizes largely activity. This is what one can see, the talking rather than the words.

I cannot recall any offhand but, for example, another patient yesterday told me that in her dream I was giving a lecture to an audience, and while I was lecturing I was masturbating her. She didn't know what I was saying, but I was talking.

Is it possible, in terms of evolutionary development, that the visual—the visual image—is not more primitive? Is Freud right that the auditory image is more primitive and that the visual is more advanced? The chances are that visual imagery is not as regressed as is auditory hallucination, for example, and that we are getting a high level function when we have dreaming. Of course the context of dreaming is important; the dream deals with activities that we see in the middle of the night. We close our eyes and we see activity. It would be strange if we closed our eyes and we heard voices. It is a shifting.

Maybe you ought to consider dreaming and not dreaming as a resistance to communicating, or the telling of dreams as communication and non-communication. I was thinking of a particular patient and my saying—and I suppose it is a little non-discriminative—that I do not want to hear any more dreams from him, at this point.

But you let him tell one last week.

Yes, I was not so non-discriminative that I did not let him tell any, but I wanted him to interact more. It was in this spirit that I felt with Irene that she was leaving something out; that her dreams are very revealing and very exciting and she has gotten better in my working with dreams. But I was making another kind of demand on her. You are quite right, I think, that she was telling me that she wanted to communicate medium-to-medium, mind-reader-to-mind-reader and not get involved. But now I think we must try to analyze the resistance to her boy friend, to her involvement with her father, to her staying on this unconscious-to-unconscious or mind-to-mind relationship, to discover what it means.

Let's stay on this point another moment. Although I recognize the generality of what I am about to say, I wonder if there is any truth to the idea that you can conduct the entire analysis of a patient on the basis of one dream or a number of dreams he might have. Theoretically, perhaps, a single dream of a patient should contain the total dynamics, that is, the latent and the manifest content of the dream should reveal the neurosis.

What is your reaction to the assumption that one could conduct an entire analysis using only the dreams. For instance, I wonder whether you could interpret Irene's resistance by means of the dream. Suppose we take Irene's dreams. You should be able to find in her dreams, if she does not relate to the father, reflections of her difficulties in relating to him and reasons for them. You might ask: How is it you never have a dream in which you relate to your father?

This patient has already had a dream in which she has intercourse with the governor of her home state, who is a father figure. But she only knows that she's been to bed with him, that she's going and then . . . that it is over, and what the experience was is blanked out.

Suppose you say to her: How about having a dream in which you remember the experience. What do you think would happen then? Do you think that this would be less valuable to her than if you said: Now I want you to have the experience with me. She cannot in fact have the experience with you anyway. She can only have a fantasy experience with you. Then why should the fantasy in transference be more acceptable to you, the analyst, than the fantasy in the dream?

I do not know now for sure whether I am trying to rationalize my position or not. But this was her daydream with her father. Maybe he would come to her while she stayed in that remote room and she would keep fantasying about it. Perhaps it is necessary as a prelude to her being able to have the full relationship with her boy friend that she at least first have the fantasy, have the dream before she can have the reality with him. However, I feel there is something very significant in the extent to which she never reacts to me, never to me personally, except just before and after the session.

So there is something fantasy-like about the experience within the analytic situation. Why does she have to keep it a fantasy relationship? She is really trying to avoid something in reality. What you were just saying reminds me of a borderline patient. I think the patient was really very disturbed. This woman used to spend hours and hours of her time before a mirror narcissistically exhibiting herself. In this mirror she saw the three men of her life: her father, a first lover, Henry, and her husband. She said again and again in the course of a year of therapy that these three men really loved her, that they were the only three persons in her life who were absolutely uncritical of her, who accepted her completely, and saw her as beautiful, as intelligent, as desirable, and never found anything wrong with her. And yet she continued to have the fantasy in which they ooed and ah'd and praised and enjoyed her. One day the therapist said to her, "If it's a fact your husband, Henry, and your father always loved you and always accepted you in reality, why do you need this fantasy that you have now and have had over the last 20 years of your life? Why are you spending these hours in front of the mirror having such fantasies?" With this, the patient broke down for the first time, after a year of treatment, and admitted that it was not true, that the reality was that her father, and Henry and her husband never found anything good in her; that her father had always been tremendously critical of her, had never expressed any acceptance of her, any love for her. She had been damaged by the father in his total rejection of her in reality, just as Henry had rejected her. And in order to deny the reality, she created the fantasy. The repetitive fantasy supported the denial of the very hostile father relationship.

I wonder, if Irene can relate to the analyst only in fantasy, only through dreams, why is it necessary that she do this? What is she covering up by insisting that her father come to her only in fantasy? Is it possible that her father came to her in reality? And she has to deny this, because if she lets the reality reach her, she will have to communicate that she has experienced this before? In other words, the fantasy and the dream are used here defensively, it seems to me. But what are they defending against? I thought of the other patient, because in her case fantasy gave gratification by continuously supporting denial of reality.

One of the things Irene reports is that she remembers, as a very little girl, her mother urging her to allow her father to embrace her, and her feeling disgusted and trying to push the father away. She has always rejected this. But in her dreams in the past, and this has now been largely worked through, she used to have repetitive dreams in which her mother would always catch her with a man. The mother would always be threatening, and Irene would have an anxiety attack and wake up as from a nightmare. The mother would catch her. Of course, she may actually have sensed her mother's ambivalence about her being with her father, or some feeling of guilt about her wish for the father, or sensed his ambivalence but it suggests that she really was afraid of her mother's threatening her if she came close to the father. Now in a recent dream, the mother tells her that she has to sleep with the governor. Her boy friend is married, but has not slept with his wife in several years. They are talking about his separating from his wife and marrying. But Irene is beginning to feel very sorry for the wife and she is feeling, I think, it is either her life or her mother's. She loved her mother, too, and her mother loved her, and perhaps she does not want to destroy the mother. But she may feel that if she moves toward the father either she will be killed or the mother will be killed. She must have felt that she would be killed if she moved toward the father.

Well, you are leading up to the next problem. I don't know why we go back to Irene. You were starting to develop the question of various ways of approaching the dream. But before we do this, let me say that you really are going into the problem we talked about earlier, namely, in what way the dream uses and reflects the language of insight. In Irene's case you must have some feeling that the work on dreams and changes in the dreams are really not insightful, because apparently, for some reason, she is unable to accept the change in the dream and put it into activity in reality.

This cannot be true because, even though we have concentrated pretty exclusively on dreams, she has for the first time in her life made an ongoing relationship with a man, although he is married. She feels very involved with a man for the first time in her life, feels that he is very involved with her. She enjoys sexual intercourse as she never has before, and her pleasure keeps growing.

In what way has she been using dreams resistively?

I feel that the only residue of resistance, and maybe this, too, can be worked through by working exclusively with dreams, is that she has not reached an orgasm and that she is not direct with me except through dreams.

One of the functions of the dream is relieving tension, solving problems and to prepare us for activity. If dreams are related to insight, having changes in the dreams in terms of the kinds of activities one can undertake might be a preparation for having similar kinds of activities in reality. If the emotional weighting of the dream is positively and gratifyingly nonanxious, is not an anxiety-provoking experience, it may help us in the direction of new kinds of activity. As insight we know that dreams sometimes move ahead of reality, and reality sometimes moves ahead of dreams. For whom is the dream material insightful? Is the dream insightful for the analyst or for the patient, or for both?

Well, it is important for the analyst to understand the dream. One of the striking things about Irene is that she has changed her activity as a result of the dream analysis. She associates very well to the dreams and there are changes in her life and the action she takes in contrast to Alice who brings in very long, very elaborate dreams. In Alice's dreams it is extremely difficult to get at the heart of the matter. Her dreams seem to be much more obscuring than insightful, unless it is just a reflection of my own incompetence and my getting lost in the maze of these long dreams, so long that she can take up almost an entire session telling one. Perhaps we should say that Irene is not using the dream so resistively, while Alice is.

You say there are long dreams and short dreams. Have you any associations to that?

Some patients come in with long dreams, handwritten or typewritten, several pages long, and the theme of the dream may be very hard to find. The patient is all over the place in a dream. For example, I have one patient that does much better and really feels better and has improved since we paid less and less attention to these very long dreams. And it turned out that in presenting these long dreams she was feeling that she had to report to her mother what was wrong with her. As I got some insight into this and said I want to hear what is good about what is happening, with the idea that I could endorse what was good in her life, this patient began to improve.

What has been happening with her dreams?

She has not been reporting dreams much lately, but she is having a much better relationship with people outside, and to her boy friend. Apparently the dreams were associated with presenting sickness, and as we paid less and less attention to her dreams she has made some really big leaps forward.

Are you doing repressive-inspirational therapy rather than psychoanalysis with this patient?

That remains to be seen. So far she seems to be flourishing under this approach. I am enjoying her activities. And, I think, because I'm a mother to her, this is a new kind of experience, a kind of working through the mother problem with her.

What do you think about the emotional tone surrounding the dream? Some analysts routinely ask the patient, "How did you feel when you awakened?"

I almost always ask, if I cannot get the emotional tone of the patient in the dream, "How did you feel in the dream?" I think this is indeed very important to ask, because sometimes patients leave out this relevant aspect. The affective response, the feeling of the patient in the dream, is very often an insightful key to the patient's relationship to the analyst, or to persons in his outside life or in his original family. As in the group, when a patient says "I've got a father on you," my reaction is that I don't know what you're talking about. Tell me how you feel about this first, how you feel about your father?

I think there is a difference between when you feel "I've got a father on you" and how you feel about "having a father on someone."

Let us return to a dream we were talking about earlier. In the dream this woman sees herself as a little boy; she puts her knees into the back of her mother who is leaning over some other person, and breaks her back. In the dream she felt extremely hostile, it is quite clear, to the mother. But her feeling about the dream is one of horror. It was a nightmare. There are two different sets of emotions here.

There is the feeling in the dream and the feeling about the dream. It seems to me that it is the feeling about the dream that often causes the censorship of the dream, and the feeling in the dream that causes the censorship (dream work) in the dream. It is not the feeling in the dream but the feeling about the dream that makes us want to repress it, because if we do not like the feeling, that is, if the feeling we have about the dream is one of discomfort, we will tend to forget the dream. The feeling in the dream can be sexually loving or hostile, and yet about either one of these two we might have a different set of reactions.

I recall a dream that may illustrate this point. I mentioned earlier the patient who dreamed that the devil told him, "You like expensive clothes, don't you?" And his response was, "I'm dubious about that, but I know you're right." In the dream there was a struggle between the devil and the patient who makes various incantations to ward off the devil; the patient is a religious person. In the last part of the dream, a homosexual man is acting very seductively toward his wife who has a cat's head mask over her head. Her face is uncovered, but his association to the cat's head is that this is also devilish. He is very alarmed in the dream, that the homosexual man is so exciting for his wife, that he might seduce her. At one time, the patient was actively homosexual but fell in love with this woman whom he married. I think he is saying he has to make a superego incantation over his own sexuality which he sees as wrong, that is, as homosexual, that he judges it as devilish whether in himself or in his wife, and he wakes up with horror at the dream. But in the dream at one point he admits that the devil tells him what he really likes, namely, the luxury of expensive clothes and the pleasure of sensuality with his wife, but he tends to divorce himself from this sensuality as devilish and will make an incantation of a "religious" and superego nature against his sexuality. I think it is probably true that the dream may contain within it both the pleasureful gratifying wish and the horror, but the horror may occur only on waking.

There is one part of this dream, in the beginning, that I did not mention. It's a longer dream. Something interesting perhaps to think about is that I had asked the group members how they would feel about introducing a woman, an alcoholic to the group, who might come in drunk to meetings, who might not be easy to handle, who might create certain problems. Now the man who reported this dream had the strongest negative reaction because he has a long history of having to serve and take care of his brother, and take care of his father, and take care of his mother. He was the problem-solver in the family, and they all turned to him. For a long time he compulsively re-enacted in the group this role as a caretaker, something he is still struggling with. He is not so compulsive anymore that he has to take care of all these projected figures in the group, but he just did not want anybody else he would have to nurse along. He is very warmly related also to the analyst and feels that if the analyst wants it, maybe he should go along. But he was really, in his deep feelings, very resistant to the idea of having this woman in the group, and he had great difficulty talking about it. In one part of the dream, he orders a bunch of drunks out of the cellar of his house, and he is very vigorous about it and very verbal. I do not know that he actually recalled the words nor can I recall them, but he was very verbal about it in the dream in contrast to his nonverbality in the group.

In still another part of the dream, however, his brother is lying in the same cellar on a mattress. His brother is sick and vomiting and hurting, and the patient does not know what the trouble is. But he takes his brother upstairs to a bathroom where his mother says of the brother, "Oh, he'll be all right." But the patient is very sensitive to his brother and feels his brother is trying to communicate something which he senses, that is, that the patient senses, that the mother does not. Somewhere, of course, the patient identifies with his brother and is trying to say something to the mother that he cannot verbalize, and this also characterizes the patient. He has great difficulty in verbalizing and making clear some of the things he thinks and feels. But here is a situation in which he expresses, very directly to me, his protest against the alcoholic patient.

Without putting it into words, except in transposing the dream images he is able to report the dream.

Perhaps without putting it into words and again, like the brother, he has difficulty in communicating some feeling of his own.

What kinds of information, what kinds of insights do you think you, as an analyst, get from the dreams of patients?

It is extremely difficult to work analytically with a patient who does not present dreams. One important function of the therapist is to try to analyze the patient's resistance to dreams because dreams do present us with understanding, insight into patients' basic and repressed conflictual material, with what is going on unconsciously. And since a primary analytic function is to make what is unconscious conscious, dreams are a basic avenue or access to what is unconscious and what needs to be made conscious.

The dream also tells us the nature of the censorship and from whom censorship came, from what familiar figures. The dream tells us about the relationship of the patient to original family figures. The dream tells us how we can anticipate the projection and the reenactment of these relationships with the analyst and with other persons, such as co-patients in the group. The dream tells us something of the kind of distortions, displacements and condensations the patient is likely to make in acting them out in lateral transference behavior in the therapy group, or in behavior with the analyst, or in behavior with members of his family. So the dream is one of the richest, perhaps the richest source of information about what the patient has done, is doing and will continue to do. It suggests, therefore, in the repetition of themes, what plans to lay out to deal with the patient therapeutically.

The dream also tells us, so long as we do not concentrate exclusively on its pathology, what are some of the constructive yearnings of the patient, constructive yearnings which can perhaps be fulfilled in reality, or partially fulfilled in reality, or sublimated if they cannot be fulfilled. The dream may tell us which wishes are so archaic that they simply need to be brought out of repression, made conscious and frustrated with full awareness of their inappropriateness in the present reality.

The dream may tell us how much the patient is locked in fantasy. A dream is a kind of fantasy but it may also tell us why the patient is locked in fantasy. The dream, concentrated on too exclusively, may also give us the key to why the patient cannot act on some of his dreams and provide clues on how to help the patient act on some of the positive wishes in the dream. For many and perhaps for all patients it is important for them to dream and recall the dream. To take an extreme example, there was a patient who was always acting, and my struggle with him was to get him to fantasy, to tell dreams, to think, to feel rather than to act, because his acting was a resistance to exploring the healthy and the pathologic character of his acting. I tried to get him to think and feel about something, to hesitate, and in a way a dream represents a hesitation. It is an exploration and effort against impulsive or compulsive action. It is interesting to think of a dream as giving the patient a time to hesitate, a time to explore. Again we ought not to be non-discriminative about this, because some patients can live in dreams, live in fantasy, live in autism as a way of evading action. But even then the dream itself may give us clues as to why the patient remains in fantasy.

The moment of hesitation is the moment of decision, of choice between healthy and pathologic alternatives; it is a braking action on impulsive and compulsive necessities; it is the awareness of reality in any activity based on illusion. The dream as a time for hesitation is a defense against acting out. That is, if the dream gives a person a chance to play it out in the fantasy, he may be less likely driven to act it out in reality. It may thereby be an attempt to drain off strivings to fulfill wishes, or give gratification, or express aggression without having to go through the activity in reality. In this sense the dream may be related to what is known as the M response in the Rorschach. It is a projection into the inkblot of a human movement, a human fantasy, the illusion of the human condition. It, too, reflects a defense against acting out. The dream mirrors what are the typical modes of defense against anxiety, against acting out, against aggression, against sexuality.

We have discussed what are the many kinds of insights that the analyst might get by looking at dreams. Let us reverse the question. What insights does the patient get by having dreams?

The patient gets insight into his unconscious psychodynamics. For example, the patient Marge kept insisting that there was nothing but love between her and her mother and that her problem was with the father. Lately she is beginning to dream about battles with women, gun duels and wars among women. And I have been asking: Why is there this kind of aggression between her and a woman, or other women. And as I raised the question I suggested that maybe it is not all so very loving between the two. And as I have been doing this, she has been finding actual corroboration in her life experience to indicate that there is something to it. That is, she had to block out of awareness certain of her own competitive and aggressive feelings toward her mother and experiencing them from her mother. This is a reality which she has not been seeing. Dreams, then, are a source of bringing material out of repression into consciousness, so that the patient can relate in a new perceptive way about what is really going on. They can help in breaking through the defensive pattern of denial and projection.

Do you think of the dream as preconscious? I'm assuming that there are things that are repressed. If they are repressed they are not directly available to us. There are also facts, events, feelings and experiences that are forgotten, but with attention and effort we can recall them. These are called preconscious. Generally we say that in the dream repressed, not preconscious material is to be found. But once it comes into the dream would you then not say it is entering into consciousness? It is in that transition phase between being repressed and coming to consciousness. And entire dreams can be repressed. Is that re-repression?

In a patient who says he does not dream, or does not remember his dreams, or remembers a dream on waking and then loses it, the forces of repression are stronger. The fact that a person dreams and remembers and reports it and associates freely about it, suggests that this material is in preconsciousness. If he is not remembering his dreams it remains in repression. This in itself is an important step in the prelude to making the material conscious.

Yet, just because he dreams, does not mean there is no or lesser repression. If this were true, why do we need free associations, why do we need to unravel the dream work to get to what is repressed? Yes, if a patient presents dreams the repressed material becomes available to consciousness; it is not immediately available.

The patient is in less resistance if he is dreaming. I think this is important for the analyst to know, that a patient who is dreaming, remembers his dreams and is reporting them is less resistive.

That might well lead us to a stage where the person is dreaming so much that we recognize that repression has broken down, that the ego is failing, that the ego processes involved in secondary elaboration are ineffective. For example, in a schizophrenic patient the dreams are so overtly filled with primary process material the chances are that the repressions which we feel are necessary in order not to be flooded by unconscious material, have given way. I can imagine a person dreaming in such a way that I would want to help build up the repression of certain kinds of material. I might even suggest to a patient not to report dreams, even not to have them, just as I might suggest to one patient to avoid intercurrent material and to focus on historical data, or to another patient that he give up free association and fantasy for realistic reporting, and other individualized variations. The fact that psychoanalysis seeks to make the unconscious conscious cannot be non-discriminatively followed. It will depend on which patient is being treated, what the nature of his psychopathology and psychodynamics is, and what unconscious material we wish to help make conscious.

There is more to unconscious processes, the unconscious, than what has been repressed. It has been said that the unconscious knows what the conscious seeks but never knows. But knowing, it seems to me, is apparently not enough, not even conscious knowing. We have all had the experience where a patient has a dream or many dreams in which he has a healthy, positive sexual experience with a member of the opposite sex. And yet he is unable to have such an experience in reality. What does this mean regarding insight? What does this mean in terms of making the unconscious conscious, or an unconscious "knowing" what the conscious will never know? There is a big gap between dream (inner) reality and the external reality, the psychologic reality and the reality of acting and interacting.

I was thinking of patients, and by thinking about them perhaps we can come to something. A paranoid patient, Joe, has made some progress, but not a great deal. He has made progress to the point where he has an improved relationship with a woman. He is married, he has a child. All this is constructive. He loves her as he has never loved any woman before. But he perceives all analysis as a destructive assault on him and he uses his analytic observations to attack other people. He does not have insight into this, and any attempt to show it to him he perceives also as aggression against him.

Another patient, Mike, in his second group session started asking questions about how the process works. Or if the members of the group go out after a regular session with me and have dinner together, he has an impulse to say "Let's not have dinner together; let's go right to work again;

let's start the alternate session." This man somewhere does not want to get emotionally involved with people, or he avoids it for one reason or another. He is looking for answers. While looking for answers and getting insight are important, this man uses his looking for answers as a resistance to a meaningful encounter with others.

Joe also avoids constructive emotional involvement with people, because what he acts out and re-experiences all the time is the hostility from both his parents and his hostility toward them. That is, he persists in using what could be insight, to re-enact the old detachment and hostility. This can become a problem in therapy where the analyst is trying to provide insight, and the patient incorporates it into his acting out.

There must be some difficulty here with regard to the nature of the relationship between dreaming and reality. I'll be more specific. In view of the ego processes in dream formation, is it your experience that as the patient improves the dreams become more realistic?

Maybe we can think in the context of the progressive development of that set of dreams of the man who could not find his keys, found them in the keyhole, and so on, who came to make his dreams less distorted, less symbolic, more in correspondence with his waking feelings, so that he no longer had to see himself or his wife symbolically, but could see himself and his wife in a dream. The dream becomes less condensed, less covert, more consonant with waking wishes. I find that as patients get better they do dream in a less disguised way and in less symbolic terms, but in terms that correspond more with realistic waking thoughts and fantasies.

Does that mean they have more repression or less repression?

I would say they have less repression, but also these patients have more ego. You raised the question before about schizophrenics. You recall that analyst who wrote a paper on the genesis of a hallucination; his patient was not ready to dip into all this unconscious material to the extent he did. The ego should have been built up first, so that he could cope with this unconscious material. His primary process material was overwhelming for the weak ego he had.

What happens to the primary process material when the dreams become more realistic? Let us assume that a patient after analysis or toward the end of the analysis starts dreaming less symbolically. He loves his woman; his woman is his wife; and he wants to have intercourse with her; so he has a dream he is having intercourse with his wife. What happened to the symbolic material? Where are the primary processes? Does he still have primary processes? Where are the unconscious processes? Is there no more id? Is the censorship now working better? Or is the id disguised now in the form of reality?

A good deal of primary process material has been worked through. There is some residue of primary process material. It is never totally worked through. But this man is now able to recognize that he has wishes, that he has a penis of his own; he is no longer threatened by his father's set of keys; he can distinguish between some man and his father; he can distinguish between his wife's father and his father, between his mother and his wife; and he recognizes his own legitimate rights to gratification in reality that were denied because of the projective approach to life that he had before.

Are you saying then that it is possible to work through so that a person no longer transfers? I have had the opinion that we can never be rid of our transferences; that transferences persist so long as we are alive; that transference is a part of our history and we shall always continue to have our history with us; that history is never worked out in the sense that it has disappeared. But the necessity to act historically is worked through in that we can recognize what is the here-and-now relationship and what is the "as if" relationship, and we can act upon the present in terms of the present realities and present necessities. This does not mean, therefore, that we do not have a history. What you seemed to be saying is we no longer have unconscious processes; as one works it out and through in analysis we even have less primary process.

I would say that the primacy, if you like, or the quantitative and qualitative intensity of unconscious processes is diluted by the new experiences the patient is giving and is given in his interactions with his analyst, his co-patients and others. In the new experience he also does not play such a provocative role and is convincing himself again and again that the man that he meets today is in fact no longer his father and that the woman is no longer his mother. He has the experience now of swimming instead of drowning. He has been given new experiences and resources and help that enable him not to act upon and provoke and elicit the same archaic set of circumstances which injured him in the first place. His repressions are not totally lifted; primary processes never totally disappear but they are not exercised so much. From a lack of exercise there is a tendency for them to atrophy. The patient understanding this and struggling with it continues to operate in a new way, and while it never eliminates primary processes altogether, it nevertheless leads to atrophy from disuse. I really think that transferences do atrophy; they never disappear entirely. If the provocation is great there is always the tendency, the likelihood, and if the provocation is great enough the certainty that the transference will reassert itself, but it takes more provocation to elicit the transference than it did before.

In other words, after analysis we have greater resistance to unconscious material than we had before.

I am not saying we have greater resistance to unconscious material, because now the material is more conscious and therefore the patient is more able to cope with what before was unconscious.

It is not transference if it is conscious; by definition, transference is an un-conscious reaction, isn't it?

Transference is unconscious, but the patient is more able to become aware of what he is doing and to struggle with what he is doing. A healthy person, of course, dreams and makes transferences. But let us go back to a patient from which we might try to generalize, to formulate theory. The patient begins to develop a transference to the analyst as a father figure, with positive and negative attitudes, but she is continually being made aware that while it has something to do with the analyst it also has some-thing to do with her father. As she becomes aware of this she experiences the love, and the sensuality, and the incestuous feelings, the competition and resentment of her mother, and the frustration of having to give the fa-ther up. But it is experienced on a conscious level. I think that the fact of experiencing this out of repression makes it unnecessary to repeat to the extent the patient had to repeat it before in acting out with one married man after another, without consciousness of what she was doing. There may remain some tendency still to repeat. But I think there is less of a necessity to do it because she can catch herself in the act of moving into this and can make more conscious choice to relate to an unmarried man whom she can marry, because she no longer finds it necessary to re-enact the archaic role.

Can you give me an example of what you would consider an instance of an "unhealthy dream," that is, the dream of a person who is still struggling with repression? And can you give me an example, even using the formula-tion of the keys of a "healthy dream" in which the person is not struggling with repression.

It may not be possible to do this, because maybe there is nothing in life or in thinking, feeling or doing that is not "contaminated" by health and ill-ness. I am thinking of an "unhealthy dream" where a female patient is with the symbolic mother and father and instead of moving in the direction of relating more positively to the father has a homosexual relationship with the mother figure. In the sense that the patient is trying to get the mother figure out of the way in this homosexual act, even though this has its path-ology, it may be an indirect means of trying to reach the father. In the same way, one could ask why in that so-called healthy dream in which the man dreams of his wife, becomes erotic and wakes her up, why he had to dream about it in the first place, why he did not have this erotic feeling before he went to sleep. Or maybe there is even hostility in waking her up and not letting her sleep. So perhaps one could say that pathology gets less and health gets more apparent, or that there is less psychopathology as patients go on in analysis but there is never a total or absolute end to psychopath-ology.

But what is the latent content of the dream in which he has erotic feeling for his wife and he has intercourse with her? What is the latent content of that dream? Since dreams obviously have manifest and latent content, what is latent in this dream?

It should first be clarified that actually this dream was the dream of a woman and maybe the latent content of it was that with the kind of husband she had, she had to dream about it. I am not sure of this, but one of her husband's problems was that he tended to receive her as the father and that he was not a particularly responsive person. She was dreaming a wish here that would be hard to consummate. She had to make it rosier than it could be in actual achievement. She was using the fantasy as a substitute for life. In retrospect, perhaps this patient was discharged prematurely, because what should have been analyzed here was her making a rosier picture of her husband than was appropriate. She was repressing her actual disappointment with him in that she was dreaming of his being marvelous. Of course, she did wake him up, and he did have intercourse with her but this was because he was a very sensuous person, and he would have intercourse with her anyway. But the question is with whom was he having intercourse? This might have been something she was not looking at. For example, I have a patient now who has sexual relations often with many men, and "everything is wonderful," and "everything has always been wonderful" about every man she has ever met. But behind this I feel there is much disappointment in and resentment of men. She has got to make it rosy so she does not get depressed. But are you implying that we cannot help our patients?

No, I am not saying that nobody ever gets any better. What I think I am saying is that valid generalizations about dreams are difficult to make, the dream process for each person is as different as his fingerprint; that we have no clearcut conception of what the dream function is with regard to reality and unconsciousness; and that what we are doing always is to operate empirically, as we do in most other areas of therapy, and use the dream in terms of our conception of the necessities of the particular patient. What seems to happen is that if the dream in its manifest content provides us with the necessary material to move the patient in the directions that we think the patient ought to go, we do not bother to analyze the latent content. But if the dream does not provide us manifestly with the kind of data we think we need to help the patient, we then analyze the latent content. We then say there is a resistance to or is a disguise of the real wish for the direction in which we think the patient realistically desires to go. Obviously, we are still working with most of this dream material quite non-specifically but adapted to the specific needs of the particular patient. This may be good analytic therapy, and I am not suggesting it is bad. But it may be bad science.

That is a matter of the analyst's art and skill. Some therapists, if they listen, do not seem to hear the patient, like the one who did not heed the patient's warnings in the dreams and elsewhere that foreboded the birth of the hallucination. The question is why some therapists can hear a dream, and after hearing it are able to make that kind of interpretation or to select what to interpret in the dream, or not interpret and say what will be most ego building if that is necessary, or insightful if that is necessary, or emotionally reactive if that is necessary, or propose an action if that is indicated, or whatever is indicated in terms of therapy for the patient, rather than perhaps always doing the same thing in response to a patient's dream.

It may not be appropriate in response to every patient's dream to interpret it, or to interpret it fully. It may be appropriate to interpret a part of it; it may be appropriate not to interpret it at all. It may be appropriate to try to pay no attention to it, but to remember it. There are different indications for different patients and this is part of hearing a dream, to know in the process of just hearing it and the associations what is indicated to do with it.

I know a young analyst who is too limited in dream analysis, who seems much better able to interpret what the patient is saying or doing apart from the dream, or to work with other dimensions of the patient's indications of pathology and health than the dream material. He seems lost or blocked with dreams. One sees this even with patients, and especially in the group. Some are quite helpless with dreams, and others have a fantastic perceptivity about catching in a discriminating way the meaning of other people's dreams. For some it is not so discriminating; for some it is that they are so schizoid themselves, they live so much in unconscious material, that they can grasp something about the symbols of the dream. They are so immersed in pathology like John Rosen's nurses who were formerly his patients, whom he now uses as adjunct analysts, that they tell him what a schizophrenic patient is communicating or thinking or feeling. For example, he asked one of his nurses, why he could not get a patient to sit down, and she told him immediately, "Because he does not want to be a woman." They can express quite spontaneously this kind of explanation which, as far as Rosen felt, and even the patient admitted it, had really hit home. But I think there are other people who are not so schizoid, who seem to have creative faculties, sometimes this creative faculty is also associated with the schizoid patient, to get at the heart of an obscure part of a dream or of a whole dream that most of us have missed, and perhaps this is as hard to understand as it is hard to understand creativity.

Do you think that with experience we grasp more easily the repetitive patterns in dreams? Since neurosis has a repetitive core, we get repetition in the dream, from dream to dream, and the repetition of entire dreams.

The repetitive theme in a dream is probably a condensation of many things or it may represent different things in different patients, or different things at different times in the same patient. It might be a defense against other constructive alternatives. It may also be the patient's attempt to communicate to you, to the analyst, what his problem is and to communicate it to himself as well. The repetitive theme may be a quest for certainty, for familiarity, for looking for the security and haven with the familiar figures now represented by surrogates.[111] The repetitive theme, as in a traumatic neurosis, may satisfy the wish that the patient be not destroyed, in fact.[98] If one works analytically with the patient and watches, one sees that the character of the repetitive theme becomes a way of trying to work through toward new possibilities. Now, this is saying the opposite of its being a defense against other alternatives. In the course of therapy as you work with the repetitive theme you discover that the patient is getting beyond the point of fixation. The repetitive theme may be an attempt to resolve the dilemma rather than only to repeat it, so that it contains this contradiction within it. The patient comes to the therapist, with his neurosis, not only with his dream, with the repetitive character of the neurotic operations in the hope that the analyst will repeat the old operation of the parent, and in the hope that he will not, but instead will give the patient a new experience that will be more liberating and more gratifying. The contradiction operates within the transference itself, as well as in the dream.

There is then repressed material in the dream as well as current reality and distortion. But when a patient dreams in therapy, everything in the dream, including the dream itself, may be viewed as a manifestation of an action in transference or on transference to the analyst. The patient dreams for the therapist in the analytic relationship. If one wants to understand the dream or dreaming, it cannot be extrapolated from the context in which the dream is being dreamt. In other words, if a patient brings in a dream today and we had a session yesterday, what we were discussing in the session must have some bearing on some connection with what is being dreamed today. One cannot ignore the intercurrent reality of the therapeutic context in the material under discussion, the associations of the analyst as well as the patient and his co-patients that were exchanged in the preceding session. In this sense, the dream is not an exclusively intrapersonal process. The dream can be viewed as an interpersonal experience, rather than intrapersonal process. Certainly the patient created the dream, but he made it up in relationship to the knowledge, the conscious as well as unconscious knowledge, that the dream is to be told to the analyst, that he is going to come to treatment the next day, and he is going to tell his dream to the analyst and to the group.

When we dream outside of analysis there may be similar motives, but certainly within the analytic frame the patient is fully aware that, if he has a dream he remembers, he is going to tell it to his therapist. The nature of the dream itself has something to do with the motivation, the relationship, and the way the patient sees the nature of the relationship to the analyst. What is said in the dream and the dream process itself is in some way connected to the relationship with the therapist and the patient's understanding of the rules of the game.

The content of the dream is in some way selected, disguised, told, not told, censored, repeated, and so on, with an eye to the analyst. One of the areas of confirmation is the dream within a dream, which, to the best of our knowledge, occurs or is available for reporting only in treatment. Last night, I was dreaming that I was dreaming, and in this dream that I was dreaming that I dreamed, I dreamed that so and so happened. Clinical experience indicates that the dream within a dream often occurs when the patient is saying to the analyst, "I had a dream, I told you this dream, you didn't hear me, you didn't understand it, and so now I am dreaming a dream about the dream to tell you that in the dream that I dreamed, you did not hear me, you did not respond." The patient seems to feel that the analyst did not understand him. At the same time, the dream within a dream is also a distance making mechanism in that it contains a piece of resistance. The patient withdraws further from the analyst by saying, "Because you did not understand me, I am hurt. I am now cloaking the dream within a dream." It is a kind of further symbolization because the relationship in some way was disappointing, punishing or frustrating.

I do not think there are patients who are non-dreamers. The patient reports no dreams. Such a patient does not voluntarily say to the analyst, "I never had a dream." If a patient in the course of an analysis never brought in a dream, it may be that he did not have to, because the therapist was not interested and did not work through the resistances to reporting dreams. The patient is reporting dreams because he thinks they are related to his motivations with regard to the analyst. If the therapist does not want dreams the patient is not going to bring them in. Patients, for example, today tend to bring in dreams almost automatically. If you reject the dream, if you refuse to work with it, if you do not gratify the patient in some way for bringing in the dream, the patient is not going to bring in more dreams. You can stop any patient from reporting dreams. If the patient brings in dreams every day, you can stop that merely by refusing to be responsive to the dreams for a few weeks. At all events, there is enough material in the dream for any therapist, of any persuasion to use it in the interests of patients, as he sees them.

8. Working Through

The theoretical and practical problems of working through represent one of the most neglected, yet most important aspects of psychoanalysis, whether in the individual or in the group setting. Some therapists are convinced that human behavior is not determined by original provocation and specific laws. They believe that man's function is accidental, a consequence of impulsivity and inspiration, self-generated and unrelated to causality and etiology, and directed by a mystical unconscious. They contend that subscription to principles and plans in psychoanalysis eliminates the participants' spontaneous choice. Therefore, conscious, lawful and reflective intervention on the part of the analyst or the patient is contraindicted or even futile. Human beings become the blind and passive victims of a fateful unconsciousness. The patient is indoctrinated with an unseeing faith in destiny, an undiscerning predestination and an intertia in pathology.

But the patient's behavior, his illness and his health are consequences arising out of original causes, his history. Transference in the present is the repetition–compulsion of an earlier relationship, and working through is the resolution of this pathology by a radical displacement of the persistent negative history in the course of treatment. Taking history, causality and the laws of psychology for granted, the analyst does not reject accident, spontaneity, inspiration and choice, but tries to discover their motivation, etiology, development and the laws that govern their present operation. He consciously and expertly enters into the therapeutic relationship with the purpose of facilitating freedom from compulsion by dispelling projective illusions. Freedom is attainable only by grasping the laws of reality, toward which the analyst is guiding the patient in the working through process. A genuine independence is not an illusory license for disregarding psychological laws, but is an increasing awareness of them and their appropriate

---

Modification and elaboration of material appearing in refs. 139 and 146.

application in human relations. Unless the therapist and the patient come to understand the psychodynamics of transference, they become unconscious victims of its inexorable recurrence. The progress of the patient is possible only if his behavior in all of its modalities, including thinking, feeling and doing, is thoroughly investigated for its conscious and unconscious components. And he can work through to independence only by resolutions based on developing insight. Pathology is a product of the patient's history which has made him a servant of transference. Psychoanalysis, by providing him with a more liberating, nontraumatic, but planned and organized body of current experiences, sets him free.

The patient is in conflict and inner contradiction. He is inwardly embroiled in a struggle between illusion and reality, between repetition–compulsion and conscious choice, between regression and growth, between disorganization and organization. In the context of this dynamic opposition, what the analyst does determines in large part which way the patient will move, toward the entrenchment of transference or the development of new resources. The conflict between archaic pathology and working through, between destructive, conditioned responses and more realistic, evolutionary prospects is the basic psychodynamic in the patient. The analyst can help resolve this opposition by allying himself with one trend or the other. If he chooses to befriend unconsciousness, the outcome is further irrationality and psychosis. If he joins forces with the patient's consciousness, he consolidates gains in reality. Working through is not a fulfilment of primitive pathologic yearnings, which always leave the patient frustrated, because it abandons him in regression and disintegration. Working through is the struggle for the fulfilment of mature, healthy aspirations, which leave the patient satisfied, because it sponsors him in growth and integration.

In working through, the analyst points the way toward the diminishment of anxiety and the resolution of conflicts by constantly posing more valid, realistic and constructive alternatives which, when chosen, confront the participants with new problems to pursue, but always on a higher level of development. Whereas, among plants and animals, sudden changes and mutations appear in the course of natural selection, in man changes are accomplished in the main by conscious planning. Having discovered the dynamics of the patient's pathology, the analyst, then, carefully maps a course of action to deal with it. Improvements the patient makes do not arise impromptu. They are the result of the cooperative effort of analyst and patient within the context of a thoughtful and flexible treatment plan. In their rational exertion the participants differ from lower forms of life which simply exploit their natural surroundings without awareness, adapting themselves and influencing their environment without consciousness. Men can change themselves by conscious effort, and direct and change external reality by forcing it to gratify their purposes. It is the struggle to reach objective and realistic common goals and to manage and control his life according to a hope, a vision, a design and a fulfilment, that distinguishes man.

The analyst, grounding himself in knowledge of the pathology that rules patients, strives to see in advance that if he treats them thus, he will imbed their pathology, but if he treats them so, he may move them to new insight and reasonable adjustment. The analyst's awareness that he will elicit a transference reaction if he countertransfers, that yielding to the temptations of acting out is bilaterally defeating, and drawing upon other generalizations, derived from clinical experience, enable him to attempt to predict the consequences of an act, to apply the proper timing to his interventions, and to introduce them with appropriate technical skill and consideration for the patient's needs. Instead of deluding himself that he knows patients through his own projections, he realizes that just to the extent that he countertransfers, he knows them and himself less. He is aware of the necessity that his subjective chaff has to be sifted from the grain of true discernment. He knows that insight develops when patients can see the mutually destructive nature of projection; that understanding develops further in the exercise of learned ways and means to respond instead of yielding to obsession; and that an acute wherewithal can replace compulsion only in the light of reason. He realizes that, if he knows enough about a patient and himself, their relationship and their culture, together they will be better able to achieve a mutually constructive outcome.

Conscious, planned and goal-directed application is essential in the analyst's endeavor to help patients. Their potential cannot be realized unless he reflectively and discriminatively follows a deliberate strategy aimed at achieving realistic solutions determined by the existing circumstances. To accomplish this purpose the analyst should be willing to use his judgment and exercise his responsibility. Instead of reducing his intervention to countertransference, to disequilibrium catalysis, or to doing nothing constructive because patients are possessed of occult, self-reparative powers, he actively demonstrates to patients that they can, in some measure, outgrow their pathologic history in the context of current and future experience. He accomplishes this, in part, by providing the possibility for a healthy interpersonal relationship as the initial healing environmental influence.

When treatment induces patients to take first steps toward establishing better human contact with the analyst, they are fortified by insight gained from a consciousness of the process and begin to make efforts to relate more appropriately. Gradually pathology withers from disuse as they function more realistically. The better the analyst understands the particular details and dynamics of this process in patients, the more accurately he can guide the course of treatment. The more the patients see that he knows what he is about, the readier they are to join him in accomplishing their ends. Only that analyst can play a decisive role in treatment whose therapeutic intervention is in the well-defined service of his patients.

In working through, impulsive, fragmented patients yield to and utilize the analyst's consciously directed flexibility and freedom to choose. Out of the conflict between illusion and reality, between outmoded transference reactions and the awareness of new choices,[111] patients sense refreshing possibilities. These new concepts mobilize their hopes, lead them to plan new activities and integrate them for untried enterprise. They discover fresh reserves of energy to apply in new pursuits, while their former disorder atrophies from disuse. The patient unable at first to participate consciously in an understanding of his conflicts, is enabled, through the insight provided in the course of treatment, to level a conscious attack on his pathology. Therapy, releasing creative possibilities, opens the door to his further development.

A genuine change for the better in the patient cannot be achieved instantaneously, at the impulse or whim of either participant. Recovery is possible only under certain objective conditions, in which the analyst knows how to intervene, times his interpretations properly, and knows why he is saying or doing this and not that. In order to effect positive change, it is not enough that the patient understand the undesirability of behaving as abnormally as he has in the past. It is necessary also for the analyst to make such a discriminating analysis of illusion that it can no longer dominate the patient's life. This is not a countertransferential attack. It is a considered examination of more reasonable alternatives and a recognition of the frustrations to which projection leads. Only when the patient no longer wants to function in his old way and illusion can no longer maintain itself, can analysis be said to be taking effect. While the potential for constructive change exists in the patient, it will not blossom under assault; once having burgeoned, growth cannot proceed in and of itself. For the patient to realize his potential, the analyst needs to apply himself with resoluteness, devotion, self discipline and technical skill.

Working through, like most other psychoanalytic procedures, relates to the treatment of the individual patient. In the group setting new dimensions arise requiring of the analyst additional perceptions and often different technical skills. Working through is a consciously determined activity of the analyst and arises at any point in the course of an analysis. A necessary precondition is an understanding of the stereotyped forms of behavior and their psychodynamic origins. For this reason a period of working out personality structure and function precedes working through. Generally, working through is assigned by most analysts to the more advanced stages of treatment leading to termination.

In an analytic group, transference is elicited and resistance broken through more readily by the multiple interaction of the members. Repeatedly they confront one another's irrational behavior, explore more deeply into its meaning, and offer a variety of alternatives. Nonverbal, concealed and disguised reactions are often penetrated. One member objects to another's dozing, day-dreaming or autism. Another comments on a co-patient's worried look or draws into discussion someone who is feeling hurt, left out or abandoned.

Working through takes place for each patient not only of his relationship to the analyst but to the other group members as projected figures of his original family. There is an easier resolution of authority projections, first because the disparate views of the analyst force patients to re-examine their distorted perspective in the light of other perceptions of him. In addition, the projected father, mother and siblings in co-patients shift from one member to another, and often are recognized and analyzed there more easily. The varying responses from group members, misperceived as familial figures, induce the patient to study, question and finally correct his distortions. Insight into the dynamics of the actual behavior of group members with their varied perception of any other member including the analyst, stimulates the individual to question the relevance of his responses.

Another valuable source of insight is provided by an examination of the disparity in thought, feeling and behavior at regular and alternate meetings. Patients confront one another in the analyst's presence with these variations and seek his help in understanding them. The alternate absence of the analyst, the projected parental authority, permits the sibling-peers to explore their affect, thinking and activity on their own and to find their own way. Growth goes on, then, in the presence and in the absence of the analyst. He provides thereby a climate of wholesome attention and wholesome inattention and the patient develops autonomy, independence and authority. Both healthy and neurotic leaders emerge at regular and alternate meetings. Positive leadership is always welcomed, but pathologic domination and monopoly require and get careful analysis.

Group members acquire an increasing ability to perceive one another's psychodynamics, to interpret unconscious processes, and successfully to engage one another in more appropriate ways of dealing with their problems. Doubts about and astonishment at their acuity are replaced by increasing confidence in a capacity to be helpful, which is recognized and supported by the analyst. In this way patients become more and more aware of their insights, egos are strengthened and authority and peer problems are diminished. Understanding then is not derived from the analyst alone but from the new-found family, the co-patients.

The shifting position of helper and helped, of leader and follower, of being independent and dependent, encourages patients to give up compulsively helpless or compulsively authoritarian roles. Two or more patients may, on occasion, share a problem and work on it back and forth with exploratory associations, and come to an earlier resolution than might be possible without such mutuality. Even where one member's difficulties seem more foreign to another, they are often not met with as destructive recriminations as in the original family, for pathologic responses are sooner or later subjected to analysis. While recriminations do occur, no patient is ever completely isolated in the group. He always has at least one ally. Sometimes support comes from a peer, sometimes from the analyst.

But the group is invaluable for the patient who cannot mobilize the strength at first to become aware of or express his feelings about the authority invested analyst. Here the faltering member finds ready, encouraging allies among his peers, until he can manage alone. Ego-support comes from co-patients through the awareness that a person has friends in expressing his feelings and ideas and by being witness to his neighbor's success in dealing with the analyst.

Control moves gradually from the authority figure to the peers to the self. An occasional patient can often 'hear' more easily what his peers are saying than he can absorb the same comments from the threatening therapist. For some who are intimidated by authority, the analyst's words are heard sometimes only through less fearful intermediaries. At times, group members identify with one patient's archaic or constructive id, ego or superego, offering emotional support out of their own pathologic and healthy needs. It is at such times that the analyst steps in to identify motivations and underline directions that seem bilaterally positive. While the principle of consensual validation generally holds true in the group, the therapist is alert to the possibility that the majority may be on the wrong track and he pursues his own perceptions or sponsors the view of a single patient at odds with the group. For the most part, however, the others point out for each member that there are more reasonable alternatives. Patients encourage and appeal, make practical suggestions and propose plans to act on these more constructive alternatives. The group members not only offer insight but become a matrix for increasingly reasonable adjustment that draws the patient into the same struggle against unreality. The manifold strivings for more positive and conscious ways and means impel the individual to join the others in their therapeutic objectives.

Speculation with regard to working through is the analyst's first consideration after the discovery of pathologic patterns. It is important that he not permit disturbed interaction to go on too long. This merely intensifies and entrenches it. Meetings may then become chaotic, confused and the members bewildered and frustrated in verbal acting out. It is the analyst's function, and patients will follow his lead in this, to confront, interpret and work through expressions of pathology.

We have never been witness to a whole group in an advanced or terminal phase of group psychotherapy. Only one or another individual has been so improved, and no two were so identical in sickness or in health that they could be said to be making exactly the same kind of progress. To assume that a group advances en masse is to anthropomorphize the group, to give it a unity and homogeneity that it does not, in fact, possess. This tendency in group psychotherapy is discussed at length in chapter 10. The coalescent view of patients as a group is an antipersonal, antianalytic distortion, a countertransference problem. With regard to working through in advanced phases in group psychotherapy, we refer only to the individual in interaction and not to the whole group. Because, in our experience, no group proceeds to termination as a group, we prefer, among other reasons, to work with continuous rather than closed groups.

It is to be noted that reference is made to the patient in exchange with his fellows, not as an isolated person. For while we would not lose the individual in the group, some group members are recognized to have strong reparative influences on one another. It is an awareness that patients stimulate and evoke each other's pathologic responses as well as healthy resources that impels us to do group therapy in the first place. We say, then, the individual in interaction, for just as there is the tendency, on the one hand, to treat the members as a group, there is the opposite inclination to do individual psychoanalysis in the group with little tolerance or regard for the members' interrelation.

In the advanced stages of treatment a central problem is that of working through vestiges of pathology. Here too a discriminating estimate of the uniqueness of each patient's disturbed psychodynamics and, therefore, the particular devices to be used to move him toward a more reasonable adjustment have to be studied, planned for, and employed.

Let us, for illustrative purposes, consider one member who is extremely impulsive in expressing his feelings, but who considers thinking things through as resistive and controlling and regards planned activity as too frustrating compared to immediate yielding to affect. Working through this problem for such a patient would entail a discriminative review of the kind of emotion he indulges. If it is irrational, our struggle with him is to bring him in time to the expression of more appropriate feelings. But having progressed so far, he has not yet reached the optimal therapeutic experience. It is necessary, further, that we help him see the value not only of relevant affect but of thinking things through and of planned activity.

Let us now consider a second member who withholds feelingful responses but exults in his intellectual and interpretive productions. Here an adequate resolution of the problem calls for an analysis of the patient's resistance to his own emotion in order to liberate it, and a corresponding demonstration to him of how his compulsive intellectuality is equally defensive.

Reference has often been made in the literature of group psychotherapy to the emergence of group leaders and auxiliary therapists among patients, particularly later in therapy. A note of warning is in order to caution the analyst against the patient's exploiting such a role in resistance to his participating affectively. By engaging as a leader and interpreter of other members' difficulties, the patient may well conceal his own affective detachment, his underlying compulsive seniority or his competition with the therapist. The latter, in his ready appreciation of help from all resources in the group, may be too readily inclined to condone whatever analytic aid he can get in the group and accordingly be misled into tolerating what may at times be a resistive maneuver. This is not to say that analytic observations coming from patients on occasion may not be evidence as well of their budding resourcefulness, in which case their interpretations can be welcomed in both the donor and by the recipient as bilaterally therapeutic; but it would seem reasonable to say that only the analyst is the leader in terms of expertness, that while patients can certainly play reparative roles, they have neither the knowledge nor the training to be considered auxiliary therapists. If they are so regarded by the group or so regard themselves, their activity may well be examined for its disordered significance. And if the analyst looks upon a patient as an auxiliary therapist, he may well explore his perception for countertransferential content.

A third member may defy impromptu activity to the neglect of thought and feeling. He is accordingly very active physically in the group—he cannot stop moving. Where one patient is verbally tender, he embraces; where one member speaks his anger, he is ready to throw something or strike; and where one man weeps, he rather tears his hair. Here, working through involves the exercise of control over such indeliberate activity, the quest for more planned operations and the pursuit of the uses of reason and affect. A fourth member may be compulsively devoted only to those activities which are in essence defenses against repressed material rationalized as strategically reasonable. Here the resolution of the problem lies in the analysis of his behavior as defensive and compulsively repetitive lacking in the sensible planning that might lead to the fulfillment of his real potentials.

In all these instances, we are interested in each of the three dimensions of thought, feeling and behavior, in the kind of intellectuality, affect and activity, as well as in which form of these is pursued to the neglect of the others.

The same discriminatory emphasis is required in the study of what temporal accent the patient gives to his productions. If he is enmired in an exclusive preoccupation with his past, we are interested in his present and his future. If he is engrossed primarily in here-and-now experiences of the moment, we would lead him to an exploration of his history and a consideration of eventualities. If he is wrapped up with his future, we want to know more of his background and current necessities. If the patient is absorbed in sexual matters, we would direct his attention to his interpersonal relations apart from his sexual obsession. If he excludes sexual content from his revelations and seems exclusively consumed with social relationships, we would attempt to analyze the resistances that exclude consideration of his sexual needs.

One member, prepsychotic or psychopathic, may need stronger superego controls. A second, overconscientious and bound by rigid inner monitors, may need some relaxation of an incorporated sense of duty. A third, a borderline, whose ego has been weakened by schizophrenic parents, may require ego strengthening as the primary therapeutic intermediation.

Another member, too readily given to value only his unconscious productions, may have to be led to lay store by conscious activity. Still another, inattentive to unconscious material, should be demonstratively guided to a more serious contemplation of underlying motivation. One patient, preoccupied with dreams, may have to be induced to explore other dimensions of his life in waking experience. Another, who never reports dreams, should be induced to pay attention to this voice of his unconscious.

One member, too involved with the other patients, should be directed to develop and explore his extra-group contacts. Another, detached from the group but seemingly involved with people outside the group, must be induced to extend his interaction in the group.

One patient, haunted by his parents, may not be able to let others intrude on his continuous involvement with his forbears and require a weaning toward the admission of nonparental associates into his limited circle of experience. Another, divorced from his family, and in reeling flight toward nonfamilial figures, may need a careful review of the real and projected defenses that keep him from a wholesome acceptance of his parents.

These examples are sufficient to illustrate the importance of the analyst's maintaining a discriminative view of the particular pathologic dynamics of each patient, so that he can keep in mind the specially indicated means to work through. In so doing, he also makes group members aware of their uniqueness in terms of their needs as well as their potentials, so that they are not so commonly impelled to demand from the therapist that he treat them the same way. Even in the most homogeneously organized group, there are always enough differences in character structure, psychopathology and resources to call for such differentiated study and treatment. Moreover, when the analyst is thoroughly aware of these distinctions and the need to treat them differently, he no longer feels threatened by the patient's complaint that, "You don't treat me the way you treat him." But if the therapist persists in making discriminating estimates of each member, he finds before too long that group members soon follow his lead, cease demanding undifferentiated responses from him and, in their own interest, recognize the value of differences and complementation.

According to some group therapists[31] the leader is somewhat more active in the end phase than during the middle phase of group psychotherapy. Here again, we believe a discriminative view of the therapist's activity, passivity or neutrality must be taken and, if he is any of these, consideration should be given to the timing of his interventions as well as to the kind of engagement he chooses to serve the patient's positive evolution at this moment or in the future. With a member who is initially silent, the analyst may choose to be active or passive, depending on which maneuver he believes will best call forth a response. With an initially verbally monopolistic member, the therapist may have at first to intervene very actively in analyzing his narcissism and, in a terminal phase, just as active in esteeming his allocentrism. With a shy, withdrawn patient the analyst may in the beginning be quite active in encouraging him to participate, in a middle phase be just as energetic in appreciating his more vigorous communication and nearing termination more passive as the patient appears to be doing well enough on his own. These differences in patient requirements point up once more why a non-discriminative, stereotyped prescription for the therapist's role at so-called group phases can no more be appropriate to the needs of all than to the needs of one patient in different periods of his progress.

The analyst's or a patient's analytic comment to member A may apply as well to patients B and C. But even D and E may get something out of it by virtue of comparison, learning to appreciate their differences from A, B and C and gaining insight by contrast. Understanding here occurs then not only out of identification but out of difference. The analyst is careful, when he generalizes from one patient to the next. A collective interpretation tends to obscure specific differences that may vary with each patient. A generalization may enable a member to resist deeper and more refined insight into his unique dynamics. Still, the therapist seizes the opportunity, when a recollection or dream brings insight to one patient, to encourage exploratory reactions of other members to the same recollection or dream.

One of the most fundamental roles of the analyst in all phases of treatment, but particularly in the advanced stages, is concerned with his traditional neutrality. In individual therapy, it is easier to maintain for the most part a consistent regard for the interests of the patient and thereby not to jeopardize his confidence in the therapist as a dependable ally. Even in those instances where the therapist is at variance with the patient, subtle and gentle means may be used to guide him to a more reasonable adjustment. In the group, however, where irrational contention so commonly arises between two members, it is more difficult for the leader to maintain neutrality without abdicating his therapeutic functions entirely and losing the regard not only of the contestants but of the other patients. A word is in order here with reference to the doubtful value of pursuing such a course of abstention which in time may assume the countertransferential character of indifference with all the hazards in patient responses that such an attitude entails. For the analyst to assume an absolutely impartial position suggests that he has no values, no judgment, no appreciation, no discrimination, which he can exercise in resolving the seeming impasse between two patients. And if he does not step in with an attempt to heal the breach, he begins to lose the affection and respect which his position demands, if he is to go on securely in his role. So he cannot continue, under these circumstances, to maintain a non-discriminative detachment without alienation.

Yet, how can he take sides in an issue between two patients without hurting one or the other? Here again, if the analyst keeps in mind the particular constructive evolutionary needs of each contestant at this particular time, it is unlikely that he will go wrong. If the patients' differences have arisen from the one's acting out his compulsive intellectuality and the other's acting out his irrational affect, the therapist may analyze the bilateral intrapsychic pathology without taking sides. If, however, the contesting patient is just beginning to break through his defenses to express an unreasonable feeling, he needs at this moment the leader's unqualified support. It is only when these emotional outbursts threaten to become entrenched in pathologic repetition that the analyst can begin to take issue with them and point the way to more reasonable alternatives. The excessively rational member will need the leader's support as resistance begins to give way before emotional needs pressing for release. While the therapist's aim is for ultimate reasonable interaction, he must, therefore, be guided in taking sides, by the principle of working through for each contestant the special psychodynamics of the individual. In the advanced and final stages, the therapist will find himself sharing more and more the increasingly sound reactions of the recovering patient. While at first the latter may require the leader's endorsement of his behavior, in time he becomes able to pursue his own judgments without affirmation from the authority figure.

Certainly in an open group, with a recovered member leaving and an inexperienced new patient replacing him, no two patients are improving at the same rate, so that the group as a whole can hardly be said to be at one in an advanced or terminal stage. In a closed group, where the improved are detained until tardier members catch up, it may be that there is finally some uniformity in terms of common progress, though it hardly seems fair or therapeutic to a patient who has recovered to hold him, until his fellows have come abreast of him. It would seem more rewarding to all concerned to encourage a recovered member to try his wings. This is not only appropriate compensation to the member who has struggled so hard to achieve his gains, it is a heartening demonstration to the remaining patients that rehabilitation is, in fact, possible and may one day be in store for them. The departure of a recovered member also endows the remaining ones with unspoken, but nevertheless covertly understood and acknowledged privileges of seniority, not the least of which is to break in a patient newly joined. There is also value in the open group to the introduction of a new member, who out of his unique personality and problems, evokes new and old transferences, elicits previously unseen healthy potentials and enables the patients to test their responses to a novel provocative agent.

The departing patient may be advised that, should he at some time feel a recurrence of his neurotic disorder, he should feel free to consult with the analyst again, and if necessary, will be permitted to rejoin his group. At the same time the therapist may warn him that, for a period after termination, he may experience some return of symptoms at times, that are likely to pass without the help of professional therapy, if the patient applies the tools made available to him during treatment. But failing in this, he should reapply for more expert help.

It cannot be assumed that working through is the therapeutic activity engaged in only in the advanced and terminal phases. The resolution of psychopathology may begin as early as the initial stage and continue in the middle phase. However, it is appropriate in the advanced and terminal phases to review our objectives to see if we have attained them, and, if not, to speculate as to what further means to employ to achieve our goals. As in any psychotherapy, the group therapist must ask himself and his patient in the end phase whether both of them are reasonably, and non-perfectionistically satisfied with what has been accomplished.

If a patient has approximated the goals we have described in chapter 12, he may be said to be in an advanced or end phase of treatment. But there are also practical guides the analyst may use to estimate the patient's readiness for discharge. One of these is his improved interpersonal relations both in and out of the group. It will be noted that he is wholesomely closer to his family, his friends and his associates at work. He may have some regrets about leaving the group, but he looks forward with pleasant anticipation to turning completely and actively to life apart from therapy. We find him to be more reasonable and temperate in his responses which are more commensurate with reality. He is more rational, flexible and discriminating in all his activities. He is less narcissistic and more positively involved with people. He has lost the impulsivity or compulsivity that characterized his earlier behavior.

It is important to bear in mind that the therapist ought not to adhere too strictly to notions of ideal conditions and perfectionistic goals. For in practice, we generally fall short of complete attainment and must realistically settle for lesser objectives. This is not to say that the patient will not go on developing after termination. But goals often have to be adjusted, adapted and modified in the end phases of treatment. Sometimes we start with reduced designs in the face of seemingly serious pathology, not infrequently a countertransference problem. But the patient may make such unexpected and remarkable improvement that we can raise our sights and project more advanced achievement. At other times, we find we have set up unrealistic and unattainable goals and are accordingly obliged in terminal phases to shave our objectives down. The therapist's pursuit of a perfectionistic denouement may make treatment interminable and infect the patient with similar idealistic strivings, so that he is always disappointed, with his progress. Accordingly, the analyst may have to reduce his aims in the light of disappointing clinical experience with a given patient, or raise his goals in the face of another's surprising and easy advance. When confronted by newly emerging limitations or resources in the patient or his environment, flexibility in modifying previously determined objectives is indicated. We cannot be governed by extravagant, impractical and rigid ideals of limitless attainment. When a patient can use the tools of analysis to resolve his problems on his own, he is through with treatment. One aim of therapy is to be free of the therapist. If the analyst keeps this in mind, he is less likely to set up theoretical, improbable and unreasonable goals. Otherwise, in his idealistic quest, he is liable to keep the patient in treatment longer than is good for him and away from living apart from therapy that can become endless.

A good test of a member's readiness for discharge is the proposal, whether emanating from the analyst or the patient, that his leaving the group be considered. When the suggestion is made, the group leader asks each member to evaluate the progress of the patient. As a result, valuable clues are uncovered in interaction which indicate in review the extent to which he has recovered and the amount of residual psychopathology. The patient who has really improved may, if he is shown that he still has some minor problems to resolve, agree to remain for some time longer. Or he may convince us, out of his readiness to remain in the group and tackle his few remaining difficulties, that he is, in fact, able to do this on his own. Or we may discover our own perfectionistic or rivalrous demands in expecting him to stay. When the proposal for departure comes from a patient who is attempting a resistive escape from resolving his distortions, group interaction and discussion shortly reveal his request as a pathologic maneuver.

Sometimes an advanced patient is subjected to two or three such reviews of his progress over a period of three or four months before we can agree to his readiness to take leave of us.

The patients themselves can never certify to a member's adequate maturation. Their estimates are welcome contributions, and the therapist may be influenced by their perceptive observations as to a patient's need to remain or go. The group assists just as the patient's self estimation does in helping the analyst come to a decision. The various members participate, suggest, counsel and appeal, but it is the therapist, as expert in appraising psychopathology and health, who determines in the end a patient's fitness for leaving.

The advanced patient, near termination, will exhibit increasingly a lesser tendency to become embroiled in entangling transferences with other members in distinct contrast to his earlier neurotic involvement. His essential friendliness and earnestness in trying to maintain realistic communication under these difficult circumstances will be apparent, however, and distinguishable from the kind of withdrawn, indifferent or hostile detachment, which is itself characteristic of intrapsychic disorder.

The recovering patient shows growing signs of developing his own autonomy, independence and authority at the same time as he welcomes a responsibly unneurotic interdependence. He becomes increasingly perceptive about his own and others' psychodynamics, in the interpretation of unconscious processes and more successful in engaging other patients with a view to discovering more appropriate means of dealing with their problems. As a result of his edifying development the peers are encouraged and pursue their further evolution with more zest for the work. They take good example too, from the fact that he is sufficiently resourceful to take a position and defend it reasonably and yet flexible enough to be influenced by the divergent view, while he grants the other the right to see things differently.

The patient approaching recovery exhibits less preoccupation with his own thoughts, feelings and behavior. Or, having originally been messianically devoted to the demands of other members, he will begin to attend to his own needs. From these poles of self- or other-centeredness the improving patient moves toward a bilateral consideration of his own and the other's ideas, affect and activity, toward a nonisolative mutuality. He begins to recognize the complementary value of differences, so that he no longer seeks a homogeneous environment that will merely mirror his egocentricity and narcissism, but a heterogeneous climate that will stimulate him to new endeavors at the same time as it complements what he has to offer.

A quality that characterizes the advanced patient and that endears him to the other members is his open-mindedness. While he refuses to yield to rigid and doctrinaire positions, he demonstrates by his lively attention to our remarks that no one of us is in exclusive possession of all the facts. His ability to attend us all, sift our comments and come to a new synthesis based on his own review, testifies to his high level of integration. He becomes a force in the group devoted to reciprocal consideration, interpersonal communication and bilateral insight.

A common problem of the advanced and terminating phase is concerned with the ultimate hesitation in expressing positive affect, feelings of warmth, tenderness, affection and love. Not infrequently patients find it easier to lend themselves to ventilating competitive, aggressive and hostile emotion. It has been our experience that when the therapist deals with this problem fairly early in treatment, it need not in the main appear as a difficulty in ending. There are, however, some patients, whose esprit de corps cannot be mobilized until their repressed resentment has been ventilated and resolved.

The advanced patient will exhibit an increasing freedom in verbalizing his warm, tender and affectionate feelings. Not infrequently he will have developed a loving relationship with a woman and end therapy in a constructive marriage. Or, if already a husband and father, he will have deepened his positive relationship to his wife and children.

One of the indices of recovery in a patient is his ability to move the majority of the group to more cooperative exploration of their communications leading to some realistic consensual validation, whether the problem is his or another's. As his responses become more reality-centered, the other members feel more impelled to seek him out for understanding and to share his warmth and good sense.

A useful guide to the analyst as to the patient's readiness for discharge is the change in the nature of his dreams as well as the more obvious evidence of his overt behavior. For these unconscious dramas also certify to his basic progress. As he improves, there is in them less symbolic disguising of latent content, less frightening ambivalence and conflict and more open suggestion of wholesome choices that correspond to waking fantasies. As anxiety is replaced by calm, the corresponding nightmare is replaced by the more freely expressed wish in dreams.

In an advanced phase of treatment the members have become increasingly familiar with one another's distorted patterns of behavior, their origins and the provocations that elicit them. Spontaneously every group applies itself in offering proposals to the patient caught in repetition–compulsion to try to adopt more reasonable alternatives. Whenever a proferred alternative to the neurotic behavior seems constructive, it is helpful if the analyst gives the suggestion his support. This appreciation of more wholesome substitute designs offers some reward to those who tender them, approval which is particularly valued, if the patient, who can most profit from the counsel, rejects it. The therapist, in esteeming the positive expedient, thereby indicates to the group what his value is, namely the constructive alternative as opposed to the irrational compulsion. His affirmation also keeps these salutary proposals coming, for the recipient, in repeatedly setting them aside, tends to reduce the donors to despair. Finally, the therapist's underlining more reasonable choices in behavior plays a significantly additive part in influencing the patient to relinquish his disordered manipulation for more appropriate transaction.

In an advanced stage of treatment, when the detail and variety of transference responses have been made manifest, the analyst may take the lead in confronting each member with the disparity between his perception and that of the other patients in order to get him to question the reality and appropriateness of his impressions. With some patients, however, this process of working through by comparing divergent estimates of one another can be initiated as early as the initial and intermediate phases of treatment.

Group psychotherapy, by providing a milieu of peers, permits patients to explore the ways in which they relate to one another on a horizontal level. While this is a salutary procedure for all, some members may use this avenue of interaction to resist examination of their vertical relationship to the analyst. Where this occurs, it is the function of the expert to encourage examination of attitudes toward him with a view to the exposure and resolution of hierarchical problems. Some members postpone the study of this vertical relationship until an advanced stage of treatment, but the therapist may, if patients seem defensively to be avoiding him, push for appraisals of him at an earlier time.

Other patients may be overly attached to and dependent upon the leader, particularly if he is an adherent of routinely combined treatment, limits the frequency of group meetings or denies the membership the privilege of alternate sessions without him. Here pathologic dependency on the analyst may become a difficult terminal problem at the same time as peer relations are curtailed and unresolved. Or, if the leader manages to work through the patient's difficulties in the authority vector, he may, by isolating him too much from his fellows, leave unsettled the ego-strengthening experience of peer interaction.

What may occasionally replace an insidious attachment to the analyst is an equally morbid dependency on the group. This is particularly true if the group is allowed to become a pathologic subculture in which bizarre and distorted attitudes and behavior are permitted successive indulgence without analysis and working through. For the patient may then persist in maintaining or acting out his disorder in a fraternity which sanctions neurotic behavior rather than correcting it. It becomes the analyst's function here so to unearth the unhealthy character of the patient's intra-group pre-occupation, to free him for extra-group life.

Commonly, the group's attitude toward a recovering member is one of increasing regard and affection in sharp contrast to previous mixed feelings about him. When he is at last indeed ready to take leave of us, there is generalized expression of regret at his impending departure, some fewer displays of envy at his achievement, but in the main, a prevailing pleasure in his wellbeing. These positive responses to him are in themselves often a good measure of the extent to which he has improved. The remaining patients frequently bring ceremonial food and drink to his last group meeting or tender him a final party to testify their warmth.

9. Routine Individual Sessions

No attempt is being made here to describe psychoanalytic theory and practice or the various methods by which psychotherapy may be done in an individual or group setting. We have combed the literature for material about concomitant or concurrent individual and group therapy, generally known as combined therapy. We have organized and integrated the general arrangements and rationalizations for variations within this context, and we have become aware of the confusion concerning the functions of a combined treatment plan, which includes routine individual as well as group experiences.

The utilization by psychotherapists of many different kinds of approaches in helping people to solve their problems is laudable and necessary. Introducing new and different techniques within any one treatment frame or supplementing the treatment process by additional kinds of experience, however, must be evaluated carefully for theoretic and therapeutic implications as well as outcomes.

We have, therefore, summarized the literature in the field of combined therapy and extracted from it some of the implicit and explicit contradictions, some of the pervasive themes and motivations. Our definition of combined therapy is specific; namely, it is the routine practice of prescribing concurrent individual and group sessions. We are aware that others have defined or have structured the combined therapeutic experience in other ways. Our criticisms are largely of the regular use of parallel individual and group sessions. Some conclusions about individual and group therapy instructive in other contexts have also been added.

Individual, group, and combined therapists are often unclear about the nature of therapy done in groups. Not all forms of treatment are psycho-

---

See ref. 114.

analytic. The term *group therapy* may obscure the real nature of the experience. The point of departure in our review is the combination of psychoanalytic therapy done with individual patients in an individual setting and psychoanalytic therapy done with individual patients in a group setting. There are quantitative and qualitative distinctions in the content, structure, method and goal of therapy in the various settings. Often the qualitative differences are most obscured.[113]

Some psychotherapists take the antipsychoanalytic viewpoint that the motivations of the therapist are of no consequence in what goes on in therapy. By extension this attitude could lead to the position that the motivations of patients also are of no consequence. Clinical experience has demonstrated that motivations affect what one does, that the therapist's feelings are very often implicit rather than explicit, and that the choice of theory as well as practice may, in part, be a consequence of motivation. Moreover, it is not always practice which follows theory, because theory itself is derivative of practices. In psychoanalytic work with patients, practice can precede theory in that a patient may engage in improved activities without full consciousness. Later when the patient becomes aware of these activities, he can discover the reasons why such changes have taken place. Then he can come also to a clearer understanding of the earlier, less rational premises on which his prior activities had been based.

A number of analysts trained to work in individual settings are doing therapy in group settings and in various combinations of arrangements. Many of these therapists approach the group with an orientation derived from working therapeutically in the individual setting. Such therapists may misperceive the nature of the group therapeutic experience as well as the qualitative and quantitative differences in working in these two settings. Although opinions exist concerning outcomes, it is still a matter of research and more objective measurement of results that will determine the usefulness of the many kinds of combinations of individual and group experiences which may be made available to selected patients or patient populations.

Combined therapy has been interpreted variously as an individual therapeutic experience preceding treatment in the group, the group process being a rounding out of individual therapy. On the other hand, it has been conceived as prior group experience in preparation for individual treatment. In our view, combined therapy is the parallel or concurrent use of group and individual sessions with either the same or a different therapist. Ideally, one might think that such an arrangement would be optimal; but in practice, combined therapy often leads to a lessening of the effectiveness of both methods.

Contradictory Claims

With the development of psychotherapy in groups, conflict has arisen over the relative merits of individual and group therapy. The individually oriented therapist may take the position that his approach offers better treatment than the group method. The analyst, traditionally geared to the dyadic relationship and now entering the field of group therapy, tends to homogenize the group, to treat the group en masse, or to treat the individual in the group, and so limit peer interaction. Moreover, the individual therapist is sometimes so immersed in uncovering intrapsychic pathology that he is disinclined to give proper place to interpersonal psychodynamics and social psychology.

The group therapist, on the other hand, tends to deify group processes, to claim that even the one-to-one relationship is group activity, and that the same dynamics obtain whether the group is made up of two, eight, or eighty. He argues that the individual does not exist alone but only in relation to others and that there is no individual psychology. Some individual analysts (and even some group therapists) say analysis cannot be offered in the group; consequently treatment is not deep. The group therapist recites clinical experience with patients with extended individual analysis to certify to the movement and depth of treatment only after they have joined therapeutic groups. Conceivably, combined therapy might be a happy marriage between the benefits of individual and group psychotherapy. How better resolve the conflict than by juxtaposing them for mutual enhancement.

Baruch and Miller[8] report that with allergic patients group and individual treatment "seemed to supplement one another," that "individual therapy went deeper more rapidly" and "the group stimulated ideas that could then be brought into individual sessions."

McCartney[71] writes that he has "used group psychotherapy to facilitate the readjustment of the patient, and to shorten the time necessarily spent in individual sessions . . . Although patients can seldom be readjusted by group therapy alone, anything that will cut down the time necessary for individual therapy is welcome to the armamentarium of the psychiatrist."

Hulse[51] states that "thirty-four (of the forty-six psychotherapists answering a questionnaire) use individual and group psychotherapy concomitantly. Some apply this combined treatment to all patients, others use it occasionally. Only eight do not use it at all."

Shea[119] reports "in some patients," analytic group psychotherapy "constitutes a treatment setting which makes possible the dissolution of resistances which are intractable in individual therapy . . . In still other patients, whose resistances would eventually succumb to individual therapy, group psychotherapy greatly speeds up the process."

Durkin[21] remarks, "it seems obvious that even with a small group many . . . problems cannot be fully followed through without using the individual interview also. Large groups of seven or eight would certainly seem to be better off if they were combined with individual interviews, though doubling or tripling the number of (group) interviews a week might well serve the same purpose."

Papanek[83] finds that the "double exposure and the mutual interaction of the two situations (in combined therapy) afford the opportunity to explore the patient's goal and style of life and to gain understanding in it. The neurotic pattern changes when the patient has been helped to overcome his exaggerated feelings of insecurity and inferiority by encouragement through both his relationships in the group and with his therapist."

Berger[10] conceives of the group as aiding in the examination of transference resistance in individual therapy, as preparation for intensive individual therapy, and as valuable in cases where the intensity of the transference requires modification.

Bieber[13] believes that "the combination of individual treatment with group sessions is preferable because it is in the individual sessions that the atmosphere, the time and the structure are provided to investigate fully, develop and follow the unfolding of the processes underlying the manifest neurotic difficulties of each patient." And she later elaborates a theoretical base for understanding the interpenetration of concurrent treatment processes.[14]

Foulkes and Anthony[31] state that "some, none, or all the members of the group may be receiving individual psychotherapy as well. Experience has shown that the most effective combination is for individual therapy to be followed by group therapy as a 'rounding-off' process, or for individual therapy to be preceded by group therapy as a preparatory measure. These combinations are to be preferred to the concurrent use of both, which, if done at all, should be done in an open group and with all the members. The important principle is not to isolate any patient by different treatment or bad selection."

Shaskan[118] in describing the course of treatment with one patient refers to it as group with supplementary individual therapy.

Fried[36, 37] claims that individual sessions are necessary to enable the analyst to acquire fuller understanding of the patient. Other combined therapists say that group sessions are required to provide a more thoroughgoing picture of the patient. Abrahams[1] contends that the group breaks down defenses; while Fried vouches that the group builds up defenses. Bieber[13] asserts that the group affords an opportunity to see and attack

character defenses. Furthermore, Fried cites the danger of premature interpretations in the group as a hazard which makes individual sessions necessary. We, however, have not found early attempts to provide insight offered
by co-patients to be perilous, partly because these proferred insights are in
the horizontal vector and partly because the patient awaits confirmation by
the therapist.[109]

Fried believes that in private consultations the patient is given a chance to
act out, that through this opportunity to express pathology he breaks
through. But other combined therapists charge those who concentrate their
therapeutic work in the group with sponsoring more acting out. The claim-
ants for the greater validity of combined therapy contend that their method
yields better results because the constructive forces of both individual and
group processes are "cross-fertilized,"[36, 37] or at least additive. A more
mechanistic if not mystical view[124] holds that in combined therapy insights
are combined.

There are as yet no research results to demonstrate the truth or falsity of
these and other claims with regard to combined treatment. Our main objection is that they seem to be based on a persuasion that few if any healthy or
positive things can occur among patients in a group, that no patient ever
gets sympathy or support from another patient, that every member is mo-
mentarily in defenseless jeopardy at the hands of his associates. With such
a view of group membership as sado-masochistically constituted of victims
and aggressors, it is inevitable that the therapist rationalize himself into the
position of peace-maker, arbiter and judge exclusively in his private cham-
bers.

All of these contentions have some clinical validity. To argue for one or
the other is really to waste precious time. No one can object to the idea that
every therapy needs to be kept flexible, free of the orthodoxy that rigidly
excludes new, constructive approaches. And good clinicians try to adapt
their techniques to the reconstructive needs of specific patients. Individual
therapy has many variations and methods, and so too has group therapy.

Our position is to try to get away from an exclusive choice of one form of
treatment *or* the other. So too for a combination of the two. We are not for or
against combined therapy. We are for what is most effective for what kind
of patient under what kind of circumstances. We are against the confusion
with regard to any form of therapy that leads to abuses. We, too, do combined therapy, but in special circumstances.

What we are concerned about is the implicit bias against doing therapy
in the group and the view that the individual situation is the primary condition in which therapy can proceed. The group is put in a subordinate or supplementary position; in the dyadic relationship *real* therapy takes place.
Combined therapists view the group mechanistically as if additional patients

provide only quantitative dimensions, such as more or less transference, more or less acting out, more or less resistance, more or less psychodynamic material, more or less catalysis, and sometimes go so far as to deny the existence of qualitative differences in the group. By contrast, the individual situation is evaluated in terms of emphasizing its superior quality. If the combined therapist concedes that the group has some therapeutic quality, it generally remains vague and undefined.

Its Non-Discriminative Use

While we do not subscribe to the non-discriminative position that every patient needs combined treatment or to the equally rigid view that no patient should ever be seen in parallel individual therapy, the contention for combined therapy has generally been so overestimated, that we are inclined to show how the exclusive application of combined therapy limits the effectiveness of group therapy. At the same time we would like to make clear that we believe there are specific indications for individual hours in selected instances and in certain periods of treatment.

We would ask the combined therapist, What are you really combining, for what reasons, and with what objectives? And what are the pitfalls of any of these combinations? For individual sessions may at times be used to resist group participation. Or the group may be misused in order not to relate to the therapist. Or the patient may exhibit constructive behavior at group meetings and destructive behavior at individual sessions, and the reverse. Or there may be a tendency to avoid reporting in group meetings what has transpired in individual sessions. Or the anxiety of the therapist with regard to the presumed dangers of peer interaction may lead the group into disintegration.

If the analyst overestimates the therapeutic importance of the private hour, patients soon begin to devaluate the significance and relevance of group meetings. If the therapist views the individual sessions as less fruitful, repetitious, monotonous or boring, patients before long look to group meetings for help. But each climate has a special, a unique importance. The private interview is meaningful for certain patients under certain conditions. The regular group meeting is essential for all patients in group therapy, under particular conditions. The alternate session, the group meeting without the therapist is vital for some patients at particular times in the course of treatment.

Preference for the Individual Setting

A survey of the writings by combined therapists indicates their general preference for the individual session. A variety of reasons is offered ranging from a sincere conviction about what the individual or group session inhibits and facilitates to an honest confession of personal need.

Lipshutz[65] remarks, "only when it (the individual session) is used continuously and side by side with group therapy, does it enable the therapist to observe the dynamics of each patient in the group from close range . . . A large number of group patients fail to present certain material in the group; others are incapable of taking part in group discussions; and still others, for long periods of time, present relevant, but comparatively insignificant material." We find such patients to be in the minority, and it is just as common for patients to delete relevant material in individual sessions and save their self exposure for the group. So too, there are many who remain relatively noncommunicative in private interviews but are more significantly participant with their peers.

When Lipshutz says, "in group setting . . . the possibility of efficient management is reduced in proportion to the number of patients present," we are naturally led to inquire, why do group therapy at all? When he remarks that his "more immediate goal in persuading (a particular) patient to join the group, was to divert her from the person of the therapist in the transference climate which was created in the individual setting," we are inclined to ask, why was the patient encouraged by private interviews into regression in the first place if afterwards she had to be diverted from this cultivation of pathology? When he notes further that "after a short time of group therapy, (she) . . . made this transfer to a female patient in the group," may we not ask, is this not the common experience in group therapy that patients make similar transferences to one another which are in most respects counterparts of projections on the leader? There is, therefore, little indication for extracting them from the group to cultivate these distortions in private.

Finally, Lipshutz says that "for the practicing group therapist, the individual session will always be welcome, if only to relax for a while behind the reclining patient. Using Grotjahn's analogy of the mirror, I am certain that we would prefer to be the single mirror behind the patient, than to be working in front of a gallery of mirrors which are curved and focused upon our countertransference feelings." Here the individual session is justified as giving the therapist an opportunity to relax. It seems to us that the therapist's need for repose has to be discounted in the treatment situation. If the therapist is more comfortable with one patient than with a gallery of them, he ought to do individual treatment. If the therapist feels a number of patients will more readily focus on and elicit his countertransferences, obviously he will prefer the safety of seclusion with one patient. But are any of these considerations genuine indications of patient needs for combined therapy?

Klapman[60] states that "the antagonist of narcissism obviously is object-love, love of others. The group is the implacable enemy of narcissism." In light of this observation, the therapist's insistence on the essentiality of the dyadic relationship in the course of group therapy, may, in some instances, be a competition in narcissism. In contrast to the opinion of other combined therapists, Klapman holds that "there is reason for believing that group psychotherapy is a fairly effective way of dealing with the transference neurosis, as well as the transference itself."

Rosow and Kaplan[91] report an experience in combined treatment with the male therapist conducting group meetings and the female therapist seeing each patient individually, the result being that "the tempo and depth of therapy became accelerated . . ." They hold that routine "individual interviews are indispensable because they enable the working through of individualized repetitive behavior patterns, specific personality strivings, and special reality problems. Similarly, dream material is more effectively used in individual sessions because of its specific personal nature." By contrast, in the group setting we find patients' associations invaluable with regard to identifying the individual's repetitive behavior, clarifying the latent significance of dreams and pointing the way to more constructive alternatives.

Bieber[13] contends that the therapist cannot pursue an exploratory and therapeutic line in the group, because there are too many interruptions, too many wills at cross-purposes. Our experience in groups is that the analyst can still follow a trend and work through in the group itself despite interruptions. Besides, there is discontinuity in individual treatment too, and we would say an essential discontinuity that itself serves a constructive end. Inhibitions of continuous unconscious production are a necessary part of therapy if treatment is to be effective. We find that these interruptions of associative streams are in themselves meaningful both to the patient who is turned aside and to his obstructor and that blocked and blocker derive more from an exploration of their interaction while in the group than in isolation.

Many combined therapists prefer the individual session and this position reflects ambivalence, anxiety and conflict about the use and value of the group. We would urge the combined therapist to make explicit why he uses the group, what specific values it has in his work aside from such nebulous objectives as "cross-fertilization," "double-exposure," "additive" and "catalytic" effects.

The Group as Adjunctive or Preparatory

Many combined therapists regard the group experience as a mere preparation for therapy which goes on in individual sessions. The group is simply an adjunct to individual treatment. They utilize the group to break impasses and to get other help for individual therapy.

Lucas[69] describes how the treatment of young children in a group was a valuable *supplement* to individual treatment. Individual treatment served "as a medium where the child could bring out the reactions stimulated by the group. Such reactions could be worked with when the children needed more intensive help than was possible in the group situation . . . The group served as a catalytic agent in individual therapy . . . Group treatment supplementing individual treatment could accelerate treatment progress." There is, however, the conclusion, "On the basis of proper selection, group treatment might even meet some of the needs of some of these younger children without involving the use of individual treatment."

Klapman[59] states that, "as catalyst . . . group therapy will be found efficacious in speeding the dissolution of resistances. When in individual interview the patient ceases to produce any material, 'shuttling' him into a group session may not only help in overcoming resistance, but even be of diagnostic importance."

Dreikurs[20] has reported that in 1929 he discovered that treating patients in groups yielded therapeutic benefits not afforded by individual psychotherapy alone, and that since that time he has employed group therapy as an adjunct to individual treatment.

Wilder[132] remarks, "The patient was instructed that group sessions will be a minor adjuvant only to individual analysis . . ." No wonder that one of his patients, "extremely frustrated in his interpersonal relations" in a group that met as infrequently as once or twice a month, expressed his protest in the remark, "Why, this is no group at all; this is nothing!" We are struck by the caution with which Wilder allowed the group to meet. Even he hints at this in the comment, "Only time can tell whether a more aggressive and courageous use (of the group) might not yield even better results . . . The results in this group were impressive (but) I have not yet decided whether to give in to the frequent desire of the patients for more group sessions."

Wolberg[134] describes group therapy as an adjunctive aid in psychotherapy. In combined treatment, he states, "the therapist is able to deal, at an individual session, with the manifold resistances and responses to the group which the patient is unable or unwilling to bring up in the group setting. Greater exploration of vital patterns is also possible during the alternate individual sessions. For these reasons, it is likely that the goals reached in combined therapy are more extensive than in group therapy alone." In citing evidence for the value of combined therapy, he employs the comments of patients who received such treatment. It is to be noted that each patient's remarks certify to the usefulness of his group experience with no reference to the efficacy of private interviews.

Morse, Gessay and Karpe[78] report "that group therapy can be used profitably as a technique for the reduction of resistance to individual therapy. . . ."

Lipschutz[64] presents no arguments to convey the impression that the group is adjunctive. He demonstrates rather the auxiliary role of individual sessions. When he describes a "male patient who could freely identify himself with the analyst in the group, but returned to his passive, dependent status during the individual sessions," Lipshutz is presenting evidence of the pathologically regressive movement in private interviews and the more constructive value of group sessions.

Abrahams[1] and others stress the primacy of the individual setting by using the group to evoke transferences and to develop pathology which is then analyzed in private consultations. Here the group is merely a preparation for the individual session and non-discriminately viewed as a medium to excite disorder. The group experience becomes an incubationary antecedent to therapy. We see the treatment of the patient taking place in the group setting, and in instances where transference ties to the therapist are intense, individual sessions may become potential media for deepening pathology.

There are contradictions among combined therapists regarding the meaning, use and value of the experience in the group. We have long since conceded the value of individual analysis as well as the therapeutic potential of appropriate individual sessions. Combined therapists continue to resist therapeutic endeavors in the group setting.

The conflict about accepting the analytic usefulness of group sessions cannot be resolved by clichés such as "catalytic," "socializing" or "adjunctive." When therapists describe psychoanalysis in groups as adjunctive, we would ask, adjunctive to what? Doing psychoanalysis is not doing psychotherapy adjunctively, and we do psychoanalysis in groups. Implicit in the word adjunctive is the attitude that patients cannot be treated in a group setting and that what happens there is adjunctive to therapy which goes on only in the individual session. If the group experience is seen as merely adjunctive, it is necessary that therapists define what its objectives are, what functions it serves, and why they employ the group at all.

Authoritative Control and Limited Peer Interaction

If the group is seen as playing a background Greek chorus to the major drama going on in individual sessions, this approach abuses the meaning of the group setting. Such therapist-centered treatment rejects peer interaction and is contemptuous of peer potential. Transactions among group members are reduced in the rationalization of the therapist's omnipotence. Peer interaction is kept at a minimum because it tends to be perceived by the therapist as primarily pathologic. In some instances, the peer is allowed to participate only to the extent that he confirms the therapist's judgment.

We do not mean to imply that combined therapy does not offer the patient an intensive therapeutic experience. Because combined therapists limit therapeutic activity in the group setting they do not make available to the patient the kinds of communication and interaction that characterize intensive group psychotherapy. The routine introduction of individual hours drastically changes the climate of group sessions, so that peer interaction is diminished and authoritative control reinforced. It is even questionable whether under these circumstances any therapy goes on in the group setting. Perhaps a more appropriate phrase to characterize such treatment would be individual therapy with some group experience, rather than combined therapy. In fact, Sager[92] approaches the problem from the position: can group therapy harm the individual analytic experience?

Hill and Armitage[50] state that "familiarity with each patient is best obtained in their individual analyses . . . (that) silences based on stubborn, hostile motives were better handled in private hours." But they note too that the group "members settled down to a period marked by a multitude of topics frequently reflecting their private hours." Is this therapy then not too leader-centered? Might not the patients, permitted more to interact in the group setting rather than to be focused on the therapist, reveal facets of *their* inter-relatedness not so exclusively determined by and limited to the leader?

Feldman[26] has demonstrated in a social group therapy setting that for certain passive dependent patients, unless they interact, unless there is a material experience with regard to peers, no therapy can take place. And there is no therapy with an analyst in individual or group therapy unless there is experience with peers.[146] Social group therapy provides a structured alternate session, a forced interactional experience before such patients can make progress in treatment. For the very passive, inactive, schizoid, character-disordered patient, this arrangement has proved valuable; but these patients may also be reached by psychoanalysis in groups. The main point, however, is the prior necessity for an intensive interactive experience on the horizontal level.[109]

The non-discriminative use of combined therapy tends to make treatment too leader-centered. While no therapy is possible without a therapist,[146, 149] the relegation of group sessions to a minor role in combined treatment forces patients to minimize their reparative resources with one another and to turn too exclusively for help toward the authority figure.

We find that there is a correspondence between the readiness to do combined therapy and the reluctance to permit patients to meet without the therapist.[149] Such a trend represents a movement toward activity which clusters around the therapist and away from peer interaction. This attitude seems motivated largely by the therapist's concern that patients—unless they are under fairly constant supervision—are likely to act only pathologically and consequently need authoritative surveillance. As a result the therapist hovers so over his brood of projectively helpless and aggressive patients that they are all herded into what is essentially individual therapy, infantilized and prevented from exercising their own resources in mutual give and take.

The emphasis on peer relatedness and interaction in regular and alternate sessions is a movement toward equality and away from the pathologically bound intensity of parental transference that may be cultivated by individual hours. The private hour can become a movement toward excessive dependency and regression to the suckling stage. Such a transaction may be necessary in some degree, but if therapy is to go on, seclusion with the parental surrogate should be offered in lessening proportions. Otherwise it fosters a hierarchic, dependent relationship. The combined therapist's insistence on the necessity for the authority-centered relationship may demand repression and regression. The combined therapist increases resistance by rejecting peer interaction. There is less likelihood of entrenching transferences to the therapist in the group setting, and such an outcome is desirable. There is no implication here that transference neurosis does not occur in the group setting. Peer interaction tends also to lessen the possibility of irrational authoritarianism on the part of the therapist.[109]

Surely the combined therapist is a well meaning individual with an open mind who feels the group is in some way helpful. But even with good will, combined therapy becomes primarily a matter of working individually with patients in isolation from their fellows without fully exploiting the provocative and reparative reactions of patient to patient. The group method to be truly effective requires a more active invitation to the peers to participate.

Merry[74] states, "In considering the relative values of the group and individual therapies . . . , it is my contention that the most important single factor to be taken into account is the transference situation, created at an individual level." That is, private interviews are used to induce regression. But our experience is that the development of transference to authority figures is not limited by the group except in unusual instances and may in the group situation even be intensified. Merry says further, "There is very often a clear fluctuation in the symptomatology, corresponding inversely with the amount of attention exhibited by the doctor . . . The threat of rejection by the doctor will precipitate a collapse . . . As one patient put it . . . 'I have got you fixed inside me. Every time I think of you I get a little bit of strength. If I feel down, I think of you and that bucks me up.' "

Here individual sessions are used to cultivate a passive dependency, while there is no working through of problems with authority. No wonder then that with such seduction neurotically to misuse the one-to-one relationship, "Most of the patients cling to the belief that treatment only occurs at individual interviews with the doctor. . ." But Merry admits to limited goals when he says, "It may be argued that the concept of treatment described here may result in excessive dependence on the part of the patient. We must face up to the fact that the neurotic *is* a dependent person and that we here do not fundamentally change him . . ." We see these limited objectives and results as largely the consequence of providing the patient with extensive overprotection by the therapist in the individual situation.

Baehr[7] presents an investigation "designed to test the hypothesis that . . . treating patients by a combination of group and individual psychotherapy is more effective than treating them by one method alone." But, "The criterion of therapeutic effectiveness employed . . . is *discontentment.*" Using this doubtful criterion, Baehr finds that "the methods rank with respect to therapeutic effectiveness as follows: group-plus-individual therapy, individual therapy alone, and group therapy alone (the least effective)." Since when is it possible to use a criterion like discontentment alone as a measure of the therapeutic effectiveness of any treatment? The most regressed schizophrenic reduced to passivity in the psychologic equivalent of continuous sucking at the mother's breast may appear very contented as long as his dependency is not interfered with and becomes very discontented with attempts to sponsor his independence. And have we not all encountered pathologic contentment with the neurotic and psychotic *status quo*? Is it also not part of good health in our search for new ways and means to develop ourselves and explore and change our environment to be discontented in some measure with what we are and what we know?

Fried[36] states the responses of the hostile withdrawn patient "need not be admitted and examined on the spot (that is, in the group); this can be postponed for subsequent individual sessions." Why this examination has to be postponed for study and working through in individual sessions is not made clear. Perhaps an explanation is forthcoming when she says that "in group treatment premature attacks by group members on the patients' projections are unavoidable. The therapist, aware that hostility should be worked through before projections are attacked, is nevertheless not able to convey his own sense of timing to group members. The latter are aroused over the distortions of their hostile, withdrawn, paranoid colleague and attempt to prove how irrational they are. This fact serves to emphasize how important it is in such cases to have a chance through parallel individual treatment to help the patient acknowledge and work through his hostility."

Our experience has been that if patients' attacks on one another's projections are premature, the therapist's explanation of the wisdom and necessity to allow for the particular development of emergent regression only too often leads to as highly a pathologic group culture as any therapist may require.[146] In general we take a different view of the patients' objections to one another's irrationality. We rather see it not as necessarily premature but as a wholesome demand to recognize inappropriate responses and to seek more constructive alternatives. Furthermore, we cannot make the fine distinction Fried does between irrational hostility and projection. Also, patients do not have to acquire the therapist's refined sense of timing to be useful to one another. Either their observations are rejected because they come from peers or they are more seriously considered for the same reason. In any case, they do not always carry the same quality as when offered by the leader.[109]

Fried goes on to say that "the dependent patient also resists release of aggressive feelings steadfastly in individual treatment. In this instance the reason is that he does not wish to endanger his dependency on the therapist." But it would seem to us that if the aim is to release aggressive feelings which the patient dares not do in fear of losing the therapist, why cultivate his neurotic dependency further by providing him with regular individual hours? Fried states, "it is necessary that in cases of deep-rooted dependency needs the infantile excessive oral drives be partially gratified if they are to be eventually reduced." One question is the wisdom or necessity of gratifying the patient's regressive needs at all at any time. Another question is whether such a problem cannot for such a patient be resolved by providing individual sessions at indicated intervals rather than as regular fare. When Fried says that "the negative and critical responses of group members to the patient's attempts to lean, in the face of frustration and danger, on protection by a supposedly powerful figure act as a reality pressure," she is remarking on the good judgment of group members realistically critical and opposed to parallel individual sessions which entrench dependency.

It is important at this point to add a note that anxiety and neurotic dependency are dynamically related. In the group, dependency problems and the anxiety underlying them can be worked through not only with the therapist but also with peers; they represent parental as well as sibling transference objects.

Bach[5] contends, "no one has been able to provide convincing proof of the theory that the therapy group, as we know it today, is a self-sufficient medium for intensive psychotherapy." Whereas Powdermaker and Frank[86] working in hospitals and clinics, report that for many patients group psychotherapy without private consultations has proved to be very successful, Bach finds in his private practice, "new patients expect individual treatment and demand it." It would seem to us that if *clinic* patients do so well in treatment confined to the group, therapists must begin asking themselves what motivations lead them and their patients to request regular individual interviews in private practice. Such a question seems especially pertinent in the face of Bach's admission "that neither Powdermaker and Frank nor this writer are able to distinguish, in terms of either speed or depth of therapeutic movement, between those patients who seek individual consultations less often, or not at all."

Bach states further that "group members undergoing concomitant intensive individual therapy fail to keep pace with most other members' change from ego-centered to other-centered communications." He finds that "the patient's tendency in the individual sessions is to use them as an opportunity to involve the therapist neurotically (transference) or to bathe in the fantasy experience of complete acceptance, or to flee into the past." In his technique, then, "these three tendencies are interpreted as resistance to looking at some repressed element in the patient's interpersonal experience in the group."

Despite these negative developments in private consultation, Bach believes that " 'group-centered' individual sessions are extremely helpful to the patient. They bring into focus new perceptions and insights gained in the group. By looking at the group participation from the relatively safe vista of the individual session, the patient gains that amount of distance which experiments in perception have proved to be a necessary condition for new problem solving. Furthermore, focusing his interest in the here-and-now group behavior strengthens the patient's feeling of cohesiveness with the group. Identification with the therapist's evaluation of the importance of the group as a major operating ground for therapy also reinforces the patient's involvement in the group . . . By assuming a group-centered attitude during the individual sessions, the therapist can prevent the drainage effect of parallel individual treatment."

It seems to us that the therapist can just as easily and with more benefit to all the members bring into focus new perceptions and insights as they develop in the group setting. As to the necessity for distance, the therapist may just as planfully return to a particular dynamic at a subsequent group meeting as at a later private one. While Bach's emphasis on the here-and-now is valuable, we would regard such persistent attention to current behavior as non-discriminative unless it included equal regard for the past and future. Furthermore, if the analyst conceives of the group as the major operating ground for therapy, why introduce regular individual sessions to convince the patient instead of employing the group setting itself for these demonstrations? Finally, if private interviews produce potential drainage effects, their use to establish their misuse would indicate the wisdom of suggesting only occasional rather than regular individual sessions.

We, too, are in favor of the occasional appropriate and realistically necessary individual session. We, too, believe such individual sessions must be group-centered and that the patient should be encouraged in due course to tell the group the transaction of the individual meeting. But we do not concur in the opinion that the group offers a homogenized experience in the here-and-now and the individual session a homogenized experience in the there-and-then.

Bach goes on to say that "the group-centered individual session is the most effective procedure for the release of group-generated tension. When, for practical, economic, or for transference reasons patients cannot make auxiliary use of individual consultations, it can be observed that the group participation of such patients is more defensive, less self-perceptive, more other oriented, more general and less personal." We have yet to understand why the group itself cannot be the forum in which to release group-generated tension. And our experience has been that if the therapist presses for such adaptation the patient is generally responsive to leadership within the group. When Bach refers to economic reasons, among others, as factors which interfere with the use of private sessions, we are led to wonder how often their availability is determined by the patient's economic status rather than by his genuine need, particularly when we know that clinic patients do so remarkably well without the therapist alone.[86] As to the other resistances enumerated by Bach, we have yet to find that these cannot, in general, be dealt with in the group session.

Bach states that "the negative effects of 'parallel treatment' are recognized by most group therapists, who follow Slavson's recommendation that the individual and the group therapist should be the same." Our experience is that where the individual therapist has a positive attitude toward group therapy, where the group therapist shares such feelings about the value of individual therapy, and where the therapists consult together occasionally, the patient usually can profit from having two different therapists. But when the individual therapist is critical of group practices, or vice versa, in rivalry with each other or possessive about the patient, serious problems in treatment follow. Even when the collaboration of two therapists is at its best, the problems arising out of combined therapy as discussed here, may still be unresolved.

Bach apparently finds himself in a contradictory position with regard to his views on combined therapy, for he concludes his remarks on the subject by saying, "the factor of the therapist's centricity . . . suggests a policy of restricting individual contacts to a minimum. Experience has shown that individual consultations increase dependency on the therapist and that they may encourage neurotic contact operations involving the therapist. Individual contact may have the effect of overemphasizing the centrality of the therapist's position in the group. This would affect the development of a patient-centered group culture adversely."

Fromm[38] points out some of the dangers in a pathologic one-to-one relationship against which both the patient and the therapist must guard themselves. He discusses the constructive roles of parents which have considerable bearing on the therapist's readiness to allow the patient a fuller group life as against overprotective exclusion with the authority figure. "In the ideal case, mother's love does not try to prevent the child from growing up, does not try to put a premium on helplessness. Mother should have faith in life, hence not be overanxious, and thus not infect the child with her anxiety. Part of her life should be the wish that the child should become independent and eventually separate from her. Father's love should be guided by principles and expectations; it should be patient and tolerant, rather than threatening and authoritarian. It should give the growing child an increasing sense of competence and eventually permit him to become his own authority and to dispense with that of the father."

A period of dependence on the projected parent may occasionally be necessary. But for therapy to be effective, the current need is to learn to interact, to grow up in the presence of authorities and peers. We say to the patient that he can surely depend on us as occasion arises for support. But we can assure him as well of the value of the group as a testing ground in which his peers can also be reasonable authorities without his always requiring the confirmation of the therapist. The combined therapist says in effect, I will let you get together with your peers, but not too much.[23]

The group therapist who sees all his patients regularly in individual hours has too little conviction with regard to the therapeutic efficacy of the group method. He may not consult privately with the patient according to a real need for an individual session but to bind the patient to him more closely. Such a procedure may be justified as the necessity to cultivate regressive transference as a prelude to working it through, but this requirement is unusual. For as resistances are removed in the group, even pre-oedipal and nonverbal distortions come to the fore and can, in most instances, be resolved in the group. Some therapists extract the patient from the group to intensify transference;[129] this is frequently the manifest rationalization for latent countertransference.

Therapist's Motivations

We have explored some of the motivations for doing combined therapy. For one man, it turns out that his groups are made up exclusively of women, so that they may compete for him. His criterion of selection is womanhood and positive transference compelling a scramble for the father. Another therapist prescribes individual sessions for attractive women. For the one, placement in the group is determined by an affection for the leader and a readiness to fight for him; for the other, placement in private consultation is determined by the therapist's positive countertransference.

Green[45] states, "When the new member of the group realizes that the physician spends considerable time with certain patients in an effort to help them, he begins to hope that one day he too will have private interviews. During these interviews he will have the psychiatrist all to himself and will not have to share him with others as he does during the group therapy sessions. This goal becomes something that most patients begin striving for . . ."

Here individual sessions and the therapist are dangled before the patients like precious prizes to be longed and competed for. But, Green says, "The psychiatrist must not promise anything to the patient. The latter's desire to spend more time with the physician, and the subconscious wishes which accompany this desire, originate within the patient." Green has conceived of the therapist as such a choice object of the patient's consuming desire that we wonder if this passion does not in some instances rather originate within the therapist. When he says, "This turning toward the therapist often marks the first step on the road to improvement and, perhaps, recovery," we are rather inclined to explore this movement within the group itself for its regressive content and possible countertransferential tendencies in the therapist.

A colleague, questioned as to what criteria he used for placing patients in combined therapy, admitted that those patients he liked he invited to join him in private hours, and those he disliked he limited to group therapy alone. Although such motivation for combined therapy is rare, other examples give the impression that countertransference problems, like overprotection and possesiveness with regard to patients, may be factors that motivate the analyst and lead to rationalizations as to the necessity for individual hours.

Another therapist conceded that he put patients into groups because he felt he could give them so little in individual treatment. One therapist admitted to placing patients in groups because he felt hopeless about his patients, about their ability to improve and his ability to be a force toward constructive change. Here combined therapy was employed because individual hours did not seem adequate to effect therapeutic movement, and the group experience was added to facilitate positive development. Most combined therapists, however, contend that group therapy alone is an inadequate therapeutic medium and, therefore, introduce individual sessions to make treatment more effective.

On occasion the invitation to a patient to join the therapist in private sessions is surely motivated by a countertransference problem. An example came to our attention recently while supervising a group therapist who reported that an attractive female patient in a group had developed such a strong positive transference to him, that he had advised her to avail herself of individual hours in order to resolve the regressive impasse. Before long it became apparent that the analyst's underlying motivation in inviting her to join him in private sessions was based on his own seductive interest in her. Other examples can be cited to illustrate the tendency on the therapist's part to use individual hours to act out (or act in) rather than to work through.

Pathology Combined with Pathology

There is the therapist who believes that the center of therapy is pathology, that what needs to be combined is the analyst's and the patient's pathology or patient-to-patient disorder. Here the function of the therapist is to intensify morbidity[129, 146] and he, too, may invite the patient into individual sessions, the better to combine, that is, to act out, their respective disorders.

Or a therapist may find the group a more facile medium to cultivate multilateral fragmentation. Such a form of therapy is also leader-centered. But here the authoritarianism is masked, for it suggests that the therapist has no status and foregoes leadership, that by assuming the position of patient, both he and the real patient get well. Such a therapist is commonly a vigorous advocate of the alternate meeting, because no expert is present there. Such a therapist commonly becomes discontented with individual treatment, the pathology elicited in the one-to-one relationship being too limited. The group fascinates him because it is a better arena, as he uses it, for stimulating morbid "contagion." Such a therapist maintains an autocratic leadership toward disorder and chaos by denying his wholesome and constructive authority. He presents himself to the group as helpless and like the parent who does this with the child, reverses roles. The therapist becomes the patient in order to act out his pathology and to seek what he calls therapy for himself from the group.[109, 129, 146, 147]

We have described some of the motivations of some combined therapists who see too little positive potential in peers or who regard them primarily as a source of pathology. But the status-denying therapist values the peers as a wellspring of disturbance. For him, combined treatment merely gives the participants more and varied opportunity to cultivate their illness. Whereas combined therapy is more generally used to control both pathologic and healthy potentials of patients, the status-denying therapist uses combined therapy to stimulate pathology and limit remedial resources. In all these distortions of group therapy there is a misconception of the value of the therapist as well as of the peers, an unresolved problem with regard to authority and peer relations.[109]

Choice of Field

Still another factor contributes to the patient's and the analyst's conviction that parallel individual hours are always necessary. It is the tendency on the part of the therapist to withhold, in general, his interpretations and interaction in the group or, if he does participate, to make generalizations that lack specificity for each patient and to save his therapeutic endeavors for individual hours. If the therapist does little analysis during group sessions and more in private hours, patients react with a correspondingly diminished activity during group meetings and a parallel increased participation in individual sessions.

The therapist's view of patients in group sessions as a homogeneous mass, his tendency to anthropomorphize the group while he works with it,[109] and his opposite inclination to see the individual patient with his specific needs in private sessions are potent forces in immobilizing constructive interaction and intercommunication at group meetings.

Knowing that they have access to the therapist after the group meeting, patients save their significant or strong or confusing reactions for the hour with the analyst alone, who assures them in so organizing his treatment plan of the greater value of time spent with him rather than with the group. The membership, led to believe that they can profit most from time with the therapist, may withhold dreams, fantasies, interaction and mutual exploration in the group and turn more and more to the analyst for help. The result is that the combined therapist is convinced before long of his good judgment.

Patients are generally responsive to the open or latent convictions of the therapist. He is the expert and if he believes that private consultations with him are the central medium for therapy, they cannot easily, in inexperience, gainsay his prescription. On the other hand, if the analyst is convinced that group sessions are the core of therapy, applies himself actively to executing his therapeutic role during group meetings and looks with some hesitation on routine consultations with him alone, patients try and succeed in the main in working through their problems within the group itself. What is required is simply that we allow patients to interact freely at group sessions and for the therapist to apply there all his therapeutic skills if he is to discover the extent to which intensive psychoanalytic progress can be made in the group itself.

The indiscriminate use of individual sessions may as often lead to their abuse in resistance as to therapy. Not infrequently the patient, knowing that he has regular and private access to the therapist, will fail to express in the group his reactions to other members and prefer to save them for exposure to the leader alone. Such a procedure leads to the cultivation of indirect and devious trends rather than to working through to more straightforward responsiveness. Moreover, such tactics prevent the participants from discovering and exploring one another's provocative roles. It inhibits reality testing and a detailed and active mutual investigation.

In summarizing the therapist's choice of field of operation, we recognize four possibilities which may be combined: routine group sessions, routine individual sessions, selected individual sessions, and alternate sessions. A fifth possibility which is purely theoretical so far as we know at this moment, is selected group sessions. Nine possible combinations of these four elements may be described.

1. Group sessions without individual or alternate sessions.

Such an arrangement provides group interaction before the authority figure but denies peer interaction without him, and denies the exploration of the exclusive one-to-one relationship with the therapist.

2. Group sessions without individual sessions but with alternate meetings.

This combination permits the fullest exploration of intra-group relations in the presence and in the absence of the therapist. But again the private relationship with the authority figure is excluded.

3. Group sessions with routine individual sessions and alternate meetings.

Such a clinical procedure is rare.[46] Although this combination would tend to have the limitations already described for combined therapy as we have defined it, the utilization of alternate meetings with the concomitant increase in peer transaction would tend to lessen the deleterious effects of the hierarchic vector. Therefore, if combined therapy with routine individual sessions is conducted, alternate sessions could be introduced as a safeguard.

4. Routine individual sessions without group or alternate meetings.

This is individual therapy and we have never taken a stand against the usefulness of psychoanalysis done in an individual setting. We have already indicated, however, some of the seemingly special benefits to be derived from a group experience. We wish to re-emphasize the consciously discriminative application of psychoanalysis in the individual and in the group setting.

5. Routine individual sessions with alternate but without regular group sessions.

Once again, we know of no such clinical method. Where the patients of an individual analyst happen to get together, it is generally regarded as acting out. The possibility of such a combination being organized as part of the therapeutic experience needs to be explored experimentally for its positive and negative implications.

6. Group sessions with selected individual hours but without the alternate meeting.

This arrangement provides the maximum utilization of the regular group session but limits peer interaction.

7. Alternate sessions without regular individual or group sessions.

In our experience only two such leaderless groups have sought therapy without a therapist, although the membership of both groups were all therapists. Neither of these groups was able to continue without a leader. The development of an exclusive pathologic sub-culture precluded therapeutic outcomes.

8. *Group sessions with routine individual sessions but without alternate sessions.*

This is combined therapy as commonly practiced, and the subject matter of this chapter.

9. *Group sessions, alternate meetings and selected individual consultations.*

This is our clinical procedure of choice which we identify as psychoanalysis in groups. It provides the optimal exploration of horizontal and vertical vectors and the maximal therapeutic usefulness of each procedural variation in the therapeutic fields of operation.[109]

Discrimination in Selecting Patients

It must be reported that a number of combined therapists have attempted to be discriminating in their assignment of patients. There is recognition of some patients' need for individual therapy and the need for individual sessions for some patients in group therapy. The validity of the criteria used is still to be determined.

As early as 1927, Burrow[17] raised some questions relevant to the problem of combined therapy. He said, "What the scientific inquirer is really interested to learn primarily, after all, are the advantages, if any, of the group method of analysis as compared with the restricted method that limits the analysis to conferences between physician and his individual patient. First it should be pointed out that the group method of analysis by no means excludes individual conferences between physician and patient. In point of fact every patient's analysis begins with such personal interviews, and he is at liberty to return to them as his need demands."

The patient "comes into group relationships which, while in no sense critical of his ingrowing habits of self accommodation, do not permit him to regress into the privacy of his own introversion . . . In our group procedure this condition of a patient's dependence upon his physician is from the outset precluded. We know very well that the essence of the neurosis is the mother–child relationship, that this is the neurotic patient's unconscious impasse, that fixation is his unremitting quest. But, in the group, the mother–child relationship is from the very beginning submitted to consensual observation and study, and no surrogate for this relationship such as obtains in the usual technique of analysis is permitted to creep in unconsciously and defeat the real purpose of a psychoanalysis. I do not mean for a moment that there is not in each patient the tendency toward such a fixation or transference in the group situation. It is constantly present. But under conditions of group association naturally there is not the opportunity favorable to its secret lodgement and entertainment as is the case in the private work involving months of solitary confinement with the individual analyst. What would be the individual transference in a private analysis becomes neutralized in the social participation of many individuals in their common analysis."

Ransberg[87] is discriminating in her selection of patients for combined treatment. She refers to "the need of some patients for individual psychotherapy." In contrast to Green's report with regard to the frantic competition for individual hours,[45] Ransberg says that after one patient was given private interviews only three additional men in two groups asked for them.

"One of these did not ask for individual help until after twelve months of group therapy. To another, who requested it, we denied it for some time for therapeutic reasons. The third benefitted little from individual therapy and he was asked to continue in the group. He has done much better in the group since that time. . . Out of nineteen men, individual therapy was given to eight for brief periods. The chief criterion for selection of these cases was inability to express basic problems . . . Of the four who were assigned, there seemed to be more gain through the group than through individual treatment in three cases."

Hallowitz[49] reports that "at the Jewish Board of Guardians more than seventy-five per cent of the group therapy caseload consists of children who receive activity group therapy exclusively; (that) this trend developed out of increased awareness of the therapeutic possibilities inherent in activity group therapy. . . ." Hallowitz is discriminating with regard to the use of particular treatment, whether combined or any other. He says, "only on the basis of a dynamic understanding of each child can one prescribe correct treatment. For one child it may be placement in a foster home or institution; for another, hospitalization; for a third, individual treatment; for a fourth, group therapy; and for a fifth, a combination of techniques. Activity group therapy . . . should . . . be used . . . on the basis of the need of the individual case."

Hulse[52] says he has "always considered each case separately and individually; only selected patients . . . are receiving additional individual psychotherapy for varied periods." In contrast to other group therapists, he reports an "increased tendency to act out in individual sessions" rather than in group meetings. He finds "that material which has been long withheld from the group could be brought up in the group after it had been 'tested' in an individual session." We find the opposite to be just as common, namely, material long withheld from the analyst may first be brought up in the alternate session. Apparently these divergent experiences depend on the variable dynamics of a given patient.

Hulse reports further that there is "strong intensification of transference phenomena in patients undergoing the combined treatment regime. . . . Patients who are treated exclusively in group psychotherapy are made aware by other patients of their lack of intensive transference neurosis. Often they are 'taken in' by the intensive transference manifestations of other members of the group who are experiencing the effects of combined therapy."

In psychoanalysis in groups there is generally no difficulty in eliciting the manifestations of transference. If individual hours are provided to intensify one-to-one pathology, we must indeed raise some question as to what end pathology is developed in the therapeutic process. If, as it might be claimed, pathology must first be revealed before it can be worked through, we could agree with such a necessity. But our clinical experience has been that projective distortions in sufficient variety and depth are provoked in group interaction to satisfy the most searching therapist devoted to ferreting out pathology.

We are dealing with a complicated problem in trying to evaluate the usefulness of combined therapy as against other treatment arrangements. There is a need in trying to come to definitive conclusions for more experimental groups in order to compare what kinds of therapy can facilitate cure for what kinds of patients and under what kinds of conditions. It is likely that we shall find individual treatment the method of choice with certain kinds of patients, group psychotherapy with others and combined therapy with still others. We may discover that for some individuals the alternate session does them a disservice, while for others the alternate meeting may be vital. Until more of the evidence is in we must make our clinical decisions on the basis of theory and practice developed up to now. We are dealing with a great number of variables: the way in which the therapeutic situation is structured, the tone established by the therapist's conscious and unconscious preference of operational field, the therapist's personality and the patient's diagnosis, among others.

We cannot compare a poor group therapist with a gifted individual analyst, or vice versa. Nor can we easily compare the results of therapeutic application when an analyst applies his highly developed skills in private hours but not during group sessions. And we have the same problem with the group therapist who exercises all his therapeutic talents at group meetings but is bored into passivity by private sessions. The achievement of results involves the therapist's values, his clinical judgment, his theoretical fitness and his willingness to seek confirmation from colleagues in psychoanalysis and other social sciences.

Perhaps we are beginning to have more experience and consequently we may become more selective with regard to the type of patients who need combined treatment. Fried[36, 37] has reported on the value of combined therapy for the hostile withdrawn and the hostile dependent and orally frustrated individuals with paranoid character trends. Papanek[82] recommends parallel treatment for the "paranoid schizophrenic and the very depressed patient, who may become self-destructive without strong support from the authority figure." In a subsequent paper,[83] Papanek recommends combined therapy for borderline cases but also then includes neurotics in general. Hill and Armitage[50] recommend combined therapy for patients with schizoid, obsessive-compulsive and aggressive defenses. Baruch and Miller[8] suggest that the allergic patient does well when one form of treatment supplements the other. Hulse[52] recommends concomitant therapy for depressed patients and in character disorders of long standing. We have found that very sado-masochistic patients may require associated individual therapy.

Although there have been attempts to be discriminative in selecting or eliminating particular patient categories for combined therapy, it may be noted that the varieties seem to include the entire gamut of diagnostic possibilities. Selection criteria are not explicit. The problem still remains for more adequate clinical experience and research.

Obscuring of Differences

There is a tendency among therapists of whatever orientation, and the combined therapist is no exception, to obscure differences.[147] There is the inclination, for example, to extinguish the differences between therapist and patient,[45] between fantasy and reality, between conscious and unconscious processes, between analysis and psychotherapy. In one current vogue,[129] the therapist and patient are alike, one patient equates with the next, the child equals the adult and health and pathology are the same.

Differences are obscured when we are preoccupied exclusively with the patient's pathology, with his affect or intellect, with his motility or inactivity, with his talking or nonverbal productions. Differences are obscured when we are singularly attentive only to the patient's past history or the present moment, or obsessed with his future.

Some group therapists foster an unhealthy uniformity by organizing homogeneous groups, whether on the basis of sex, age, diagnosis, symptom or other identifying characteristic. Some go so far in beclouding individual uniqueness that they project the group as one person, treating the group as if it were one patient, so that no wholesome differentiation has a chance to develop.

The group therapist who rejects the alternate session on the assumption that all his patients will exploit such a climate to act out homogeneously, denies differences among human beings. We believe the group therapist must distinguish between a social and a therapeutic group, between social dynamics and psychodynamics.

The tendency to do combined therapy can also be used to obscure differences, to conceal the particularity of a patient's behavior in one context and another, to confuse the special value of the individual, the regular and the alternate session. One group therapist eclipses distinctions by recommending individual treatment in the group setting and having patients relate to the therapist rather than to each other.[13]

The non-discriminative extraction of every patient from a group for private sessions obscures the uniqueness of each member, the difference of one patient from the next.[147] It would be more appropriate for the analyst to ask himself in each instance why he wishes to offer this or that member private interviews at this particular time. Will individual sessions facilitate treatment just now? Will they offer the patient something that cannot be accomplished within the group itself? Will they cater to the patient's resistance? But to invite all members at all times to avail themselves of private therapy is to disregard the personal differences and requirements of patients at different times.

Discussion and Conclusions

We have attempted to distinguish between psychoanalysis in groups and traditional combined therapy which regularly and indiscriminately offers parallel individual and group sessions. Surely the combined therapist is motivated by values, by the wish to overcome some of the limitations of individual treatment, and by the conviction that both group and individual experience are beneficial to the patient. But it seems that such an arrangement is not necessarily a group therapeutic experience in our sense. Certainly there is nothing wrong in providing the patient with the flavor of group transactions, but there is some question as to the accuracy or relevance of calling such a method therapy in a group setting. It might be more appropriate to refer to it as individual therapy with a group experience, but not combined therapy. A truly combined treatment would make a more thoroughgoing use of patient interaction in the group, and a more selective and discriminating utilization of individual sessions only when indicated. Combined therapy which non-discriminately runs parallel private and group hours is not necessarily either good individual or good group therapy.

Some less well motivated combined therapists have turned to the method as a way of getting in on the current vogue for group psychotherapy, using the group approach because it is *à la mode*. With the increasing popularity and demand for group therapy a large number of therapists trained exclusively to administer individual treatment and untrained in group therapy have nevertheless undertaken the clinical practice of treating patients in groups. They have gotten on the bandwagon of group psychotherapy, with no real conviction, special training or experience with regard to the techniques or effectiveness of the group method.

We are recommending psychoanalysis in groups rather than combined therapy primarily for adults, not for children. It may be that individual play therapy is a necessary preparatory requirement for children. Some children, adolescents, acting out neurotics and psychotics require a degree of supervisory control, but this is true in individual as well as group treatment. Individual direction can be exercised with the patient in the course of his group experience often just as effectively as in individual sessions.

A patient who cannot function without the constant support of the authority figure is likely too ill to live outside a hospital. As an in-patient he is not available for out-patient therapy. As long as he is ambulatory and able to participate in life experiences, he is likely to tolerate the conditions of psychoanalysis in groups. If the patient is so helpless and dependent as to require the psychologic equivalent of spoon feeding and diapering, he is no longer ambulatory, needs the exclusive support of the therapist and cannot avail himself of the group. But even here the analyst, in order not to infantilize the patient further, may before long have to take a trained, calculated risk by placing him in a group.

If the patient is so isolated from social interaction that he cannot join a group or participate in it, he is also frequently not available for individual psychotherapy. In some instances the patient needs the one-to-one experience with the maternal surrogate before he can join and participate with his siblings and peers. On the other hand, there are patients who cannot avail themselves of the dyadic relationship until they have had a multiple freeing experience among their peers.

An occasional group therapist may invite the patient into individual sessions on the presumption that if the patient hides out in the group or evades a one-to-one relationship he needs the dyadic experience to resolve bilateral problems. But it is a misconception of therapy in a group to believe that one-to-one relationships do not operate or are lost in group interaction. Dyadic contacts are not obscured in the group. Such a view can be maintained only if we fall victim to the mystique of group dynamics or misconceive the nature of psychoanalysis in groups by attending only pathologic intrapsychic processes.

Too often the use of combined therapy is a subtle demonstration of the analyst's conviction that group members have no reparative powers and, if allowed to interact, they will become hopelessly enmeshed in transference and countertransference, and in acting out. On the one hand, there is a good deal of talk of the value inherent in group processes, of belonging-ness, of togetherness, of cohesiveness, of group dynamics. But underneath, the combined therapist is apparently doubtful, if not skeptical and cynical about remedial potentials in his assembled patients.

We are not opposed to combined therapy if its results with patients demonstrate its clinical usefulness. In our experience, however, combined therapists have not exploited the therapeutic value of the group setting and have, therefore, unwittingly deprived patients of the rich potentiality of the experience. We ask that the evidence be made available. If the combined therapist can show that he maximizes the resources of the individual patient by such special structuring of the therapeutic settings, we are receptive to such persuasion.

We are led finally to a position where we can accept combined therapy if we combine the positive capacities of the therapist with the positive capacities of patients, where we can see the validity of constructive work in each setting. If patients have problems with authorities and peers, as they all do, they cannot easily solve their difficulties by being limited only to vertical or horizontal relations. We would offer them an authority oriented experience in the individual hour, a peer experience in the alternate session, and the interaction of both at the regular meeting, the core of the group analytic process. We prefer to use the individual session only as necessary to work through special problems. And we are in no way opposed to this form of selective or discriminative combined therapy. But to demand that all patients under any and all circumstances, regardless of special need, submit regularly to private hours, seems to us to subvert certain inherently constructive potentials of psychoanalysis in groups. In our arrangement the regular meeting is projected as primarily familial, the individual hour is projected as parentally, more commonly maternally, supportive, and the alternate session becomes a preparation for termination, for life. The discriminate use of the private interview is directed toward the resolution of infantile needs. The regular meeting sponsors and works through unresolved problems of family life and growing up. The alternate session addresses itself to the development of fuller maturation and independent adulthood. The combined therapist says to the patient in effect, I am a good parent; I will let you play with other children, but only under my surveillance. We say, The only way you can grow up is to take increasingly independent steps apart from the parental surrogate; if you go back into the womb, into isolation, you cannot mature, for then your dependence is absolute.

10. Misuse of the Group

One current source of conflict among psychotherapists who work in groups is subsumed under the term *group dynamics*. Various conceptions and misconceptions have been called by that name, masking an anti-individual, antianalytic, and antiscientific trend when applied to psychotherapy. We shall attempt to explore this problem.

We are not rejecting groups or group dynamics. We are as interested in groups as the next person; one of us (Wolf) has been practicing psychoanalysis in groups for over twenty years. Let us, therefore, have this basic understanding: our mutual interest in improving therapeutic work in a group setting. We are not opposed to flexibility, to experimentation with new ideas and their incorporation into psychoanalytic therapy, if these ideas are constructive. We are not opposed to change. We are not opposed to group dynamics as a new developing social discipline, as a new phase of social psychology.

The Existence of Groups and Group Dynamics

As group therapists, we believe groups exist, are real. Let there be no confusion about this. The existence of groups can in no way be denied. Do individuals form groups, however, or do groups create the individual? What is their relation? Without the existence of individuals there can be no groups. To believe that we can have groups without individuals is a misconception. There are group dynamics as well as individual dynamics; social psychology as well as individual psychology; the interpersonal as well as the intrapsychic. Group structure, climate, contagion, trends, values, mores, and prejudices operate whenever and wherever individuals assemble. Moreover, group dynamics do have validity as a descriptive, phenomenologic

See ref. 112.

science concerning what goes on in group life. Group dynamics provide a useful body of knowledge enabling us to understand more richly the totality of human experience. But we are concerned here with how this knowledge is used by the psychotherapist.

Cartwright and Lippitt[18] say, "Groups exist; they are inevitable and ubiquitous; they mobilize powerful forces having profound effects upon individuals; these effects may be good or bad; and through a knowledge of group dynamics there lies the possibility of maximizing their good value" (p. 90). This may be true of groups in general. But the special problem of the individual in a group concerns itself with issues other than those attended by group dynamicists.

We use the term *group dynamicist* to refer to those social psychologists who are interested in describing behavior in and of groups. Group dynamicists are devoted to the study of the laws of movement or change in and of groups, group dynamics. In this view, the individual assumes anonymity and plays a subordinate role. We use the term *group psychodynamicist* to refer to those psychotherapists working in a group setting whose function and responsibility are limited to the treatment of the psychiatric patient, but who pursue group phenomena and neglect individual necessities. According to Scheidlinger,[97] Bion and Ezriel illustrate this position. As Foulkes[30] remarks, "If you treat the group, the individual will take care of himself." Group psychodynamicists assume the group has an individual psychology, called group mind, governed by group psychodynamics. In our sense, a *group dynamicist* is not a therapist. A *group psychodynamicist* is a therapist who seeks to apply group dynamics as therapy.

We may encourage the patient in the course of therapy to join a constructive group, but he needs more technical and expert help to achieve intrapsychic change. Additionally, we have a commitment to psychoanalysis. There may one day be better modes of therapy, but for the present we believe psychoanalysis is the preferred therapeutic orientation. If therapists want to experiment with group dynamics as a mode of treatment, they must define what they mean by group dynamics, and then demonstrate their usefulness in the therapy of the individual. This they have not yet done. If group psychodynamicists can demonstrate that by attending group themes they can achieve more therapeutic results, we should learn how they do it, and incorporate their techniques.

Some changes proposed by therapists may be in the direction of greater pathology;[146] other changes may be toward health. Therapists who plead for eclecticism are not necessarily doing bad therapy. But there are therapists who are so intrigued by group dynamics that they claim the group treats the patient. There is no clinical evidence for this assertion.

Group dynamics are not in themselves a mystique. It is the utilization of group dynamics as treatment that is the mystique. The use of group dynamics in psychoanalytic therapy is based upon an illusion, a distortion as to what is appropriate to select in psychotherapy. Moreno[75, 76] long before the current fad, made a significant contribution to group dynamics by his invention of sociometry and sociometric techniques, but he never once suggested that sociometry is psychotherapy.

One group psychotherapist[122] is so critical of the inappropriate application of group dynamic concepts to therapeutic groups as to state, "Not every compresence of persons is a *group*" (p. 132). We do not go so far. Surely, every group is a group. Some have more or less cohesion, unity, and other group dynamic dimensions. In his resistance to group dynamic formulations, Slavson[122] rejects even the concept of cooperation among patients. He says, "In a therapy group collaboration is not a virtue. At most times it is entirely absent, at others it is present to a minimal degree and is fleeting. Patients in groups do not collaborate . . . for any length of time. They *react* to each other and at times help one another, but are not engaged in a *common* (collaborative) project or process, and therefore no ties among them are, or should be, established" (p. 145). We are not so blinded in bias against group dynamics that we would reject a concept because it seems tainted through usage by group dynamicists. We rather think collaboration at times can be a virtue. Of course, patients establish neurotic and healthy ties which we analyze. This analytic procedure requires and gets collaboration, else therapy in a group would be impossible.

In the literature on group psychology, reference is made again and again to Freud's classic work[34] in which he utilized church and army to demonstrate the individual's transferential attachment to leading figures. On the basis of this one study, Freud's contribution to group psychology is often described as related only to large and irrational groups. This is a denial and misunderstanding of his over-all position. Freud's basic formulations stem from his recognition that human activity can best be understood within the context of the family as the primary group within which the human being is born and develops. It is erroneous to see him as attempting to understand individuals apart from groups. There is nothing in Freudian psychodynamics, psychopathology or psychotherapy, in theory or in practice, that does not relate specifically and concretely to the nature of the individual's interaction within the family as the prototypal group. Freud's therapy was not group dynamically oriented, although the individual's psychodynamic operations arose in the family. His pessimism and cynicism, however, led him to a rather non-discriminative position on the inevitable regression in group relations. He tended to see in groups largely the pathologic transferences and acting out. He neglected the provocation, the interpersonal or interactive aspects of behavior, as well as the healthy resources of group members.[110]

The Group is Not an Individual

The position has been advocated by some group therapists that the group *qua* group becomes a collective authority. It is said to establish its own values and mores. It is even said to establish its own more tolerant superego, so that the group acts as a collective but more flexible authority. We have not yet adequately understood the nature of group living and of social interaction. This social psychologic problem is as obscure in many places as individual psychologic problems. But to misapply individual psychologic concepts as explanatory for the group is to destroy the operational and phenomenologic characteristics of group activity. It is just as inappropriate to misapply social psychologic constructs as explanatory for the individual.

Group activity exists and is different from individual psychologic activity. A problem arises when we begin to anthropomorphize or to amalgamate the group into an individual and ascribe individual functions to it. The group is not an individual. It is an aggregate, a mass, a composite, a complexity of individual complexities. To use an analogy, a table is made up of atoms, but a table does not function like an atom even though it contains them. The atom is in constant flux and fluidity, whereas the table is not, even though it is constructed of nothing but atoms. The qualitative difference between atoms and table is obscured by an attempt to say the table itself is an atom. The table, too, has existence, but is a different kind of element of nature. To superimpose the laws of functioning of the atom onto a table simply because it is made up of atoms is to obscure and to mystify the nature of a table.

A group does have its own laws of movement. To attempt to make the group fit the laws governing the individual is to propagate a mystique. We would be equally mystical, if we rejected the existence and function of groups. We have begun elsewhere to define the parameters of groups. A parameter is a constant variable in the therapeutic experience in a group as distinguished from any other kind of setting.

Group Dynamic Terms

Group dynamics as psychotherapy is a mystique, because it jumps frames of reference. The social psychologists do not use such terms as group ego, group superego, group id, group mind, group soul, collective unconscious, collective conscious, group resistance, or group transference. The group psychodynamicists who use such terms are trying to reconcile disparate or discrete formulations. They are condensing ideas which are valid in the context of individual psychologic theory with perceptions of group processes appropriate to the group context. As a consequence, projective distortions, as in dreams, are the result. It is like taking a valid concept, for example, individual physiology, individual respiration or individual perspiration and calling it group physiology, group respiration or group perspiration. Everybody in a group may perspire, but is it group perspiration? Is there a group skin? A group liver? Or a group mind? Can there be an individual mind without an individual nervous system? Can there be a group mind without a group nervous system? If we are speaking figuratively, let us not act as if it were really so.

Some group therapists with little or no training in the field of group dynamics have become enamoured of its terminology and non-discriminatively use its technical terms, such as belongingness, togetherness, gregariousness, group loyalty, group contagion, group morale, and group cohesion. This is a problem, too, which also fosters the mystique. The group dynamicists mean one thing, the group psychodynamicists another. In addition, group psychodynamicists and other group therapists use the same terms differently. A *group dream,* for the therapist, is a patient's dream which includes group members. A *group dream* for the group psychodynamicist is everybody in the group having the same unconscious perception. There is similar confusion with group analysis or group therapy as contrasted with analysis or therapy in a group. We do not treat or analyze the group. We do not do group therapy or group analysis. We analyze individuals in their interaction in a group.

It is of some interest to examine the mystical and magical terms used by the group psychodynamicists. The writings of psychoanalytically oriented therapists with considerable clinical experience in group psychotherapy are especially curious. Frank[33] refers to "group cohesiveness, viewed as a property of the group in itself" (p. 54). Bach[6] writes of the "healing function of the group" (p. 64), "the group as a whole" (p. 65), "togetherness" (p. 67), and "group situational pressures" (p. 67). Slavson[122] observes "that there should be emotional contagions (in groups) is . . . inevitable" (p. 142). Elsewhere he[120] refers to "the tribal unconscious" (p. 18), a "group ego" and a "collective superego" (p. 21).

Foulkes and Anthony[130] speak of "treatment of the group-as-a-whole" (p. 21), and say that "the compelling currents of ancient tribal feeling" permeate "to the very core and . . . all subsequent interactions are inescapably embedded in this common matrix" (p. 216). They remark further, "The group is a more fundamental unit than the individual, which goes beyond the more usual emphasis on interpersonal relationships and reactions" (p. 216). They note that "every psychotherapeutic group develops in time a characteristic rhythm of its own . . . There is never any need to push or pull the group along. It moves at its own tempo governed by a constellation of forces, progressing and regressing, integrating and disrupting, ceaselessly opposing change and ceaselessly changing, never the same" (pp. 209 f.).

Liff[63] writes, "My thinking . . . hypothesizes that there is a group dynamic force which can be utilized to increase the effectiveness of the group analytic process. Of course, we have been aware of the various therapeutic contributions made by individual group members, but there has not been a complete awareness that this operates on a group dynamic level. A strict adherence to the classical analytic concepts would desensitize the group analyst to this force. For example, Freud did not explicitly mention the healing function found in therapeutic groups" (p. 8). And further, "The group can do more for its members than the therapist can do for his patients alone . . . The emphasis is not merely on the analysis of transference and resistance, but also on the mobilization of the group healing force" (pp. 9 f.).

For some group psychodynamicists, the group represents a new essence, an oversoul with suprahuman, divine, healing powers. So Bach[6] says, "The theragnostic process . . . depends on the freeing of the mutual aid and self-help tendency inherent in group life. The therapist, and the *patient as therapist*, form a healing group which together has the courage fully to explore *all* aspects of the self" (pp. 69 f.).

Slavson[122] rejects every application of group dynamic concepts to psychotherapy but conjures up a mystique of his own. He remarks, "The basic integrating force that assures the survival and achievement of ordinary groups is what has been described as *synergy*" (p. 133). He refers also to the group's "unitary synergic effort" (p. 145). He formulates, moreover, a concept of couple dynamics. "Psychoanalytic studies have thrown light upon and adequately described the relation of the child to each parent as individuals and to them *as a couple*. This fundamental formulation has made palpable to us some of the most baffling aspects of human personality" (p. 140). He subscribes to the view that a group has its own phases, ebb and flow, nodal and anti-nodal rhythm, mathematics. He writes, "The periods of nodal aspect of group behavior are characterized by mounting animation and communication . . . When the noise and chaotic atmosphere reach a high level of intensity, sudden quiet sets in. This alternation is observable in all free gatherings" (pp. 146 f.).

Group psychodynamicists are preoccupied with the dimensions of leadership, cohesion, climate, contagion, group role, common group tensions, the emergence of group themes and other collective responses in group psychotherapy. But we cannot accept the existence of a *group mind*, a *group mentality*, or a prenatally derived collective unconscious. Nor is the therapeutic group a microcosm of society. Neither can we discern a group id, group ego, or group superego. Such formulations are projections onto the group, the misapplication of constructs which are appropriate within the frame of reference of individual psychology.

Cohesion, a group dynamic term, deserves more than passing reference. Seashore[115] states, "Members of high cohesive groups exhibit less anxiety than members of low cohesive groups." But group cohesiveness does not necessarily determine the individual's response. Certain persons join cohesive or non-cohesive groups as a result of their individual history. The group dynamicist abandons the individual by disregarding personal motivation for joining a particular group. Frank[33] notes, "An important safeguard against a therapy group's becoming cohesively resistant is that it can develop cohesiveness only by incorporating the standards of the therapist" (p. 61). But this is authoritarian. Apparently, in order to belong, the patient must submit to the group. Now in the interests of cohesion, the group must submit to the therapist. No analytic therapy can take place in such a hierarchic setup, in which the patient becomes therapeutized by incorporating a piece of the leader.

Cohesion does not exist in the air. There is no one formulation that will hold for all cohesiveness. It follows from the particular family history of each person in the group. Cohesion is many-faceted. As with belonging, so too with cohesion; the motivations of each member are different and many levelled. Preoccupation in therapy with group identification, an aspect of cohesion, is another group dynamic which may limit the examination and working through of the specific nature of neurotic identification in each instance. An emphasis on identification may become a kind of imitative behavior leading to a denial of individuality in order to be accepted by the group. The therapist's over-valuation of identification in the interests of cohesion creates problems in conformance and submission. His overattention to any group dynamic process tends, in general, to divert him and his patients from exposing and resolving transference distortions.

The Relevance of Group Dynamics

It is appropriate to inquire whether group dynamics are relevant to the therapy of the individual in the group. There is as yet no clinical evidence demonstrating that attention to these phenomena is useful to the understanding and treatment of the patient in a group setting. How do group dynamics help achieve a healing objective?

While some group dynamicists have evidenced an interest in therapy, a good many reject the processes involved in treatment. As a result, their approach is largely philosophic and descriptive, with little or no relationship to psychotherapeutic practice. They have no theory of personality. They have no theory of psychopathology and health. They have no theory of the cause and cure of mental illness. The group psychodynamicists insist group cohesion, climate, and belonging have therapeutic usefulness for the individual patient. We however, cannot assume the relevance of a mystical parallel which holds that while in individual analysis we therapeutize the individual, in psychoanalysis in groups we treat the group. Scheidlinger[94] suggests that the group dynamicists are interested in group dynamics apart from the presence or absence of improvement in the patient, that is, apart from therapy of the individual. They are interested in how group forces operate, in the phenomenologic. They are not really interested in psychodynamics.

Any greater knowledge about individual or group activity in any kind of setting has value in advancing our understanding of human beings. The group dynamicist is in part attempting to work out a theoretic and philosophic view of the nature of man, of his gregariousness, of his operations as a group animal. We are for such explorations, not against them. But the literature indicates that changes taking place in the individual as a consequence of group dynamics are viewed as haphazard, chance phenomena, and not the outcome of therapy. On the other hand, changes to which therapy is directed are a consequence of consciously applied therapeutic activity and not of group dynamics. Changes take place in living; when human beings live together with other human beings there may be good and bad effects of such living; but this must not be confused with therapy. Although therapy is a living experience, it is not synonymous with life. It is an experience in which one learns how better to live, but living takes place outside of therapy.[117] Therapy is a very specialized kind of experience directed toward achieving realizable, consciously determined results in changing human behavior from more pathologic to less pathologic modes of operation and for this purpose, within this context, we are defining therapy. Group dynamics do not have these objectives; group dynamics are not dedicated toward the improvement of the psychiatric patient.

There are reparative experiences in life, in groups outside of therapy, as well as in one-to-one relations. There are reparative experiences in social groups, professional groups, work groups, occupational therapy, chess clubs, athletic clubs, social and political movements, and family groups. These may be health-promoting or health-destroying as in fascist groups, the psychotic family group, the delinquent gang, the Ku Klux Klan, or homosexual groups. There are democratic and autocratic groups, constructively or destructively permissive groups, constructively or destructively controlling groups, depending on what is being permitted or controlled. There are constructively and destructively cohesive groups. Our emphasis is that the changes brought about by these groupings sometimes called by group dynamicists, true or natural groups, have nothing to do with technical psychoanalytic therapy.

Some of the ideas derivative from group dynamics, like milieu therapy, work therapy, common project therapy, and identification therapy are attempts to rationalize a non-analytic approach in treatment. They are attempts to define a non-analytic activity of the group as therapy. If identification therapy is as described, namely, the patient's treatment through vicariously experiencing someone else's behavior, then there is no need for the patient to experience and understand for himself, to examine his anxiety, to resolve his conflicts, to struggle to work through his own problems. There is room for milieu or work therapy. But these are not analytic treatment which would make unconscious processes conscious. There is room for art therapy and music therapy, but these, too, are not insightful. There is room in treatment for a group experience, for group relations, for group interaction, for a dramatics club. But none of these is analytic therapy.

We are concerned also about the view of some group psychodynamicists that the patient *catches on* to the traditions of his particular group. This is the kind of group dynamics which has little therapeutic usefulness. This is not insightful. There is no exploration of the nature of the *catching on.* There is no evaluation of the traditions to see whether they are valuable or not, realistic or not, necessary to perpetuate or not. There is no examination of the traditions to see if they are rational or irrational, healthy or pathologic. Just to accept the traditions of a group in itself is not sufficient. This is an example of the mystique of group dynamics.

Living in groups is good. I-ness and we-ness are integrated by group living. But group interaction is not scientific psychotherapy. Some of the generalizations of group dynamics may fit more than one patient, but many of these generalizations have little to do with significant alteration in personality. The fact that assembled individuals create a particular group climate is not too relevant to the analytic process. But the fact that all the members make transferences is valuable to understand, so that their resolution for each can be achieved. Just as some therapists are too non-discriminately preoccupied with the patient's psychopathology with little regard for his reality-bound and healthy potentials,[110] some group therapists are inappropriately concerned with group dynamics.

We, too, believe the patient needs to feel that he belongs to the therapeutic group and that good therapeutic climate is conducive to therapeutic work. To organize the group heterogeneously, to discourage routine use of individual sessions, to require alternate sessions, to arrange the treatment room so that the patients are seated comfortably in a circle with the therapist as part of that circle, and to see that therapy is conducted neither under klieg lights nor in darkness and not against a background of competing noises is to be concerned with climate, the climate that facilitates therapy. These as well as other environmental considerations in and of themselves are not therapy. To be preoccupied with the climate is to emphasize the less relevant and leads to the neglect of the more relevant aspects of the work of doing psychoanalysis.

Emphasis on Group Dynamics is Antitherapeutic

A sharp distinction must be made between the therapist's recognition of group trends, the enrichment of his knowledge of the group as a group, and his activity as a therapist for patients who constitute the group. In some way, hidden behind the group psychodynamicist's position is a rejection of therapy. There are various kinds of groups, therapy groups as well as other sorts of groups. One may then use the group in order to study group dynamics or to accomplish other purposes such as education. Or one may use the group therapeutically. The tendency to use group dynamics in the therapeutic situation is a way of anthropomorphizing the group and looking for group dynamic laws as if the interpretation of these to the group would be therapeutic in some way.

The field of group psychotherapy is already crowded with conductors, leaders, and counsellors inadequately trained in psychoanalytic psychotherapy. To these ranks are now being added the group psychodynamicists who are attempting to do therapy with inadequate means. What is even more startling is to discover how many psychoanalytically trained therapists are trying to make indiscriminate use of group dynamics in treatment. Such emphasis suggests either a disregard for or a lack of knowledge of the principles of psychoanalytic therapy. If we focus our attention on group dynamic processes, we cannot also at the same time easily attend diagnosis, psychopathology, individual psychodynamics, dream analysis, resistance, transference and countertransference reactions, provocative roles, multiple reactivities and other relevant parameters. Concentration on group dynamics can become an avoidance of the necessity for good analytic training in psychotherapy and a rationalization that treatment equates with the elaboration of group dynamic processes.

While group dynamics may apply to all groups and have usefulness in understanding groups, the interest and preoccupation with group dynamics in therapy groups may be a reflection of resistance and countertransference in the therapist. Scheidlinger[97] notes that Bion and Ezriel "suggest some useful hypotheses regarding the utilization of group dynamic elements in the service of resistance" (p. 34). Frank [33] states that the "universal tendency of members to continue interacting outside of the regular group meetings may be viewed as a manifestation of their efforts to become cohesive" (p. 55). Such seeking one another out after regular group meetings may be less a search for cohesion than a compulsion to act out. Frank's search for a group dynamic explanation leads him to an extra-analytic one. He says further that "a well-established therapy group . . . resents newcomers, and the behavior of the regular members vacillates between attempts to integrate and to exclude them" (p. 56). A group never reacts so generally, en masse, without differentiation. The group may manifestly accept or reject some new member, but each member does so for different and personal latent motivations. Here Frank is denying individual differences and rejecting unconscious motivation.

Frank [33] remarks, "A cohesive group not only exerts pressure on members to change, but strengthens their ability to maintain the changes it has helped bring about. Allegiance to a group helps members to hold to their decisions. If these decisions arise out of group discussion and have its sanction, the member feels that he cannot let the group down by recanting. It has been shown that group discussion leads to more permanent change of behavior than individual persuasion. It seems likely that the more cohesive a group is—that is, the more each member feels himself a part of it—the stronger their force will be" (p. 61). This is true provided all the members of the group change in the same direction. Such a consuming demand for allegiance imposes submission on the individual, else he will be excluded. Where is the individual patient's resistance? Has he none? Is not the individual in such a view bludgeoned into conformity by submission to a destructive homogeneity? Here uniformity and sameness become the social and therapeutic goal and ideal. Frank observes further that "by putting pressure on them (the patients) to continue communicating, it can often carry them to a successful resolution based on deeper and more accurate mutual understanding" (p. 62). For us, a satisfactory working through becomes possible only if communication is analyzed in terms of resistance, transference, and countertransference.

Bach [6] states, "It is possible to explain the fact that the patients do 'grow up' as resulting from a need to maintain group cohesion, i.e., the need to make themselves as attractive as possible to each other. The therapeutic growth is not solely mediated by identification with the therapist, it is rather the group-dynamic force of cohesiveness that moves the patient forward" (p. 75). It is group cohesion that leads to growth rather than because the therapist leads the way and stands for growth. Furthermore, identification with the therapist is not therapeutic except for patients with weak superegos. In most instances, identification with the therapist is compulsive, pathologic, needs to be analyzed as resistance and worked through.

In connection with the growing antianalytic trend in group psychotherapy, of which the group dynamic inclination is merely one facet, it is worth noting how little attention is paid these days to the brilliant contributions made by that pioneer in the field of psychoanalysis in groups (Trigant Burrow[16, 17]). It may be, because he was rigorously oriented to the individual in the group. It is our impression that the group dynamic emphasis is antipsychoanalytic, because it is anti-individual and disregardful of individual differences. It ignores individual necessities with regard to growth and maturation. By attending the group the central analytic problem of timing is further obscured. Resistances may be bolstered, defenses attacked and activity initiated without reference to the readiness of the individual patient. The group dynamic emphasis tends to homogenize the membership, to create an apparency of psychologic uniformity and so to block the emergence of divergent transferences and healthy differentiation. The group dynamic point of view sponsors a false belief in the value of mediocrity. The group dynamic orientation is anti-rational and anti-multidimensional. It emphasizes structure and neglects content and process. The stress on group dynamics is anticlinical and antitherapeutic in its devaluation of history and diagnosis. When a therapist takes a unidimensional, exclusive position which ignores individual genesis and individual relatedness, treatment cannot take place.

Group Dynamics and Depth Therapy

One of the reasons why Slavson[122] and Kubie[61] do not believe group therapy is as profound as individual therapy may be the group dynamic resistance to doing therapy, its resistance to the necessity to understand the individual, his unconscious and transference problems. The pre-eminence given to group processes and the deceptive homogenizing of individuals inevitably leads to a neglect of each patient and his deep therapy. Any therapy which does not attend the individual, *his* history, *his* psychodynamics, *his* dreams, *his* pathology, and *his* health, remains superficial. The group psychodynamicist provides the patient a group experience without therapy.

The conviction that deep therapy cannot be done in a group is confirmed by the combined therapist, who often does not apply his analytic skills in the group setting but routinely supplements group meetings with individual analytic hours when deeper therapy is attempted. Apparently the combined therapist merely uses the group to provide a kind of catalytic experience. It would appear that both the group dynamicist and the combined therapist start out with the assumption that the group situation is not one in which the individual can be perceived or dealt with in a therapeutic way.

Liff[63] takes the position of the analyst who tries to amalgamate group dynamics and psychotherapy. He says, "The almost infinite variables with which we are confronted in attempting to understand the multiple of interacting psychodynamic processes, both group and individual, have rendered most of us inadequate to specific prediction and control. We have adopted what appears at this time as a transitional compromise in our widespread emphasis on combined group and individual treatment. This compromise is probably a healthy development in view of the lack of exact understanding of what takes place in the therapeutic process of perceptual unlearning of distortions to new realistic learnings. At this stage, the individual sessions provide us with a closer scrutiny of the unconscious conflicts and the defensive organization" (p. 11). It seems as if the group therapist's preoccupation with group dynamics in group sessions removes him from his analytic role, to which he returns during individual hours. The group psychodynamicist, therefore, needs combined therapy in order to do therapy at all.

The position of the combined therapist seems to be that it is not possible for a patient to reach the depth of his repressed needs, pathologic and wholesome, unless he is under the guidance of the therapist alone. This is a reason why the combined therapist rejects the alternate session as well. There seems to be, moreover a very curious grandiosity inherent in the assumption that the patient will only and always expose himself more to the therapist than to the group. And clinical evidence points to the fact that the opposite is just as often true. There is a more subtle grandiosity in the assumption that by assembling patients they become a group which then has an inherently healing quality or acquires it from the therapist who had the vision to unite them in the first place. Why, for the combined therapist, this therapeutizing inherence is not sufficiently restorative, is not made clear unless he is not group dynamic enough. For the group therapist who rejects alternate meetings, it would now seem as if the group can retain its reparative gifts only for as long as the therapist is present. If he is there, patients are capable of comprehension, understanding, insight, development, maturity. If he is absent, they are confused, helpless, infantile, neurotic, decorticate.

The Primacy of the Group

The concept *group* has acquired in certain group-oriented circles such fundamental status that the group is projected even where it does not exist. There are those who see even in the individual the unseen group. He is seen as a group in the sense that he has incorporated aspects of his fore-bears. He is seen as a group if his libidinous self narcissistically makes him-self the object of his love. He is seen as a group, if he is fragmented into various selves.[146] He is seen as a group if he is alone but experiences a sub-jective sense of anxiety or aggression against fantasied persons with whom he populates his mind. There are those who regard two associated individ-uals as a group, or three, or four to eight, or eight to thirty, or thirty to several thousands, or unlimited numbers.[66]

There are even some for whom the group is so deified, it can be healthy, even though it is made up of sick individuals. Foulkes,[30] for example, states that "the deepest reason why . . . patients . . . can reinforce each other's nor-mal reactions and correct each other's neurotic reactions is that collectively they constitute the very norm from which, individually, they deviate" (p. 29). This is a mystique. Somehow, when you homogenize pathologic individuals in a Waring Blendor, out comes a healthy group. The deifica-tion of the group produces not an I–thou relatedness, but an I–it relation-ship, that is, an I–group relatedness. Here the group replaces the thou. The group is used to obscure and replace the thou, so that interpersonal related-ness is eclipsed. Such a glorification of group dynamics encourages rela-tions to things, to masses, rather than to persons.[131]

There is a trend in the culture to invest the group with a primacy over what is happening to the individual, to emphasize what has been called me-diocrity, in which the individual gets lost in the group. The group psycho-dynamicist too endows the group with a supremacy that enables it to pre-vail over the individual, so that he cannot readily be explored in difference and in uniqueness. The prejudice that one cannot do as good therapeutic work with patients in a group as one can in an individual setting is con-firmed by virtue of creating a situation dedicated to establishing a pre-eminence of group phenomena. The group dynamic emphasis views the group as a whole and searches for a group mentality. This would put the group before the person and lead to a form of repressive inspirational psy-chotherapy.

The group dynamic emphasis brings with it a failure to differentiate one patient from the next and occupies itself instead with phases of group de-velopment. "Individual problems become reinterpreted as group prob-lems"[70] (p. 29). The group is the organism to be studied. Cartwright and Lippitt[18] state, "Most infants are born into a specific group. Little Johnny may be a welcome or unwelcome addition to the group" (p. 87). But the child is not responded to in one way by the whole family as a group. To assume so is to obscure the personal reactions of individual family members to the new child.

Bach[6] remarks, "The group is a stage or projection screen onto which the total repertoire of conscious, preconscious, and unconscious needs are externalized, projected, acted out, recognized, and corrected through a group-centered therapeutic work process (theragnosis)" (p. 69). Here the group is elevated to the point where it exercises all functions. The group diagnoses and treats, not the therapist. He has no function. The group becomes the therapist. Bach implies the group is the screen, the mirror, the therapist. So the analyst is no longer necessary. We do not believe in such noninteractive therapy, whether in individual or group treatment. The patients are not neutral. They always have necessities and psychodynamics of their own. Nothing is so static. Bach now makes the group the neutral mirror to replace the neutral analyst. This is a mystical misuse of the group.

Frank[33] observes, "Group standards and codes which a member has internalized may be relatively independent of the particular members of the group" (p. 53). If this were true, then a culture ought to be independent of the individuals who constitute it. If this were so, we could say that only the family is responsible for what the child is, not the father, the mother, or the sibling. If this were valid, it was the Nazi movement, not Nazis who destroyed Jewry rather than Jews. He notes further that, "the attitudes of a professional soldier . . . are determined to a larger degree by the codes and standards of the army than by the personal characteristics of his fellows" (p. 53). This would deny individual responsibility. The codes and standards of the group are symbolically signalized while the soldiers who give them shape and meaning are vitiated. This accentuation of the group over man would depersonalize him and leave only the organization man, the marginal man. But patients do not "work toward a common end" (p. 59), but toward individual ends. For Frank,[33] "each member is helped to clarify his self-image, at least in respect to those aspects of himself that are relevant to the group's functioning" (p. 62). What is analyzed then is only what is relative to the group's functioning, not to the individual's needs.

From the foregoing it would appear that the group psychodynamicist obscures the individual's psychodynamics and reinterprets the personal response in terms of group reactions. Group dynamics replace psychodynamics. Individual acting out is disregarded for group reaction. If the individual acts, he is acting out. If the group acts in seeming concert, it becomes a group reaction. The personal act becomes neurotic, a defense against the group response. A non-discriminative sanction develops of all communality as healthy and a corresponding depreciation of all individuality as unhealthy. Individuality is made synonymous with competition and communality synonymous with cooperation. Such a view is a distortion of real-

234 / Psychoanalysis in Groups

ity. There are healthy and unhealthy resources both in individual and in communal living. We must also be able to appreciate the positive in the individual as well as the negative in the group.

Group Dynamics and Status Denial

Liff[63] imputes to the group a healing force not too different from the self-generative repair process of Whitaker and Malone.[129] By virtue of a group of people getting together they conjure up a magically therapeutic power; this must be an occult art. Apparently one of the functions of the therapist is to mobilize this force, to get it in motion, to catalyze it. This notion implies not only the therapist's status denial but his grandiosity as well. This projection on to the group of remedial inherence is not objectively and realistically to be seen.

The idea that the group itself provides a mystically healing power is reflected especially in such statements as the following. "It is the patients themselves who provide the greater therapeutic force."[63] Scheidlinger,[97] in referring to the work of Bion says, "He is quite emphatic, however, in denying the suggestion that the leader's ideas or personality influences a group. Quite to the contrary, according to him (Bion), the leader and the group members are at the mercy of 'Basic Assumption' forces" (p. 4). The expert function of the therapist is denied or becomes meaningless in such a view.

The Denial of Individuality and Difference

We are not unmindful of the importance of knowing how the I and the we are related. We see the necessity of the individual, especially the narcissistic person, to substitute for the I–orientation a we–orientation. But to do this routinely is non-discriminative and denies the individual his right to discover himself as a person. An exclusive attention to group phenomena imposes on therapy the weaknesses of nonanalytic psychology in that personal motivation is neglected. The group psychodynamicist looks for motivation outside the individual. Scheidlinger[97] observes, "A fundamental problem lies in the distinct failure by Bion and Ezriel to relate group concepts or phenomena to the personalities of the group members. The impression is thus conveyed that in group therapy it is *the group and not the individual* that is being treated" (p. 34).

Bach[6] states, "In order to 'see' group-generated healing forces one has to adjust the lenses of the psychoanalytic looking glass, or borrow some other frame of reference" (p. 66). The proposal made here is so to change our focus that we do not see the analytic and concentrate on the extrapersonal.

Frank[33] also notes, "With respect to hostility toward fellow members, the kind of patient who most often receives the group's ire is more easily defined in terms of his effect on the group than his underlying psychodynamics" (p. 56). But how can a patient's effect on other members be separated from him? Apparently, the compulsive focusing on the group renders everything extrapersonal.

Cartwright and Lippitt[18] write that ". . . the individual needs social support for his values and social beliefs; he needs to be accepted as a valued member of some group which *he* values; failure to maintain such group membership produces anxiety and personal disorganization. But, on the other hand, group membership and group participation tend to cost the individual his individuality. If he is to receive support from others and, in turn, give support to others, he and they must hold in common some values and beliefs. Deviation from these undermines any possibility of group support and acceptance" (p. 91). The group dynamicists insist that groupness destroys isolation; that belonging to a group involves "fission," a "chain-reaction" linking the members constructively to one another. But one can join a fascist movement and still be isolated. The delinquent joins a group of delinquents who are basically unrelated. The individual then can often find further isolation and detachment in a group, even in a democratic group. There is more joinerism in the United States, yet more alienation than elsewhere. Grouping can end in pseudo-closeness, in the lonely crowd. Deviation in the group need not undermine any possibility of group support and acceptance, if the group accepts a discriminating nonconformity as one of its ideals or goals. The group dynamic principle is that the group demands conformity.

The individuals within a group still function, still exist, still have to solve for themselves their individual problems. The group *qua* group cannot become the means by which its members resolve intrapsychic difficulties. The need for such differentiation led us to change our concept of the psychoanalysis of groups,[135] to that of psychoanalysis in groups.[142] We do not treat a group. We must still analyze the individual in interaction with other individuals.

Lewin, the father of group dynamics, emphasized the understanding of individual and group behavior in terms of the precise momentary setting. This is in contrast to the psychoanalytic system which lays simultaneous stress upon genetic, causal, and explanatory concepts. Although some therapists emphasize primarily the here-and-now and reject historical exploration, this is largely an antianalytic development. So long as the genetic is not seen in the momentary interaction, the analytic or transference view of the historic determinants of current behavior tends to be denied.

An analytic orientation involves attention to intrapsychic processes of the individual and the way in which they facilitate or interfere with his relationship to others. The group dynamicist is engaged in defining generalized group processes which obscure personal and unconscious motivations. The use of group dynamics as interpetation and as a means for effecting change in the individuals that constitute the therapy group is a misperception and a rejection of both intrapsychic and interpersonal processes.

Behind the group dynamic concepts of cohesion, identification, and belonging lies a pressure for conformity, homogeneity and a denial of the right to deviate. Under the guise of sponsoring the democratic group, there is here an actual denial of the democratic process.

Perhaps what some group therapists do in their orientation toward the group-as-a-whole is to sponsor what is misperceived as a democratic position. So they go along with the consensual position as healthy and valuable and fail to see that underneath this *manifest* concord there are unique differences. Bion[15] speaks of a "group mentality" by which he means a "unanimous expression of the will of the group, contributed to by the individual in ways of which he is unaware, influencing him disagreeably whenever he thinks or behaves in a manner at variance with the basic assumptions" (p. 16). It seems to be assumed here that if the individual can be taught to conform to the group will, his pathology thereby disappears and he becomes healthy. It is assumed further that so long as he does not submit to group consensus, he is unhealthy. But there is a difference between democracy and group agreement, and between both of these and psychotherapy.

The group psychodynamicists are concerned with facilitating and sponsoring democratic trends within their groups. The misconception seems to be that if the group is democratic, the group is therapeutic. Here democracy is equated with therapy. But the keynote of group therapy is not democracy. While democracy in groups is a valuable form of social organization, it is not treatment. The keynote of group therapy is good therapy. If it is good therapy, then certain democratic processes will arise both in their positive as well as in their negative aspects, be scrutinized, examined, and where they are pathologic largely worked through.

Let us consider the group dynamic concept *belonging* to which healing functions are ascribed. The group is said to offer a therapeutic balm by providing a social milieu in which the isolated patient can feel included. He is supposed to develop a sense of belonging out of group identification or cohesion. But belonging has dynamics which are highly complicated. Belonging in a group can become a serious hazard, if it is non-discriminatively cultivated. It may destructively entrench a patient's attachment to group members who come to represent a pathologic subculture which tolerates his neuroticism rather than work it through. Such pathologic belonging may intensify a patient's dependency and seriously limit the need to develop a life apart from the group. We are wary of the kind of pseudo-belonging in which a patient, by neurotic identification or submission to consensual standards, has to belong to the group only on its terms. This is not unlike the demand of certain cultist psychoanalytic schools which exclude original or divergent thinking from prescribed true faith.

If a patient can belong to a group only by giving up his wishes and values, this is pseudo-belonging, repressive inspirational belonging, neurotic irrational belonging. Much perhaps of the joining tendencies of Americans with an associated denial of individual needs and differences, is really part of this pseudo-belonging. In psychoanalysis in groups, if we focus on belonging, we are liable to neglect the necessity to achieve tolerance for and acceptance of differences, the wholesome need to interact with one's personal uniqueness, the value of disagreeing and still being friendly.[147] While each patient belongs to a group in a cooperative enterprise directed toward a goal, the group itself has no goals which are equal for all. There are no group therapy goals. The goal of each individual member is his individual therapeutic outcome in the form of successful personal resolution of problems.

If it is true that as people become healthier their individuality disappears and communality takes over, then we are leading ourselves into a mediocracy of the *group mind*. We are entering Orwell's world where a *group will* begins to supplant personal identity. This is a rejection of individuality. It is a denial that the individual who is healthy may preserve his special uniqueness and difference, and be tolerant of other people's distinctness and diverse necessities. It is a denial that persons are able to work cooperatively in the achievement of common objectives for their mutual enhancement and fulfillment without the suppression of dissimilarity. It is an attempt at a reductionistic explanation to find a single, simple answer to the highly complex phenomena of individual and social psychology.

The therapist is involved in a process of levelling, when he demands a group function as if it were a uniform group. Such obscuring of disparity applied to the family group would repudiate the reality of the difference between parent and child, between older child and younger child, between girls and boys, between father and mother. Although the family may seem to function as unit, it is unreal to view it as if it were constituted of mirror images within the family structure. These unlikenesses are rejected in the implication that there is a basic family dynamic, a family unity, which contains within it no place for independent motivation, personal history, variance in one's own reaction even to the same family traditions, structure, and heritage. The second child is not entering the same family as the first child or the third child. With each birth into the family it becomes a new one where a new fragment of history is added and a new generalized structure is developed. Each succeeding child must deal with the family as a changing family. Its structure changes as distinguishable children are added to it.

Group dynamics in psychotherapy is based on the assumption that by changing the environment, you change the intrapsychic pathology. This may be possible. But it is not psychoanalytic therapy. It is a concept of a world utopia where everyone does good things, where everyone is good, kind, and homogeneous, where there is no conflict, no transference, no resistance, no ambivalence. This is a brave new world of undifferentiated, homogenized nonindividuals.

Therapy pursues individual reactions. Whenever the therapist sees a manifest group trend and lets it prevail, he encourages conformity, totality. Therapy is a movement toward diversity, toward complementation, toward the cohesion of nature, which is healthy cohesion in difference, not in uniformity, not in pathologic identification, not in homosexuality. The therapist, like the patient, may fear deviation, uniqueness, as being disruptive, conflict-producing. There is value in conflict as well as in harmony.

Homogeneity and Heterogeneity

If a group dynamic emphasis rejects individuality and difference, it embraces homogeneity rather than heterogeneity in group organization. There is an impression current that if patients do not have a large common point of departure, they cannot tolerate or understand one another. We see this as a problem to be worked through rather than catered to by organizing a monolithic group. The more the members are like one another, the more they will have to become different from one another. Furst[39, 40] reports that even if one starts with a so-called homogeneous group, patients become wholesomely differentiated, unless it is forbidden by the therapist. If one really does therapy, the group becomes more and more heterogeneous.

We have indicated that a fundamental human value is to accept the stranger.[147] It is inappropriate to organize a therapy group on the basis of common syndrome, sex, diagnosis, clinical manifestations, character structure or psychosomatic symptom. Homogeneity and group dynamics run hand-in-hand in excluding variety in the group and in failing to sponsor the therapeutic necessity for its development. The homogeneous group, as in Alcoholics Anonymous, may be salutary, but is not a good medium for scientific psychotherapy. A homogeneous group, as in the classroom, may be constructive, educational, but does not necessarily provide that composition which would best facilitate analytic treatment. A homogeneous group imposes certain destructive pressures that a heterogeneous group does not. For example, the demand for uniformity and conformity is conceded to only if the individual is isolated from other influences.[147] The presence of multiple elements in a mixed group is, therefore, a valuable safeguard against a destructive conventionality.

Several quotations from the literature will illustrate the group psychodynamicist's inclination to homogenize the membership of a group into a single mass. Foulkes[29] for example, claims "that the group associates, responds, and reacts as a whole" (p. 51). Cartwright and Lippitt[18] report, "those individuals who deviated from their own group's norms received fewer sociometric choices than those who conformed" (p. 94). The homogeneous orientation implies then that it is difficult to like or accept a person whose standards are different from the group's standards. Frank[33] remarks, "Common to all patients who are strongly attacked by the group is that their behavior tends to disrupt the group's cohesiveness or prevent its increase" (p. 56). Here it is suggested that anyone who is different moves the group away from an over-valued homogeneity. We, on the contrary, would see constructive group development in movement toward self-defining heterogeneity. Slavson[122] notes, "When an individual's superego functioning is at too great divergence from that of the group, he will either withdraw, or the group will reject him. An individual whose superego is either too lax or too strict, as compared with the standards of the group, generates anxiety and guilt and is rejected as a consequence" (p. 137). Here the denial of diversity and multiformity tends to impose the illusion that the group is one patient.

Homogenizing the group membership is not infrequently a countertransference problem. Just as some patients sometimes perceive the whole group as one projected, parental figure, it is conceivable that the therapist similarly invests the group with unifying quality on one basis or another, which is then rationalized. The habitual inclination to see and treat eight or ten patients as if they were one is a denial of the therapist's responsibility for each and undermines their own individual responsibility for their actions. The therapist cannot avoid his accountability for what goes on in the group as well for what goes on with individual patients. Nor can he encourage the patient to neglect personal accountability for his activity. The blending of the membership into one nebulous and amorphous body subverts these differentiating necessities.

One latent motivation of the group therapist in rendering the group uniform may be due, in part, to an unconscious wish to manipulate it. For the group is more easily wielded if it is stereotyped, than if it is dispersed into differentiation and, therefore, not accessible to a manipulative technique. For example, one group therapist uses the group primarily to confirm his impressions and suggestions made in individual sessions. Here the therapist wants the mass to respond in terms of his choices and his position.

Massed individuals can be more easily dealt with when they are levelled in a single direction. But to be reduced to a mass the pathology must be provoked and brought to the fore. So long as his healthy resources predominate, a person will not permit himself to be homogenized into the group.

Another latent motivation for homogenizing the group may be a blind but misconceived faith in democracy in which equality is confused with sameness. This may be linked to the therapist's desire to be a social reformer. Still another possible motivation for homogenizing the group lies in the therapist's wish to avoid involvement in the multiplicity of problems, if the diverse nature of nature were seen in his patient group. By obscuring differences, some therapists may deny the difference between therapist and patient; the homogenized group may then be interchanged with the therapist, and the therapist as patient may expect help from it.[146] The possibility also exists that some combined therapists may prefer homogeneous groups in order to restrict acting out to the group situation. Others may prefer the homogeneous group in the belief that in such a group, interaction among the patients is diminished, and with it, acting out.

It may be that the group psychodynamicist is looking for a short cut in group therapy to evade the necessity for detailed, specific, and differentiated analysis of the individual and his problems. Some therapists inappropriately look to this or that patient to be an auxiliary therapist. The group psychodynamicist may be looking to the group itself as an auxiliary therapist, hoping that somehow group activity will therapeutize the individual without any particular exploration of his unconscious psychopathology. Not that there is anything wrong with looking for short cuts. We are interested in all the means we can acquire to give us more rapid and effective therapeutic results. It remains, however, yet to be shown whether homogeneous organization is a short cut.

The trend to homogeneous groups and the current preoccupation with group dynamics impose upon the group a demand of the therapist that patients respond in one way. For example, some therapists[129] value only the expression of irrational affect. Others emphasize the recurrent need to express hostility, a narrow and limited view of what is required of everyone. Still others require that all reactions must immediately be analyzed before the patient can have an affective experience, whether wholesome or pathologic. Some therapists limit the group only to verbal exchange, forbidding patients to touch one another, or to see one another outside the group therapy room. The assignment of such categorical limitations imposes a homogeneous demand of the therapist.

Perhaps the therapist himself has a misunderstanding of individuality and difference. Historically we have separated the very unique, psychotic person, removed him from the community and institutionalized him. The creative individual too has in his own time often been rejected by his contemporaries as a deviant from the group, regarded as an eccentric or bohemian, and accordingly isolated. It may then be that even the therapist has a confused concept of nonconformity and singularity and regards all difference and deviation as pathologic, and does not sufficiently recognize the creative, positive, and wholesome side of constructive initiative. The homogenizing process then not only disregards interactive and intrapsychic dynamics, it also repudiates individual productivity and expansion.

The search for universal laws in group dynamics, like the search for pathologic unity in homogeneity, is related to the quest for certainty.[111] Perhaps one factor that leads the group therapist to elaborate a theory of group dynamics is a defensive reaction to the individual analyst's criticism and doubts about group psychotherapy. The group therapist may feel this as a demand to prove his value to the professional community. So he pursues means to prove and justify group processes screening them with absolute certainty. But this may be an inappropriate defensive maneuver that has no bearing on therapy of the individual. The group therapist may have no real conviction that therapy takes place in the group situation. He may then attempt to justify and to rationalize the kind of work he does by creating mystical ideas concerning what goes on in the group. In this way he is not compelled to answer the individual therapist's challenge on his own terms, namely, to demonstrate specifically the effectiveness of group dynamics in the improvement of the individual patient. The avoidance of meeting this question directly suggests a sense of underlying inadequacy and uncertainty in the face of the individual analyst's skepticism. How better to vindicate group processes than by simply asserting their absolute superiority to individual psychodynamics and thereby gaining unchallengeable certainty. Let us be less defensive rather than more group dynamic.

Our hunch is that most therapists who stress group dynamics in the group setting probably do routine combined group therapy. Analytic work is done in the individual situation, but analytic work is not done in the group setting. Here the group is conceived as exercising an innate reparative function confused with consciously applied therapeutic intervention. Combined therapists are probably attracted to group dynamics because then the individual and his analysis may be reserved for the private setting and avoided in the group.

Group Dynamics and Di-egophrenia

Wherever there is weakness of the ego, whether in the schizophrenic, the borderline,[132] the di-egophrenic,[137] the psychopath, the impulsive patient or the hypnotic subject, there is a tendency to be swept along by the other or the seeming other homogenized as the group. Perhaps this is true in the present gangland phenomena where the members act out the aggressive and irrational demands of the leaders. In the degree to which a person has ego strength he will be able to value his own perceptions, judgment, and constructive uniqueness, and pursue his own line against the domination of other egos. To the extent to which the therapist emphasizes the group dynamic formulation he underlines the *we* of the group, the negative egos that foster split ego problems. By denying personal aspirations ego resources are weakened, and di-egophrenic pathology is cultivated.

We do not wish to be non-discriminative in seeing only the negative in homogeneous group operations. Individuals in the group are frequently mutually helpful, supportive, sympathetic, understanding, and emphatic. They often identify with one another and put themselves in the place of the other despite differences in background and experience. To the extent that group members do this for one another they have in some respects achieved a constructive homogeneity which the therapist can welcome and support. There is positive value in group living and in human interaction. No one would deny this. But what is the therapeutic usefulness of this idea? How can we technically utilize our awareness that when human beings are loved by one another there is reparative value in their mutual feelings? Does this mean that the function of scientific therapy is to be secured by our loving one another, by creating an atmosphere of love? This is actually to deny the possibility of conscious intervention based upon an understanding of the nature of psychodynamics. Even though there is value in patients relating to one another, feeling positively for each other in support of faltering egos, this is not to be equated with scientific psychotherapy.

A glance at the literature on group psychodynamics indicates how this mystique sponsors borderlineness. Slavson[122] states, "The condition of belonging to a group is *partial de-egotizing* of the individual so that a portion of his ego is given up to the group, and especially to the leader as its representative. In other words, the individual has to submit to the group in order that he may be a part of it and groups come into being and survive because of this partial de-egotization of its members. It is out of these 'discarded' portions of the individuals' egos that a 'group ego' emerges" (p. 136). At least here Slavson tells us where the group ego comes from. If this were true, the group would break down the self and produce di-egophrenia in all participants. In reality, patients do not give up their pathology in order to become part of the group. Nor does group membership entail relinquishing one's ego.

Slavson notes further, "A part of the ego . . . of each of the constituent members is given up to form the 'group ego.' This is part of the process commonly referred to as 'socialization' or 'assimilation'—a process essential for human survival" (p. 136). As we see it, socialization does not require a loss of ego function but rather a greater ability to use one's ego and to develop a constructive superego. Slavson remarks, "The more 'individualistic' (neurotic) a person is, the less can he give up of his personal ego and is therefore less capable of becoming part of his social milieu. In mobs, for example, a much larger portion of the individual's ego is given up so that he is guided less by it than in democratic deliberative group" (pp. 136 f.). Cannot a person be individualistic without being neurotic? What may be true for a mob is not necessarily valid for a therapeutic group. The mob encourages acting out. The therapeutic group analyzes it. The therapeutic group is not a mob led by a demagogue in a di-egophrenic relationship. Slavson says, "Superego judgments are weakened in each member by the group's primary code, its sanctions and approval" (p. 137). Apparently groups are very destructive, for patients become decorticated by them. Slavson then goes on to say, "The libido thus freed is invested in the leader who becomes the representative of the 'group superego' " (p. 137). After patients are "de-egotized" by the group, the therapist becomes the group's ego and superego.

Bach[6] states, "I see the therapeutic group as a generator of pressures on its members which go beyond the kind of influence exerted by a psychoanalytic group therapist" (p. 66). The group becomes a crowd that backs the patient into a corner exercising a "pressure" that enforces allegiance or submission. Frank[33] remarks, "Criticism of a member because he is behaving in such a way that the group cannot integrate him into their activities seems especially likely to eventuate usefully. When a patient yields to such an attack and modifies his behavior accordingly, he is promptly rewarded by experiencing a greater sense of acceptance by the group. This may shield his self respect from the damage that it would otherwise have suffered and also reinforce the new pattern of behavior." Here, too, health comes from submission to the group. And cohesiveness depends on a denial of individuality and an acceptance of group standards. The way to group acceptance then is to undergo a splitting of one's ego. Frank observes further, "A paradoxical example is that of the submissive member who, in compliance with the group's standards, forces himself to act aggressively, that is, he acts aggressively because he is basically submissive. This pseudo aggressiveness, bolstered by his allegiance to the group, may lead to beneficial changes in his relationships with important persons in his life" (p. 61). A therapy based on capitulation to group dictates is authoritarian. Basic therapeutic changes do not come about through deference to group fiats but by working through.

Foulkes[30] states that as a group works together, there emerges "less contradiction between individuality and community." If, by this statement, he means that in a therapeutic group what develops is increasing differentiation with some conflict perhaps about different points of view but ultimately more and more appreciation and acceptance of complementary and opposing points of view, we can heartily agree with him. But if he means that the individual obediently conforms to the communal point of view and thereby avoids conflict, we cannot see eye to eye with him.

Scheidlinger[95] writes that "in becoming part of a group each individual perceives a number of people with their complex behavior patterns as well as broader group factors which are expressed through verbal or non-verbal channels of communication. From these he selects certain dominant aspects to which he responds in line with his unique adaptive patterns and which now become part of the broader network of group inter-relationships" (p. 669). But what meaning does this theoretic formulation have for treatment? Is not Scheidlinger saying, in effect, that when a patient enters a group, he becomes susceptible to the prevalence of a group dynamic which is homogeneous, which demands compliance, repression of his own positive ego, and the ambivalent submission and rebellion that characterize the di-egophrenic? Not only is such a climate of no use in therapy, the changes that follow in such an atmosphere are generally in the direction of pathology.

It seems to us important, that we should take a strong stand against any group dynamic interpretation whether offered by a patient or a therapist. Otherwise, successions of generalizations inappropriate to therapy do further damage to already weakened egos. If the analyst does not insist upon the recognition of individual differences and strengthen personal independence but rather makes so-called *group interpretations,* he leads the group toward a uniformity in pathology and away from the wholesome reality of human diversity. He denies the patient that freedom and autonomy which is one of the therapeutic objectives of any good analysis. A therapist who emphasizes consensual validation creates a borderline problem for the patient in the sense that he is not endorsing the right of the individual to non-compulsive differentiation from general orthodoxy, thereby permitting an oppressive *group authority* to prevail.

The Manifest and the Latent in Group Dynamics

Slavson[122] takes issue with the group psychodynamicists when he observes, "What seems at first a 'universal' feeling or attitude in a therapy group actually is not so, for the uncovering of reactions shows that there are those who are affected by it deeply, others only slightly and still others remain indifferent" (p. 141). While Slavson is making a plea for individual distinctions, he is inclined to see these refinements as quantitative. We would emphasize the qualitative discrimination and note as well that the group psychodynamicist attends the manifest content, while the analyst scrutinizes the latent material.

In this sense a group therapist who occupies himself with group dynamics is catering to the patient's resistance. To contemplate the seeming homogeneity of response is to give undue importance to the superficial and obvious reaction and to disregard the covert and unconscious individual responses. It might be well to illustrate clinically an example of this process. In a therapeutic group, patient B helplessly and childishly demanded a constant suckling from the maternal breast projected onto each patient. At first he monopolized group sessions, and the members catered to his passive claims by being very supportive, reassuring, directive, seemingly maternal. The therapist tended under these circumstances to view the group as responding homogeneously in a group dynamic way to the patient's pathologic need. At first, attempts on the analyst's part to penetrate beyond this apparent, uniform reaction met with resistance. But persisting on exploring the underlying and personally differentiated psychodynamics in the seeming maternal figures, he discovered a specific transferential, identifying or other psychodynamic operating which was not at first apparent.

For example, patient A finally reported at one point that he had to keep B talking, that B's silence made A very anxious. When asked to associate to this feeling, A recalled an older brother whose glaring angry, depressed silences would frighten A as a child. A used to seek relief from his brother's intolerable, mute anger by getting him to verbalize his aggression. In this catharsis A discovered that his brother would loose a good deal of his oppressive wrath and A became less frightened. B was then a brother figure for A, who had to keep B talking in order to relieve A's apprehension. It became clear that A was not offering B a psychic maternal breast. He was instead acting out in an entirely personal way a part of his past history.

Patient P, when asked to explore her reactions to B, reported that he was not unlike her hurt father whom she felt obliged to support and protect, all the while feeling a mounting resentment against this constant obligation to him, an animosity she dared not express for fear of hurting her father still more.

Patient M, pressed for associations to her dealings with B, recalled how deprived she felt as a child of physical closeness to her mother and uncovered repressed yearnings, in fact, for the maternal breast. She handled this problem in her childhood by playing mother to her little dolls, which were images of her own denied infantile self. And B came to represent this deprived self that she was again impelled to feed. At other times B assumed for her the transferential character of a younger sister, for whom M had to take responsibility.

For patient K, B was a father figure who was stingy and self-denying, depriving K of the fulfillment of many of her legitimate aspirations. K always felt obliged to yield submissively to her father's example and dictates. So she felt she had to sit quietly by acting out her childhood role while B prevailed.

And so it turned out for each member that he was not in fact playing the *manifest* role of breast feeding B, but was acting out a personal unconscious psychodynamic of his own. Such a discovery is possible only if the therapist does not inappropriately homogenize the group but rather explores individual unconscious processes. There is a parallel between the therapist's accepting the group's support of B as a group dynamic breast-feeding and the therapist's accepting the manifest content of a dream as the reality rather than a distortion to conceal the underlying reality. The therapist's choice of the group dynamic as a process to work with, to enlist, to do therapy with, is a misperception of the reality underlying this manifest distortion. If group dynamics present the resistive superficialities as basic and permit the unconscious material to remain concealed and real motivations repressed, the resistance and acting out of patients are thereby encouraged.

Scheidlinger[97] stresses the fact that " ' . . . group behavior should be viewed as the behavior of *individual* personalities in a special process of social and emotional interaction.' It always comprises two interrelated sets of factors: (a) *Individual personalities* with their genetic and dynamic properties, some conscious and some unconscious. (b) *Group dynamic elements,* such as climate, structure or code, constituting the product of the interactions within the group" (p. 36). If this is true, it means that in order to treat, one still has to analyze individuals. In order to understand group dynamic elements, one must understand the individual personalities in their interpersonal reactions within the group setting. It seems, therefore, that there is a contradiction in Scheidlinger's position. Though he insists that group dynamic elements must be understood, by his own definition they are a consequence of individual personality interactions. Therefore, the meaningfulness of interpersonal responses is lost if the therapist obscures the latency of psychodynamics for the manifestation of group dynamics.

The acceptance of the apparency of homogeneity as a real homogeneity is a rejection of the idea that individuals function in different ways. The apparency of homogeneity, viewing groups of people, whether they are families, crowds or mobs, as if they were one person, is one of the pitfalls in social psychology. To assume that each person's motivation and identification with the group are the same is to deny psychologic reality. A group may have seemingly uniform behavior, but closer scrutiny of each member's springs of action shows them to be quite different from one another. Psychologists must seek to understand not only the apparency of psychologic uniformity of behavior in a group, but also individual differences which are predicated upon the person's life history, the needs and motivations for his

activity at the moment, and the meaning to him, both conscious and unconscious, of his participation in what looks like a *group action.*[67]

If, in the therapeutic group, the patients move toward the expression of
themes, the therapist is overvaluing homogeneity and denying individual
differences. It is in the nature of human beings to be diverse as nature is diverse. Allowing a group theme to prevail is not unlike the situation in some
pathogenic families where the child must conform to the parental demands,
values, and ways of behaving. Such a point of view does not fit the analytic
conception of individually differentiated psychodynamics and psychopathology.

The therapist working with patients in groups might then inquire, what
is the correct therapeutic handling of group dynamic manifestations such
as themes? We would respond, if the therapist sees a group trend or theme
developing, he ought to test it by exploring the patients individual by individual, to see whether he has been deceived by manifest conformity and
missed the latent diversity. If the therapist will regard such themes as manifest and explore each individual's latent reactions, he will be able to penetrate the manifest content, generally resistive. To encourage the theme is
to encourage the resistance, homogeneity, conformity, pathology, and the
denial of individual differences. It emphasizes a closed rather than an open
environment, an illusion of cohesion rather than the reality of cooperation,
an overcontrolled climate rather than a liberating one. By analyzing the individual in interaction with other individuals in the presence of still others,
including the therapist, the analyst fosters morale, cohesion, constructive
heterogeneity, and complementarity of values. Authority and autonomy
remain with the individual patient where they belong. The psychoanalyst in
groups needs to know enough about the group dynamics to be able to dis-
count them, and so get on with the business of doing therapy.

Integration

Advances in social psychology have given rise to interest in group dynamics and the study of small group behavior in nontherapeutic situations.
An ancient philosophic and psychologic problem has been raised once
again; namely, the relation between the individual and the group. The
widespread acceptance of the possibility of doing psychoanalysis in a group
setting compels the group psychotherapist to reconcile the seeming contradiction. The obvious alternative, "If you treat the individual, the group
will take care of itself," and "If you treat the group, the individual will take
care of himself," really obscures the problem.

We are concerned with creating the best possible procedure in which
what is realistically most useful for both therapist and patient is consciously
and technically applied in professional therapy. The use of group dynamics

as a method of treating psychiatric patients has yet to be demonstrated in clinical situations. Experience with psychopathology, psychodynamics, and working through cannot be replaced by nonclinical constructs. When group therapists turn to group dynamics as the fountainhead of therapy, they are participating in the current cultural trend toward togetherness and groupism. They thereby identify themselves with a movement which denies the value of the individual, which accepts unreality as the greater or transcendent reality, non-intellect as the higher intelligence and inappropriate feeling as the healthier feeling.

The realities of doing psychoanalysis in a group setting include an awareness that individuals exist and groups exist; that there are useful observations about individuals and about groups of individuals; that theories may be constructed concerning the laws of change of individuals and of groups. The reality which primarily concerns us here, however, is the professional treatment of the patient. The nature of the disturbance of the individual can be understood only on the basis of an implicit or explicit theory of personality including its healthy and unhealthy functioning. Group dynamic concepts are misapplied to the treatment of the disturbed individual, because no generalized theory of cause and cure of a psychologic disorder has yet evolved from them. As a consequence, group dynamic observations have been distorted by forcing them to fit into accepted individual psychologic theory. The result has been to suggest such inappropriate formulations as *group mind, group superego, group ego, group id, group transference*, and *group resistance*. Here we have group observations misrepresented in an attempt to make them fit or be equated with concepts which make sense only in the context of a consistent, coherent, individual psychologic model.

The mystification of legitimate group realities is further seen in the group therapist's awareness that living together with other human beings may be reparative, whether in the family, the social group, the work group, the educational group or the political group. Many human beings have positive growth experiences as a consequence of being a member of a group. But here, too, the cautionary must be emphasized that not every form of group living is necessarily reparative for every participant. The group therapist cannot help but become aware that individual patients seem to take strength from group morale and group dedication to the work at hand. Some group therapists then tend to forget, however, that as individuals improve with treatment in the group, they improve not because of an inherent mystical quality in the group experience, but because of the specificity of therapeutic work done under the conscious leadership of a trained therapist. The status-denial trends, especially among group therapists, are part of their generalized projection that the group and not the therapist is the healer. We have attempted here to make explicit the differences between health-giving experience in social living and the specific application of technical intervention in a treatment situation.

In studying the meaning of group, Sapir[93] said, "In the discussion of the fundamental psychology of the group such terms as gregariousness, consciousness of mind and group mind do little more than give names to problems to which they are in no sense a solution. The psychology of the group cannot be fruitfully discussed except on the basis of a profounder understanding of the way in which different sorts of personalities enter into significant relations with each other and on the basis of a more complete knowledge of the importance to be attached to directly purposive as contrasted with symbolic motives in human interaction. The psychological basis of the group must rest on the psychology of specific personal relations . . . Group loyalty and group ethics do not mean that the direct relationship between individual and individual has been completely transcended . . . The psychological realities of group participation will be understood only when theorizing about the general question of the relation of the individual to the group gives way to detailed studies of the actual kinds of understanding, explicit and implicit, that grow up between two or three or more human beings when they are brought into significant contact. It is important to know not only how one person feels with reference to another but how the former feels with reference to latter when a third party is present . . . No matter how impersonally one may conceive the behavior which is characteristic of a given group, it must either illustrate direct interaction or it must be a petrified 'as if' (i.e., transference) of such interaction."

A social theory is not necessarily the answer to resolving individual psychopathology. Some therapists think that individual analysis focusses on the individual and therapy in groups focusses on the group; that the intrapsychic is attended in the individual setting and the interpersonal in the group setting. This is a misconception of the nature of good analysis done in any setting. Any thorough-going therapy will be concerned with both the patient's inner life and the way he relates to other people. They are not separable. No good analysis can be done if it emphasizes only one or the other. Therapy is concerned with how to harmonize a patient's oneness with his other-relatedness. We would have no language unless there were individuals to speak it, and no language unless there were others with whom to talk. A therapy which emphasizes purely the intrapsychic is as meaningless as a therapy which emphasizes purely the interpersonal. The self helpers neglect the multilateral aspects of therapy. The group psychodynamicists deny the patient's independent identity. The individual entrepreneurs err in rejecting the endeavors of others, and the social reformers make the mistake of devaluating the individual. You cannot have one without the other. Their separation leads to pathology. Neither the individual nor the individual members of the group can be denied.

11. Values

The growing awareness that the analyst, too, is human and the increasing emphasis on his personality, his values, and his strengths and weaknesses, are characteristic of the recent period in the history of psychoanalysis. There was a time when the therapist was not supposed to have or to express values, when the emergence of values in therapy was viewed as antitherapeutic. In itself, such an attitude is a reflection of values.

As we see it, all people, including patients and analysts, have values. Part of our task is to make explicit the values which often remain implicit. We are presenting a philosophic chapter based on clinical experience. We are raising a large number of questions about which we have done some thinking.

What do we mean by values? A value is that which is good. The word good is synonymous with values. By good is meant ethical. So when we say values, we are speaking about what we believe is good. In psychologic terms, values are long-range attitudes, convictions, wishes, hopes, dreams, faith. They are what we hold near and dear and good. These are values; the principles we live and die for, so to speak.

Values, then, lie largely in the realm of ethics and ethical behavior. They have to do with attitudes, motivations, and convictions, with real and fancied choices. They are primarily social in scope and application. Their sphere lies in all human conduct in which significant alternatives are available. A choice must exist, and we choose one mode of behavior as better when compared with another. Values are always hierarchically integrated; that is, they are related in terms of a greater or lesser degree of desirability. Without choice there is no value judgment. What determines one's choice is the sense of values. This is what we mean by values.

Some therapists, for example, hold as good what we would hold as bad; and we hold as good what others do not believe is valuable. Some do not believe that the very fact that you are part of a group is good. They think that being alone with somebody is better. Perhaps neither of these alterna-

---

See ref. 147.

tives in and of itself is good, but still another choice: a combination of a happy, appropriate, reasonable, and significant measure of each of these varieties of experience.[114, 142]

We also want to raise the question whether what is therapeutically good is also healthy. Are values synonymous with health? As healers, as practitioners of the healing arts, may we affirm that anything that is healing, anything that is health-promoting, is good and whatever is health-denying or health-depriving is ipso facto bad? Can values, in this way, be translated into terms of health?

The therapist has values, the patient has values, and there are prevailing values in the community. Need these sets of values be consonant with one another, need they be in harmony? Need the values of the therapist and the patient be congruent? How much divergence can be tolerated? Clinical experience, for instance, seems to indicate that when the values in the family are significantly different from the values of the community, problems arise in the children. If the values of the therapist and the values of the community are significantly different, will such a state of affairs lead to problems in patients?[99, 100] Can the therapist do therapy and yet hold that certain conditions are health-giving if the community holds that they are health-denying, or the reverse?

Are there, moreover, general values, general human values, that supersede the particular therapeutic situation and specifically therapeutic values? Need they always be the same or are they always different? Can good therapy be done if these basic human values are in opposition to the values of therapy?[4, 102]

We think it is good that a therapist has values and we hope they are constructive values, for they will determine the effectiveness of his therapy. The therapist has values whether or not he admits or is aware of them. They are important in his selection of patients, his treatment practices, and his choice of goals. We wish to help make conscious the values of the therapist, especially the analyst who works in groups, to bring into awareness what his values are, so that those which are bad may be scrutinized, rejected, and worked through. Those that are good can then consciously be fostered, facilitated, and reinforced. Nor do we believe that the therapist must have only mild values, as some analysts think, as if strong convictions and strong feelings are prima facie bad. We feel, on the contrary, that the analyst's attitude of not wanting to take a firm and consistent position is bad.

We shall now attempt to specify some of the general human values, some of those related to psychoanalysis, and more especially those that are specific to doing psychoanalysis in groups. No claim is made that we have thoroughly explored any of them or that our list is exhaustive.

(*1*) The analyst's choice to do therapy in an individual or group situation is an expression of his values. The way the therapist perceives what is good and what is bad in himself and in the group affects the quality of the therapy. A dominating or authoritarian therapist, for instance, who sees the group as one person or who will not let the group meet as peers without him, may not do therapy as well as the individual therapist. He may demand extraordinary superego controls. But the patient stands a better chance of achieving a wholesome set of democratic and constructive attitudes toward his peers and the therapist in a group situation than with an authoritarian analyst alone.[135, 142]

A therapist can influence patients to become very much like himself, or submissive borderline egos who act out his schizoid or conflictful demands, or who act out their own id forces. Whatever the therapist's attitude—whether he is too detached, or too aggressive, too overbearing or too compliant, too rational or too irrational—his problems can be better coped with by a group of patients than by the isolated patient. This is not to say that we go along with the belief that the therapist's problems are treated by the group.[129, 146]

The resources of patients can be better mobilized by their interaction in a group setting than when having to deal with the therapist's problems in an exclusive, dyadic relationship. Patients working together in a group are likely to be better able to resist the therapist's irrational demands or his emphasis upon pathology than patients who work with the therapist alone. The choice of a group as the medium for therapy by the therapist as well as the patient is recognition of how the group setting can be a factor in moving the patient as well as the therapist toward more wholesome values.

(*2*) The group is a radical departure from the position of the patient on the couch, with the analyst seated behind. It is a geographic set-up in which the patient is seated facing not only the therapist but also his co-patients. He is forced into interpersonal interaction and intrapsychic exploration. The value of forced interaction already has been demonstrated for the dependent, passive, detached, and isolated patient. Most people in our society, though seemingly interactive, in many respects are really very isolated. In the group, patients have to look at one another and at the therapist. Out of forced interaction, we move toward intrapsychic exploration.[145]

When a patient sits in a group and does not look at the people he is going around on, when he sits gazing at the floor, group members soon complain that he is not looking at them, that he is not involved with them, that they want to see his eyes, they want him to talk to them. If he starts speaking to one member and the whole group does not hear, they demand that he be heard. If he addresses himself exclusively to the therapist, the group protests. The members force interaction.

How different this is from the traditional analytic arrangement. An individual analyst, for example, came to his supervisor and complained that for the past months the patient on the couch had spoken so softly that he did not hear her. What should he do about it? He was very surprised when the supervisor said, "Why not ask her to talk a little more loudly?" This could never happen in a group. Another instance is that of the patient on the couch who would fall asleep early in each session. The therapist took the position that if the patient felt like going to sleep, this was all right with him. Then there is the therapist who writes his letters, papers, and books while the patient is on the couch.

Some analysts seem too ready to permit the patient to isolate himself in intrapsychic fantasy, pathology, or sleep. Such a therapist permits—and sometimes even encourages—no interaction. He rationalizes this behavior by saying that he must encourage, teach, or develop frustration tolerance in the patient. Supposedly, one learns better to tolerate frustration by experiencing more frustration. We feel that one may be better able to tolerate frustration by being secure, by being less anxious, rather than by experiencing continuing frustration.

The principle of forced interaction is an important therapeutic process in the group. From the inception of psychoanalysis in groups, patients have been asked to "go around," to involve everybody in interaction.[135, 142, 145] From the interpersonal transactions we then can examine the behavior in terms of what stands in the way of more wholesome interaction. This is an important and constructive principle which both the patient and the therapist in the dyadic relationship often abandon.

We wish to warn against the practice of some therapists compulsively to impose pathologic interaction between patients and therapist and among patients.[129, 146] This is a seeming, pseudointeraction which is really non-communicative, fragmented and fragmenting, transference and countertransference. Our concept is quite different from that kind of forced, pathologic noninteraction in isolation. For us, the individual also must be given the opportunity to explore his own intrapsychic processes on a reasonable, healthy basis. In addition, he must have an opportunity for genuine, appropriate, and realistic inter-communication.[106, 109]

(3) In choosing to do psychoanalysis in groups, the therapist is expressing a belief that out of conflict and controversy come gains. In the group, patients become more aware of their differences and disagreements.[32] They learn to reach compromises, a more harmonious balance. They learn to sublimate some of their wishes, make concessions to one another, and be more flexible with each other. The therapist necessarily must examine conflict, difference, disharmony, disagreement and help patients to reach some sort of harmonious, relative agreement in compromise. What the

therapist values in this scheme is not conflict for itself but compromise, sublimation, the necessity to reach some partial fulfillment for the contestants.

(4) The analyst who works in groups accepts the fact that the patient must examine critically not only himself but also others. The group therapist believes that it is socially, psychologically, politically, humanly valuable for the therapist, too, to put himself in the position of being examined, criticized, challenged, questioned, that this is a valuable experience for the patient and an important value in life. We do not mean to foster rebellion which may already be a problem of the patient. We distinguish between rebellion and the wholesome necessity to examine leaders or persons in authority positions. Patients often need to learn that they can have the right and the courage to examine leadership critically. The critical reactions of the individual patient to the individual analyst is not always rebellious and resistive.

The patient in individual analysis has no feedback except the analyst. There can be little or no consensual validation of his critical view of the analyst, who can irrationally maintain his position of omnipotence. The group, on the other hand, provides opportunity for sharing and comparing experiences, for confirming or denying whether the reaction to the therapist was transferential or appropriate.

By virtue of the fact that he puts himself before a group, the group analyst exposes himself consciously to the possibility of criticism and the confirmation of its legitimacy. The therapist is not so different from other human beings that he can never be wrong. This makes him much more human and leads to the possibility of greater equalization.

An individual analyst once said, "You know, if any patient of mine called me by my first name I would throw him out of analysis." It is not calling the analyst by his first name that we are proposing. What we are pointing out is the attitude that I, the therapist, must never be perceived as a human being, as having a first name, as having any name but "The Analyst," in the orthodox sense. The classic anonymity of the analyst prohibits his exposure to consensually validated, realistic criticism.

Distinction must be made, however, between our position and the concept of status denial where the analyst not only subjects himself to criticism, but becomes more of a patient than the patients themselves.[79, 129] This is not what we mean by the therapist being subject to critical examination by group members. We do not mean sponsoring or acceding to a patients' or therapists' demands to establish a co-pathology, co-delinquency, or co-psychosis.

Implicit here is the right to criticize authority and the need of support for that right. Experimental and social psychologic studies of the authoritarian personality,[4, 99] support the value of being legitimately critical of authority, and also of the therapist making a legitimate mistake without having to hide behind the mask of anonymity, omnipotence, and omniscience. There are objectivity, critical value, and positive potentials, also in patients, in peers, in the child, in subordinates.

(5) We believe in the importance of the value of democracy. By democracy we mean not the absence of leadership or the absence of differences, but the value of each person in the interpersonal experience. A person has value in and of and for himself. Psychoanalysis in groups tends to encourage a more democratic way of relating. It rejects the absolutism of authority, the noncritical view of the therapist, and, at the same time, recognizes the value of peers. Not only parents, but also children have values; not only therapists, but also patients. The one does not exist without the other; together they constitute a reciprocal unit.

Interaction between therapist and patient is valuable, but so is the interaction among patients in the group. The interaction among peers is not only, always and exclusively negative, destructive and pathologic. The nature of a relationship to a co-patient is different from a relationship with the therapist, but nevertheless of value. Peers permit the possibility of a patient not only to be helped but also to help; not only to be supported but also to support; not only to depend upon but also to be depended upon. It attenuates the fiction of the benevolent giving by one person, the therapist.[101, 142]

The fact that a therapist chooses to apply therapy in the group situation says something about his valuing and his wish to explore a patient's relationship to peers as well as to authority figures. He is interested in providing a medium for the exploration of horizontal as well as vertical relationships, and the necessity to work these through. Moreover, problems with the authority figure can be more readily worked through with the support the individual receives from peers. The group facilitates the working through of authority and peer problems because both vectors are simultaneously present. The interplay of authority and peer vectors is present also in the relation of one patient to another.[109, 114, 135, 142, 149]

The patient in individual treatment often feels that he has no value, no position, no status, no consideration, no ego, no adequacy, unless he is alone with the therapist. Alone with the therapist he has value, he is regarded, he is felt, he is considered, he is a person, but once he is with another person or a group of persons, he is lost, he is inadequate, he is inferior, he has no position, no status. Psychoanalysis in groups mitigates against the preservation of such an irrational attitude, which must be worked through whether it is considered in the therapy group, in the family, in society, or in a democratic community. Such a patient needs to learn that he has position, status, equality, an ego; that he is a person who is valued, valuable to others and to himself; that his contributions are important; that we value him in the community and in the therapeutic group.

A common problem of patients is the difficulty they have in viewing themselves as peers, as equals. For example, whenever one man in a group is asked whether he is anybody's equal, he characteristically says, "No! I'm either superior to the next fellow or I'm inferior. I am never equal." He sees himself compulsively in this hierarchical position. We all suffer from this attitude in some degree. Perhaps, in some respects, it is also a true perception; in other respects, it is a distorted perception. The reality is that we are different. The question is whether this difference really makes us unequal. The group permits one to explore and understand differences.

(6) Differences are not to be ignored. The demand of society, of parents and even of psychoanalysts for conformity, adjustment, and sameness contains a denial of the value of difference. The preference among some group therapists for homogeneity is, in our opinion, the less valuable choice for the organization of therapy groups, for it reflects an attitude that tends to deny individual differences.

Differences can have equal value, but difference and equality are not on the same continuum. One can be equal in difference, because differences can have equal usefulness, acceptability, and validity. In psychoanalysis in groups it is possible to lose the sense of uniqueness without losing the sense of difference. The feeling of being unique is very often involved in pathologic formations and can be worked through. A sense of uniqueness can be given up and yet the validity of being different can be accepted. One can have a private life as well as a public life; one-to-one relationships as well as relationships to groups. One can have an individual and a group relationship. These can and should be integrated. It is possible to integrate a difference and a sameness without having to take either extreme, in uniqueness or loss of difference.

In individual analysis the therapist says, "I am the analyst, you a patient. You may be superior to me as a philosopher, as a technician, as a teacher, as a butcher, as an athlete, or in many other ways, but here, as analyst, I am superior to you." In psychoanalysis in groups, by providing a different atmosphere of peers, the patient is able to work out this problem more readily. In the group, the patient experiences the difference between patient and therapist, but simultaneously the sameness of his status with regard to other patients; they are peers. Yet each one is different, even though in the status structure of the group therapeutic situation they all are on an equal level. They are all equal before the therapist. They are all equally valuable and equally important to the therapist. The structure of equality and difference is conjointly present. They are men and women with different histories and different problems and in the group they can experience directly the possibility of being equal in the difference. This cannot be experienced first hand in the individual therapeutic situation.

The patient who feels he has no equals assumes that all human beings are hierarchically related. As long as he rigidly holds to this assumption he can never resolve the problem of equality and difference. Only when he accepts the fact that human beings can be horizontally related is the perception of equality in difference possible. There is no less value in the human quality of the person who is able to fulfill himself in his role in society as a mechanic than in that of the banker, or philosopher, or scientist. The difference in their contributions may be very great, and we may regard them differently, but without the mechanic the others cannot fulfill themselves in terms of their own life's plan. The fulfillment of the one is as necessary as of the other in order for humanity to progress. They have equality of necessity, of value, of responsibility, if you wish, in terms of the larger human picture. This does not mean that they are the same. It does not mean that they are equal in the sense of no difference. But they are equal in the sense that they have value, and we can hold the recognition of differences as being valuable in itself. The difference between male and female, between illness and health, between therapist and patient must not be obscured.

We are aware of the compulsive quest for diversity, which may then become the pathologic addiction to divisiveness and diversion. On the other hand, science seeks to simplify in order to lead to clarification, but it does not deny diversity as a state of nature. The one-sided pursuit of sameness or difference can be equally pathologic and misleading.

(7) We hold that there is an appropriate place for differences of opinion, even between analyst and patient; that controversy in and of itself is not bad, and that one can be critical, argue, and disagree and still be friends. We are opposed to those who believe it is base to think independently, to get into criticism and controversy.[32] Conformity and submission can be the only end products of such an attitude.[101, 108, 142]

This value is often neglected in the experience with the individual therapist because the patient does not really fight with the therapist, unless the therapist is counterattacking. But in the peer situation of co-patients, it is possible for attack and counterattack to occur and for the patients still to know that they can be friends. They can work together, despite the fact that they have attacked one another or even acted out with regard to one another. It is a striking admission on the part of new members of a therapy group when they indicate their amazement of how the others can express considerable ambivalence and hostility toward one another and yet walk out of a group meeting in the friendliest way and continue to work together. A new patient often feels startled by the way in which group members can dispute one another and still maintain a working relationship.

We are aware of the patient who must compulsively fight every individual before he can show any affection. This is the only way in which he can relate. There are also patients who compulsively emphasize only their feelings of being different. To be able to relate to only one kind of person, to be able to relate or function in only one way, is limiting and limited.

(8) We reject absolutism, totalism, and exclusivism. The principle of multiple reactivity and complementation represents an important value of psychoanalysis in groups.[109, 114, 135] It leads each patient to question the particular nature of his compulsive activity. It demands of him an examination of his prior and present modes of living. It helps him explore the possibilities of functioning in different ways. Group members question each other about the particular ways their competitive patterns limit them. Patients are forced in their exchanges with one another to seek compromises, to find a golden mean, to give up a totally isolated and egocentric position. They learn to recognize the distortion in total potency or total impotency, and to struggle for the acceptance of partial human capacities in their interaction.

The therapist and the patient must learn to accept their similarity with other individuals and their difference, as well as the different roles each single individual is called upon to play in different situations and relationships.

In individual analysis there is generally only one kind of activity the patient can perform. He, the taker, is dependent upon the therapist, the giver. What the patient gives are his "free-associations." This is his work, his giving. Theoretically, the role of listener is the therapist's; the patient does not have to listen. There is no real alteration of roles, in part due to the fact that the analyst has no right to seek fulfillment from the patient. When the patient becomes healthier and attempts to alter the nature of the roles, the therapist may interpret this as resistance and not permit the change.

Psychoanalysis in groups sponsors the recognition of the necessity in all human relations to assume different roles. In the group, the patient can now, this moment, be helped; but it demands also that within a short space of time he be a helper, that while he is listened to now, shortly he must listen to the other. It demands of him now that he pay attention to his own feelings, but that the next moment he attend the feelings of the other; or even that in the moment of expressing his feelings, he must consider their impact upon the feelings of the other. Now he can be attentive to his own affect; in the next moment he must be reasonable about the feelings he has expressed. While he can give vent to his feelings, he must apply some reasonable attention to the needs of other people. While this moment he may be impulsive, the next he must be more considerate. This shifting of roles makes a healthy demand on him to be responsible and to relinquish the resistive and rigid pattern of an exclusive way of relating.

We have already suggested that an exclusive way of relating is limited, whether only with authority figures or only with peers, only in the one-to-one relationship or only in the group. Even in the group therapeutic situation, if the patient is always the giver, always the helper, this can be resistance. The occasional assumption of such a role is healthy, but always to be in the role of helper is just as unhealthy as always to be in the role of being helped. It is part of totalism.

We believe it is good that peers and authorities can be examined in the variety of their aspects because of the multiplicity of interactivity and stimulation. A person can relate to, be stimulated by, and interact with many kinds of persons. In individual therapy, the patient must relate in a complementary way only to the therapist. In the group, the uniqueness of resources in the therapist is complemented by a multiple set of other persons. In the group, the patient has greater freedom to choose with whom to react, to what degree, and in what way. In individual analysis, the patient has no such choice except in reporting outside experience or in fantasy.

(9) In psychoanalysis in groups the patient learns to understand that he has no right to expect from all people the same kind of detached, objective understanding that he gets from the therapist; that the therapist's position is, in some respects, artificial. The therapist does not behave this way in his relationships outside of the therapeutic situation. If the therapist is attacked outside of therapy, he may withdraw or counterattack, or he may be hurt, or have a variety of human responses. If the therapist is always nonreactive to the patient's provocative role, then the patient never really learns to perceive his provocative role except insofar as the individual therapist wishes to interpret it as transferential. The patient may, however, have a provocative role which is not always transferential, but related to how he functions and what kind of person he is. With the therapist alone he may never become aware of how other people feel about him and how they see him. This benefit arises only in the therapeutic group.[135]

The patient also needs to learn about how his peers in the group react to him. In this way he comes to recognize the effects his rational and irrational expressions have produced in his peers in the group, as well as in society; in this way he gets to know his provocative roles, both positive and negative, with regard to peers as well as authorities. He becomes aware also of the difference between his peers in the therapeutic group and those in the community.

The patient has no right to the exclusive possession of the therapist or the other person. This misconception exists even in marital situations where one partner will demand the total and exclusive possession of the other. Exclusive possessiveness is mitigated by the group. However, there may be patients, as for example, the severely orally dependent type, who need a period alone with the therapist, perhaps projected as mother, before they can make a more wholesome transition to siblings, to peers, to the group, and relinquish the exclusive possession of the therapist. It would be unreasonable to refuse to perceive the patient's irrational needs for exclusive possession and to demand that he forego them at the moment. For this reason, individual sessions where they are really needed are appropriate. It is bad, in our estimation, for a group therapist to say, "I never hold an individual session."

(*10*) Just as relationship is important, we believe relationship cannot occur unless there is communication. Good communication is nonambiguous, open, direct, a free expression of feelings, thoughts and attitudes. One of the aims of any psychotherapy is to establish communication, for without verbal intercourse we cannot achieve real understanding.[101, 108, 109]

We think it is good if people have relatively uninhibited conversation with one another. Social intercourse can be relatively uninhibited. If one is as honest as is realistically appropriate to the relationship, this is a desirable kind of communication. We think that intercommunication, even in psychoanalysis, is as important as intracommunication, that is, communication with oneself or one's own unconscious processes.[109, 142]

We believe that to interpret to patients that they have experienced telepathic communication and that this is the "real," the unconscious-to-unconscious communication, is destructive. We reject, moreover, the value some therapists put upon inappropriate or irrational means of communication, namely, in sleep, in dreams, in telepathy, in nonverbal contact.[129, 146] Their emphasis upon irrational and isolating pseudo-communication is a preoccupation with destructive values. We wonder how much they try in their working through, to get the patient in therapy to communicate in a more appropriate way.

There are some people who can communicate in a one-to-one, private, secret relationship, whether good or bad. But the moment they are exposed to the more public situation of a group, they remain separated, withdrawn, detached, depressed, hesitant, and uncommunicative. Other people seem to be able to communicate only in the public relationship; in the group they seem related and interactive. In the intimacy of the one-to-one situation, they become isolated, hostile, anxious, uncommunicative. The presence or absence of the authority, the therapist, seems similarly to affect communication in some patients. Psychoanalysis in groups attempts, then, to provide a harmonious balance of individual and group experiences.

(*11*) In contrast to some analysts who prize isolation, we hold that relating, interacting with other human beings, in and of itself is good. We hope that in the therapeutic situation we shall be able to examine the nature of that relationship and to help make the relationship more constructive by working through the destructive elements and distortions and by fostering positive relatednesses. But relating to other human beings, as such, is valuable, as opposed to insulation and separation, as such. Aloneness, the absence of social interaction is dehumanizing.[101]

The group provides a happier medium for the evocation of problems in social living and the possibilities of a struggle toward their resolution. In its emphasis upon the interactive, the possibility of increased relatedness is offered by the group. If striving for equalization of parent and child, of teacher and student, of analyst and patient, is an objective in therapy, the attainment of this socialization is facilitated in the group by providing peers who can help the individual work through his tendency to attach himself to or over-invest in the authority figure, and finally come to a more wholesome approximation of equality.

Socialization is vital to the development and preservation of man. A human being is a socialized human animal. It seems to us valuable for him to be placed in a social context to humanize him further. The good therapist, whether he works with individuals or with groups, accepts the concept that man needs about him other human beings in order to mature, to be able to live adequately with other human beings. The analytic group is an excellent matrix in which to reconstruct the family, to provide an extra-familial group in which to make the transition from the projected family to nonfamilial wholesome associations, and to enable the patient to return more positively to his original family, once his projections have been worked through. Through his contact with other patients in the course of his struggle for growth, the patient learns to cooperate for the continuity and gratification of self and the group.

It is true that the patient in individual analysis may work out his problem with the family as reanimated in successive transference projections on the therapist. The group, however, facilitates the resolution of these problems because the whole canvas emerges more quickly and is, therefore, available for more lucid examination and working through. One gets a better picture of the multiple transferences operating in the family at the same time.[142]

(*12*) We believe that the group has value in and of and for itself. This does not mean that we do not value individual experience in therapy and in life. Living in a group, experiencing interaction in a group, is a maturing, fostering and broadening experience for human beings. The individual exists only by virtue of the fact that there are groups, and the group by virtue of the fact that there are individuals.

The purpose of being in a therapeutic group, however, is not so much to live as to learn. Therapy and the therapeutic group exist to provide a learning experience. This objective must be clear to both patient and therapist. Here patients are learning how to live, but the living takes place not in the group, although it is a living experience, but outside the therapy group, outside of the function of therapy. It is in the therapeutic group that one learns to live better, to live with more fulfillment, to live more constructively with other individuals and groups.

The group therapist, however, must not be misled and allow the group interaction to become the patients' substitute for social living and socialization. The individual analyst, aware of the aloneness of his patient, may encourage him to interact with other people and to socialize. The group therapist, providing a situation in which interaction with other people, the other patients, takes place, may tend to overlook the fact that this can be an isolating experience. Patients before they come into a therapy group may have relations with friends and family. They may give up these contacts and seemingly regress into the group and react exclusively with members of the group.

The ultimate objective of the therapeutic group, like the individual therapeutic experience, is that the patient will find social and sexual life and fulfillment outside of the relationship with the therapist and other patients. This pitfall must be kept firmly in mind by the group therapist or he can become seduced by the apparency of interaction into encouraging the aloneness and isolation of the patients. Patients may misuse the therapy group as the invested experience of socializing and thereby isolate themselves as some patients isolate themselves within the individual therapy situation. This possibility must be consciously pursued by the group analyst, especially if he uses the alternate session, one of the benefits of which is socializing. By providing patients with such an opportunity, further isolation from the larger social group can occur.

Moreover, it is an error of psychoanalysis in groups to allow patients to see the subculture of the therapeutic group as a microcosm of the total society, to see all of society as a generalization of the therapeutic experience. As the patient gets better he should want to slough off his more pathologic associates. It is, therefore, not only resistance when, after improvement, a patient wants to leave the group. To view this development only as resistance is to miss its positive implications. Furthermore, it is resistance to change for a patient not to want to leave the group, to resist getting well, because here is a controlled social life, a provided social life. Just as the family may be used as a means of not relating to people who are different, so the therapy group may be a way of not relating to or avoiding relationships with those who are different, those who are not members of the therapeutic group.

(*13*) Although we see value in real belonging, we recognize a current, phony concept of belonging. It is often a pseudo-belonging as, for example, in the group patient's inability to attach himself positively to someone outside the group. It is an apparent, transferential, pseudo-belongingness that isolates him in therapeutic relationships.

This happens even in life. We are reminded of the case of a young woman whose father said, "You can belong to me and be loved by me, but only on my conditions, only on my terms." That is, only if she accepts the irrational demand of the superordinacy of the parent and the subordinacy of the child. This is a kind of transferential belonging which is different from real belonging. Transferential belonging can occur in the group, and the therapist may unwittingly encourage and accept it as if it were real. One sees pseudo-belongingness also in individual analytic relationships where, for example, the therapist develops an intimacy with his patient and sees her only during analytic sessions, but makes no real relationship with her outside of this fantasy one.

(*14*) We reject the tendency among some group therapists to permit a pathologic subculture to develop where one patient will say to the next, "Well, what do you want of me, that's my neurosis." This attitude is sometimes seen in individual analysis and is even cultivated by the individual therapist, when he tries, no matter what, to understand the patient and permits him to go on acting out his pathology.

Psychoanalysis in groups recognizes that the patient must become increasingly aware not only of himself but of others. This contrasts with more orthodox individual analysis where too often the patient becomes almost exclusively preoccupied with his own intrapsychic processes.[109] In such a case, we say, it is poor individual analysis. The group, however, by its very nature demands forced interaction and interpersonal communication. The patient must be attentive also to the problems and resources of the people around him. The group demands that he be creatively adaptive to the individuals with whom he is associating. He not only can adapt himself, but he tries to adapt the environmental situation to himself.

Psychoanalysis in groups precipitates areas of interpersonal conflict and forces the individual to scrutinize his and others' roles in creating the opposition, the impasse. The antagonists must seek means to resolve and work through the intrapsychic pathology that has led to the interpersonal conflict.[32, 145]

Psychotherapy has been too largely devoted to the elucidation of psychopathology and given less attention to the necessity for bringing out and developing the patient's healthy potentials.[110] Too little attention has been paid to the problem of working through.[146] In working with groups, one is impressed by the extent to which patients confront one another spontaneously and healthily with the demand to try constructive alternatives. Questions occur like, "Why don't you try this?" Or, "Don't you see that . . .?" Or, "Can't you make an effort to . . .?" It is noteworthy that the group is generally more impatient with, less tolerant of, and less interested in psychopathology than the therapist. This is a positive value in human beings who are patients, who do not have the kind of interest, sometimes obsessive, that the therapist has in psychopathology.

(*15*) We reject the view that health rises out of pathology. We see it, in its extreme, in the form of the "therapeutic psychosis." The assumption is made that out of illness, through the expression of pathology, you rid yourself of the demon that possesses you. Then you will be healthy. It is true that healthy potentials will be freer if the psychopathology is worked through. But we have the feeling that if we work more with the constructive potentials in patients, the freedom to use those potentials is increased and pathologic barriers to freedom will atrophy. But it is a misconception to believe that the source of what is health-giving, of what is constructive and creative, is the pathology. Some therapists value pathology more than health.[110, 129, 146]

We do not hold that catharsis results in health. Indeed, catharsis is valuable, but like pathology it is not the via regia to mental health. Merely to cathart, to express pathology, is not in itself curative. Something has to be done with it. To insist that it is healthy if one can express unconscious material directly is a mistaken value. It overemphasizes intrapsychic material. Nor are psychodynamics equal to therapy. Psychodynamics knowledge, like diagnostic information, provides material for therapeutic work, but together they do not constitute the therapeutic process. This is pars pro toto reasoning. To view therapy and dynamics as one is to misconceive the analysis of the dynamics as the cure. Moreover, psychodynamics and psychopathology are not the same. A good psychodynamic understanding of the patient includes all of his functioning, positive as well as negative. We want to know his motivations for health as well as unhealth.

With regard to psychoanalysis in groups, it is true that the group stimulates psychodynamics and that the alternate meeting in particular stimulates psychodynamics, but not only the psychodynamic pathology but also the psychodynamic healthy potentials in the patient are stimulated. What happens reconstructively depends on how the therapist uses the pathologic and healthy psychodynamics.

(*16*) We feel it is valuable to understand that in all situations, including psychoanalysis in groups, there is structure, process, and content, and that each is related to the others. Values are implicit in which of these we stress and how we use each of these. Those who stress content, for example, generally miss the unconscious, the psychodynamic material. They miss also status and interaction problems which arise out of the nature of the structure. The structuring of the therapeutic process also implies values. To emphasize the structure as opposed to process or content, namely, in what setting, as opposed to how and with what material you choose to therapeutize, is also one-sided and non-discriminative. It leads to limited therapeutic results.[114, 142]

(*17*) Psychoanalysis in groups provides an excellent opportunity to evaluate old values and learn new ones. As one experiences through interaction and intercommunication, and shares values, convictions, and attitudes with other members of the group, one learns to evaluate one's own traditional, familial values and, at the same time, to learn new values. Values arise in the interaction between individual and individual, group and group, and between the individual and the group. In the individual analytic situation only one of these three sources for the derivation of values is provided by the therapy. In psychoanalysis in groups, all three exist.

The values we have discussed so far are those that have specificity with regard to psychoanalysis in groups. We feel that they have application to all therapy as well as to the individual in society. Nevertheless, we have omitted a number of genuine values, some of which we must list, no matter how briefly. We are not elaborating even those we include here, but we recognize that they lie *au fond* and provide the substructure for the values of psychoanalysis in groups.

(*1*) We have reached an unfortunate point in psychology, as well as in the culture in general, where it is believed that experiencing and expressing affect are more enlightening than logic or reason. The value of intelligence and reason is often neglected. We are not advocating an exclusive view of human function. Affect and action also are valuable. Thinking, feeling, and doing must be integrated and the compulsive pursuit of any one of them to the exclusion of the others is not good. Nevertheless, we wish to state our belief that human desires may be directed by reason. "The voice of the intellect is a soft one, but it does not rest until it has gained a hearing," Freud said. "Ultimately, after endlessly repeated rebuffs, it succeeds. This is one of the few points in which one may be optimistic about the future of mankind, but in itself it signifies not a little."

(*2*) We believe that there is value in the funded wisdom of human experience. Culture, training, human interaction, and exchange are valuable. History and context must not be pursued in and for themselves, but they are useful.

(*3*) We believe that flexibility and judgment are good.

(*4*) We esteem educability and change. One of the ordeals of the psychotherapist is the patient's enduring resistance to change. Yet a patient with no resistance would be psychotic or the totally passive and dulled instrument of the therapist. In many ways, it is overcoming the patient's resistance that makes psychoanalysis such a fascinating experience for the therapist. The patient's tempering his rigidity in the face of insight is an endlessly exciting and wonderful experience. It is intriguing to observe his opposition begin to defer to reality. The patient whose resistance takes the form of utter compliance is not nearly so interesting, until his passivity yields to self-assertive claims. But the possibility of change is one of the most stimulating, rational gratifications available to both patient and therapist.

(5) A comprehensive view of human behavior includes not only the manifest act but also the motivation. Behavior and motivation may be either consciously or unconsciously determined.

(6) It is necessary for human beings to learn in the family, in therapy, and also in life the difference between right and wrong. In therapy the analyst must refuse to yield to a patient's pathology and in so doing strengthen the patient's sense of values. The sense of what is right and what is wrong is a consequence of human interaction, never of mystic intuitive inheritance.

(7) Freedom is good. It implies a rejection of false necessity, of fate. We mean the concept of choice, selectivity, discrimination, parity, and spontaneity. In freedom one can survey, understand, and accept the possibility of multiple alternatives and to make a choice within those. It implies, too, an awareness of responsibility in anticipating the consequences of the decision for the self and for others. We do not mean the encouragement of the illusion that limitlessness and license represent freedom. Liberty is not derived from acting on impulse or in compulsion. Too often the patient's and the therapist's insistence upon the "right" to have every kind of experience is simply a rationalization for acting in pathology. Their freedom is lost unless they discriminate sufficiently to choose reality as more valuable than oceanic fantasy.

(8) Mutual aid and cooperation are good. Not only does the human being need to be supported, but also to support others; to protect and to be protected; to help and to be helped; to love and to be loved.

(9) Since problem-solving is one of the characteristics of the human being, what facilitates this capacity is good. Psychoanalysis, science, rationality, propose that problem-solving be based upon scrutiny, causality, observation, comparison, and reason rather than upon authority and revelation.

(10) Finally, we hold as bad the growing tendency in current psychotherapy to reject training, clinical experience, social interaction, and rationality. Speculation and philosophizing need more than subjective confirmation. They must be based upon human experience and tested in clinical and life situations. The present withdrawal into mysticism among certain psychotherapists as a more adequate substitute for reason reflects a bewilderment and a sense of inadequacy before the inexorable logic of science. An irrational school of therapists is regressing to magical notions of treatment while announcing them as an advance. For the idolatry of the past they are substituting glorified illusions that security lies only in the momentary satisfaction of pathologic strivings. But our experience shows that whenever we build a structure on unreasonable foundations, no good can come of it. We cannot gain more understanding by resigning our rational responsibilities or by resurrecting antiquated and cabalistic devices when sounder means are available. To relinquish our hard-won victories over mystification is to submit once again to a despotism of unreason and the destruction of values.

12. An Application

The history of psychoanalysis has amply demonstrated its usefulness not only in treatment settings but also in other areas of human activity. Psychoanalytic theory has furthered the growth of the behavioral sciences such as anthropology, history and sociology. Psychoanalytic thinking has been applied successfully in order better to understand such a wide range of human problems as language and communication, folklore and literature, art and work, family life and diplomacy. Our psychoanalytic forbears recognized the dynamic similarity between child rearing, government and psychoanalysis.[34] The analyst is committed to freedom and change, and he has applied his tools to every aspect of the human condition.[54] Having investigated the roots of neurotic and psychotic development in childhoood he turns to education as an important experience outside the family in which prophylactic measures in the furtherance of good mental health must be stimulated. It is in this context that we have drawn from our understanding of psychoanalysis and psychoanalysis in groups these formulations which may be suggestive for the teacher, the educator. As we shall discuss in our final chapter, there may be a better future if psychoanalysis for treatment is coupled with psychoanalysis for prevention.

We have already investigated the differences between psychoanalysis in groups and individual psychoanalytic work. In the group there are, in general, observable quantitative increases in security, interaction and stimulation. One of the most important qualitative differences between individual analysis and psychoanalysis in groups lies in the nature of the hierarchic and peer relationships. In individual analysis equality can never be achieved, because, by its very structure, the vector is always in the direction of the vertical relationship. The hierarchic position of the analyst, no matter how benign it remains, takes the growing edge off the patient in individual or group therapy. Although the aim of all good psychoanalytic therapy is the actualization of the human equality of patient and therapist, it can never be fully achieved in a vertical relationship.

See ref. 145.

This structural asymmetry can in fact be a negative force in relation to the patient. There are times when the psychoanalyst is defensive and strives to maintain his position of authority. The following is a case in point. A psychoanalyst was sitting behind the patient who was lying on the couch. The patient complained that the analyst was not paying attention. The analyst had been reading a letter and not listening. Nonetheless, his response to the patient was "You're always looking for attention." In this way the analyst repeated some of the patient's traumatic experiences with parents and teachers who could never be wrong. Not only was the psychoanalyst's unrealistic interpretation destructive, but it made the appropriate feelings of the patient unacceptable to the analyst and to the patient. The analyst confused further the patient's capacity to differentiate between projection and reality. This kind of situation can rarely take place in the group. Here the psychoanalyst sits as part of the circle, and the peers—the other members—give strength to the patient to face the father or mother in the analyst with whatever affect is being experienced.

The group, therefore, provides anchorages in reality. There the distortions of the psychoanalyst are not accepted by patients so readily. When the analyst's authority is questioned, he may respond in different ways. He may deal with the issue as the patient's problem, he may admit his mistake if he has made one, or he may become defensive. In the group there is greater likelihood that the analyst will be seen as a human being. It is easier for the group than for the individual alone to demand of the psychoanalyst a basic humanity in the interpersonal relationship. It is easier also for the group psychoanalyst to maintain a healthy regard for the symmetry of human relations.

In the group, the individual may discover that it is possible to fight and still be friends, that it is possible to have differences of opinion and still be members of the group without losing membership or face. The group experience, then, is different from that in the original family. Furthermore, the arrangement of the group offers an important possibility for contact and emotional exchange of feelings. The circle in which the patients sit and the looseness of the chairs make for greater physical contact and more genuine horizontality than do the couch-chair or across-the-desk arrangement of the individual therapeutic setting.

In psychoanalysis in groups the patient is not obliged to choose only the analyst with whom to relate. He has no need to perpetuate the idea that he must become involved with only one person or one kind of person. In this way problems of divided loyalty, prejudices, submission and rebellion are more easily perceived and worked through. In the group, feelings can move in both the peer and the authority directions. The group permits feelings to be experienced between any two individuals in the group, in the vertical or horizontal direction.

Many patients come for treatment seeking emotional fulfilment in the analytic relationship. It can rarely be found in the individual setting because the psychoanalyst does not ordinarily enter the therapeutic situation seeking fulfilment from his patients. On the other hand, all patients in the group want fulfilment. What cannot be experienced directly with the psychoanalyst may be experienced with other patients. Some individuals who have never been able to gratify themselves in the presence of the family manage now to express overt feelings toward others in the group with its approval. Some people who feel hopeless about ever being accepted or loved may be re-educated by the group.

Of course, not all fulfilment is necessary or desirable. The encouragement of fulfilment may lead to acting out without full understanding of the transference feelings involved. Compulsive acting out, with its mutually- or self-destructive trends, needs to be controlled, and the group is effective in this respect. Patients who come into the group with a sense of being unacceptable and a need to be loved sometimes experience growth through the analyst. Where fulfilment of the need to be loved is sought in the peer relationships, most patients can recognize limits. Sometimes the therapist's stand for health sets the limits on acting out; in the main, however, the group sets its own limits. As Thelen puts it, "A member has expectations for certain ways of behaving in the various situations in which the group finds itself. He is aware of performance standards, and of limits to expression; of criteria of relevance which he can use to control and direct his behavior in such a way that he can obtain reward for participating."[126]

Some psychotherapists nevertheless believe that the group tends to foster acting out. Among the forms of patient behavior the one most feared by the therapist seems to be acting out. Thelen observes, "Our point of view is that through social interaction, conversation and expression of feeling, the group exerts influence on the individual and the individual on the group; the problem of control is not to prevent these kinds of influencings but to try to obtain a quality of influencing that improves learning."[126]

Any activity of the patient, including acting out, can be used constructively in therapy. There is a tendency among psychoanalysts to threaten patients with punishment or abandonment if they act out. This is not therapeutic. Acting out, permitted to go on unanalysed, is destructive, and the psychoanalyst should take a stand against it. But if it occurs, it can frequently be used positively for a productive working through by demonstrating its self-destructive nature.[144] Sometimes, acting out remains within the group frame. This is one of the advantages of the alternate meetings from which the analyst is absent. At these meetings patients let their hair down and express their feelings to one another more freely. When the therapist is present, he is sometimes seen as a forbidding figure of authority. Often, the patient uses the alternate session in order to test new-found personal strength. There is always, however, auxiliary strength which resides in the group and which the individual secures from the group in the expression of either love or hostility.

Just as there are differences between individual and group psychoanalysis, so there are differences between the analytic group and the educational one. Every therapeutic group is educational, but not every educational group is therapeutic. The purpose of education is not very different philosophically from that of therapy; namely, to encourage the freedom of the human being to grow and develop to the maximum of his potentials as a social animal. Here psychoanalysis can offer to education a series of theoretic ideals. One objective may be formulated as the freedom to explore the self and the environment, to try the new and the different, to disagree with the told, leading to a fuller self- and outside-awareness. Another goal involves freedom from compulsion and rigidity, with the capacity to accept and direct change, a flexibility resulting in new ways of being and relating, in changed attitudes toward foreign ideas and material things, and a capacity to tolerate errors and differences in oneself and others. Still another aim is the capacity to tolerate frustration and postpone the immediate gratification of needs, an ability to accept an altered aspiration level. Another set of anticipated outcomes can be stated as the attainment of mutual respect, cooperation and help, the capacity to put the other before the self, or the self in place of another, and the ability to change attitudes toward children, parents, students, teachers, minorities and authorities. Finally, in the struggle for reintegration, we hope to achieve a capacity to work and to plan, to play and to struggle, to love and to be loved.

These ideals shared by psychoanalysts and educators are not pursued in the same fashion. The structure, materials and methods of the two processes are quite different. The educational group is not voluntary. People generally come to the psychoanalytic group voluntarily. For both, the experience serves as the basis for change, and the right to influence others is vested in the authority of the teacher, the analyst, or the setting.

Both the educator and the psychoanalyst are expected to provide good conditions for human growth. The teacher, however, affords an original learning which follows on the school of the mother's knee. In one sense, the teacher, like the analyst, does remedial work by allowing students to experience anew with the teacher ideas and attitudes which were badly or traumatically acquired in the family. This re-educational process, however, is not consciously pursued in the educational group. A therapeutic group experience is predominantly a corrective one. The educational group is sometimes remedial, sometimes preventive, but most often instructive. The acquisition of information and attitudes becomes the largest part of the educational group's activity.

These two kinds of groups work with different subject matter, but the methods each group uses to solve its problems characterize the chief dissimilarity. In the educational group, the emphasis is almost exclusively upon content. In the psychotherapeutic group it is less upon content and more upon feeling. The possibility of extending the right to freedom and growth is bound to be richer and more meaningful in the therapeutic group than in the educational group. Parallels, however, can be drawn and extended.

Teachers cannot be expected to convert their classes into psychoanalytic groups. The popularization of psychoanalysis has created confusion among teachers and laymen by assuming that only psychoanalysts and the psychoanalysed really know what is going on. The psychoanalyst's word must be taken as the last word. In this way, parents and teachers lose spontaneity and become self-conscious. They begin to see themselves as the cause of all problems. Psychoanalysts, thereby, unwittingly interfere with the free exchange of feelings between parents, teachers and children.

Finally, the conclusion is reached that all people need to be analysed; that no one can really understand the working of the human mind and interact as a human being without having been analysed. Parents tremble in anticipation of what they are doing to their children. The analyst is held in reverence, and this attitude is encouraged, unfortunately, by some psychoanalysts. Too many parents today hesitate to make a move toward the child without first consulting Gesell, Spock, or the psychoanalyst.

There is a tendency for the psychoanalytically oriented person who approaches the educational process to look upon the children and their behavior from the point of view of psychopathology and disorder. There is little positive that one can do from this position. It is important not to superimpose psychoanalytic concepts upon education with little appropriateness or practicality. Psychoanalysis can give to the teacher insights into disturbances within himself, in the child and in group relations. But the educator must not view himself as a psychoanalytic private eye, a Sherlock Holmes ferreting out psychopathology. This approach would destroy education as an emotional environment dedicated to the freedom of the child in his self fulfilment.

It may seem that we are denying that psychoanalysis has any usefulness in education, but this is not true. Psychoanalysis, like education, must seek to free the child from blocks and inhibitions in order to achieve maximal self realization. Character building, a goal of all education, is certainly directed towards the intensification of the purposeful human relationships dedicated to the achievement of emotional goals.

Moreover, psychoanalytic understanding has value in teacher selection, curriculum construction, and pupil placement; in diagnosing and resolving pupil disabilities; and in facilitating parent–teacher and student–teacher relations. But we do not believe, as do some psychoanalysts, that only by being analysed can the teacher be a good teacher. Such a position would deny that there are any psychoanalytic insights more directly applicable to education.

It is a matter of accident that "of all the social sciences, education has availed itself least of the potential resources of psychoanalysis."[125] It is largely because psychoanalysts have continued to maintain that the psychoanalysed teacher or pupil is the answer to the problem.[84, 99, 125] It would be better, it seems to us, that the contributions of psychoanalysis be reduced to specific and concrete ideas that are directly applicable to contemporary educational procedures without demanding a reconstruction of the teaching personnel or of the philosophy and practice of formal education. We, as analysts, prefer to stimulate the imagination of educators to explore new possibilities and new alternatives rather than impose upon them a doctrinaire position.

What, then, are some of the things that the educator can learn from psychoanalytic therapy? It seems to us that the hierarchic relationship between the teacher and his pupil is never lost. The teacher wants high marks from his students; if he does not get them, he punishes his pupils because he feels that he in turn will be punished—as part of the hierarchic system—if they do not achieve success.

Despite this hierarchic vector in education, there are ways in which the teacher can encourage students to interact and so help them work out some solution to their own problems of acceptance and growth in relation to authority as well as to their peers. If the teacher is able to create a warm atmosphere and does not remain detached, he encourages the students to interact more warmly. There is also less likelihood, then, that the class will attack the teacher. If the teacher maintains the vertical position unbendingly, if there is no contact either between teacher and pupils or among the pupils themselves, the teacher invites attack which is somewhat analogous to the acting out of patients. It is not easy to describe how a warm atmosphere is created, or to measure the extent of warmth. The teacher's role, nevertheless, must be one of responsiveness in a democratic, more symmetrical atmosphere with a healthy respect for the children and their resources, and especially their capacity to develop and make decisions on their own. Without being overprotective and worrisome about their ability to follow their own inclinations safely, one can help the child and the class in the discovery of their resources and limitations.

If the teacher is overdirective, he tends to infantilize the pupils. Some students who act only on command are unable to function without direction. The overt expression of the teacher's interest in his students, even physical contact between the teacher and the pupils, builds a positive climate.

In this connection, it may be of value to alter the formal arrangement of the classroom in order to facilitate greater physical contact among the pupils and between pupils and teacher. In psychoanalysis in groups, the looseness of chairs and their arrangement in a circle with the analyst as part of it, diminishes the formal aspects of the vertical relationship. By contrast, in the school the authority vector predominates. In the typical classroom, students have no relationship with one another, no peer relatedness except that which is permitted by the teacher. All eyes are on the teacher. All attention must be directed toward the satisfaction of the demands of the teacher. Any energetic interaction among the pupils is frowned upon, or even punished, by the teacher.

In this kind of structuring, the children never see the faces of other children except by sly unapproved glances. Only when students leave class are they permitted to have a relationship with each other. Unfixed seats not only provide opportunity for increased motility, physical contact and closeness among the members of the group, they also foster the breakdown of the superimposed verticality of the classroom.

In the fixed seat situation, where the teacher demands all attention to be focused upon him, the fulfilment of oneself in relation to one's peers is blocked. Piaget[85] has pointed out that the socialization of the child is best affected through peer relationships. This dynamic seems to have been overlooked in the usual school where children sit fixedly and are passive receptacles of adventitious information.

As has long been known by educators, the size of the class is of consequence. The experience we have had in psychoanalysis in groups indicates that once the group gets beyond the number ten or thereabouts, its group character tends to diminish. Then cohesion, identification and interaction are also reduced, and we have a group only in the most artificial of senses. We would assume, therefore, that students in a class numbering more than ten have little feeling of belonging.

The teacher's role includes encouraging the imagination and the expression of it. Emphasis upon facts, upon dates and upon data, all tend to limit the child's capacity to grow and to feel about himself, the others around him, and the world in which he lives. It is true that it is difficult to grade, to give marks, to an expression of the imagination. Perhaps the whole idea of marking and of evaluating other human beings—not in terms of their individual growth and potentials, but in competition with one another—is to be questioned.

The teacher should be aware of his own needs so that the kinds of countertransferences we see in psychoanalysis can be avoided. The teacher may demand that some of his needs be satisfied by the class. He may expect love from his students; he may want gratification from particular pupils or from the class as a whole. If the group has cohesion and identity of its own, if members of the group are related and interact, the irrational demands of the teacher will be more successfully resisted by the group. The teacher cannot then so easily dominate the class or compel it to conform. When teachers, like psychoanalysts, insist on homogeneity and conformity they are, we feel, masking a drive to dominate and control.

It is essential that the pupils' activities be directed not only toward the teacher but also toward each other. In group psychoanalysis, this is accomplished by the encouragement of emotional interaction. Pupils can be stimulated to react to one another, to be honest in their feelings about one another. They can learn to accept feelings expressed toward one another, whether these feelings are of a positive or negative nature. As has already been pointed out about therapeutic groups, patients learn that they can fight and still be friends, so it should be possible in the classroom for one pupil to express an unfriendly feeling toward another and still be friends. By facilitating such interaction, greater freedom, expressiveness and mutual respect can be achieved.

The teacher, like the analyst, may be concerned about going too far, about limits. As we suggested earlier, self-imposed discipline and limits can be expected, in the main, from most people. The individual tends to derive the necessary strength from the group as well as from the presence of the authority figure to set his own limits to his destructive tendencies. This applies also to the classroom. When students recognize acting out as self-destructive and hurtful to others, the tendency to act out diminishes.

We are aware of the teacher's conflicts in attempting to resolve the choice between freedom and discipline, between anarchy and control, between integration and disintegration. We are aware of the boring repetitiousness of the patterns of education. We understand the teacher's resistances to change and how his exercise of authority becomes marked by complacent rigidity. We believe, however, that it is possible for students and teacher cooperatively to come to some resolution of these conflicts to the benefit of all.

Children as well as adults hunger for a group experience, to be part of a group, to belong. This does not mean that there is a loss of individuality, a loss of individual difference. One can be related to authority, have feelings of self awareness and self esteem and, at the same time, have group membership. Belonging helps to overcome a sense of extreme difference, of uniqueness. The opportunity to be a member of a group, to be supported by it, often does away with the need to act out.

The significance of the educational group is very complicated. A good deal more research will have to be done to understand its complexity. By its nature, the classroom permits less freedom than is to be found in the psychoanalytic group. This does not mean, however, that greater freedom cannot be achieved by an increased awareness of its necessity on the part of teachers. The teacher seems less willing to allow freedom than the group analyst, because the teacher fears blame if the children get out of control, blame from administration, parents and fellow teachers.

One of the most important recommendations we should like to make is that for every class, students be provided regularly with a period of time in which to express their feelings toward one another, toward their school, toward their courses, toward their teachers and toward anything else they would like to express feelings about. One might arbitrarily set aside a given part of each day to allow the class to express these feelings. If the teacher shows an interest in the pupil's feelings about him or about others, the teacher may soon learn to ask, "Did I make you feel bad?" For the teacher to make such an inquiry implies the possibility that the teacher may do something to hurt students. Even to be willing to countenance this thought involves a gigantic change in pupil–teacher relations. This procedure would enable children to find their proper places as human beings in relation to one another and to authority. It might also help the teacher to know better what he is doing; what effect he is having on the feelings and on the life of his students.

This expression of feeling, in which children are encouraged to talk without fear of punishment or retaliation, will improve human relations in the school, the home, the larger community and social group. The class now becomes a place for testing feelings, thoughts, attitudes and rights in relation to other human beings. In this way, the class permits the ventilation of feelings which might otherwise be pent up and inappropriately displaced on to other situations and persons.

Just as each pupil and each class need time at the end of the day to express feelings which have accumulated, so the teacher also ought to have such opportunities. Perhaps the teacher does not need this opportunity every day; perhaps the teacher needs the opportunity, but it cannot be made available every day. It should be possible, nevertheless, for teachers to meet together regularly in groups and express their feelings toward one another and their pupils. They may wish also to tell each other what the students have said in their group sessions about other teachers and about themselves. We are aware of the teachers' need for group support quite independent of their activities in the classroom. These group sessions will help teachers to ventilate some of the repressed feelings and attitudes which are often displaced unconsciously upon pupils.

As a consequence, teachers and students will come closer and develop a healthier respect for themselves and for each other. In an ideal sense, this experience might also be provided for groups of parents, for groups of parents and teachers, and parents together with their children. How far we can extend this opportunity must be guided by realistic limitations. However, it does not seem too much to expect within the contemporary educational system that students as well as teachers be provided with such opportunities regularly.

Psychoanalysis offers no panacea for human beings in societies or in educational situations in which the structure itself is pathogenic. There are realistic limitations of time, space and other conditions which cannot be surmounted easily by the teacher or by the students. The group setting, however, can be utilized more consciously as an important educational experience and a profound human experience, if interaction among members of the group is encouraged by those in authority, so that authority is somewhat levelled and peer relationships strengthened.

It is by the struggle to achieve greater symmetry in human relations, regardless of the formal structure of the situation, that self acceptance and self realization can be achieved. We do not recommend the complete analysis of the child or of the teacher. We do not recommend that analytic concepts be superimposed upon education. Psychoanalysis offers a better way of understanding human behavior. Experience from individual analysis and, more especially, psychoanalysis in groups, may stimulate teachers to think along new lines and to try out procedures that have been demonstrated to increase the intellectual and emotional freedom of human beings in social situations.

13. Synthesis

This chapter is an integration, a pulling together of what has gone before. It is an overview with the purpose of anticipating what is still to be done. Its presents similarities and contrasts, an explanation of variations in psychoanalysis when it is applied in a group. We are not attempting to demonstrate the advantages of practicing analytic therapy in an individual or a group setting. Good analysis can be done in either. We are interested rather in exploring variations in process, material, content and activity.

Two people getting together, and eight or ten people getting together, make for quantitative and qualitative differences in behavior both of the therapist and the patient. The person who rigidly maintains the same kind of activity, be he analyst or patient, whether he is in the one-to-one or in the group situation, is resistive or distortive.

While the patient or therapist may choose the individual or group setting in which to work, it can be assumed that if he has problems in the group situation, he has problems also in the individual situation, and vice versa. Perhaps certain kinds of difficulties become more acute in one or the other setting, but all of us have problems in both climates. There may be an actual or seeming easier participation in one milieu, but closer study reveals limitations in both. A man who has sexual intercourse has not necessarily solved his heterosexual problems; nor has a man who lives in group situations necessarily solved his group problems.

Therapist's Motivation

The individual analyst generally believes that the intensity of the dyadic relationship is a motivating and curative force. He subscribes to the necessity for complete concentration upon one person as the way in which unconscious material can be uncovered more effectively. He is convinced of the need to work through a single transference relationship, specifically with regard to the parental figures, as the core problem. The group analyst,

---

See ref. 113.

on the other hand, has conviction about the importance of interaction, about the value of peers, and working through sibling transferences as well as parental projections on them, rather than exclusive dependence upon authority.

Group therapy seems to attract, among others, both an authoritarian and a self-devaluating type of therapist. The aggressive therapists, in general, seem to regard individual analysis as a more profound therapeutic experience than the group, even though they do group therapy. The self-devaluating therapists seem to prefer the group perhaps because they do not esteem their own expertness and overinvest patients with potentials for offering one another and the analyst help in treatment. The therapist's preference for a field of operation may have both healthy and pathologic determinants.[143]

Privacy and Exposure

The individual analytic relationship is a more secure one, from the point of view of privacy, and the group leaves the individual less certain in terms of exposure to outsiders.[111] But clinical experience has shown that extra-group revelations are rare, usually anonymous and, therefore, no serious detriment to treatment. If we encounter a patient who is a compulsive gossip, our means of trying to cope with him is to analyze this necessity rather than to exclude him from the group. If, however, the group life is threatened too much by such a patient, he may have to be extracted and the problem worked through before he can be reintroduced to a group.

Patients are wary at first of joining a group, more intimidated at the prospect of their privacy being invaded by the group, than by exposure to persons beyond the group. Here the anxiety revolves around the fear of being discovered with shortcomings, and condemned for them.

A form of mental suffering which many neurotics endure is the guilt of dishonesty or the belief that they are wicked behind a façade of respectability. It is the burden of having to maintain a spotless reputation that keeps some people from psychotherapy and forces others to seek out an analyst who may understand and relieve them. For some patients the therapist's forbearance is not enough. The feeling remains that he is unique and God-like in his tolerance, that if the truth were more widely known, all patients would be outcasts. For these, the analytic group is a more practical sanctuary, for there they can test out the compassion and sympathy of a more diverse community. For those, then, who overvalue the opinions of others, for those for whom the mischief lies not in immorality but in being discovered in it, the group is a very salutary influence. Not infrequently these very patients, themselves so victimized, become the self-righteous guardians of morality in the group, pretentiously condemning deviations among the idealists, poets, and dreamers, as if these were now the renegades from respectability. It is as if by assuming the appearance of outraged militancy before lack of principle, they can more readily conceal their own aberration.

Tolerance

We are led to the question of the relative tolerance of group members and of the analyst, and the effect of permissiveness on the course of therapy. The question is sometimes raised as to what factors make for tolerance of the individual patient by the others in the group. Some group therapists project the group as so intolerant of difference, so hostile, that they try to make the group as homogeneous as possible, rather than to help each patient work through to the tolerance of healthy differences in every other patient. The factors in the group that make for tolerance are empathy, mutual wholesome identification, pathologic identification with each other's abnormality, bilateral inclinations to act out and gratify archaic urges, acceptance of cultural and experiential differences, and a sense of equality as patients.

Sometimes the group is also much more intolerant of the repetition of pathology than the therapist may be. The therapist's preoccupation with and exploration of it, make him at times too tolerant of persistent psychopathology. While the group tends to permit acting out, at the same time it makes vigorous demands for more constructive alternatives. There is probably more of a tendency in a group to tolerate conflict and differences of opinion, than in individual analysis. Else why do we so often see—with the possible exception of Freud—so many professional analysands end treatment sharing the theoretic orientation of their analyst? It is interesting that Freud had many disciples who took divergent courses from him.

Relatedness

The question of tolerance is not far removed from the problem of establishing close relations. Some patients are able to develop a closer relationship in the individual setting, if there were no siblings for example, or if in the patient's past history contact with extrafamilial figures was curbed. Such patients tend to seek out individual therapy. In general, however, patients establish much closer relations with one another than they do with the analyst. Sometimes these relations are transferential, but in many instances there is a larger component of realistic, friendly interaction than in the vertical contact with the therapist.

Closer relations must be examined in terms of their appropriate or distorted content. Good analysis, whether in the individual or group setting, leads to discriminating multiple relations. What has to be analyzed in any interpersonal intimacy is whether the relationship is pathologic, transferential, compulsive or reality-bound, appropriate or discriminating.

In individual analysis the relation between therapist and patient can be closer than the relation between patient and group therapist. If we define this closeness in terms of a deeper involvement in the details of the nature of the relationship, if we define this intimacy by the amount of detailed exchange of experience, there is more interpersonal contact between patient and therapist in the individual setting. But by its nature, the individual therapeutic relation is one of isolation and limited fulfillment. It must, therefore, remain largely in fantasy. The nature of the relationship with the individual analyst, although it carries with it the aspect of intimacy and closeness achieved with more difficulty in a group setting, is always more illusory and frustrating than the patient's relation to group members. In the group situation, the relationship with the analyst may appear to be equally close, if a large number of private sessions are provided as in combined therapy. Within the group, unless specifically forbidden by the therapist, contact with the peers is always closer than with the analyst because of the opportunity for at least some partial fulfillment with one another. This relatedness is realistic and transferential containing elements that are positive and constructive as well as pathologic and acting out. But the possibility of experiencing one another in reality is always greater with the peers than with the therapist.[112] Therefore, the closeness of a relationship must be measured in terms of illusion and reality.

The relation with the therapist, whether in the individual or group setting, is more closely identified with illusion. Relations with peers, co-patients, are more closely identified with reality. Individual analysis provides only one-to-one contact. In the group, multiple relationships may exist simultaneously; more than or other than only dyadic relationships exist. It is a limited view of relatedness that a human being is capable of relating only to one person and only one person at any one time. Such a narrow view would encourage the isolation of the individual.

Closeness is related also to the degree of mutual understanding. But patients are not required to understand one another in the same way as the therapist. His understanding must always be different from that of a patient. Even in the dyadic relationship, to obscure the nature of the difference in understanding to be expected of patient and therapist, is not to see the difference between patient and therapist or between person and person. There is no generalized common base, a single dimensional thing called understanding. People can work together with limited understanding; people can work together with a great deal of understanding. Some people cannot work together with a great deal of understanding. The less they understand each other, the easier it is for them to work together, to wit, some husbands and wives.

Reality

If relatedness is determined by reality and illusion, an exploration of reality factors in the individual and group setting is in order. Hopefully,[146] ideally, and probably in fact, the therapist is the most reality-bound person in the group, and the more reality-bound person in individual analysis. However, he confronts the patient with a particular kind of reality. As long as the group therapist selects patients heterogeneously, the reality-boundness with which each is confronted has great variety. It is in part this diversity, these different kinds of reality in the group, that demand of the patient a flexible and appropriate modification in character structure. He learns, moreover, that realistic alternatives do not stem only from one source, for example, the analyst. Also, seeing others in the group making various kinds of realistic adaptations attenuates the necessity to conform. The fact that he may draw on his own resources and those of his peers rather than accept a given view is ego-building and enlarges his view of reality.

One of the criticisms of psychoanalysis in groups is that multiple transferences limit the ability to perceive reality. In individual analysis transference is fairly consistent and persistent, so that the therapist is more easily able to parse out what is real from what is irrational. While in the group multiple projections may go for a period unperceived and unanalyzed, they ultimately come under scrutiny. The general experience that every patient in a group kaleidoscopically projects a variety of familial figures depending upon outer provocation, suggests that such distortions are operating all the time, even for the patient in individual analysis. The color, variety, and transience of these penumbral projections often remain unreported and unperceived by the individual therapist. Multiple transferences may provoke for the moment greater unreality, but in working through, material for a more thorough resolution of wider aspects of psychopathology is provided.

Another dimension of reality is concerned with the extent to which the therapist reveals himself in the two settings. In individual analysis the therapist generally reveals less of himself than in the group. In the face of the stimulation and needs of eight or ten different patients with whom he sits in a circle, he tends to respond in ways which ordinarily are not exposed in the individual setting. There are, however, some therapists who expose less of themselves in the group, where they detach and isolate themselves, whereas they become interactive in the individual setting. The group may stimulate the analyst to show more of his healthy and pathologic responses but will inhibit his sexual acting out. The exposure of more of his real self to the group is used differently by patients. It may provoke healthier patient responses. Some members, however, may utilize these additional reality points for their own pathologic needs. The exposure of the real personality of the analyst is not good or bad in and of itself. What is relevant is what the patient does with it and how this is analyzed by the therapist.

There is then more subjectivity and more objectivity in a group. When, however, the analyst alone with a patient becomes subjective, he is more damaging, for there are no group members to check him with their scrutinizing roles. A more realistic examination of the therapist is possible in a group out of a sharing of impressions, out of contrast and comparison. An orthodox analyst might contend that the therapist must remain anonymous, an illusion. We believe rather he should be an interactive person with many flexible sides.

The Intrapsychic and the Interpersonal

A consideration that bears on relatedness and reality is concerned with intrapsychic versus interpersonal emphasis. One central therapeutic factor introduced by psychoanalysis in groups, sometimes neglected in individual analysis, is the social necessity, while expressing one's own thoughts and feelings, to consider also the ideas and emotions of other people, an interactive process that demands more reality-boundness. This socializing experience does not permit a dangerous regression into autism. It calls his provocative role to his attention. It enables him to explore not only the internal but the external consequences of his behavior, without denying him the freedom to associate.

In individual analysis, by virtue of the illusion created by the therapist who does not generally respond with subjective feeling to the patient's communications, the analysand has little experiential opportunity to develop a sensitivity to the needs of others. One of the outcomes of a good analysis should be not only self awareness but awareness of the other. This experience is largely rejected by the nature of the individual analytic orientation which implies that almost anything the patient says to the therapist is inapplicable to him. This is a kind of grand illusion he creates, and not infrequently a self-protective mechanism. As a result, the patient tends to become rather isolated and self-involved.

The analysis then of intrapsychic material as a result of forced interaction among members is a new dimension that is not available in individual analysis. The therapist does not interact with the patient on the kind of emotional level that patients do with each other. To the extent the patient is permitted to proceed in free-association to intrapsychic exploration he may become isolated. Individual analysis, unlike the interaction in the group, is a kind of extended self scrutiny which is self-concerned, self-initiated and self-responsive in an ideal sense. Individual therapy then is a more homogeneous experience with less correction or feedback except insofar as it is provided by the therapist.

Some group therapists focus from one individual to the next, doing individual analysis in the group. This is not, however, what we would call psychoanalysis in groups which studies also the individual in interaction with his fellows, his co-patients, his family, his therapist, his associates outside the group. [142] Furthermore, psychoanalysis in groups is not a preoccupation with antianalytic social psychology or group dynamics.[112] In individual analysis, there tends to be a focusing on interaction primarily with the therapist. In better individual treatment, a good deal of attention is paid to the patient's relations with his family and associates. The only interaction the therapist can be witness to is the interaction between the patient and himself. The group provides other possibilities for interpersonal relations to which the therapist can be witness.

Isolation and Socialization

Isolation and socialization are intimately related to the question of intrapsychic and interpersonal dynamics. Many individually analyzed persons are inadequately oriented to group life and group relations. Occasionally they end up in greater isolation and are referred for group therapy to socialize them. It is conceivable that, subjected largely to intrapsychic exploration, patients may be forced into increasing detachment. The possibility has even been raised of conducting an individual analysis "from beginning to end without the analyst ever having said a word."[73]

The individual analyst is wary of the social possibilities in the group which may be turned into resistive maneuvers and acting out. But the alert therapist can analyze such manipulations and sponsor the positive and constructive aspects of socialization.

A problem from which many people suffer, namely, that of feeling left out in a social situation, is more vividly re-experienced and re-enacted in group than in individual psychotherapy. Patients in a group frequently report their unhappiness and sense of isolation at the time of its occurrence, and we can trace more readily the intrapsychic and interpersonal dynamics that led to the real or imagined dissociation as well as its familial antecedents. It is a striking experience for the therapist who has had a sizable number of patients in groups with prior individual treatment to discover how commonly this problem emerges in a group setting and how less frequently this difficulty showed itself in the earlier private analysis. Very likely the one-to-one relationship in which the therapist is completely attentive to the patient alone counteracts the exposure of this dilemma. Psychoanalysis in a group accents the process in action by which a patient manages to isolate himself by re-enacting withdrawal or rivalry with a parent or sibling figure who is preferred by another familial surrogate whose acceptance or love the patient wants.

Principle of Forced Interaction

The patient in individual treatment may find it easier to maintain his detachment, to avoid getting involved, because of the therapist's observing, relatively noninteractive role. It is more difficult to remain uninvolved in the group where the membership is impelled into interpersonal reactivity. Group members encourage the patient into activity. The therapist tends to be less aggressive, less forceful than group members in demanding that the patient move in a new direction. The therapist may be fearful of the effect this can have upon the patient, who may interpret it as rejection or an oppressive demand to which he must conform. Or the analyst may be concerned that his long-range systematic plan of the therapeutic procedure will be disrupted.

The patient who is in a symbiotic relationship to the therapist has in a sense no place to go. That is, in the life-long development of his neurosis, the patient has acquired a circle of relatedness which fits into his neurotic adaptation. Therefore, to suggest that he try new patterns of behavior with the people with whom he comes into contact every day may not be very realistic. These others may resist his new functioning, since his neurotic behavior meets their own neurotic needs. They may not tolerate an alteration in the nature of their relationship. They do not demand but discourage an alternate way of behaving.

In the group, however, patients tend to be less hesitant in demanding new alternatives. They insist on exploring new kinds of action. They offer the patient illustrations by their own example or provoke new ideas and feelings which are not stimulated by the therapist. In a heterogeneously constituted group, realistic as well as projective needs for other ways of behaving exist. Members offer and support other possibilities and make demands upon the patient not to relate exclusively only to the therapist; there is, therefore, greater urgency put on the patient to move forward.

The presence of other persons who insist on the consideration of activity beyond verbal insight is an imposing force for health. The alternate session, too, encourages new ways of relating by providing opportunities to interact in the absence of the therapist and makes it possible to explore these new ways without having the continuous help of the analyst. The presence of the peers without him permits the possibility of competition among them for leadership roles. When he is present they may become less concerned with each other, but may seek to relate primarily to him. In the group setting, the fact that siblings are always present, however, provokes competition among them for his attention and consideration. In the individual setting the patient may accept the illusion of the exclusive and total possession of the analyst's interest, except insofar as the patient is aware of other patients. The opportunity and acceptability of realizing a symbiotic relationship to the analyst is, therefore, more limited in the group setting. Moreover, other patients offer examples of other kinds of behavior which the analyst cannot offer except by suggestion.

Forced interaction impels the patient in a group toward an oscillation or alternation of roles. The more reasonably flexible the therapist and the more varied the roles of the patient, the more healthy and pathologic material emerges. Treatment is facilitated by the heterogeneity and the different ways of functioning that characterize the assumption of different roles. And forced interaction helps the individual into such heterogeneity that enlarges his personality and gives him a multidimensional character. Forced interaction, variation in roles, the value of differences, and heterogeneity are all interrelated.[147]

Homogeneity and Heterogeneity

If heterogeneity facilitates therapy, it is appropriate to consider which climate, group or individual, is more homogeneous. The chances are there is more uniformity of reaction to be anticipated in individual analysis than in psychoanalysis in groups, even if the group is homogeneously constituted. The group rarely reacts as a unit.[149] Some members align themselves with regressive compulsion, while others are more impelled toward a struggle for health. The therapist by contrast pursues a consistent line. His activity, values, attitudes, responses, and interpretations are directed along a single course that make for greater homogeneity in the individual analytic climate than in the group, no matter how undiversified the group's constitution.

It is difficult for a therapist to homogenize a group and impose his will on a number of persons; the patient alone with an analyst is subject to greater pressure for submission. A therapist may attempt to assign to the patient in the individual or group setting only one kind of role such as moment-to-moment reactions or the exclusive emphasis on affect. He may limit explorations only to genetic material, concentrate on motivations, emphasize only ego functions or non-discriminately demand only conscious responses. By assigning such fixed roles he imposes on patients a homogeneous way of functioning. Such uniformity is antianalytic, in that it does not allow for other dimensions. The therapist who rigidly limits what can be expressed, whether in individual or group therapy, homogenizes the treatment setting and limits therapy.

Multiple Reactivities

The phenomenon of multiple reactivity[109] is characteristic of the group setting and is facilitated by a heterogeneous rather than a homogeneous group. Multiple reactivity is not available in individual analysis except insofar as the therapist elicits varied responses. Of course, it is available by indirection for analysis in terms of the patient's responses to people outside the therapeutic situation. But here the therapist's skill is called upon to a greater extent to perceive through the patient's distortions in his reports of what occurs on the outside. The therapist is able to witness how the patient in the group responds to different kinds of situations and persons. The group provokes through the diversity of its stimuli a larger canvas of the patient's pathology at the same time as it requires from him a more challenging and comprehensive adjustment in health toward a wider variety of realistic and unrealistic demands.

The group member learns a valuable lesson in interpersonal relations not so easily acquired in individual analysis. He learns that identical feelings do not rise up as responses in all people at the same time to the same provocation. He discovers that when he is in one mood, his friend is in another; that when he is eager to share an emotion, his companion is just as anxious for some private introspection; that just when he wants to entertain his neighbor, the recipient of his good will is about to punish him for a real or imagined hurt at a prior meeting. As many instances of mutually responsive interactions, of course, also occur.

Multiple Transferences

The therapeutic group immediately and continuously provides the patient with many provocative figures who elicit multiple transferences more readily than the individual therapist alone. In the course of any group session the therapist can become aware of the variety of transferences a patient may project on others. In individual analysis such projections on the therapist rarely occur in a single therapeutic hour. The shifting distortions in the group are the result of multiple interaction and the changing relations of one member to the next. In individual analysis transference tends to be more rigid and fixed. With some very unstable patients similar alternating projections may be seen also in individual treatment.

One sees a phenomenon in the group that is not available in individual analysis, namely the pathologic homogenizing of patients into a single transference figure. Here the therapist is projected as one parent and the group as the other. This problem is often not ventilated into awareness in individual treatment and can be dealt with more readily in the group, where the patient must be encouraged to respond to the membership as individuals, to differentiate them, one from the other, in order to work through this distortive tendency.

In individual treatment the more prevalent kind of distortion is a parental transference; sibling projections tend to be neglected or disposed of too casually, because they rarely occur with the same intensity. In the group there is a larger opportunity to express and see sibling transferences, so that they can more readily be scrutinized and worked through. There is a greater chance of working out the larger familial picture in the group.

It would, however, be non-discriminative to say that the group is perceived only as family, but surely this is a consistent and generally reliable phenomenon. Greater possibility exists in psychoanalysis in groups of dealing with the shadowy transferences of siblings. But peer transference can be both parental and sibling in character. And the projection on co-patients of a parental figure is generally less oppressive than its counterpart on the therapist and leads to an easier working through. Similar transferences on the analyst are generally more intense and more laden with authority significance. Certain patients tend to provoke extremely strong parental transferences, but here, too, the reality of the peer relation attenuates the projective intensity.

It is of some interest to compare how transference is dealt with in the two climates. The analysis of transference becomes almost the exclusive prerogative of the therapist in the individual setting, whereas in the group, patients may point out distortions and suggest more constructive alternatives. Even the patient under scrutiny also has the opportunity to analyze projective reactions in others. If a patient suggests that the therapist is in countertransference in the individual setting, this may make the analyst defensive and he is liable to interpret the patient's remark as a distortion. While a co-patient too may resist the implication that he is in transference, he is less likely to avoid the suggestion, particularly when the distortions are bilateral as they generally are between any two patients. This readiness on the part of co-patients to explore their mutual projections enriches the understanding of transference in its bilaterality. The provocative role of the other person with regard to transference is more clearly defined in the group than in the individual situation. The therapist by comparison tends to deny his own provocative role in eliciting patient distortions even when he has played such a role. He cannot accomplish this so easily in the group setting. Transference reactions, then, are generally analyzed in the group as bilateral. In the individual analytic situation transference responses tend to be analyzed as unilateral.

In the group, the more stable transferences are projected on the therapist. They are more fixed, because at first they are subject to less frequent scrutiny than the projections patients make on one another. In individual treatment transferences to people outside the therapeutic relationship can be only inaccurately perceived. In the group these transferences are available for study and working through within the therapeutic frame. Transference to the analyst is less intensively worked with at first because of the opportunity to examine distortions with regard to co-patients. In individual treatment, if the therapist works out transferential feelings directed toward people in the reality situation of the patient's life, it becomes much easier to resolve transference responses to the analyst. If the procedure is reversed, if the therapist attempts to explore and work through projections on himself as an initial process, he generally meets with more resistance. Also in the group, then, it is a commonly better procedure to analyze transferences to co-patients before attempting to work with projections on the analyst in order to avoid a resistive impasse.

As a rule in individual analysis the strength and persistence of transference is greater than in the group. The intensity and rigidity of projection is encouraged by its dyadic character and its isolation. In the group, parental transferences are made on co-patients, but because they are also seen as peers and because there is such freedom of movement in selecting various members for projection, transferences are less intense, more flexible, more easily moved away from to more constructive alternatives. While quantitatively and qualitatively these projections on patients are different, their repetition with peers helps the patient ultimately to cope with the more authority-weighted transferences on the analyst.

It is likely that no therapist is ever completely free of countertransference problems. To the extent they exist, the analyst has difficulty in being objective about the patient. In the group the therapist's countertransferences are more readily perceived with some objectivity by group members and, therefore, more easily dealt with. So the group therapeutic setting as a medium becomes a better safeguard against the distortions of the therapist.

Sometimes the countertransference problem of the analyst takes the form of obsessively trying to get the patient to develop a transference neurosis. But this develops in any case.[114] In so exclusively directing the patient's attention to the analyst, the patient is isolated from valuable and salutary relations with others.[146] The group tends to operate against such a limiting eventuality.

Displacement

Patients often displace feelings on one another as a way of avoiding reactions to the therapist. This is both an advantage and a source of resistance. A patient may in individual treatment say he feels thus and so about a person, when he really feels this way about the therapist. In the group, a patient may similarly be reacting to a co-patient or to all of the members of the group as an extension of the analyst. Or a member may displace a response from one patient to another. There seems to be greater chance of concealing displacement in individual treatment because the provocation that leads to such substitution is often not available.

Acting Out

The analyst by his training is not prone to act out. There are instances, however, where the therapist is provoked by his or a patient's instability to act out.[114] Here treatment loses a rational, scrutinizing, evaluating observer. In the group, the therapist is more obliged to maintain an observing role, because group members provide one another with reality anchorages and support against the analyst's acting out.

Every therapeutic group sooner or later sets limits on the acting out of patients. One source of this control is the constructive resource in individual patients, generally healthy elements in various superego and ego functions. Another resides in the projections of authority that operate to restrain irrational activity. The therapist, his presence at regular sessions and his presence in absentia at the alternate meetings or afterward, also exercises a controlling influence. Patients know that their behavior will sooner or later be reported, so that acting out tends to be controlled by an awareness of this eventuality.

Surely there is more activity in the group than in the individual setting. If there is more activity, there is more activity of every kind, whether healthy or unhealthy. The issue is not whether there is more or less. There will always be acting out as long as we treat persons who are sick. The question is why we are so afraid that the acting out should occur within the therapeutic frame. In individual analysis the patient's acting out is limited within therapy, but he may act out beyond the treatment setting without the analyst's knowing. The opportunity to expose his acting out within the group makes it more available for therapeutic working through.

Control

Group therapy, like civilization, would easily become disorganized and irrational if each member were encouraged to act impromptu on every sudden thought or feeling. Just as in society where we are obliged to circumscribe our activity to meet the demands of the social order, the therapeutic group controls acting out that threatens the cooperative struggle against satisfying unconscious pathologic yearnings.

If a patient is given to impulsive or compulsive behavior, it is necessary to explore how and where this lack or excess of control was fostered. If little control was exercised in the home, he may seek out an individual therapist in the expectation that no reasonable restraints be imposed on him. If the encouragement to the acting out of pathology was outside the home, he may choose the group. The reverse may also be true: in the hope of discovering a parental surrogate who will in fact control him, the patient may choose an individual therapist. Or, in quest of a group of peers, who, unlike his original peers, will discipline him, he may choose the group.

The direction of movement, of the development of control is from outside inward. Control moves in therapy from the authority figure to the peers to the self.

Repetitive Patterns and Flexibility

In individual analysis repetitive patterns may become visible earlier than in the group, partly because the therapist tends to be more rigidly projected as a particular transference figure, so that the repetitive pattern in relation to this familial surrogate emerges more clearly. But repetitive patterns appear in the group as well and with more diversity since there are more transference figures available from the start. Initially it may seem to be more difficult to define repetitive patterns in the group. The patient seems to have a larger flexibility than he has in fact, because he is showing many more repetitive patterns in the group. As time goes on, the fixity of these designs with reference to particular projections emerges more clearly on a broader basis.

Perhaps a word is in order about flexibility in the two climates. In individual analysis the patient is less called upon to make more diverse and flexible adjustments to many shifting demands. The therapist alone may or may not make varied healthy demands on the patient determined by his conception of what the healthy direction is. Group members make many salutary injunctions. At the same time, they make distorted demands that he adjust to their pathology.

The individual therapeutic situation tends to foster repetitive patterns, based on a conception that a consistent relationship is necessary for analysis. Deviations tend to be analyzed as resistance to the continuous repetition of the patterns of therapeutic behavior. Individual analysts refer to the first phase of therapy as making the person a patient, the idea being that consistency becomes the core around which analytic work is done. The individual therapist is critical of group therapy in that consistency of ways of relating seems not really to be found in the group, because the members do not appear to persist in their responses. The therapist may feel that there is little basis for anticipating how they will react to one communication or another. But if he looks deeper, he will discover an actual consistency of responses even in the group. At the same time, the patient is afforded the advantage of actual increased flexibility and range of reactions, the freedom to shift from the expected response, the right to choose another alternative.

A factor in the group that makes for more flexibility is the heterogeneity of its construction. For the id-dominated patient there are present in the group several members whose entrenched superegos act to control his impulsivity. For the patient overwhelmed by the demands of conscience, there are others to encourage him to relax the pressures of duty. The presence of peers also operates to provide a less oppressive and more flexible corrective influence than the projected and real authority of the therapist whose blandishments are experienced as more executive. Flexibility arises too out of the simultaneous and concomitant presence of peer and hierarchic vectors.[109] If just one dimension is present, either horizontal or vertical, there is more rigidity and tightness, less freedom and flexibility. The fact of a concurrence of the two makes for easier movement in both directions.

Hierarchic and Peer Vectors

Transferences in the group can be better understood if we realize that in the setting of a number of patients we provide a peer vector, that is, interpatient relationships, as well as a hierarchic vector in the patient's reactions to the therapist. The addition of a horizontal dimension to the verticality of individual treatment gives the patient the freedom to have peers and the difficulties of having peers, such as the necessity to compete with them.

The hierarchic vector operates more strongly in individual analysis, in which the patient may feel intimidated, dominated, or over-protected by the therapist as a projected parental figure. In the authority-laden dyadic atmosphere it is often difficult for the patient to communicate his thoughts and feelings. By providing a setting of peers, the group removes this threatening quality from the environment in some measure, so that communication can take place more readily. There are exceptions in which the reverse is true, where telling the authority figure is less anxiety-laden than telling the peers. A patient may relate also to other patients or homogenize the group as the same or the other parental figure, so that even peers, co-patients may be related to in a vertical direction.

If the therapist is in fact given to assuming an authoritarian role in the vertical dimension, the multiplicity of peers in mutual support enables them to make both reasonable and unreasonable challenges of his supremacy. For some of the patients this is a healthy struggle, for others a compulsive one, but one which in any case unsettles the therapist, who cannot so easily in group as in individual treatment dictate ways and means.

In individual therapy, the horizontal vector is not so immediately and directly available for experiencing and working through as the vertical vector. Actually it is never available in the therapeutic situation itself in individual analysis, whereas the group provides within the therapeutic frame for the elicitation of both hierarchic and peer problems and accordingly for their working out and working through. The concomitant presence of both dimensions makes it possible for the patient to move back and forth from one vector to the other depending on where he needs support, so that he can turn for respite and help now to the projected parent in the therapist and then to the peers as siblings or parental figures depending on his needs.

All good analysis tries to achieve parity, but real equality is not experienced in the framework of the individual setting, whereas it can be experienced through the peers within the group. The realization of parity in the group increases the possibility of equality even between patient and therapist. In individual analysis, where the analysand is always in the position of being helped by a helper, a wholesome sense of equality in difference is more difficult to accomplish. There are some few individual therapists who view the patient as all child, regressed, pathologic and inferior and regard themselves as all mature, all knowing, and with all help residing only in themselves.[146] In accepting the idea of conducting analysis in a group such attitudes are rejected. Here some healthy potentials and helpfulness are seen also in patients, and the therapist does not view himself as the only and exclusive resource for support, change, and motivation for activity.

The individual therapist's position of omniscience tends to foster illusion. Since he is the only other person in the individual situation, there is only one other set of associations, only one other means for testing and comparing the nature of reality. Reality and unreality are supplied by various other persons who contribute simultaneously within the group therapeutic setting.

Equality, Freedom and Hostility

Wherever there are inequality and loss of freedom, hostility and hate follow. Hostility exists where equal opportunity does not exist, and equal opportunity can exist only in a climate of freedom.[147] The essentially hierarchic nature of the individual therapeutic situation limits the patient's feeling of equality. Moreover, if the therapist tends to emphasize the patient's pathology, his disordered behavior, the patient tends further to feel unequal, inferior.

Equality and freedom are more closely approximated in the group. There is in the group more freedom to express less intense hostility as well as a sense of positive relatedness, a greater opportunity for sympathy, empathy and wholesomely loving feelings than in the individual setting, where loving and hostile affect is more generally symbiotic, regressive, and transferential, that is, unequal.

Patients analyzed in groups, however, occasionally treat each other with a harshness that is unnecessarily cruel and causes them a good deal of mortification. We do not believe that suffering is a requirement of good psychotherapy.[110] Too often it represents a masochistic inclination in the recipient of aggression and a sadistic bent in the aggressor. Frequently, the offensive patient is acting out a negative transference and his victim a submissive one. Where this occurs, it is the function of the therapist to analyze the respective projections as soon as possible to protect the members from prolonged hurt. For sympathy and forbearance with one another cannot be acquired in endlessly belligerent and victimized surroundings—they can flower only in a happier climate. Enmity cannot generally lead to good will, except for the patient who has never been permitted to be angry. And even he has to work his way back into the group's good graces after his outbursts. Malevolence commonly is met with counterattack or secret resentment. The therapist in the group has to be alert to the sickness of brutality.

Retaliation and Fulfillment

In the group there is both more retaliation and more fulfillment of archaic and real needs. It is the role of the therapist to point out the destructive nature of neurotically interlocking activity and to encourage the fulfillment of more appropriate needs. The artificial immunity against retaliation as well as against the fulfillment of archaic needs that supposedly exists in individual therapy by virtue of the neutrality of the analyst and the isolation of the experience may not always be a constructive force. The need to over-protect the patient from co-patients has something to do with the therapist's attitude toward them and the somewhat inappropriate feeling that they will in fact dangerously aggress against each other if they are allowed their full expression of affect. Patients turn out really not to be so damaging to one another; in the act of becoming patients in the first place, they reveal potentials for health, for growth, and for decency.

There is a tendency to view the bilateral reactions of patients as equally meaningful and penetrating as those in which the therapist is involved. Patient-to-patient interaction is less powerful because it is on a peer level. A reaction from the therapist can be devastating; sometimes it can be neurotically fulfilling in the patient's wish to involve or frustrate the parent. In psychoanalysis, whether individual or group, the authority is both real and projected. To view the authority of the analyst in the individual setting only as projective and the social authorities of the group as exclusively real, or the reverse, is to misunderstand the nature of authority in both the individual and group situations.

The group therapeutic experience is in part so successful because it does not frustrate the patient in exploring his multidimensional feelings about real and unreal authorities and peers. There is more opportunity to retaliate and fulfill himself in reality and in illusion in both the horizontal and vertical directions. These fulfillments, healthy and neurotic, in which he is helper and helped, listened to and listener among co-patients, have an important function in psychoanalysis in groups.

Support

It is of some interest to explore the parameter of support especially in terms of the vertical and horizontal vectors. There is more certainty in a group where there is greater likelihood of finding members who support the patient's healthy or pathologic strivings. The patient alone with the therapist is always less certain of finding acceptance of his aspirations from one other person. There is, therefore, more of this type of security in the group setting.[111]

Support is a necessary component of all therapy. Support is a way in which the resources of the patient are encouraged. Through his positive potentials, the patient is stimulated to expose his problems, the pathologic material, the affect-laden history and so on. Support from the therapist is limited in that it comes in the vertical vector, and is of the kind which he feels appropriate or necessary. The analyst may withhold support for fear of entrenching dependency problems. In the group, support comes from the peers as well as from the therapist. The supportive use of the peers is especially to be seen in the alternate session, where very often material is exposed by some patients for the first time and only with the encouragement from the peers is the material brought into the regular session in the presence of the analyst.[148] Some patients have to be supported by the therapist in individual sessions before they are able to expose certain material to the group. Nevertheless, the opportunity to find support in either vector in different therapeutic climates makes for the possibility of greater and various kinds of support arising within the therapeutic context. Distinction needs to be made between support which comes from the peers and support from the analyst. The nature, quality, purpose, usefulness, and the more discriminate application of therapist-support are quite different from the more spontaneous, more impulsive, or compulsive support from co-patients.

A characteristic of man that facilitates analysis in a group is his readiness to extend himself for a neighbor in adversity. The group member is a witness to other people's misfortune. The honest exposure of difficulty elicits an equally feelingful response. The patient in distress who looks round the group for something to sustain him, in whose eyes there is a plea for relief, is not easily resisted. Patients, like men everywhere, act to relieve each other's suffering with an ingenuousness that is as candid as the expression of pain.

Happiness, too, may bind patients in closer relations. The patient in adversity needs more than sympathy for his pain; he needs optimistic, realistic support. There is the danger of encouraging a patient always to present himself as the underdog in difficulty in order to get attention. Moreover, group members may reject the disturbed patient, especially if he is a compulsive sufferer. Occasionally there are patients who cannot stand tears, suffering, and unhappiness, or who feel all affect is phony. Compulsive supporters or servers are, at times, to be found in the group; their need never to reject a plea for help or sympathy has also to be analyzed. But if the deepest affect could be ascertained, it would not turn out to be pity or tenderness for the suffering of another. The feeling that stirs us the most comes when the patient finally achieves some happiness and victory over his distress, when the misjudged are treated fairly at last, when the estranged are strangers no more. Our feelings are touched more by the humane gesture than by vexation.

Some patients try to conceal their excitement, too self-conscious of a display of strong emotion that might be looked on as affected or weak. But if the truth were known, as sooner or later it comes to be in the group, most of us want one another's affairs to prosper. Some of us are too shy to make such an admission because it sounds too much like a maudlin hope that virtue will master wickedness. This secret but ultimately apparent and expressed wish is a force in group therapy that makes members reparative to one another.

Knowing this underlying longing is common, the therapist, wherever possible, can use it to mutual advantage. For example, he makes an effort not to permit sessions to end in generalized depression over the despair of a patient whose sad recital has cast the group down. He cannot superimpose a too heightened optimism or faith that somehow everything will work out in the end. He may admit that the present dilemma is indeed cheerless but not without some bright prospect. But more than this, he must try to mobilize in the membership their basic wish to continue to struggle for a most positive solution. If he succeeds, the meeting may end on an animated rather than on a dismal note. Perhaps better than a compulsive striving for a spirited conclusion to every session, the therapist can try to convey the idea that we are not at a permanent impasse, that there is room for further exertion, that the only ground for ending in this record of failure is the close of the meeting and that we shall yet find a sounder resolution.

The therapist may indicate the persistence of vitality in the least of us, of positiveness and reassurance that enables us to hold on and withstand the present hardship. So that at least the termination of a meeting becomes also a promise in the start of the next. Just as the therapist cannot guarantee the patient the satisfaction of undivided happiness at the close of treatment he cannot end every session happily. But he can assure the patient of the continuity of struggle and the desirability and likelihood of making his exertions more rewarding. He can encourage the patient in part by showing again and again how his history, unconsciously repeated in the present, leads to the sad ending, but that he need by no means remain forever trapped in repetition compulsion. The analyst can emphasize not only the past and present but a more propitious future freer of blunder and impotence. He may underline the passing character of disappointments in the obsolete past and the neurotic present that need not substantially corrode the future. In this effort there are commonly one or more group members whose optimism can be counted on for support.

Free Association

Many analysts have expressed doubts about whether the patient can associate as freely in the group as in the individual situation. While there are greater forces for interruption of the free flow of associations in the group, to view uncontrolled, unlimited, continuous free association as desirable is to misconceive the nature of free association and the nature of cure. It is preferable to use free association more discriminately, more selectively, with greater understanding of when it is appropriately necessary. To associate freely at all times is in itself an objective which is neither achievable nor desirable. Interruption and limits are necessary in therapy as in life.

The analyst is often critical of psychoanalysis in groups on the grounds that free association is not possible because of the interruptions to which each patient is subjected by other members. The fact is that free association is both interrupted and facilitated at different times. When the individual is exploring new unconscious territory, he generally excites and holds the interest of the group and is thereby encouraged to continue. When he repeatedly acts out the same psychopathology in his streams of consciousness, the group gets bored with the repetition and reasonably interrupts to demand a more salutary alternative. When his associations are leading him to the discovery of more realistic choices, the group is enthusiastically but silently attentive, on edge with the hope that he will find his way. When verbalization seems to be deteriorating into self-destructive and isolating autism, the group will not tolerate such free association for long.

Theoretically, the patient in the individual setting provides the material on which the therapist acts. The patient acts without awareness. In fact, the more awareness he has, the less free his associations presumably are. In the group, he is expected to express himself not only as freely and honestly as he can, but he is encouraged to function with awareness—with awareness of the other person. Although it may seem like an inhibition upon his so-called free associations, the fact is that the necessity for bilateral awareness furthers his healthy resources. From such a point of view, absolute freedom to associate without reality feedback can only lead to deterioration and psychosis.

In both settings it is essential that the patient present himself with an honesty that he has not used before. The difference in a group is, however, that all the other patients are required to do this as well. Members are called upon to interact, so that each is confronted with the impact of his responses in a way that is not available in individual analysis. Each patient discovers his provocative role in terms of his pathology and health and then may rationally choose which thought, feeling, or activity to pursue.

A concern about interruptions sometimes masks the therapist's view that what goes on is really individual treatment in the group. Such an attitude tends to lead the therapist to an inadequate therapeutic use of the resources of group members. Interruptions may not only serve the functions already described, but the contributions of co-patients can elucidate the productions of a particular patient. This is to be seen, for example, in working with a dream in which the spontaneous associations of other members of the group stimulate the revelation of latent thoughts of the dreamer and provide the therapist with additional clues for the analysis and interpretation of the significance of the dream for the dreamer as well as for other members of the group. The therapist's view of co-patient contributions as interruptive actually deprives the group of these positive values and forces the group members into a competitive struggle to interrupt resulting in a scramble for attention in order to be heard. Allowing them to come in with their own associations which may be scrutinized sponsors the feeling that all the members are under analysis rather than the one patient who has the floor at the moment. It is important, therefore, for the therapist to work with any production as interactive, so that the multilateral dimensions of human behavior not be obscured. In this way the freedom to associate is enhanced rather than limited. The therapist's good intention to give the individual ample room to associate by restricting the freedom of others actually impedes the accomplishment of his very objective. In psychoanalysis in groups all of the patients are participants.

Dreams

Dreams are important whether analysis is done in the individual or in the group setting. But dreams are handled differently in the two situations. In individual treatment, the patient associates to his dreams, while the therapist rarely shares his associations. These are concealed in his interpretive or other intervention. In the group, the dreamer first associates to the dream; then other patients spontaneously offer their associations. The membership moves then toward an understanding and interpretation of its latent meaning. The therapist may step in either to integrate, clarify a point, or to ask for consideration of those items in the dream which were not touched upon, if they appear significant.

Patients who are resistant to unconscious material in individual analysis may resist and repress dreams. They rationalize their resistance by saying they cannot see how dreams can be useful to them. This kind of rationalization can be neutralized more easily in the group by virtue of seeing another patient bring in a dream, whose analysis leads to insight and change. Occasionally it is the therapist who rejects dream material. In the group it is more difficult for him to resist the demand that dreams be heard, for there are generally a number of patients who spontaneously present them. He is compelled, therefore, in the group to heed them. Even in a group, however, if the therapist rejects the presentation of dreams, they tend to be reported with lessening frequency.

Genetic and Current Material

Group interaction tends to provoke the recall of relevant history.[135] From the interpersonal response comes the genetic recollection and the intrapsychic exploration. So history is not lost in the group, unless the resistive patient or the therapist excludes it. Sometimes the analyst is obliged to take the lead in bringing the group to associate around original causes and development, the relationship of the present experience to the past. If the therapist does not do this, the group may tend to bypass it and remain non-discriminatively interactive on current thoughts, feelings, and behavior. This is characteristic of the therapists who emphasize the "here and now," whether they work in the individual or group setting.[146]

In individual analysis it is commonly believed that talking about the intercurrent material and events is resistive. The traditional fixation upon the rejection of current outside material in the individual situation occurs because so much of present events is external to and not part of the therapeutic experience. Here the intercurrency lies primarily in the transference relationship to the therapist and the developing transference neurosis. In the group, present events are an integral part of therapy. The moment, the here-and-now takes place in treatment and is subject to analytic exploration and understanding. In individual analysis—apart from reactions to the therapist—the emphasis is upon genesis, because the therapist cannot always interact, cannot continuously provide the present material and must, therefore, draw from recollection and memory, rather than upon the scrutiny of events as they occur.

Data

In individual analysis, the data are second hand, that is, they are supplied out of reminiscences of the patient to the event. The only first hand experience that is provided is the relationship with regard to the therapist. In the group, data are supplied not only on the basis of the memories of the patient but also in terms of his actual interaction with other members. In fact, the emphasis in the group is upon interaction and the interaction is then used for coming to a better understanding of the intrapsychic necessities and motivations that gave rise to the particular interaction. The participants in the interpersonal exchange share the analytic experience. In individual treatment, the interaction external to therapy can be understood only reconstructively through the projections of both patient and analyst as to what the person who is not in treatment was really doing or feeling at the time. It is conjectural whether an accurate perception can be formulated from the distorted recollections of the patient without direct knowledge of the actual provocation. In the group, there is emphasis on the interaction. The group tends to resist long, repetitive recountings of past or current material. In the individual setting an exclusive preoccupation with the relationship to the therapist can also become an isolating and illusory experience.

There are some analysts who believe they can learn more about their patients only in the individual experience. The question is, what do they learn more about and is it true that the data they gather is therapeutically more useful if it is secured in the individual setting? There is no doubt that one can learn more about some things about one's patient in the individual situation. But one can learn other kinds of things in the group which can elude the therapist in the private setting. However, the order of data is different in the two situations.

The individual analyst is limited in the dyadic relationship by the view of the patient the one-to-one experience affords him. The therapist does not see the patient in the multiple interactive possibilities with varying personalities. He does not see the patient in social interaction. He does not become an actual witness to the divergent transference reactions as they occur in life. Nor does he see the exercise of certain healthy resources in the patient. For example, the analyst gets a one-sided perception of his patient as an exaggeratedly helpless person, because the therapist is always in the position of helper. In the group, however, each member is called upon at different times to come to the assistance of his neighbor, a development which calls into being an aspect of the patient, hitherto unseen by the therapist, a supportive and reparative role.

Resistances and Defenses

Resistance is generally more easily overcome in the group than in individual analysis. The group members make a frontal attack on each patient's resistance—they will not let a sleeper sleep; they will not let a silent member remain silent; nor will they permit resistive maneuvers long to go unanswered. They demand action, change, force interaction, protest against anyone's withdrawal or monopoly, his autism or illusory relating. They demand contact, communication, clarity.

Group members, through support and attack, break through defenses more effectively than the therapist alone. Some analysts have viewed the group as a setting where defenses are attacked while the anxiety behind these defenses is to be dealt with only in the individual session.[114] Occasionally, the group therapist may have to support a defense at a given stage of the patient's development. But the notion that in the group only defenses are dealt with and that underlying anxiety cannot be exposed and worked through in the group seems like a misconception of the nature of the group experience. In individual treatment, the timing and technique for handling defenses are determined exclusively by the therapist. The breakthrough on the part of other patients, however, frequently facilitates similar breakthroughs among the more defensive who experience vicariously the insight, forward movement and resolution of the necessity for defensive behavior.

Silence

It is of some interest to explore the clinical phenomenon of silence in the group, not so much for its resistive significance, which has been elaborately studied in the analytic literature, but for its other dimensions. There is an intolerance for silence that is traditional among therapists who generally interpret all silences as always unnecessary and resistive. There are silences in treatment that are not negative but represent moments of restoration, integration, inner reflection, or deep affect without the necessity to take action or directly relate to another person.

The therapist's time in this sense is more efficiently used in a group setting. For while one patient is silently exploring an issue for himself, a second is inaccessible in resistance, and a third is too anxious to withstand scrutiny at the moment, a fourth member and a fifth are engaged in a fluid interaction that welcomes analytic examination. So that in the group the therapist can productively turn here and there while other patients are temporarily silent.

If the patient is communicative and needs to be listened to in silence, then it is appropriate for the therapist in the individual or group setting to be silent. This is his interaction, his activity. His silence is his appropriate selection of activity, which is necessary in terms of the patient's mutuality and interaction. So the therapist's silence which looks like passivity is really his determined activity, that appropriate activity which furthers therapeutic ends.

Anxiety

As defenses or resistances are threatened or removed, anxiety appears. There are some patients who experience little anxiety in the individual session but enormous anxiety at the prospect of joining a group. Such patients may have been overprotected and isolated by the mother and threatened by the external environment. Others who were originally more anxious in the family or with a given familial figure and more secure in extrafamilial situations often experience the group as more gratifying and secure. They are more inclined to enjoy the alternate session rather than the regular one when the therapist is present. The therapist also may be in the same position. He may be more or less anxious in one setting or the other depending on his prior history. Whatever the case, the patient must gradually be moved into an exploration of the source of his anxiety and toward working it through in whatever medium he is experiencing it. Else he is likely not to enter the situation eliciting more anxiety and, therefore, not to alter his adjustment but escape it.

All patients have anxiety. The question is whether these anxieties are based on reality perceptions or distortions of the nature of realities derivative of childhood. The differences that have been described in terms of where the greatest anxieties are experienced generally have little or nothing to do with reality but are based upon original early conceptions as to where threat is felt. To be able to explore the differences in anxiety in a projected threat with the analyst alone, in the regular group meeting and in the alternate session provide media for discovery of the nature of the misperceptions that lead to anxiety and defensive maneuvers.

In individual analysis, the kind of anxiety which is experienced is anxiety in the face of the projected threat from the therapist. Any other kind of threat based on reality or distortion in the external world has to come from the report of the patient. We must assume that the patient will become aware of his anxiety outside and that he will have the freedom to talk of his feelings to the analyst. The need to become aware of anxiety provoked outside of treatment is much greater in individual analysis, because in the group underlying anxiety of which the patient is not aware can be exposed more readily and rapidly in interaction.

For some patients there is more freedom from anxiety and relaxation in the group as opposed to the individual setting. The individual situation is for these more anxiety provoking since it is closer to the therapist, deals more intensively with an emotionally charged relationship in more isolation and under greater scrutiny. In the group there is a larger possibility for momentary escape from examination and therefore less anxiety. For others, the peers in the group are much more threatening. It may be that for most, given a choice, they would choose the individual rather than the group experience to avoid anxiety. The fear that in group there will be less expertness, less tolerance, more aggression, more freedom, urges most patients to choose individual analysis. In part the choice depends on the nature of the patient's historical experience with authority and peer figures, as well as culturally determined expectations regarding the treatment setting.

Principle of Shifting Attention

The fact of shifting attention in the group spares the patient anxiety by giving him breathing spells from continuous scrutiny. In individual treatment the analysand is constantly the subject of examination. This makes him resistive, defensive, and works a hardship on him that can be somewhat immobilizing. By contrast the shifting attention of the group affords the patient a relaxing interval, a time to consider what he has been confronted with, a time to assimilate and work through, a time to help rather than to be helped. The shifting of focus is itself an alternative way of behaving. It permits the possibility to see that one does not have to pursue endlessly a way of acting, that one can undertake an activity, abandon it for a while and then return to it without continuous or compulsive application.

The principle of shifting attention gives the patient a chance to expose himself at his own time and pace. In individual treatment he is always under the microscope, constantly urged to reveal himself. In the group setting, intervals free of demand that he communicate may make for resistance. This may be related to Freud's idea of having sessions every day.

Timing of Interpretations

A common objection to psychoanalysis in groups is based on the feeling that a patient may inexpertly or inappropriately impose on a co-patient a piece of insight which he is not yet ready to assimilate. The criticism is made that a premature or ill timed confrontation may be too damaging to a member who may not be able to handle the anxiety elicited by the insight. Clinical experience, however, has demonstrated that in the main patients are able to cope with insights proffered in the horizontal direction by resisting or integrating them in nontoxic doses. By contrast, when the analyst himself makes an error in timing, the patient is more threatened because the insight is in the authority-laden hierarchic vector.

The group therapist soon gets over the illusion that only he has the sensitivity to confront a patient at a particular time, that he alone can be deeply empathic. While some patients are insensitive to others, a good many show initial and increasing feeling for and awareness of the needs of others. Occasionally the therapist is overprotective about a patient's ability to withstand a piece of insight and may unnecessarily delay sharing understanding with him.

The patient in a therapeutic group cannot be expected to show the technical skill in timing of the trained analyst. But it is striking how often the inexpert patient makes appropriate insightful comments with a keenness and accuracy that are startling. It is not that the principles of psychodynamics are handily available or inherent in the minds of the untrained. It is their common sense, the simplicity, spirit and candor characterizing their observations, and the implicit wish to help that endow them with reparative power. Their directness and emotional intensity also have a deep impact on the listener.

In individual analysis timing is the exclusive prerogative and responsibility of the therapist. His errors in timing carry with them the weight and burden of authority. Provocations, interpretations and interactive reinforcements from co-patients are both more easily sloughed off and at times more penetrating in their horizontal derivation. If individual therapists frighten fewer patients away with interpretations, it may only mean that such therapists are less active than they need to be. If they are more cautious about making badly timed interventions, they may be equally hesitant in making the appropriately timed observation and thereby impede therapeutic progress. In the group the analyst can then more safely leave the interaction to the less anxiety provoking peers with less concern that their remarks will be damaging and intervene himself with more detached discrimination at those moments when his intervention can be most useful. While an occasional patient may become frightened by an ill timed reaction of another member, we cannot be blind to the value of peer interaction which generally encourages, supports and strengthens the forward movement of the patient.

Depth of Therapy

By depth of therapy the analyst generally means the extent to which repressed material can be uncovered and worked through. The formulation has been made[13] that individual analysis is a deeper experience than analysis in groups because the patient achieves a more profound regression to the infant–mother relationship; that in the group where relations are formed with later genetic figures like the father and siblings, such regressive possibilities and their working through cannot take place.[61] The artificial separation is then made that in the group we deal with character and defensive mechanisms and superstructure, whereas in the private setting we deal with basic conflicts and anxiety.

It is said that in individual analysis we work with the more basic biologic underpinning, while in the group we deal more with later historical developments.[2, 3] Such a view is artificial and deceptive. It is not possible to work through a defensive mechanism or a historical distortion without dealing with the basic conflict which gave rise to them. One cannot artificially separate the analysis of conflict and the analysis of the defenses against the anxiety arising from those conflicts. Nor can one artificially separate the analysis of regressive material from the content of that material in terms of current patterns.

It has been said that in the group setting transference neurosis does not arise. Some of those who concede that it can develop are nevertheless convinced that it cannot be resolved, that is, worked through in the group. It is our experience not only that transference neurosis develops among patients in a group, but also that infantile behavior can be worked through. The recurrent patterns of parental and sibling transference demands and expectations regarding the therapist as well as other members of the group can be elicited, elucidated, and with the conscious cooperation of the patient ultimately replaced by realistic, insightful ways of relating.

Depth then is attainable in either setting. It depends upon the patient and the therapeutic objectives. There is no limitation intrinsic to the group which demands that we do not deal with certain kinds of patients or with certain kinds of material. This depends on the particular patient, his strengths and his pathology, and his capacity to cope with his disturbance. The depth to which therapy can proceed is in part dependent on the therapist. If he encourages the exploration of deeply unconscious material and its working through, he may do deep therapy in either setting.

Speed of Therapy

It is difficult to evaluate the relative speeds of individual analysis and psychoanalysis in groups. But there are very few patients who happen to be in individual analysis who after entering a group do not become less resistive. And this is generally acknowledged by the individual therapist and patient alike. It is not easy to evaluate whether a patient would have moved faster in individual than in group therapy just as it is difficult to compare the progress of any two patients in individual treatment since no two persons are exactly alike. Generally a group is more stimulating to the analyst in terms of his own productivity, creativity, associative facility, imagination, and interpretive skills. The same is true for the patient, where cross discussion stirs up and touches off new associations and opens up new possibilities.

Activity and Passivity of the Therapist

There is a difference in the activity and passivity of the therapist in the individual and the group setting. In the group, members look more to one another for emotional interaction, for interpretation, for understanding, and insight. In individual treatment where patients look to the therapist for this kind of response, he generally gives it, when indicated. Accordingly, the therapist can in the main be more of a detached and rational observer of the interactive scene in the group. In individual treatment where all intratherapeutic reactions are directed toward him, where he is called upon to participate much more, it is more difficult for him to maintain a detached, rational, and observant role. The opposite may be true for some therapists, who become more isolated and removed in individual sessions and more emotionally involved and irrational in group sessions.

Because in individual analysis the multiple stimulation provided by other patients is not available, the therapist is called upon to be more active, to force the interaction that comes naturally to the group. The analyst in the group may diminish his activity, because the forced interaction occurs among the peers.

It is likely that analysts, like patients, prefer the individual or the group setting, because in one or the other they can be more active or passive by their own lights. A therapist may be immobilized in one climate and stimulated in the other. But we must examine the reality, unreality, and relevance to therapeutic ends of specific activity and passivity. In the traditional individual analytic relationship, the therapist is usually more passive and the patient more active. If, however, the patient is passive, the therapist may have to be more active. The kind of passive superneutrality of traditional analysis may have to be modified in the light of group analytic experience, where forced interaction turns out to be so useful. The individual therapist may discover that if he is more active in breaking through resistances, in provoking, in forcing interaction, he will save valuable time and facilitate treatment.

Where Does Therapy Take Place?

Therapy takes place primarily through the activity of the therapist. For some patients, usually in the first stages of treatment, the greatest movement may not occur in the individual session, nor in the regular session, but at the alternate meeting. Because this happens, it does not mean that therapy has, therefore, taken place. Such movement becomes therapy when the nature of the breakthrough is examined and made conscious, when the significance of the breakthrough is understood in terms of the total experience, when the underlying attitudes that gave rise to the anxiety are analyzed.

An important activity of the therapist is to activate the patient in interpersonal relations outside the therapeutic situation. There are some therapists who too exclusively stimulate, value, and attend only those activities which involve patient and analyst. This is poor therapy, because it tends to isolate the patient entirely to movement within treatment and to deny the validity of experiences outside the therapeutic frame. This occurs even in group therapy if the therapist limits patient interaction, does not encourage extra-group interaction, forbids alternate meetings, and encourages reaction primarily to himself.

Selection of Material

In individual or group settings, access to personality is always partial and selective. In individual analysis selections are determined by the nature of the real or projected anxiety in the presence of the therapist, the capacity to build a relationship of trust with him, and his assurance of nonretaliation. In the group, selections are determined by the ability to accept the reality that he will not be destroyed there and the degree of support the person may expect from co-patients and therapist. What is selected to reveal may vary from individual to regular to alternate sessions depending upon the particular kind of material, the kind of patient, the constitution of the group, attitudes of its members and the analyst.

In any therapy, the bulk of a person's reactions is not brought to the attention of the therapist. It is non-discriminative to be concerned with not missing a single reaction or with wanting to know everything. Therapy is selective—in individual analysis the therapist can select the transference relationship to him for scrutiny. He can study what is reported in the fantasies of the patient that bear upon his reality situation outside of therapy. The analyst can only examine the responses, recall, and presentation of the patient. Furthermore in the group, sufficient material arises for the therapist to select that transference reaction or defensive maneuver that he thinks important to work through. He goes after that operation which he believes is crucial, central, one of the interlocking keys. He lets scores of responses go by the board or he is not a good therapist. He has to be discriminative. He has to select for work the heart material appropriate to each patient according to his stage of development.

Focus of Interaction

In individual analysis the therapist may encourage the patient to focus his pathology on the analyst in order to work it through. In the group a good deal of this interaction is focussed on patients. There is value in being able to see the extensive unfolding that follows upon a deeply affective experience, whether healthy of transferential. Deeply feelingful interaction is not frequent in the individual treatment situation. The individual therapist limits such a development by his detachment. He lets the material play itself out. He cannot let it go beyond the nature of the therapeutic relationship with him. He must not become irrationally involved. In the group one of the primary values is that patients can be encouraged to interact with one another. There the focus of interpersonal affect remains among group members, while the analyst can maintain his rational, scrutinizing role. However, in the individual setting this role operates to inhibit the extent of emotional interaction that characterizes psychoanalysis in groups.

Dependence on Therapy

The pathologic dependence that develops upon the analyst is more dangerous in the individual than in the group setting. It is more dangerous at least in its abuse, more isolating, more crippling. While a patient may become dependent upon his group, upon his therapist or upon one or more co-patients, the fact that therapist and group members demand interaction tends to break up the isolated clique that forms the interdependency. This quality of group interaction is useful in the continuous working out and working through of the transference neurosis.

There is a risk in some groups that the therapist may be inclined to cultivate a pathologic subculture, where the members can act out interminably in a nuclear society in which patients prefer to abreact and cathart endlessly without working through toward more realistic ends.[146] In other words, regression is prolonged and rewarded. Here the analyst feeds the patient's pathology and enlarges his neurotic dependency. So we may conclude with regard to dependence on therapy that the individual or group medium may be used by the patient or the therapist to foster symbiosis or counteract it. Addiction to therapy is a possibility in any setting.

Responsibility

One of the values of psychoanalysis in groups is the sense of social responsibility it cultivates in its participants. The obligations the individual analyst imposes on the patient are largely limited to paying fees, doing the therapist no bodily harm, and not damaging his property. For the rest the relatively permissive attitude of the therapist sometimes engenders or preserves in the patient a disappointing habit of taking help for granted and grumbling if it is not immediately forthcoming, as if it were his due. If the therapist does not analyze this unreasonable expectation in an exploitative patient, his dependency and misuse of others and himself are activated. In group therapy no one can exercise such irresponsibility without being called to account, a healthy demand to which the patient must begin to respond if he wishes the group to attend him as indeed he must. This, too, is a useful aid in working through the transference neurosis.

Working Through

There seems to be a tendency to neglect the necessity for working through especially in group psychotherapy.[146] This may be due in part to the fact that many group therapists, unlike individual therapists, consciously or unconsciously reject psychoanalysis. They are, therefore, at a loss in coming to a unified theory of treatment for patients in a group setting. This is reflected in the many therapies described in the literature by group therapists.[19] On the other hand, the large amount of material resulting from patient interaction in the group as contrasted with the individual setting sometimes makes some therapists feel overwhelmed and driven to the necessary assumption that working through is not even possible.

Psychoanalysis in groups is a reality, because working through can be accomplished in the group setting. The multiplicity of material facilitates the seeing of the repetitive core of the transference neurosis and its working through. Repetition is characteristic not only of neurosis; it is also characteristic of therapy. After the expression and elucidation of the pathology and its dynamics, it is the task of the analyst repeatedly to support more realistic alternatives in behavior. A possibility that exists only in the group setting is the bilateral working through of interlocking neurotic maneuvers on the part of two or more persons. Working through different aspects of the neurosis of different patients at different stages of development is valuable for all the members of the group, since it reflects a repeated stand for reality. It is this repetition that makes for the possibility of working through to the ultimate acceptance of healthy alternatives to regressive strivings.

Termination

It is likely that movement toward termination is easier to achieve in group, because it provides the patient with extra-therapist experience, contact, and involvement. While the decision for termination in its final form rests primarily on the good judgment and expertness of the therapist sometimes the patient's constructive development is not fully perceived by the analyst and is called to his attention by other members. A special aspect of this occurs in psychoanalysis in groups which require alternate sessions. It has happened that a patient will first show his improvement there. What has to be worked through, however, is his reluctance to exercise his positive resources in the therapist's presence.

Resistance to termination can be found on the part of analyst as well as analysand. The chances that these resistances to termination will be acceded to are less in the face of the validation by other group members. This is not to diminish the expertness of the therapist but rather to provide him with more data upon which his evaluation and decision can be made. The nature of the individual analytic situation is such that the data are always provided by the patient except in the relationship with the therapist. This is a one-sided, specific kind of experience with a limited source of material. The group provides more data for coming to a better decision as to the appropriateness of termination.[139] In our experience, the patient facing termination values the judgment of the therapist with regard to his readiness to end treatment and always seeks it before coming to a decision. This is not true, of course, of the patient leaving therapy out of resistance who often seeks from co-patients agreement to the appropriateness of his flight.

Conclusion

The position assumed by some individual psychotherapists that group therapy cannot be very successful because patients are too ignorant of one another's real needs and the means of understanding and coping with them, has the flavor of the pronouncements of certain producers of mass culture for the people. These guardians of the arts justify the low quality of their product in the contention that they must adapt their more refined taste to the level of the crowd. The experience of the psychoanalyst in groups that patients develop there a remarkable capacity for mutual exploration, understanding, and reparative means contradicts both the general misconception of popular ignorance and the particular fallacy that human beings cannot serve one another well.

Until now, psychoanalysis in groups has been the recipient, the student of individual analysis. The analyst in groups has tried to bring to his work the knowledge and technique that the individual analyst has had to offer. We believe that insights, experience, and understanding derived from psychoanalysis done in groups may well improve, intensify, and enrich the character of individual analytic therapy. If analysts were to become aware of the value of forced interaction, of socializing, of becoming involved with other people, of resolving hierarchic and horizontal vectors, of dealing with status problems, of the value to intrapsychic change of multiple interpersonal experiences and so on, these would not be so neglected in individual treatment.

Analysis, whether in an individual or group setting, deals with the same basic problem, namely, the attempt to integrate and bring into harmonious fulfillment the intrapsychic and the interpersonal. The two treatment settings provide the therapist at the outset with different materials to work on to achieve that unitary frame of reference, a realistic balance between the personal and the social. In individual therapy, the analyst must work largely with intrapsychic presentations, with the fantasies, recollections, and memories of interactions, whereas in the group the actual interactions are available for scrutiny. In individual treatment the only interaction that is handy for immediate examination is the exchange between patient and analyst, whereas in the group the interchange among patients also is always accessible.

Psychoanalytic therapy is much the same regardless of the setting in which it occurs. The setting provides different facets of the interpersonal relationship called the therapeutic experience. The setting determines in part the kinds of materials and emphases that are utilized. But the nature of utilizing therapy as a health-giving experience aimed at freeing the patient's growth potential is generally the same. A harmonious integration of techniques derived from individual analysis and psychoanalysis in groups provides us with the possibility of doing therapy in a more rounded, thorough fashion.

This is not to imply that certain structural differences in the two treatment settings do not obtain; they have sometimes been felt and described as climate, but they are firmer, more specific than that word suggests. The following are some of the built-in conditions determining the content and process of psychoanalysis in groups as compared with psychoanalysis in an individual setting.

The presence of other patients brings with it the concurrence of vertical and horizontal relationships. Although the relationship to the analyst is more distant, it is closer to the peers. Transference reactions then are not exclusively directed to the therapist or stimulated only by him. Transference to the analyst in the individual setting is more persistent and consistent. The multiplicity of provocations stemming from co-patients makes it more difficult at first to parse out what is real from what is unreal with regard to patient interaction. On the other hand, the diverse set of stimulations in the group, whether provocative or supportive, offers each patient the opportunity to feel confirmed. There are more anchorages in reality and unreality in the group, and the qualities of the therapist in reality and illusion lend themselves to more intensive exploration by the patients. The possibility of sexual or aggressive acting out on the part of the therapist in the group is diminished.

The bilateral nature of transference interactions can be experienced in the group. The intensity of the transference reactions of one patient to another, however, is more easily tolerated in light of the fact that it is directed toward a peer, a co-patient. In special instances, this intense transference relationship to another member of the group is what binds the patient to treatment, whereas such intense feelings directed toward the therapist in the individual or group situation might force the patient to flee or to become immobilized. In the group, interaction is provided by the patients, and the therapist can remain less active. The opportunity for the patient to remain silent and nonparticipant, that is, to hide out, exists in the group, unless the therapist encourages interaction by requiring the alternate session and by such techniques as "going around." On the other hand, the presence of peers forces greater activity, interactivity, and reactivity. As a result then all patient relationships are exaggerated. The possibility for greater fragmentation and greater reconstructive work are simultaneously present as a consequence of the quantity and quality of patient activity in the group. Irrational interaction between patient and therapist, however, is less likely in the group. The interpatient activity leads to the analysis of the intrapsychic material.

Finally, no one patient becomes the exclusive and continuing center of the therapeutic activity. Attention from the analyst as well as patients shifts from one member of the group to another, so that the human necessity for alternating periods of activity and restitution may occur. In addition, no patient is forced into playing only one role. In the individual analytic situation he cannot alter his role; he relates helped to helper. In the group, he is encouraged to try various roles.

14. The Future

The future grows out of the past, the present and some uncharted elements chance may serve up. When postulating what may lie ahead, we would rather speculate on these bases than prophesy. At this moment in the evolution of psychoanalysis, we have reached a point where re-examination and re-evaluation of our goals, methods and dedication are in order. We are led to the conclusion that psychoanalysis will move toward psychoanalysis in groups and this in turn will lead to a new dimension in depth psychology which may more appropriately be called depth–breadth psychology. For psychoanalysis in groups will illuminate not only the complex intrapsychic dynamics of the patient in depth but will also make more explicit and specific his operations in interaction, eventually determining how he will extend his activities from the group into the real world. In other words, psychoanalysis in groups is here to stay as a psychoanalytic method. It has evolved organically from the techniques of the past and has demonstrated that it is in step with the trends toward the future.

Out of the past, and still in the present, a primitive attitude toward the mental patient has persisted on the part of the public and even of the therapist. The emotionally disturbed person was generally looked on as an object of fear. People were afraid they would be contaminated by his "madness," that despite all resistance they would be infected or possessed by it. And so the psychotic patient was isolated in dark places, chains confined him and human intercourse denied him.

The victims of such prejudices are never limited to psychotics but extend to neurotics as well. And then all deviants are included: the queer, the unusual, the different, the exceptional.

In the treatment of psychotic patients enormous strides are currently being made in the opposite direction. It is fitting at this point to examine this new trend. While treatment is still in the hands of the authorities, it is more available to outside scrutiny. Today it is recognized that isolation entrenches illness, that it forces the patient to project and populate his environment, even to hallucinate. We know that to prevent or cure mental illness we must get the patient into life, into the family, into school, profession and community; that by increasing his contacts with reality rather than by isolation, we take the patient away from subjective irrationality. Many hospitals in various countries around the world have begun to experiment with open doors for their mental patients, within the hospital and its grounds. Other institutions have gone further and incorporated the life of the hospital into the large community. And in some countries, like Belgium, there are therapeutic communities in which the psychotic patient lives with a family, and there is no hospital at all. To give a sidelight on the complexity of the situation, this particular Belgian community was founded by far-sighted individuals who realized the fact that human nature needs human contact, and they dedicated themselves to putting their ideals into action. And in our modern times, their simple, humane solution is being threatened by the complexities of society, present day economics and political and segregationist theories.

If these forward trends are so readily discernible in the treatment of psychotics, it is inevitable that therapy for neurotics and borderline cases should develop along similar lines. Though in some analyses the hangnail of fear of the patient is still discernible, inroads have been and still are being made on that concept. Few analysts behave as if they believe the patient will contaminate them. Not all analysts insist that the patient lie on the couch and the analyst sit behind him at a distance, that the analyst speak as little as possible and stay out of interaction as much as possible. And some even believe that it is not antianalytic to like the patient and perhaps to see a patient occasionally outside the analytic hour, at a social gathering, let us say.

Actually this is no radical departure from the practice of psychoanalysis as Freud saw it. He had long conversations with patients, social visits and walks. To Freud, evidently, psychoanalysis was a humanizing process that went on between two persons and did not demand isolative separation of patient and analyst.

Though the warnings of Freud as to how the transference situation might be manipulated by the patient have been taken much too rigidly and too literally by some, the general attitude toward the patient–analyst relationship has been one of steadily increasing interaction. Ferenczi introduced the more intensely personal aspect to the relationship. Though he seemed to encourage bilateral acting out, he drove the main point home in a way which could not be ignored, that the relationship between analyst and patient is central in treatment. Since then the work of Adler, Horney and Sullivan and their followers has been oriented toward a study of the patient in his cultural environment and his interpersonal relations, striving always toward increasing reality boundness.

It has already been shown how psychoanalysis in groups has combined and realized many of these new ways of viewing and treating the human being. In the open, heterogeneous group, people of different levels of illness, age and social position strive to communicate and to work out their intrapsychic and interpersonal problems in interaction. Though the analyst leads the group, he does not stand apart, he is available for interaction and subject to criticism as are patient members of the group. Moreover, the patients are asked to function on their own in alternate meetings and encouraged to develop personal worlds also outside the group.

Trust in the positive strivings of their persons can be extremely helpful in the strengthening of the patients' resources. It is true, that escape into reality can endanger the analytic process, that the patient may try to occupy himself exclusively with so-called real problems to the exclusion of his intrapsychic ones. But then, anything done to excess is a danger to analysis, if not properly handled. Concern with intrapsychic problems, to the extent that they become mystical abstractions, is just as inimical to the analytic process. The fact that caution and flexibility of observation on the part of the analyst are continually called for should be viewed as a fact of life in the practice of psychoanalysis and not as the deciding factor of whether or not a principle is valid. The alternate session, for example, has been rejected by many as giving patients too much opportunity to act out or to escape into social rather than therapeutic relationships. Of course, this may happen, but it certainly does not always happen. It does not even often happen. And the fact that it sometimes may happen seems scant reason to reject a procedure which has so much to offer.

In any event, it seems likely at this writing the movement toward encouraging patient autonomy will be reenforced in the future no matter how many conservatives resist it. This is in part a consequence of the Zeitgeist, because independent statehood and integration are trends in the world today, and deny it or not, psychoanalysis is influenced by the realities in which it exists, both negatively and positively. There are those who would entrench and narrow boundaries between nations and races. And there are analysts who would still prefer to isolate themselves from their patients. But there are others in the world and in great numbers who seek wider and more productive areas of endeavor, and they are joined by proportionately as many analysts and very especially by patients. These are the people who will find themselves gravitating more and more toward psychoanalysis in groups, as providing quite fertile ground and climate to yield more expansive results. And as this influence has already made itself felt, it will continue to feed back and enrich individual analytic practice.

It might be well to sound a word of caution here. While we would extend individual psychoanalysis to psychoanalysis in groups, where indicated, we cannot go so far as some zealous group psychotherapists who would like to bring the blessings of group psychotherapy to solve mass conflict on a national and international scale.[136] While such aims are doubtlessly well intentioned, it seems to us inappropriate to attempt to understand and resolve enormous social problems by the psychotherapeutic means applicable to eight or ten patients. These proposals are more than irrelevant, they are grandiose. The same recommendations have been made by individual analysts for disturbed governmental leaders. But some group therapists go even further. In their omnipotence they would heal the masses of mankind.

The scientific discoveries of psychotherapy are not directly applicable to the problems of economics or government, although Freud pointed out that government, child rearing and psychoanalysis were of a similar order. The categories that explain one body of knowledge, however, are not necessarily relevant to another. Besides, such urgings by group therapists are unrealistic and are, therefore, rejected by political leaders and the population at large. We ought not in our appreciation of the results of psychotherapy to try inappropriately to extend our reasonable skills. We are still in need of more insights into the dynamics of family life, education, government, international relations and how the individual relates to them, a tall enough order without becoming so self-impressed as to believe that everyone should be psychoanalyzed or that we could be equal to the task should it be handed us. The most we can hope for when speculating on these problems is that they will point out paths of research. We ought be more concerned with exploration than with immediate answers based on hopeful convictions than specific knowledge.

Let us turn our attention then to the question of how psychoanalysis in groups may evolve in the future in terms of research, scope, training of practitioners and influence in the community life of the persons it reaches.

Research in problems of psychoanalysis in groups is primary in the order of importance, for two reasons. The first is the obvious one. We simply need to know more about the human being, sick and well, and how he operates within himself and with others. But we also need detailed and concrete records of case histories, as well as experimentation, in order to convince those who still doubt, that psychoanalysis not only can be practiced in groups but it can work and how it works.

Psychoanalysis in groups was not a spontaneous manifestation. It evolved gradually from group therapy for tuberculosis in 1906, through group psychotherapy until the middle thirties, when psychoanalytic methods were first introduced into the group setting. At each stage of development resistance was encountered. This was quite natural. There is always resistance to change. Freud met it. The deviants from Freud met it. Still the evolution went on and will go on.

Group therapy began when certain medical practitioners searched for a way to influence their diabetic and tubercular patients to follow the routines necessary for the control of their illness. It was discovered that when they could discuss their common problems, patients found it easier to abide by the prescriptions of their physicians. Group therapy pioneers saw in this result the possibility of extending the group setting to the treatment of mental problems. But some of these very innovators resisted the further extension to the treatment of these disorders by analytic methods.

Group psychotherapy has from the first attracted social and clinical psychologists, social workers, group dynamicists, psychodramatists, sociometrists and others outside of or on the periphery of psychoanalysis but the competently trained psychoanalyst has so far generally remained aloof. In the future we are predicating this will not be so. The analytically trained therapist will realize that leaving this fertile and valuable field to the inadequately trained or antianalytic therapist can only harm psychoanalysis. It is not enough to decry some of the irrationalists who practice group psychotherapy or those who depend on antianalytic theories, while the analytically trained insist on staying out of the practice themselves.

Group psychotherapy needs these able, experienced clinicians and theoreticians. It needs the instructive and correctional guidance of the psychoanalysts. And we can safely promise that such an experience will not be one-sided learning. Group therapists have learned a great deal on their own and are in a position to be instructive to individual analysts as well, even in the conduct of one-to-one treatment.

One thing seems certain: the development of psychoanalysis in groups is largely the responsibility of the analyst. He has an obligation to the public in need of care and to the group psychotherapists in need of training. To the increasing numbers of patients the analyst can offer his expertness in the group setting with larger rewards and satisfactions for both sides. To the group therapists inadequately trained in psychoanalysis he can bring his greater understanding of intrapsychic and interpersonal dynamics. As long as the psychoanalyst continues to reject group psychotherapy, just so long will the personnel using the method look elsewhere for training and instruction. It would benefit all concerned for this search not to be hit or miss.

Some alternative must be offered the young, enthusiastic and impatient group psychotherapist who is impressed with the results he has so far attained and who will not be put off too long in attempts to extend his knowledge, experience and methods of work. Unless analysts assume their responsibilities fairly soon, this young therapist is showing signs of developing on his own. And the public is showing signs that it is not far behind. As increasing numbers of patients benefit from group psychotherapy and psychoanalysis in groups, at costs less than individual analysis and with results which are good, the traditional psychoanalysts may find themselves obliged by social necessities to explore the possibilities of psychoanalysis in groups. Rather than wait for the pressure of public demands, we believe all would be better served if analysts seized the initiative and incorporated psychoanalysis in groups into their training programs at psychoanalytic institutes.

That this is possible is evidenced by the inclusion for the past thirteen years of a group analytic lecture course plus a subjective experience in psychoanalysis in groups at two analytic institutes. At least one has a full two year training program in group psychotherapy to which no applicant is eligible unless he has already been certified by an accredited psychoanalytic institute. We also know of at least two groups of analysts, and there are probably more, in different cities who are contemplating the organization of training institutes for psychoanalysis in groups. What is more, analysts from remote communities and around the world are applying for training in psychoanalysis in groups. If the presently accredited analytic training institutes generally reject psychoanalysis in groups, it would seem much the wisest course to avoid further splintering of the analytic movement and to establish Institutes for Psychoanalysis in Groups led by psychoanalysts of different backgrounds and training and open to those interested in furthering their knowledge of psychoanalytic techniques by research and instruction. In the United Nations countries of different size and power, peoples of different color and political bias get together to discuss their areas of agreement and dissension. Many feel that if this place of and for communication ceases to exist, the world as we know it may perish. Is it a foolhardy dream, perhaps, to suppose that analysts might establish for themselves an institution of united methods, a UM modeled on the UN, where a sincere effort might be made to communicate and clarify, to teach and to learn, to experiment and to grow with the science as it grows? Let us hope, if not actually suppose, that this is a fantasy well in the realm of the realizably possible.

What then would be the research program of such an institute? The possibilities for speculation are endless: investigation and experimentation in family group therapy; in the treatment of the very young and very old; homogeneous and heterogeneous groups; open and closed groups. We need to explore further the problems of selection and grouping of patients; to establish better criteria of when to use combined group and individual therapy, and when not; to explore the differences in the various settings of countertransference problems. We need to experiment with various kinds of structuring of groups to see which facilitate and which impede patient-to-patient reparative processes and therapeutic intervention by the analyst. We need to discover new dimensions, new parameters in psychoanalysis in groups besides those of size, support, multiple reactivities, peer and authority vectors, the intra- and interpersonal emphases. Will we find those new dimensions by having co-therapists? Adjunct therapists in the group? By having groups meet more often or less often? With longer or shorter sessions? By placing patients in groups either with families or spouses or with strangers? By patients beginning and ending treatment with the same group or being moved about? The questions to be asked are as endless and complex as the human being himself, and the number of challenges we tackle will be a measure of our dedication. And if we find ourselves equal to the challenge, we will have earned the right to make some stipulations concerning the analyst of the future, the kind of person he will be, how he will be selected and how trained.

In all probability the future will see many of the discipline designations prevalent today in choosing candidates for certification as analysts, modified. So, the future analyst may not be *only* a psychiatrist, *only* a psychologist or *only* a psychiatric social worker. He may come from the ranks of these three, and he may also come from the ranks of other humanistic disciplines, sociology, anthropology, education, history, philosophy, religion, mythology, science and art, just so long as he has demonstrated through his previous experience and activity a genuine will to train further along psychoanalytic lines. In other words, the kind of person he is will rank high in the table of standards for selection.

It may not be demanded that he be a scholar, so much as that he be endowed with common sense, that human attribute which cannot be taught but can be encouraged to blossom and grow. And, so that he not become entrenched in a completely common sense view of life for himself or his patients, he will retain that essence of creative artists and creative scientists, the sense of wonder which enables one to see freshly again and again, to question, to accept, to transcend and to renew.

The analytic trainee of the future will have a certain kind of knowledge and a love of that knowledge, not confined to neurology or statistics or research, but including as much as possible of the humanistic disciplines as they pertain to as many facets of human relatedness as possible.

And he will be a doer. He will have demonstrated in his life that his own creative impulses and powers have areas in which to breathe outside his chosen profession. Can he sculpt? Paint? Write? Garden? Have a family? Each will find his own room and way of expansion, but in order to help his patients find theirs, somewhere, somehow,—it will need to be part of his own creative-productive experience, so that he and we will know he can function as a total person with a combination of head, hand and heart. The kind of person he is will be central, because above all we would wish the analyst of the future to be a humanizing force and for that he himself needs to be human.

The training of the analyst of the future will expand as the boundaries of thought, experimentation and society expand. He will be exposed during the course of it to the precepts of traditional analysis. He will be thoroughly grounded not only in the historical sources of his profession but also in the principles of dedication it requires. He will be made aware of the wide differences of opinion existing between schools of analysis and among individuals and will consistently be encouraged to select, through instruction, training and experience those principles of practice most appropriate to the needs of patients but which suit him best, reserving always the right to question, to improvise on his own or to turn to tradition whenever it seems best to do so. In turn he will have the opportunity if not the obligation to share his findings with other colleagues, to permit them to be scrutinized and debated. It is entirely possible that in the not so distant future individual and group analytic sessions will be televised over closed circuits, sound film recordings made of sessions so that both therapists and patients may have the opportunity to see themselves from a more objective perspective than their own memories and perceptions of themselves. Already one way screens are being used for observation, and transcontinental telephone for instruction. In the future their use will be greatly expanded.

There will always be a certain amount of authority the trainee of the future will be asked to accept without servility or rebellion. No matter how threatened he may personally feel by an idea, new or old, he will have trained himself in the habit of examining it thoroughly before he makes a decision to accept, reject or table it for further study and experimentation. And he will recall T. H. Huxley's admonition that: "All science starts with hypotheses—in other words, with assumptions that are unproved, . . . while they may be, and often are, erroneous, they are better than nothing to the searcher after order in the maze of phenomena. And the historical process of every science depends on the criticism of hypotheses, on the gradual stripping off, that is, of their untrue or superfluous parts—until there remains only that exact verbal expression of as much as we know of the facts, and no more, which constitutes a perfect scientific theory."

To accept so demanding a test of research, an inordinate amount of courage is needed—courage to create as well as to tolerate the creation of others—and then the further courage to examine those creations as objectively as possible, to accept or reject them as the evidence requires. This courage, too, requires a special kind of training. Today the analytic trainee is required to have an individual analysis in order that he know himself and come to terms with himself. The trainee of the future may also be asked to have a subjective psychoanalytic group experience somewhere during the course of his training, so that he can evaluate more clearly his capacity for communication, for receptivity to the communications of others and the general extent of his reality boundaries in terms of interaction with others. No matter what school of analytic thought he will choose for himself, the center of treatment will be the relationship between analyst and patient, the interaction of at least two people with each other, but moving always toward peerage in the analytic group and thence outward into the patient's own family and society.

In his actual practice the analyst of the future will find himself much less rigidly bound by the trappings of office. It will be of little moment whether he practices in a light room or dark, whether it is austere or homey or equipped with double doors or separate entrances and exits for patients. His concentration will not be focussed on the mystery of his person or activity, but rather on the central task of greeting each patient with warmth, friendliness and humanness, wishing to make and maintain contact, in order to discover and bring into the light the central core of that particular patient's problems and potentialities. Because he himself has had the subjective experience of how psychoanalysis in groups can expand the boundaries of communication, he will be able to help the patient toward the same experience without sacrificing their own therapist–patient relationship. In fact, as techniques of training and practice of psychoanalysis in groups are refined and implemented, that very relationship will in all probability be found to be enhanced and enriched as it becomes more operable in a tangible reality setting.

So we see the psychoanalyst of the future as one who has given up his own isolation even, as he battles to bring his patients out of theirs. He lets himself see and be seen. He looks for more and more contacts, more and more ways to function outside his office doors. And he finds the community and outside world eager to meet him, eager to implement and expand their own boundaries on community levels as well as the personal one. In accomplishing this, the psychoanalyst of the future will find himself vastly helped by his experience with groups.

The scope of activity of the analyst of the future concerns us as much as his education and training. It is important for preventive mental hygiene that potential patients be reached in their most educable period, the school years. Already three large universities in New York City are offering courses in group psychotherapy. Two of them also provide courses in which there is a subjective experience of psychotherapy in a group setting. It is likely that these programs will be extended to other universities. So far they are largely training experiences for clinical psychologists on the graduate level. As these trainees acquire more experience, they may well offer their services to college students. And one day, group psychotherapy will surely become available to adolescents in high school and to children in elementary school.

We are not advocating group psychotherapy for everyone. This would be impractical and unnecessary. But a school psychologist trained in group therapy would be in a position to counsel and guide teachers in dealing with less serious problems in day-to-day contact with students. It is probable, and to be hoped, that more and more teachers will elect to have a subjective experience in a therapeutic group, not only to stabilize themselves in their professional work and in their social lives but also to enable them to apply preventive mental hygiene principles in dealing with students and their parents.

With these innovations, public interest in group therapy is bound to grow, if only for the opportunity it offers for escape from isolation, the plague of modern man, into a kind of communication which is encouraged to be honest and free. All of us have disturbances and complaints on one level or another . . . and an opportunity to ventilate them can be beneficial . . . especially if at the same time the other fellow is encouraged to communicate his response and reaction. In all likelihood this kind of exchange session, if not outright therapy, will eventually be an experience of every school-child, perhaps as part of the present hygiene class, for in such a setting it should be possible for all matters to be discussed. But the group experience can be most useful only if the student and patient carry their new-found freedom to communicate into the larger society.

Then, too, trade unions, industrial management, parent-teacher associations and other professional groups sharing common interest may approach (some have already done so) insurance companies with a view to making group therapy available at lesser cost under enlarged health insurance plans that would cover treatment in a group. Insurance companies, finding that analysis in groups is as effective as individual analysis and less costly besides, may well take the initiative here in securing psychoanalytic treatment in a group. And for all this the analyst trained in psychoanalysis in groups will be sorely needed.

Perhaps this picture of psychoanalysis of the future seems like a tall order to fill, but it is a necessary challenge which historical development will demand that we meet. The history of psychoanalysis has been one movement from isolation into reality for the patient. And, as analysis broke through the isolation of the patient, analysis and the analyst also became less isolated. Psychoanalysis in groups was a natural development of this historical movement and it may become a core setting for the future development of psychoanalysis, both individual and group. The emphasis of therapy will move from its center in the patient–therapist relationship to as many other relationships as possible in the study of the patient's total personality. In other words, the future patient will not have a choice between depth or breadth psychology but will experience a combination of both.

Since the concentration of our effort will be on training, research and experimentation with a view to increased communication and broader reality-experience boundaries for as many people as possible it is hoped that institutes for psychoanalysis in groups will be formed which will be a UM (United Methods) of psychoanalysis. These institutes will face the historical fact that psychoanalysis in groups will grow in importance, but that all other methods of group and individual therapies will have equal rights and room to observe, theorize, experiment and teach. Difference, unorthodoxy and flexiblity will be seen as desirable and healthy manifestations of mature minds engaged in a mutual search rather than as an excuse for flight, splinterings and intoversion. Psychoanalysis needs new ideas. The world needs new ideas. And this may be a good place to remind ourselves that new ideas arise out of conflict: conflict within one's own group, with other groups and within oneself when old patterns have ceased to function well. New ideas also arise when theories, hypotheses and experiences are communicated and shared in an atmosphere of contrast and cooperation, and harmony and disagreement. Discord and concord coexist in nature. They are part of the reality of man. And it is the complexity of that reality of man, intrapsychic, interpersonal and interactive, with which psychoanalysis has chosen to deal as a science and an art.

By its very nature psychoanalysis must deal daily with the basic themes of human life, love and hate, work and play, birth and death, sex and aggression, money and power. This will call on all the resources of the analyst as a human being as well as scientist. It will also call for a constant reexamination of his dedication, his goals and his methods. Here the courage and flexibility he has, strengthened by his objective training and subjective experience, will stand him in good stead. The psychoanalyst of the future will have a provocative place in which to experiment and grow. He will have a central goal: to heal the mentally disturbed; to open the way of fruition to the blocked and, on the community level, to help broaden the boundaries of reality and productive experience on as wide a basis as possible, for as many people as possible. These are opportunities as well as challenges offered to the analyst. In meeting them we will find our own satisfaction and growth. Let us hope we are equal to this promise of the future.

BIBLIOGRAPHY

The following publications contain extensive general bibliographic references to the literature in group psychotherapy. See also the annual reviews in the International Journal of Group Psychotherapy.

1946

Slavson, S. R., and Myers, G.: Bibliography on Group Psychotherapy. New York, Am. Group Psychother. Assoc., p. 12.

1950

Kotkov, B.: A bibliography for the student of group therapy. J. Clin. Psychol. 6:77–91.

Slavson, S. R., Hallowitz, E., and Kinstler, M.: Bibliography on Group Psychotherapy. New York, Am. Group Psychother. Assoc., p. 24.

1952

Scheidlinger, S.: Psychoanalysis and Group Behavior. New York, W. W. Norton, p. 245.

1954

Bach, G. R.: Intensive Group Psychotherapy. New York, Ronald Press, p. 446.

Locke, N.: Bibliography on Group Psychotherapy, vol. 2. New York, Am. Group Psychother. Assoc., p. 29.

1956

Corsini, R. J., and Putzey, L. J.: Bibliography of Group Psychotherapy. Group Psychother. 9:177–249 (also printed separately).

1957

Corsini, R. J.: Methods of Group Psychotherapy. New York, McGraw-Hill, p. 251.

1959

Klapman, J. W.: Group Psychotherapy. New York, Grune & Stratton, p. 301.

1960

Grotjahn, M.: Psychoanalysis and the Family Neurosis. New York, W. W. Norton, p. 320.

Locke, N.: A Decade of Group Psychotherapy. New York, Group Psychother. Cent. p. 48. (Mimeographed.)

REFERENCES FROM TEXT

1. *Abrahams, J.:* Correlations in Combined Treatment by Group and Modified Individual Psychoanalysis—Read before the Am. Psychoanalyt. Assoc., Chicago, May, 1957.
2. *Ackerman, N. W.:* Psychoanalysis and group psychotherapy. Group Psychother., 3:204–217, 1950.
3. ——: Some structural problems in the relations of psychoanalysis and group psychotherapy. Int. J. Group Psychother. 4:131–145, 1954.
4. *Adorno, T. W.:* The Authoritarian Personality. New York, Harper & Bros., 1950.

313

5. *Bach, G. R.:* Intensive Group Psychotherapy. New York, Ronald Press, 1954.
6. ———: Observations on transference and object relations in the light of group dynamics. Int. J. Group Psychother. 7:64–76, 1957.
7. *Baehr, G. O.:* The comparative effectiveness of individual psychotherapy, group psychotherapy, and a combination of these methods. J. Consult. Psychol. 18:179–183, 1954.
8. *Baruch, Dorothy W., and Miller, H.:* Group and individual psychotherapy as an adjunct in the treatment of allergy. J. Consult. Psychol. 10:281–284, 1946.
9. *Bendig, A. W.:* Rater reliability and the heterogeneity of clinical case histories. J. Gen. Psychol. 203–207, 1957.
10. *Berger, I.:* Some reflections on group psychotherapy, a growing force in psychiatry. Ohio State Med. J. 52:827, 1956.
11. *Berman, L.:* Psychoanalysis and group psychotherapy. Psychoanal. Rev. 37:156–163, 1950.
12. ———: Problems in Working Toward an Integration of Individual and Group Psychology—Read before the Boston Psychoanalytic Society and Institute, May 23, 1956. (Mimeographed.)
13. *Bieber, Toby B.:* The emphasis on the individual in psychoanalytic group therapy. Int. J. Soc. Psychiat. 2:275–280, 1957.
14. ———: The individual and the group. Am. J. Psychother. 13:635–650, 1959.
15. *Bion, W. R.:* Experiences in groups I–VII. Human Relations, 1948–1951.
16. *Burrow, T.:* The Social Basis of Consciousness. New York, Harcourt, Brace, 1927.
17. ———: The group method of analysis. Psychoanal. Rev. 14:268–280, 1927.
18. *Cartwright, D., and Lippitt, R.:* Group dynamics and the individual. Int. J. Group Psychother. 7:86–101, 1957.
19. *Corsini, R. J.:* Methods of Group Psychotherapy. New York, McGraw-Hill, 1957.
20. *Dreikurs, R. R.:* Psychotherapie de Groupe—Read at the Int. Congr. Psychiat., Paris, 1950. (Mimeographed.)
21. *Durkin, Helen:* Acting out in group psychotherapy. Amer. J. Orthopsychiat. 25:644–652, 1955.
22. ———; *Glatzer, Henriette T.; Kadis, Asya L.; Wolf, A.; and Hulse, W. C.:* Acting out in group psychotherapy: a panel discussion. Am. J. Psychother. 12:87–105, 1958.
23. *Eaton, A.:* Variable Uses of the Individual Session in Combined Treatment—Read at the Postgraduate Center for Psychotherapy, New York, October 29, 1957.
24. *Editorial:* The changing culture and psychotherapeutic techniques. Am. J. Psychother. 14:1–2, 1960.
25. *Eiserer, P. E.:* Group psychotherapy. J. National Assoc. Deans Women, 19:113–122, 1956.
26. *Feldman, Betty:* Social Group Therapy: An Experiment—Read at the Postgraduate Center for Psychotherapy, New York, November, 1956.
27. *Foulkes, S. H.:* Introduction to Group-Analytic Psychotherapy. London, W. Heinemann, 1948.
28. ———: Some similarities between psychoanalytic principles and group analytic principles. Brit. J. Med. Psychol. 26:30–35, 1953.
29. ———: Group-analytic dynamics with specific reference to psychoanalytic concepts. Int. J. Group Psychother. 7:40–52, 1957.
30. ———: The application of group concepts to the treatment of the individual in

the group. New York: Postgraduate Center for Psychotherapy, 1–19, 1958. (Mimeographed.)

31. ——; *and Anthony, E. J.:* Group Psychotherapy: The Psycho-Analytic Approach. London, Penguin Books, 1957.

32. *Frank, J. D.:* Some values of conflict in therapeutic groups. Group Psychother. 8:142–151, 1955.

33. ——: Some determinants, manifestations, and effects of cohesiveness in therapy groups. Int. J. Group Psychother. 7:53–63, 1957.

34. *Freud, S.:* Group Psychology and the Analysis of the Ego. London, Hogarth Press, 1948.

35. ——: The Interpretation of Dreams. New York, Basic Books, 1958.

36. *Fried, Edrita:* Benefits of 'combined therapy' for the hostile withdrawn and the hostile dependent personality. Amer. J. Orthopsychiat. 24:529–537, 1954.

37. ——: The effect of combined therapy on the productivity of patients. Int. J. Group Psychother. 4:42–55, 1954.

38. *Fromm, E.:* The Art of Loving. New York, Harper, 1956.

39. *Furst, W.:* Homogeneous versus heterogeneous groups. Int. J. Group Psychother. 1:120–123, 1951.

40. ——: Homogeneous versus heterogeneous groups. In B. Stokvis (Ed.): Topical Problems of Psychotherapy, vol. II. Basel, S. Karger, 170–173, 1960.

41. *Geller, J. J.:* Concerning the size of therapy groups. Int. J. Group Psychother. 1:118–120, 1951.

42. *Glatzer, Henriette T.:* Selection of mothers for group therapy. Am. J. Orthopsychiat. 17:477–483, 1947.

43. ——: The relative effectiveness of clinically homogeneous and heterogeneous psychotherapy groups. Int. J. Group Psychother. 6:258–265, 1956.

44. *Goldfarb, W.:* Principles of group psychotherapy. Am. J. Psychother. 7:418–432, 1953.

45. *Green, J.:* A treatment plan combining group and individual psychotherapeutic procedures in a state mental hospital. Psychiat. Quart. 27:245–253, 1953.

46. *Greenbaum, H.:* Combined Psychoanalytic Therapy with Negative Therapeutic Reactions. In Rifkin, A. H. (Ed.): Schizophrenia in Psychoanalytic Office Practice. New York, Grune & Stratton, pp. 56–65, 1957.

47. *Grinberg, L.; Langer, Marie; and Rodrigue, E.:* Psicoterapia del Grupo. Buenos Aires, Ed. Paidos, 1957.

48. ——; ——; *and* ——: El Grupo Psicologico. Buenos Aires, Ed. Nova, 1959.

49. *Hallowitz, E.:* Activity group psychotherapy as preparation for individual treatment. Int. J. Group Psychother. 1:337–347, 1951.

50. *Hill, G., and Armitage, S. G.:* An analysis of combined therapy—individual and group—in patients with schizoid, obsessive-compulsive, or aggressive defenses. J. Nerv. Ment. Dis., 119:113–134, 1954.

51. *Hulse, W. C.:* Dynamics and techniques of group psychotherapy in private practice. Int. J. Group Psychother. 4:65–73, 1954.

52. ——: Transference, catharsis, insight and reality testing during concomitant individual and group psychotherapy. Int. J. Group Psychother. 5:45–53, 1955.

53. *Joel, W., and Shapiro, D.:* Some principles and procedures for group psychotherapy. J. Psychol. 29:77–88, 1950.

54. *Jones, E.:* A Psychoanalytic Study of the Holy Ghost Concept, *in* Essays in Applied Psychoanalysis. London, Hogarth Press, 1951, pp. 358–373.

55. *Kadis, Asya L.:* The alternate meeting in group psychotherapy. Amer. J. Psychother. 10:275–291, 1956.
56. *Kallen, H. M.:* Alain Locke and cultural pluralism. J. Philos. 54:119–127, 1957.
57. *Kaplan, N. O., Ciotti, M. M., Hamolsky, M., and Bieber, R. E.:* Molecular heterogeneity and evolution of enzymes. Science 131:392–397, 1960.
58. *Kauders, O., et al.: Advances in Group and Individual Therapy: A Symposium.* Proc. Int. Congr. Ment. Hlth., London, H. K. Lewis, pp. 93–129, 1948.
59. *Klapman, J. W.:* Group Psychotherapy, Theory and Practice. New York, Grune & Stratton, 1946.
60. ——: An observation on the interrelationship of group and individual psychotherapy. J. Nerv. Ment. Dis. 101:242–246, 1945.
61. *Kubie, L. S.:* Some theoretical concepts underlying the relationship between individual and group psychotherapies. Int. J. Group Psychother. 8:3–43, 1958.
62. *Lebovici, S., Tiatkine, R., and Kestenberg, E.:* Applications of psychoanalysis to group psychotherapy and psychodrama therapy. Group Psychother. 5:38–50, 1952.
63. *Liff, Z. A.:* Group Dynamics and Psychotherapy. New York, Postgraduate Center for Psychotherapy, 1957, pp. 1–12. (Mimeographed.)
64. *Lipshutz, D. M.:* Group psychotherapy as an auxiliary aid in psychoanalysis. Int. J. Group Psychother. 2:316–323, 1952.
65. ——: Combined group and individual psychotherapy. Am. J. Psychother. 11:336–344, 1957.
66. *Loeser, L. H.:* Some aspects of group dynamics. Int. J. Group Psychother. 7:5–19, 1957.
67. *Lorge, I., et al.:* A survey of studies contrasting the quality of group performance and individual performance, 1920–1957. Psychol. Bull. 55:337–372, 1958.
68. ——, *and Solomon, H.:* Group and individual performance in problem solving related to previous exposure to problem level of aspiration and group size. Behav. Sci. 5:28–38, 1960.
69. *Lucas, L.:* Treatment of Young Children in a Group: A Supplement to Individual Treatment. (News-Letter) Am. Assoc. Psychiat. Soc. Wkers. 13(2):59–65, 1943–44.
70. *Martin, A., and Hill, W. F.:* Toward a theory of group development. Int. J. Group Psychother. 7:20–30, 1957.
71. *McCartney, J. L.:* The use of group psychotherapy in shortening individual treatment in private practice. Int. J. Group Psychother. 2:262–269, 1952.
72. *Meier, C. A.:* Advances in Group and Individual Psychotherapy. Proc. Int. Congr. Ment. Hlth. London, H. K. Lewis, 1948, pp. 94–98.
73. *Menninger, K.:* Theory of Psychoanalytic Technique. New York, Basic Books, 1958.
74. *Merry, J.:* The relative roles of individual psychotherapy and group psychotherapy in the industrial neurosis unit. J. Ment. Sci., 99:301–307, 1953.
75. *Moreno, J. L.:* Who Shall Survive? Washington, D.C., Nervous and Mental Disease Publishing Co., 1934.
76. ——: Sociometry: Science of Society. Beacon, N.Y., Beacon House, 1951.
77. ——: The ascendance of group psychotherapy and the declining influence of psychoanalysis. Group Psychother. 3:121–125, 1950.
78. *Morse, P. W., Gessay, L. H., and Karpe, R.:* The effect of group psychotherapy in reducing resistance to individual psychotherapy: A Case Study. Int. J. Group Psychother. 5:216–269, 1955.

79. *Mullan, H.:* Status denial in group psychoanalysis. J. Nerv. Ment. Dis. 122:345–352, 1955.
80. ———: Group psychotherapy in private practice: practical considerations. J. Hillside Hosp. 6:34–42, 1957.
81. *Murray, H. A., and Kluckhohn, C.:* Outline of a Conception of Personality, *in* Kluckhohn, C., and Murray, H. A. (eds.): Personality. New York, Knopf, 1948, pp. 3–32.
82. *Papanek, Helene:* Combined group and individual therapy in private practice. Am. J. Psychother. 8:679–686, 1954.
83. ———: Combined group and individual therapy in the light of Adlerian psychology. Int. J. Group Psychother. 6:136–146, 1956.
84. *Pearson, G. H. J.:* Psychoanalysis and the Education of the Child. New York, W. W. Norton, 1954.
85. *Piaget, J.:* The Moral Judgment of the Child. New York, Harcourt, Brace, 1932.
86. *Powdermaker, Florence, and Frank, J.:* Group Psychotherapy. Cambridge, Harvard Univ. Press, 1953.
87. *Ransberg, Mary:* Integration of group therapy and individual therapy. Int. J. Group Psychother. 1:115–118, 1951.
88. *Rasey, Marie:* Psychology and education. Am. J. Psychoanal. 6:26–34, 1946.
89. *Rickman, J.:* The Factor of Number in Individual- and Group-Dynamics (1950), *in* Selected Contributions to Psychoanalysis. New York, Basic Books, 1957, pp. 165–169.
90. ———: Number and the Human Sciences (1951), *in* Selected Contributions to Psychoanalysis. New York, Basic Books, 1957, pp. 218–223.
91. *Rosow, H. M., and Kaplan, Lillian P.:* Integrated individual and group therapy. Int. J. Group Psychother. 4:381–392, 1954.
92. *Sager, C. J.:* The effects of group therapy on individual analysis. Int. J. Group Psychother. 9:403–419, 1959.
93. *Sapir, E.:* Group. Encyclopedia of the Social Sciences. New York, Macmillan, 1932, vol. 7, pp. 178–182.
94. *Scheidlinger, S.:* Freudian group psychology and group psychotherapy. Am. J. Orthopsychiat., 22:710–717, 1952.
95. ———: The concept of identification in group psychotherapy. Am. J. Psychother. 9:661–672, 1955.
96. ———: Group therapy—its place in psychotherapy. J. Soc. Case-Work, 29:99–304, 1958.
97. ———: Group Process in Group Psychotherapy—A Critical Analysis of Current Trends in the Integration of Individual and Group Psychology. Presented at the 15th Annual Conf. Am. Group Psychother. Assoc., January, 1958. (Mimeographed.)
98. *Schilder, P.:* Psychotherapy. New York, W. W. Norton, 1938.
99. ———: The analysis of ideologies as a psychotherapeutic method, especially in group treatment. Am. J. Psychiat. 93:601–617, 1936.
100. *Schwartz, E. K.:* Some trends in the development of psychology as a profession in the U.S.A. Int. J. Soc. Psychiat. 2:51–58, 1956.
101. ———: The Search for Personal Maturity, *in* J. E. Fairchild (ed.): Personal Problems and Psychological Frontiers. New York, Sheridan House, 1957, pp. 13–28.
102. ———: Is Psychology Necessary in Psychotherapy? *in* M. H. Krout (ed.): Psychology, Psychiatry and the Public Interest. Minneapolis, Univ. Minn. Press, 1957, pp. 113–134.

103. ———: Psychotherapy in Mexico, *in* Masserman, J. H., and Moreno, J. L. (eds.): Progress in Psychotherapy. New York, Grune & Stratton, 1957, pp. 216–223.

104. ———: The Meaning and Use of Dreams. Los Angeles, L. A. Society of Clinical Psychologists, 1959. (Mimeographed.)

105. ———: Afterthoughts to "The Application of Group Concepts to the Treatment of the Individual in the Group," by S. H. Foulkes. *In* B. Stokvis (ed.): Topical Problems of Psychotherapy, vol. II. Basel, S. Karger, 1960, pp. 36–37.

106. ———: An eclectic view of Freud. J. Long Island Consult. Cent. 1(4), 1961.

107. ———: Some points of view on dreams and dreaming. J. Long Island Consult. Cent. 1(3):9–14, 1961.

108. ———, and *Abel, T. M.:* The professional education of the psychoanalytic psychotherapist. Am. J. Psychother. 9:253–261, 1955.

109. ———, and *Wolf, A.:* Psychoanalysis in groups: three primary parameters. Am. Imago, 14:281–297, 1957.

110. ———, and ———: Irrational trends in contemporary psychotherapy: cultural correlates. Psychoanal. & Psychoanalyt. Rev. 45(1–2):65–74, 1958.

111. ———, and ———: The quest for certainty. A.M.A. Arch. Neurol. & Psychiat. 81:69–84, 1959.

112. ———, and ———: Psychoanalysis in Groups: The Mystique of Group Dynamics. *In* B. Stokvis (ed.): Topical Problems of Psychotherapy, vol. II. Basel, S. Karger, 1960, pp. 119–154.

113. ———, and ———: Psychoanalysis in groups: some comparisons with individual analysis. J. Gen. Psychol. 64:153–191, 1961.

114. ———, and ———: Psychoanalysis in groups: combined therapy. Read at the Postgraduate Center for Psychotherapy, New York, November, 1957.

115. *Seashore, S. E.:* Group Cohesiveness in the Industrial Group. Ann Arbor, Inst. for Soc. Res., 1954.

116. *Shames, George H.:* An exploration of group homogeneity in group speech therapy. J. Speech & Hearing Dis. 18:267–272, 1953.

117. *Shaskan, D. A.:* Must individual and group psychotherapy be opposed? Am. J. Orthopsychiat. 17:290–292, 1947.

118. ———: Individual and Group Therapy in Mental Hygiene. *In* Shore, M. J. (ed.): Twentieth Century Mental Hygiene. New York, Social Science Publishers, 1950, pp. 111–124.

119. *Shea, J. E.:* Differentials in resistance reactions in individual and group psychotherapy. Int. J. Group Psychother. 4:253–261, 1954.

120. *Slavson, S. R.:* Common sources of error and confusion in group psychotherapy. Int. J. Group Psychother. 3:3–28, 1953.

121. ———: The nature and treatment of acting out in group psychotherapy. Int. J. Group Psychother. 6:3–26, 1956.

122. ———: Are there "group dynamics" in therapy groups? Int. J. Group Psychother. 7:131–154, 1957.

123. ———: Parallelisms in the Development of Group Psychotherapy.

124. *Spotnitz, H.:* Discussion of Fried, Edrita: vide supra #36, 535–537.

125. *Spranger, O.:* Psychoanalytic pedagogy. Psychoanal. 2:59–70, 1952.

126. *Thelen, H. A.:* Dynamics of Groups at Work. Chicago, Chicago University Press, 1954.

127. *Wender, L.:* The dynamics of group psychotherapy and its application. J. Nerv. & Ment. Dis. 84:54–60, 1936.

128. *Westman, J. C.:* An overview of group psychotherapy. A.M.A. Arch. Gen. Psychiat. 2:271–277, 1960.

129. *Whitaker, C. A., and Malone, T. P.:* The Roots of Psychotherapy. New York, Blakiston, 1953.
130. *Whitman, R. M., Lieberman, M. A., and Stock, D.:* The relation between individual and group conflicts in psychotherapy. Int. J. Group Psychother. 10:259–286, 1960.
131. *Whyte, W. H.:* The Organization Man. New York, Simon & Schuster, 1956.
132. *Wilder, J.:* Group analysis as an adjunct to long lasting psychoanalysis. Group Psychother. 5:64–67, 1952.
133. *Wolberg, Arlene R.:* The borderline patient. Am. J. Psychother. 6:694–710, 1952.
134. *Wolberg, L. R.:* The Technique of Psychotherapy. New York, Grune & Stratton, 1954, pp. 569–572.
135. *Wolf, A.:* The psychoanalysis of groups. Am. J. Psychother. 3:525–558, 1949; 4:16–50, 1950.
136. ——: On the irrelevance of group psychotherapy in mass conflict. Group Psychother. 5:78–79, 1952.
137. ——: Discussion of Bychowski, G.: Psychic Structure and Therapy of Latent Schizophrenia. *In* Rifkin, A. H. (ed.): Schizophrenia in Psychoanalytic Office Practice. New York, Grune & Stratton, 1957, pp. 135–139.
138. ——: Code of ethics of group psychotherapists: comments. Group Psychother. 10:221–223, 1957.
139. ——: The Advanced and Terminal Phases in Group Psychotherapy. New York, Proc. 2nd Annual Inst. Am. Group Psychother. Assoc., 1958, pp. 66–79.
140. ——: Potentialities of group therapy for obesity. Int. Rec. Med. 171:9–11, 1958.
141. ——: Discussion of S. H. Foulkes: The Application of Group Concepts to the Treatment of the Individual in the Group. *In* B. Stokvis (ed.): Topical Problems of Psychotherapy, vol. II. Basel, S. Karger, 1960, pp. 16–23.
142. ——: Psychoanalysis in Groups: Some Basic Concepts. *In* Moreno, J. L. (ed.): Handbook of Group Psychotherapy, in press.
143. ——, *et al.:* The psychoanalysis of groups: the analyst's objections. Int. J. Group Psychother. 2:221–231, 1952.
144. ——, *et al.:* Sexual acting out in the psychoanalysis of groups. Int. J. Group Psychother. 4:369–380, 1954.
145. ——, *and Schwartz, E. K.:* The psychoanalysis of groups: implications for education. Int. J. Soc. Psychiat. 1:9–17, 1955.
146. ——, *and* ——: Irrational psychotherapy: an appeal to unreason. Am. J. Psychother. 12:300–315, 508–521, 744–759, 1958; 13:383–400, 1959.
147. ——, *and* ——: Psychoanalysis in groups: the role of values. Am. J. Psychoanal. 19:37–52, 1959.
148. ——, *and* ——: Psychoanalysis in groups: clinical and theoretic implications of the alternate meeting. Acta Psychother. 7(Suppl.)540–573, 1959.
149. ——, *and* ——: Psychoanalysis in groups: the alternate session. Am. Imago. 17:101–108, 1960.

SUBJECT INDEX

Acting out, 94 ff., 103, 107, 111, 114 ff.,
    116–120, 123, 129–135, 183,
    201–202, 233–234, 257, 277–278
Activity, 116 ff., 130–132, 277–278 (*see
    also* Acting out)
Addiction to therapy, 295–296
Adjunct therapists (*see* Analyst's role)
Affect, 14–15, 17, 19, 41 ff., 119 (*see
    also* Free association; Going
    around)
Alliances, 42 ff., 44 ff., 107–108
Alternate session, 13–15, 31, 95–128, 166,
    189–190, 197, 283, 294
    resistance of patient to, 115 ff.
Alternation of roles, 246–247, 272–273,
    299–300
Analyst's personality, 307–309 (*see also*
    Analyst's role)
Analyst's role, 6, 7, 10, 11, 19, 27 ff.,
    37–44, 73–78, 98, 101, 121, 151,
    161, 162, 171, 221, 284, 293–294
    (*see also* Working through)
Anonymity, 10, 115, 242 (*see also*
    Privacy)
Anxiety, 289–290 (*see also* Working
    through)

Belonging, 67–68, 251 (*see also* Group
    dynamics)
Borderliness, 126, 229–232

Catharsis, 112–113 (*see also* Free
    association)
Change, (*see* Working through)
Cliques, (*see* Alliances)
Cohesion, (*see* Group dynamics)
Collective interpretation, 26 (*see also*
    Group dynamics; Working
    through)
Combined therapy, 77, 92–93, 105–106,
    179–206 (*see also* Individual
    sessions)

Communication, 90–98, 126–127, 140 ff.,
    160–161, 248–249
Concurrent therapy, (*see* Combined
    therapy)
Conflict, (*see* Working through)
Conformity, 245–246 (*see also* Group
    dynamics)
Conjoined therapy, (*see* Combined
    therapy)
Contributions of patients, 4, 5, 7, 15, 39
    ff., 120–121, 135–136
Control, 188–195
Co-patients, (*see* Contributions of
    patients)
Co-therapists (*see* Analyst's role;
    Multiple therapists)
Countertransference, 88, 106, 110, 113,
    114–115, 117–118, 126, 138, 164,
    185, 227, 262 (*see also* Therapist's
    motivation; Values)
Couples, 84, 102, 212
Creativity, 159, 165 (*see also* Education)

Defenses, 288–289 (*see also* Resistance)
Depth, 86, 218–219, 292–293
Diagnosis, 8
Dreams, 6, 11 ff., 17–18, 33, 103, 135–
    161, 170, 285–286
    group dream, 15
Dyadic relation, (*see* Size; Individual
    sessions)

Education, 255–264, 310
Educational group, 258, 263
Expression, 96

Family groups, 36, 55
Fantasy, 11 ff., 22, 137, 139, 152 (*see also*
    Dreams)
Feeling, 25, 114, 259, 263–264 (*see also*
    Affect)
Fees, 8–9
First meeting, 9–11

321

AUTHOR INDEX